RELIGIOUS COLLEGES AND UNIVERSITIES IN AMERICA
A Selected Bibliography

Thomas C. Hunt
and
James C. Carper

GARLAND PUBLISHING, INC. • NEW YORK & LONDON
1988

Library of Congress Cataloging-in-Publication Data

Hunt, Thomas C., 1930–
    Religious colleges and universities in America: a selected
bibliography / Thomas C. Hunt and James C. Carper.
        p.   cm. — (Garland reference library of social science; vol.
422)
    Includes index.
    ISBN 0–8240–6648–0 (alk. paper)
    1. Church colleges—United States—Bibliography.   2. Catholic
universities and colleges—United States—Bibliography.   I. Carper,
James C.   II. Title.   III. Series: Garland reference library of
social science; v. 422.
Z5814.R34H86   1988   [LA227.3]   016.377'8'0973—dc19
88–14737   CIP

Printed on acid-free, 250-year-life paper
Manufactured in the United States of America

RELIGIOUS COLLEGES AND UNIVERSITIES IN AMERICA

GARLAND REFERENCE LIBRARY
OF SOCIAL SCIENCE
(Vol. 422)

DEDICATION AND ACKNOWLEDGMENTS

We respectfully dedicate this book to our students -- past, present, and future.

We acknowledge with thanks the assistance of many people, whose help was indispensable in the publication of this book. In particular, we wish to thank: two of Professor Hunt's secretaries, Mila Moore and Brenda Husser, who assisted in a number of ways; two of his graduate assistants, Barbara Bellefeuille and Gail Ertzgard, who worked on the indexes; Mary Whitlock and David Starkey, of the Word Processing Center of the College of Education of Virginia Tech for assembling and printing the text; Marilyn Norstedt, of Virginia Tech's Newman Library, who guided the indexing process; and Linda Wilson of Newman Library, the Rev. Nancy Jackson Gladden, of the Union Theological Seminary in Richmond, and Harriet Leonard of the Duke University Divinity Library, who aided in obtaining needed references. Finally, the editors wish to express their gratitude to the Division of Curriculum and Instruction and to the College of Education at Virginia Tech for the support they provided.

Thomas C. Hunt
Blacksburg, Virginia

James C. Carper
Washington, D.C.

CONTENTS

INTRODUCTION

During the last twenty-five years, the role of religion in shaping the American educational landscape has provoked the interest of both scholars and the general public. Most of the attention has been focused on questions regarding religion and precollegiate education. For example, scholars have explored how religion (evangelical Protestantism) spurred the common school movement of the middle decades of the nineteenth century. The general public, on the other hand, has debated frequently issues such as prayer in the public schools, state regulation of religious schools, and public funding of religious schools.

Religion has also infuenced the development of higher education in America. Indeed, the history of higher education from the colonial era to the end of the nineteenth century is in large measure the history of the "old-time" religious college. Though the secular university has become the dominant institution of the twentieth century, religiously-affiliated or oriented colleges and universities (which number over 800 and enroll more than 1,000,000 students) still constitute an important but often overlooked part of the configuration of higher education in the United States. This state of affairs, however, is likely to change. Given the resurgence of interest in religion and moral education and the widespread concern about the quality of undergraduate education, both the more "elite" religiously-affiliated institutions founded in the ante-bellum era and the post-Civil War "invisible colleges" of modest means are likely to receive more attention from the general public and scholars alike.

This selected bibliography deals with private colleges and universities that are, or have been, religiously affiliated. It is divided into several sections. There is, first, a section on the most influential general works on religion and higher education. The second section is made up of chapters which deal with government aid to, and regulation of, these institutions. Legal considerations, therfore, occupy a prominent place in these chapters.

It is the third section, however that constitutes the major thrust of this book. Here the reader will find twenty-five chapters, organized by denomination(s). Some of these denominations, e.g., Baptist, Catholic, Episcopalian, Lutheran, have a major involvement in higher education in this country, one that has extended over a long period of time. The chapters that contain their entries are, perforce, quite lengthy. There are other religious groups, such as the Free Methodists and Wesleyans, whose participation is not as extensive. The chapters that include their contributions are quite brief.

The tremendous diversity found in American private higher education is reflected in this book. This diversity represents a host of different cultural traditions, and a manifestation of the richness of those traditions. This variance created some difficulties in organization that merit mention. The lengthiest chapters are, for the most part, organized into "Institutional" and "General" categories, with the latter most often dealing with thematic issues. The institutional histories are, with few exceptions, devoid of annotations. The "General" works follow just the opposite policy.

In a few instances, chapters are organized along different lines, including the "Historical" and "Contemporary," and by kinds of entry, as in the Christian Church chapter. The chapter on the United Church of Christ institutions posed a different kind of challenge. Given the evolution that has occurred with the relationship between the churches in this group and the institutions of higher education that were founded under their auspices, the appropriateness of the title of this book came into question. After considerable thought, the proposed title, *Religious Colleges and Universities in America: A Selected Bibliography*, was retained. It was kept with the realization that it was not an exact "fit" in all instances.

Religious Colleges follows the publication of a previously edited bibliographic reference work, *Religious Schools*, which was published by Garland Publishing in 1986. It will be followed by the third volume of the set, *Religious Seminaries*, which is scheduled for publication in 1989. To our knowledge no other reference works focus on these topics. This volume, accordingly, pulls together a wealth of reference material and through selection identifies the salient works, whether book, article, dissertation, or essay. It therefore provides a much-needed resource for those interested in private, religiously-affiliated (for the most part) higher education in the United States, whether scholar, student, policy-maker, or interested citizen.

Thomas C. Hunt
Blacksburg, Virginia

James C. Carper
Washington, D.C.

Religious Colleges and
Universities in America

CHAPTER 1
MAJOR WORKS ON RELIGION AND AMERICAN COLLEGES AND UNIVERSITIES
Jennings L. Wagoner, Jr. and Timothy W. Kenney

Part I: Historical

1. Allmendinger, David F., Jr. *Paupers and Scholars: The Transformation of Student Life in Nineteenth-Century New England.* New York: St. Martin's Press, 1975.

    Examines the changing nature of collegiate populations in small New England colleges in the first half of the 19th century and the impact of social changes on student life and institutional character. An increase in the number of impoverished students markedly altered the nature of the antebellum college experience. Note is made of the impact of revivals on the religious attitudes of students.

2. Barnard, John. *From Evangelicalism to Progressivism at Oberlin College, 1866-1917.* Columbus, OH: Ohio State University Press, 1969.

    Discusses the changing ways in which students at Oberlin thought about social issues in the context of that college's religious and academic orientation from the end of the Civil War to World War I.

3. Bozeman, Theodore Dwight. *Protestants in an Age of Science: The Baconian Ideal and Antebellum American Religious Thought.* Chapel Hill: University of North Carolina Press, 1977.

    Argues that among antebellum intellectuals the distinction between the "scientific" and the "religious" was not as sharply marked as in today's world. Pursuit of scientific knowledge was considered a sacred duty certain to "lead our feeble reason from the works of nature up to its great Author." Emphasis is upon attempts to accommodate scientific and religious thought among "Old School Presbyterians."

4. Butts, R. Freeman. *The College Charts Its Course: Historical Conceptions and Current Proposals.* New York: McGraw-Hill Book Co., 1939.

    Provides a progressive historical interpretation of struggles to define the nature of the college curriculum and goals of higher education. The emergence of secular over religious conceptions of the college is emphasized.

5.   Cross, Robert D. "Recent Histories of U.S. Catholic Education." *History of Education Quarterly* 14 (Spring 1974): 125-30.

Reviews seven books published between 1966 and 1974 dealing with Catholic education in the United States. The review provides a quick guide to useful sources on the history of Catholic higher education.

6.   Findlay, James F., Jr. "The SPCTEW and Western Colleges: Religion and Higher Education in Mid-Nineteenth Century America." *History of Education Quarterly* 17 (Spring 1977): 31-62.

Examines the role of the Society for the Promotion of Collegiate and Theological Education in the West as a response of evangelical Protestants to the challenge of Western migration and the need to create a new society in frontier communities. The founding of colleges was seen as crucial in extending civilization and Christianity into the West.

7.   Findlay, James F., Jr. "'Western' Colleges, 1830-1870: Educational Institutions in Transition." *History of Higher Education Annual* 2 (1982): 35-64.

Discusses the tensions between denominational colleges and university ideals in Indiana and Illinois in the mid-19th century.

8.   Godbold, Albea. *The Church College of the Old South.* Durham, NC: Duke University Press, 1944.

Depicts the origins and development of "Old South" denominational colleges, their intellectual, religious, and social dimensions, and their responses to the challenge of state universities.

9.   Herbst, Jurgen. "Church, State and Higher Education: College Government in the American Colonies and States Before 1820." *History of Higher Education Annual* 1 (1981): 42-54.

Describes the gradual emergence of a line of demarcation between "public" and "private" control of American colleges.

10.   Herbst, Jurgen. *From Crisis to Crisis: American College Government, 1636-1819.* Cambridge, MA: Harvard University Press, 1982.

Analyzes the institutional, governmental, and legal developments in American higher education from Harvard's founding to the 1819 Dartmouth decision that gave special status to the concept of the "private" college.

11. Herbst, Jurgen. "The First Three American Colleges: Schools of the Reformation." *Perspectives in American History* 8 (1974): 7-52.

Describes the founding of Harvard, William and Mary, and Yale as Reformation "schools" rather than offshoots of medieval universities with corporate autonomy. Non-academic boards of control representing civil and ecclesiastical authorities were established with long-term consequences for the governance of American institutions of higher education.

12. Hofstadter, Richard and Walter P. Metzger. *The Development of Academic Freedom in the United States.* New York: Columbia University Press, 1955.

Covers the development of the ideal of academic freedom from the founding of the colonial colleges through the mid-20th century. Religious conservatism is characterized as a long-standing obstacle to acceptance of genuine academic freedom in American colleges and universities.

13. Hofstadter, Richard and Wilson Smith, eds. *American Higher Education: A Documentary History.* (2 vols.) Chicago: University of Chicago Press, 1961.

Offers a collection of primary source documents spanning the development of American higher education from colonial beginnings to the mid-20th century. Items depicting the role of religious institutions and religious controversy in higher education are included.

14. Hovencamp, Herbert. *Science and Religion in America, 1800-1860.* Philadelphia: University of Pennsylvania Press, 1978.

Examines the relationship between Protestant orthodoxy and the rise of scientific thought in the antebellum period. Maintains that eventually the "strictures of scientific exactness" undermined natural theology.

15. LeDuc, Thomas. *Piety and Intellect at Amherst College.* New York: Columbia University Press, 1946.

Identifies religious and intellectual currents that affected collegiate life and studies at Amherst and, more broadly, higher education in general during the second half of the 19th century.

16. Leslie, W. Bruce. "Localism, Denominationalism, and Institutional Strategies in Urbanizing America: Three Pennsylvania Colleges, 1870-1915." *History of Education Quarterly* 17 (Fall 1977): 235-56.

Examines the evolution of the denominational college with emphasis upon the survival strategies and the interest groups which gave direction to Bucknell, Franklin and Marshall, and

Swarthmore. Concludes that localism and denominational distinctiveness gave way to a more cosmopolitan responsiveness out of a desire for increased financial support and opportunities for growth.

17. Miller, Howard. *The Revolutionary College: American Presbyterian Higher Education, 1707-1837.* New York: New York University Press, 1976.

Examines the social, political, and religious roles of Presbyterian colleges and academies and their leaders from the period of the Great Awakening through the Revolution to the Second Great Awakening. Following the founding of Princeton in 1746, a "ministerial elite" of graduates of that college established six additional institutions within a fifty year period. The convictions and activities of this elite cadre help explain the unity of the Presbyterian institutions they founded.

18. Naylor, Natalie A. "'Holding High the Standard': The Influence of the American Education Society in Ante-Bellum Education." *History of Education Quarterly* 24 (Winter 1984): 479-97.

Describes the work of the AES with emphasis upon its impact on American education beyond its devotion to and financial support of ministerial education. The AES was committed to improving standards for liberal as well as theological education in the second quarter of the 19th century.

19. Naylor, Natalie A. "The Ante-Bellum College Movement: A Reappraisal of Tewksbury's Founding of American Colleges and Universities." *History of Education Quarterly* 13 (Fall 1973): 261-74.

Offers a reassessment of the criteria and data used by Tewksbury in his influential monograph describing the founding and survival rates of ante-bellum colleges. In addition to updating statistics, the author calls attention to agencies other than colleges that provided higher education during the ante-bellum period.

20. Naylor, Natalie A. "The Theological Seminary in the Configuration of American Higher Education: The Ante-Bellum Years." *History of Education Quarterly* 17 (Spring 1977): 17-30.

Maintains that the theological seminary was an important innovation of the early 19th century providing for formally organized and systematized ministerial preparation. The seminary is depicted as a prototype of the graduate professional school, a precursor of the American university, and as a force in stimulating a greater demand for higher education.

21. Noll, Mark A. "Christian Thinking and the Rise of the American University." *Christian Scholar's Review* 9 (January 1979): 3-16.

Analyzes changes in U.S. education, 1860-1930, from a broad humanistic view with a Christian orientation.

22. Peterson, George E. *The New England College in the Age of the University.* Amherst, MA: Amherst College Press, 1964.

Challenges the view that celebrates the emergence of universities as a "victory" over dying liberal arts colleges. Describes the defense made by New England colleges in behalf of collegiate principles against the competing secularized and specialized emphasis of the new universities.

23. Potts, David B. "American Colleges in the Nineteenth Century: From Localism to Denominationalism." *History of Education Quarterly* 11 (Winter 1971): 363-75.

Argues that the traditional generalization concerning a basic trend from sectarianism to secularism should be reversed. Using Baptist colleges for illustration, Potts builds a case showing that denominational identity became more pronounced later in the 19th century than was the case during the founding period earlier in the century.

24. Potts, David B. "'College Enthusiasm!' As Public Response, 1800-1860." *Harvard Educational Review* 47 (February 1977): 28-42.

Contends that, contrary to traditional interpretations, denominational colleges were essentially popular local institutions supported by and responsive to local communities. Between 1800 and 1860 small colleges increased in enrollments and experimented with flexible curricula in response to local circumstances.

25. Quillian, William F., Jr. "Changes in the Church-Related College." *Journal of Ecumenical Studies* 16 (January 1979): 133-38.

Reviews the changes that have occurred in church-affiliated colleges in the United States since 1939.

26. Ringenberg, William C. *The Christian College: A History of Protestant Higher Education in America.* Grand Rapids, MI: William B. Eerdmans Publishing Co., 1984.

Traces the history of the Protestant college in the United States from its beginnings to the present day. The book emphasizes the changing influence of the Christian world view in relation to the intellectual life of the college.

27. Rudolph, Frederick. *The American College and University: A History.* New York: Random House, 1962.

Provides a highly readable account of the development of

American higher education with attention given to the role of denominational colleges and religious life, especially during the colonial and antebellum eras.

28.   Schmidt, George P. *The Liberal Arts College.* New Brunswick, NJ: Rutgers University Press, 1957.

        Surveys student, faculty, and administrative values as well as the nature of the collegiate curriculum in the traditional liberal arts college. A companion volume to the author's *The Old-Time College President.*

29.   Scott, Donald M. *From Office to Profession: The New England Ministry, 1750-1850.* Philadelphia: University of Pennsylvania Press, 1978.

        Documents that by the 1850s the New England ministry had become a modern profession. Describes the founding of provincial colleges and theological seminaries as well as details the evolution of the ministerial profession.

30.   Shedd, Clarence P. *Two Centuries of Student Christian Movements: Their Origin and Intercollegiate Life.* New York: Association Press, 1934.

        Details the interests and activities of student Christian societies as a vital part of undergraduate life.

31.   Sloan, Douglas. *The Great Awakening and American Education: A Documentary History.* New York: Teachers College Press, 1973.

        Presents documents pertaining to the impact of the Great Awakening on churches, colleges, and academies during the mid-18th century.

32.   Sloan, Douglas. *The Scottish Enlightenment and the American College Ideal.* New York: Teachers College Press, 1971.

        Focuses upon the transforming impact of the Scottish Enlightenment upon early American higher education. Special emphasis is placed on the relationship between American religious and European Enlightenment thought.

33.   Smith, Wilson. *Professors and Public Ethics: Studies of Northern Moral Philosophers Before the Civil War.* Ithaca, NY: Cornell University Press, 1956.

        Examines the ethical and religious codes imbedded in the texts and teachings of moral philosophy in 19th century colleges.

34.   Tewksbury, Donald G. *The Founding of American Colleges and Universities Before the Civil War, With Particular Reference to the Religious Influences Bearing Upon the College Movement.* New

York: Teachers College, Columbia University, 1932.

Documents the extensive proliferation and rate of mortality of colonial and antebellum colleges. Sectarian competition and the characteristics of the denominational college weigh heavily in this pioneering account.

35. Veysey, Laurence R. *The Emergence of the American University.* Chicago: University of Chicago Press, 1965.

Details the multipurpose American university's rise to power and prestige during the 1865-1910 period. Denominational colleges and the place of religion in American higher education are shown to lose their hegemony as the secular university model emerged triumphant at the turn of the century.

36. Warch, Richard. *School of the Prophets: Yale College, 1701-1740.* New Haven: Yale University Press, 1973.

Investigates the religious and intellectual trends influencing the founding and early climate of Yale. This instititutional case study is significant as an intellectual history of pre-Great Awakening New England.

37. Whitehead, John S. *The Separation of College and State: Columbia, Dartmouth, Harvard and Yale, 1776-1876.* New Haven: Yale University Press, 1973.

Traces the origin of the distinction between "public" and "private" in American higher education with the conclusion that "a distinction between private and public or state institutions was not commonly recognized before the Civil War."

38. Whitehead, John S. and Jurgen Herbst. "How to Think About the Dartmouth College Case." *History of Education Quarterly* 26 (Fall 1986): 333-49.

Argues points of agreement and disagreement between two scholars who have studied closely the meaning and significance of "public" vs. "private" distinctions in 19th century higher education. Whitehead maintains that the *full* significance of the Dartmouth decision occurred after the Civil War, while Herbst contends that it constituted a *legal* turning point in 1819.

Part II: Contemporary

39. Ambrose, W. Haydn. *The Church in the University.* Valley Forge, PA: The Judson Press, 1968.

Examines the new role of the church in education in light of increased enrollments and changing campus scenes. Calls for an ecumenical spirit among Christians to bring direction and cohesion to seemingly unrelated activities, compartmentalized studies, and complex information.

40.   Astin, Alexander W. and Calvin B. T. Lee. *The Invisible Colleges: A Profile of Small Private Colleges with Limited Resources.* New York: McGraw-Hill Book Co., 1972.

Describes the historical development, administrative characteristics, student demographics, academic environment, and impact on students of small, non-elite colleges, most of which are religiously affiliated.

41.   Aubrey, Edwin Ewart. *Humanistic Teaching and the Place of Ethical and Religious Values in Higher Education.* Philadelphia: University of Pennsylvania Press, 1959.

Maintains that religion prevents education from becoming stagnant and at the same time education gains from religion a deeper foundation for building its programs and projecting its ideals.

42.   Buttrick, George Arthur. *Biblical Thought and the Secular University.* Baton Rouge, LA: Louisiana State University, 1960.

Asserts that "all education rests upon acts of faith" and that the secular faith is under challenge. Calls for a return to Biblical faith illuminated by modern scholarship.

43.   Carlson, Edgar M. *The Future of Church-Related Higher Education.* Minneapolis, MN: Augsburg Publishing House, 1977.

Interprets the role, problems, and possibilities of church-related higher education by questioning whether the church relationship is a viable and fruitful one for the college.

44.   Elliott, George Roy. *Church, College, and Nation.* Louisville, KY: The Cloister Press, 1945.

Maintains that Christian churches need to become more united as a "commonwealth of denominations" and that Christian professors should teach toward the goal of Christian humanism. To do less is to allow the forces of secularism to dominate our colleges and the nation.

45.   Fairchild, Hoxie N. *Religious Perspectives in College Teaching.* New York: Ronald Press Co., 1952.

Provides personal accounts by recognized scholars of their intellectual and spiritual responsibilities to students, their universities, and to society. The major liberal arts disciplines and teacher education are represented as is a range of "spiritual" belief systems.

46.   Fisher, Ben C., ed. *New Pathways: A Dialogue in Christian Higher Education.* Macon, GA: Mercer University Press, 1980.

Contains essays by ten contributors who offer a broad ecumenical perspective on the present and possible future directions of Christian higher education.

47.   Gaffney, Edward McGlynn, Jr. and Philip R. Moots. *Government and Campus: Federal Regulation of Religiously Affiliated Higher Education.* Notre Dame, IN: University of Notre Dame Press, 1982.

Discusses regulations pertaining to liability issues, government aid, preference employment principles, academic freedom, student admissions and discipline, and property relationships. Revised report of a 1979 study presented to the Sloan Commission on Government and Higher Education.

48.   Gauss, Christian, ed. *The Teaching of Religion in American Higher Education.* New York: Ronald Press Co., 1951.

Analyzes approaches to instruction in religion in American colleges, denominational and secular. Contributors are primarily concerned with the place religion should occupy in a sound collegiate curriculum.

49.   Gellhorn, Walter and R. Kent Greenawalt. *The Sectarian College and the Public Purse: Fordham--A Case Study.* Dobbs Ferry, NY: Oceana Publications, 1970.

Identifies measures that Fordham in particular and other church-related colleges in general would have to adopt in order to shed identification as a religious institution in the conventional sense and gain legal status as an independent institution of higher learning.

50.   Greeley, Andrew M. *From Backwater to Mainstream: A Profile of Catholic Higher Education.* Hightstown, NJ: McGraw-Hill Book Co., 1969.

Reports on the historical development, goals and functions, and current problems and accomplishments of colleges and universities affiliated with the Roman Catholic Church in the United States. Prepared under the auspices of the Carnegie Commission on Higher Education.

51.   Hartt, Julian N. *Theology and the Church in the University.* Philadelphia: The Westminister, 1969.

Advances the argument that at Christian colleges the chapel could become a strategic theological arena for discussion of key policy questions facing the nation in the future.

52.   Hassell, David J. *City of Wisdom: A Christian Vision of the American University.* Chicago: Loyola University Press, 1983.

           Probes questions of purpose, identity, and wholeness in a search for the meaning of a Christian university.

53.   Hesburgh, Theodore M. *The Hesburgh Papers: Higher Values in Higher Education.* Kansas City, KS: Andrews and McMeel, 1979.

           Emphasizes the importance of values in higher education because "wisdom is more than knowledge, man is more than his mind, and without values, man may be intelligent but less than fully human." The volume is a collection of papers expressing the educational philosophy of the renowned former president of the University of Notre Dame.

54.   Hintz, Howard W. *Religion and Public Higher Education.* New York: Brooklyn College, 1955.

           Proposes a clarification of basic educational purposes with an emphasis upon those essential humane values which lie at the core of the advanced classical religions, and which are mainly represented by the Judeo-Christian tradition.

55.   Jencks, Christopher and David Riesman. *The Academic Revolution.* Garden City, NY: Doubleday and Co., 1968.

           Describes the forces and commitments that have shaped the modern university and the scholar's role. Chapters on "Protestant Denominations and Their Colleges" and "Catholics and Their Colleges" emphasize the diversity that divides the academic world.

56.   Kirk, Russell. "Liberal Learning, Moral Worth, and Defecated Rationality." *Modern Age* 19 (January 1975): 2-9.

           Contends that in recent decades colleges and universities have offered a limited rationalistic curricula, purged of theology, moral philosophy, and traditional wisdom.

57.   Lowry, Howard. *The Mind's Adventure: Religion and Higher Education.* Philadelphia: The Westminister Press, 1950.

           Analyzes the forces that are pushing higher education more and more toward secularism and wrestles with the question of whether, if liberal education ignores religion, it can truly be liberal at all.

58.   Magill, Samuel H., ed. *The Contribution of the Church-Related College to the Public Good.* Washington, D.C.: Association of American Colleges, 1970.

           Discusses the historical and contemporary distinctiveness of the church-related college and explores the problems and prospects of a continuing relationship between college and church in an increasingly secular age.

59.   McKinney, Richard I. *Religion in Higher Education Among Negroes.* New York: Yale University Press, 1945.

Cites the importance of religious policies in predominately black colleges to the realization of the institutions' ultimate objectives. Policies and their significance to the black student are investigated in light of the social setting of the minority group.

60.   Messersmith, James C. *Church-Related Boards Responsible for Higher Education.* Bulletin No. 13. Washington, D.C.: U.S. Department of Health, Education, and Welfare, 1964.

Describes variations in patterns, structure, responsibilities, and relationships of denominational boards to church-related colleges.

61.   Overholt, William A. *Religion in American Colleges and Universities.* Washington, D.C.: American College Student Personnel Association, 1970.

Inquires into the roles, functions, and services offered by religious organizations present on American campuses and indicates that new styles of ministry are being sought through variety and experimentation.

62.   Pace, C. Robert. *Education and Evangelism: A Profile of Protestant Colleges.* New York: McGraw-Hill Book Co., 1972.

Analyzes the heritage, environment, students and alumni characteristic of four major categories of Protestant colleges. Survey data are used to offer profiles and allow general comparisons among the various types of Protestant institutions.

63.   Parsonage, Robert Rue, ed. *Church Related Higher Education: Perceptions and Perspectives.* Valley Forge, PA: Judson Press, 1978.

Discusses the myths, categories, examples, and essentials of church relatedness based upon a three year study involving fourteen colleges representing thirteen different Christian traditions. The volume includes background papers and responses presented at a Wingspread conference sponsored by the National Council of Churches in November, 1977.

64.   Pattillo, Manning M., and Donald M. MacKenzie. *Church-Sponsored Higher Education in the United States: Report of the Danforth Foundation.* Washington, D.C.: American Council on Education, 1966.

Examines the basic problems of colleges and universities

associated with Christian and Jewish religious bodies. Provides the first comprehensive study of the problems, priorities, and prospects of church-related colleges.

65. Sandin, Robert T. *The Search for Excellence: The Christian College in an Age of Educational Competition.* Macon, GA: Mercer University Press, 1982.

Explores the problems faced by Christian colleges in an age of heightened educational competition, economic stress, and cultural pluralism. Emphasizes the need for Christian colleges to combine religious distinctiveness with academic excellence.

66. Smith, Seymour A. *Religious Cooperation in State Universities.* Ann Arbor, MI: University of Michigan Press, 1957.

Traces the development of efforts by Catholics, Protestants, and Jews to achieve cooperative working relationships in large state colleges and universities.

67. Sweets, Henry Hayes. *Source Book on Christian Education as Related to the Colleges and Seminaries of the Church.* Louisville, KY: Executive Committee of the Presbyterian Church in the United States, 1942.

Presents a wide variety of documentary material, historical and topical, that speaks to the value of Christian education and the responsibility of churches to support schools and colleges.

68. Underwood, Kenneth, ed. *The Church, the University and Social Policy: The Danforth Study of Campus Ministries.* Middletown, CT: Wesleyan University Press, 1969.

Reports on an intensive inquiry into the religious commitments and actions of American church leaders and of their relations to the laity. Singles out Protestant campus ministries for special scrutiny since they tend to be most involved with the intellectual, social, and moral movements of the educated youth of America.

69. Walter, Erich A. *Religion and the State University.* Ann Arbor, MI: University of Michigan Press, 1958.

Explores the place of religion in higher education via essays dealing with, among other topics: church-state separation, religion in state universities, academic freedom, religion in humanities, sciences, and professional studies, campus religious groups, and the values of college students.

70. Wilder, Amos Niven, ed. *Liberal Learning and Religion.* New York: Harper & Brothers, 1951.

Presents a series of essays on the indispensable role the

values and perspectives of religious traditions play in liberal learning, the academic disciplines, and in the academic community. Contributors are all Fellows or officers of the National Council on Religion in Higher Education.

CHAPTER 2
GOVERNMENT AID TO CHURCH-AFFILIATED COLLEGES AND UNIVERSITIES
James F. Herndon

71.   "Aid to Parochial Schools: A Re-Examination." *William and Mary Law Review* 14 (Fall 1972): 128-61.

        Summarizes the Supreme Court's holding in *Tilton* v. *Richardson* (no. 211) within the general context of Supreme Court decisions on state support for church-related education.

72.   Aiken, Ray J. "Legal Problems of Control of a University: Private Sectarian Institutions." *The College Counsel* 2, Part III (1967): 81-93.

        Considers criteria set out in *Horace Mann League of the U.S.* v. *Board of Public Works* (no. 102) concerning the distinction between church-related colleges eligible for public aid and those which are not; suggests the unworkability of this distinction; defends aid to sectarian institutions on educational grounds and on First Amendment free exercise grounds.

73.   Albrecht, William E. and W. Irving Shaw. "The Establishment Clause and Governmental Aid to Colleges." *St. Louis University Law Journal* 11 (Spring 1967): 464-74.

        Describes the origin and evolution of the First Amendment's establishment clause; reviews the *Horace Mann League of the U.S.* v. *Board of Public Works* (no. 102) decision; concludes that this case has clouded the guidelines for determining the constitutionality of public aid to private education.

74.   Alexander, Kern and Erwin S. Solomon. *College and University Law.* Charlottesville, VA: The Michie Co., 1972. Supplement 1976.

        Contains cases and commentaries on "State Aid to Sectarian Colleges," discussing cases from 1891 to 1968 (pp. 121-24); and on "Federal Aid to Sectarian Colleges," reviewing cases from 1908 to 1971 (pp. 124-30); updates case listings and commentary through *Roemer* v. *Board of Public Works* (no. 189) in the Supplement, pp. 5-21.

75.   American Association of State Colleges and Universities. *National*

Imperatives for Higher Education, 1981. Washington, D.C.: American Association of State Colleges and Universities, January, 1981.

Argues against tuition tax credits as expensive and inflationary; claims that tuition tax credits would encourage raising of tuition and would most benefit upper income students in high-cost institutions.

76. American Association of State Colleges and Universities. "Policy Statement on Financing Private Institutions from State Funds." *School and Society* 97 (April 1969): 239.

Sets out guidelines the Association recommends that states follow in making direct or indirect appropriations of public funds to private institutions; adopted by the Association at its annual meeting in Washington, DC, November 11, 1968.

77. American Civil Liberties Union. "Public Aid to Church-Related Related Colleges and Universities." *School and Society* 93 (October 1965): 404-05.

Presents the official position of the American Civil Liberties Union on state or federal aid to church-related colleges; outlines the ACLU's views on constitutional principles governing such aid and the ACLU's stand on the permissibility of specific forms of aid.

78. American Council on Education. *Public and Private Higher Education: Differences in Role, Character, and Clientele.* Policy Analysis Service Reports, Vol. 2, No. 3. December, 1976. Washington, DC: American Council on Education, 1976.

Asserts that public and private higher education have many of the same problems, though private higher education is especially dependent on tuition income, while public institutions are not; considers the effects of this distinction, as well as other factors (among which are church affiliation) on academic roles and purposes.

79. Anderson, Richard E. *Strategic Policy Changes at Private Colleges: Educational and Fiscal Implications.* New York: Teachers College Press, December, 1977.

Proposes that as religious institutions of higher education become more secular in order to attract funding, enrollment increases but the institutions lose the special attributes that make them effective and attractive to prospective students.

80. Andringa, Robert C. "Problems and Issues Related to Legislative Processes: The Federal Dimension." Denver, CO: Education Commission of the States, May, 1975. Paper presented at a Seminar for State Leaders in Postsecondary Education.

Philadelphia, PA. May, 1975.

Offers reasons why increased state aid to private institutions can be expected in the near future.

81.   Antieau, Chester J., Arthur T. Downey and Edward C. Roberts. *Freedom from Federal Establishment: Formation and Early History of the First Amendment Religion Clauses.* Milwaukee, WI: Bruce Publishing Co., 1964.

Describes the practice of state support of religious schools in colonial times and during the early years of independence, at pp. 167-74.

82.   Averill, Lloyd J. *"'Sectarian' Higher Education and the Public Interest."* *Journal of Higher Education* 40 (February 1969): 85-100.

Distinguishes church-related colleges by their relationship to the organized Christian community and not by their sectarianism; concludes that to receive public funds, church-related colleges should meet regional accreditation standards, provide for academic freedom, and allow for open admission for students of all religions.

83.   Babbidge, Homer D. and Robert M. Rosenzweig. *The Federal Interest in Higher Education.* New York: McGraw-Hill, 1962.

Recounts history of church-state separation; outlines federal programs aiding church-related colleges; asks how new programs aiding religious institutions might be justified given constitutional separation of church and state; offers suggestions, at pp. 134-39.

84.   Bailey, Stephen K. *Education Interest Groups in the Nation's Capital.* Washington, D.C.: American Council on Education, 1975.

Identifies and describes groups (including those representing religious organizations) lobbying the federal government in support of a variety of goals (including support for higher education); describes the objectives of these groups and how they operate.

85.   Balz, Frank J. *Estimated Effects of the President's FY 1983 Budget on Colleges and Universities in the States: A Research Report from the State-National Information Network.* Washington, D.C.: National Institute of Independent Colleges and Universities, April, 1982.

Gives estimates of loss in selected student assistance programs in the states by institutional control resulting from the President's budget request for 1981-1982.

86.   Bartholomew, Paul C. *Significant Decisions of the Supreme Court, 1970-71 Term.* Washington, DC: American Enterprise Institute, 1971.

Contains concise statement of facts, legal questions, decisions, and reasons given by the Supreme Court for selected cases, including *Tilton* v. *Richardson* (no. 211), pp. 27-28. (Later editions were edited by Bruce E. Fein with minor changes in the title; see the edition for 1972-1973 [pub. 1974] for *Hunt* v. *McNair* (no. 107), pp. 38-39; and the edition for 1975-1976 [pub. 1977] for *Roemer* v. *Board of Public Works*, (no. 189), pp. 130-32.)

87.   Beach, Fred J. and Robert F. Will. *The State and Non-public Schools*. United States Office of Education Miscellaneous. No. 28. Washington, D.C.: United States Government Printing Office, 1958.

Summarizes and analyzes, state by state, constitutional and statutory provisions for aid to privately controlled institutions, including institutions of higher education.

88.   Beaufond-Marcano, Rafael Emilio. "A Description, Analysis, and Evaluation of the Financial Structure of Four Private Universities in the Consortium of Universities of the Washington Metropolitan Area between 1973-74 and 1982-83." Ed.D. dissertation. George Washington University, 1984.

Examines financial patterns at four institutions, three of which are church-related; reviews sources of income, expenditure patterns, financial health, effects of external factors such as enrollment demand and inflation.

89.   Bender, Richard N., ed. *The Church-Related College Today: An Anachronism or Opportunity?* Nashville, TN: General Board of Education, United Methodist Church, 1971.

Collects short papers that praise church-related colleges and that document problems in these institutions of declining enrollments and short finances.

90.   Benezet, Louis T. *Private Higher Education and Public Funding*. ERIC/Higher Education Research Report No. 5. Washington, D.C.: American Association for Higher Education, 1976.

Concludes that the financial problems of private colleges (including church-related colleges) suggest that additional public resources will be needed to preserve the dual system of higher education in America.

91.   Bennett, John. "Church and State and the Christian College." *Liberal Education* 49 (May 1963): 251-57.

Rejects the "wall of separation" metaphor, arguing that in a free society public and private support of higher education must be woven together such that what the author calls the "inner freedom" of all institutions is preserved.

92.   Bennof, Richard J. *Federal Support to Universities, Colleges, and Selected Nonprofit Institutions, Fiscal Year 1982. Final Report to the President and Congress.* National Science Foundation Report No. 84-315. Washington, D.C.: National Science Foundation, March, 1984.

            Summarizes the types and amounts of aid granted by fifteen federal agencies to public and private institutions. (Similar reports are available for earlier years.)

93.   Berdahl, Robert O. "The Politics of State Aid." In *Public Policy and Private Higher Education*, pp. 321-52. Edited by David W. Breneman and Chester E. Finn, Jr. Washington, DC: The Brookings Institution, 1978.

            Describes the politics of state aid to church-related colleges in California and New York; sets out the issues and how they were resolved through legislation, at pp. 333-36.

94.   Berdahl, Robert O. "Private Higher Education and State Governments." *Educational Record* 51 (Summer 1970): 285-95.

            Focuses on state aid in describing problems of higher education; raises questions of the constitutionality of state aid to religious institutions; discusses methods by which aid might be extended; outlines the relationship of church-state issues to state politics involving aid to higher education.

95.   Berdahl, Robert O. *Statewide Coordination of Higher Education.* Washington, DC: American Council on Education, 1971.

            Reviews approaches taken by commissions in two states (New York and Illinois) in recommending aid to private (including church-related) colleges; also considers studies made in Pennsylvania and Washington; see especially pp. 207-08.

96.   Berve, Nancy M., ed. *State Support of Higher Education: Programs in Operation or Approved in the 50 States and the District of Columbia as of January 1, 1981 and January 1, 1982.* Denver, CO: Education Commission of the States, 1982.

            Presents data for fiscal years 1981 and 1982 state support of private higher education; shows distribution of contract aid, direct institutional aid, aid to disadvantaged minorities, aid for facilities, student assistance, and aid to medical, dental, and nursing schools.

97.   Blackwell, Thomas Edward. *College Law: A Guide for Administrators.* Washington, D.C.: American Council on Education, 1961.

            Emphasizes the history and development of government aid to private institutions in a section on "Constitutional Restrictions on the Use of Public Funds for the Support of Church-Related Colleges," pp. 32-34; discusses constitutional limits, as of 1960; lists the early cases.

98.   Blackwell, Thomas Edward. *The College Law Digest 1935-1970.* Washington, D.C.: National Association of College and University Attorneys, 1974.

   Discusses and summarizes the legal questions concerning public aid to church-related colleges in a section on "The Constitutionality of the Use of Public Funds for Church-Related and Other Non-Public Institutions of Higher Education"; lists cases in state and federal courts from 1938 to 1970; lists bibliography for the same period.

99.   Blank, Ben. "The 1971 U.S. Supreme Court and the Religious Clauses: The Wall Becomes an Indistinct Barrier." *Baylor Law Review* 24 (1972): 565-76.

   Traces background of the Higher Education Facilities Act of 1963; describes the filing of suit in *Tilton* v. *Richardson* (no. 211); summarizes the decision in this case; examines views of Thomas Jefferson and James Madison on church-state questions; finds that the Supreme Court exceeded provisions of the First Amendment; invokes the First Amendment free exercise clause to conclude that public aid is a threat to the independence of church-related colleges.

100.   Blanton, Harry A. "Entanglement Theory: Its Development and Some Implications for Future Aid to Church-Related Higher Education." *Journal of Law and Education* 7 (July 1978): 359-422.

   Summarizes cases through *McNair* v. *Hunt* (no. 107) in the body of the article and *Roemer* v. *Board of Public Works* (no. 189) in a supplement; analyzes cases in light of the Supreme Court's three-part test, with emphasis on "entanglement"; isolates elements courts are likely to examine in ruling on the sectarian character of colleges; makes recommendations to colleges for securing funding.

101.   Bloland, Harland G. *Associations in Action: The Washington D.C. Higher Education Community.* *ASCH-ERIC Higher Education Report No. 2. 1985.* Washington, DC: Association for the Study of Higher Education, 1985.

   Outlines the history of the development of higher education associations in Washington since 1960, including those representing church-related colleges among others; sets out the issues raised during this period of time and how they were dealt with by these associations.

102.   Boles, Donald E. "Church and State and the Burger Court: Recent Developments Affecting Parochial Schools." *Journal of Church and State* 18 (Winter 1976): 21-38.

Describes Supreme Court decisions by the Burger court on public aid to church-related colleges; relates these decisions to the Burger court's treatment of civil liberties generally; discusses "Legal Distinctions between Elementary Schools and Colleges" in separate section (pp. 30-35); describes state evasive actions; concludes that the Court will apply more rigorous standards of church-state separation to elementary and secondary schools than to colleges.

103.   Bolick, Ernest Bernard, Jr.   "A Historical Account of the Controversy over State Support of Church-Related Higher Education in the Fifty States." Ed.D. dissertation. University of North Carolina at Greensboro, 1978.

Describes historical development of state aid to church-related colleges and universities in the United States; identifies participants in the debate and their positions, and summarizes outcomes of the debate in court decisions, including *Hunt* v. *McNair* (no. 107), *Tilton* v. *Richardson* (no. 211), and *Roemer* v. *Board of Public Works* (no. 189); projects trends, including the possibility that sectarian colleges may become more secular in order to qualify for state aid.

104.   Bratton, Daniel L.   "Confronting a Loan Default on Facilities Financing." *Educational Record* 65 (Spring 1984): 46-47.

Relates how Kansas Wesleyan University coped with crackdown by the U.S. Department of Housing and Urban Development on a delinquent loan; offers recommendations for other institutions in similar circumstances.

105.   Brubacher, John S.   *The Courts and Higher Education.*   San Francisco: Jossey-Bass, 1971.

Discusses, among many other topics, issues in sectarian education, with emphasis on aid to religious institutions (pp. 82-89).

106.   Bryson, Joseph E.   "Church-State Relationship-Recent Developments." In *School Law Update-1977*, pp. 107-23. Edited by M. A. McGhehey. Topeka, KS: National Organization on Legal Problems of Education, 1978.

Summarizes issues decided or pending from November, 1976 through October, 1977, including aid for higher education. (Similar articles appear in NOLPE-published volumes annually; editors and titles vary.)

107.   Byrne, Jerome C. and John A. Kokinnen.   "Constitutionality of Federal Aid to Sectarian Universities." *Catholic University of America Law Review* 17 (1967): 139-62.

Places *Horace Mann League cf the U.S.. v. Board of Public*

Works (no. 102) in the context of earlier Supreme Court decisions; asserts that what the Supreme Court would do with this case is unclear; recommends that church-related institutions begin to consider their place in higher education and the role religion should play in the educational programs they support.

108.   Carlson, Edgar M. *The Future of Church-Related Higher Education.* Minneapolis, MN: Augsburg Publishing House, 1977.

Delineates differences between public and private higher education, with emphasis on the desirability of diversity and the support of public purposes provided by private colleges; stresses the need for private, church-related colleges to survive and the corresponding need for society to make that possible.

109.   Carnegie Commission on Higher Education. *The Capital and the Campus: State Responsibility for Postsecondary Education.* New York: McGraw-Hill, 1971.

Treats relationships between the state and private institutions in Chapter 8 ("The State and Private Institutions," pp. 63-73); describes forms of state aid to private institutions, discusses the constitutional and political feasibility of such aid, and makes recommendations for continuity and change in Chapter 10 ("Public Funds for Private Higher Education," pp. 87-98).

110.   Carnegie Foundation for the Advancement of Teaching. *The States and Higher Education: A Proud Past and a Vital Future.* San Francisco: Jossey-Bass, 1976.

Lists ways of aiding private institutions and ways in which private institutions make themselves accountable to state governments.

111.   Chaffee, Ellen Earle with David A. Whetton and Kim S. Cameron. *Case Studies in College Strategy.* Boulder, CO: National Center for Higher Education Management Systems, May, 1983.

Describes and summarizes how a sample of colleges, including nine church-related institutions, dealt with declines in revenues during 1973-1976.

112.   Chambers, M. M. *The Colleges and the Courts, 1962-1966.* Danville, IL: The Interstate Printers and Publishers, Inc., 1967.

Contains section "Cooperative Interactions between Public and Private Agencies in Higher Education" (pp. 171-78); examines litigation involving direct public funding of sectarian colleges, property sales to religious institutions at nominal prices, bequests, and public acquisition of property owned by church-affiliated colleges. (Earlier editions covered the periods 1936-40; 1941-45; 1946-50; and 1950-60; later editions were published in 1972 and

1973; publishers and titles vary.)

113.   Chambers, M. M. "Public Aid for Privately Controlled Colleges and Universities." *Educational Law and Administration* 2 (July 1933): 53-63.

Outlines amounts and distribution of the limited amounts of public aid being given to private (including church related) colleges and universities in the early 1930s.

114.   Chronister, Jay L. "Implications of the Evolving Relationships between the States and Independent Higher Education." *Peabody Journal of Education* 57 (July 1980): 233-39.

Recounts the history of state government involvement in private higher education; shows the increase in interdependence of states and private higher education; details emerging pressures and controls; and calls for public officials and institutional representatives to say what contributions private education can make and then shape public policy to elicit those contributions and protect values uniquely associated with private higher education.

115.   Chronister, Jay L. *Independent College and University Participation in Statewide Planning for Postsecondary Education.* Washington, DC: National Institute of Independent Colleges and Universities, 1978.

Reports results of a study of participation of private colleges in statewide planning for higher education; concludes that nearly every state has means for involving independent colleges and universities in planning efforts, though differences do exist between planning agencies and independent college associations on how to involve private institutions, on activities in which private schools may participate, and on how to measure success; suggests that if states wish to achieve efficiency and effectiveness in higher education they should see all institutions as potential resources.

116.   Cleveland, Robert E. "Legal and Political Issues of State Aid for Private Higher Education." Ed.D. dissertation. University of Tennessee, 1975.

Identifies patterns of state support for private higher education in all 50 states; compares opinions of selected Tennessee leaders with existing legal parameters; finds relatively large segment of leaders unaware of the Supreme Court's three-part test for determining the constitutionality of public aid to church-related institutions.

117.   Conrad, Clifton and Joseph Cosand. *The Implications of Federal Education Policy.* Washington, DC: American Association for Higher Education, 1976.

Traces role of the U.S. federal government in higher education, with emphasis on the Education Amendments of 1972; stresses the insufficiency of current student aid funds, seeing private colleges as hard pressed to provide additional aid to students not eligible for federal or state programs; recommends increasing federal assistance to higher education, with institutional grants for instruction to be used as a major means of supplying federal aid; suggests direct institutional aid be complemented by student aid programs, especially for disadvantaged students.

118. "Constitutionality of Federal Financial Aid to Church-Related Colleges." *Harvard Law Review* 77 (1964): 135-68.

Describes the Higher Education Facilities Act of 1963; challenges the grounds on which Congress sought to defend the Act against an attack based on the First Amendment; considers the issue of standing to sue as it would affect anyone seeking to challenge the Act in court.

119. Cote, Denise. "Establishment Clause Analysis of Legislative and Administrative Aid to Religion." *Columbia Law Review* 74 (October 1974): 1175-1202.

Analyzes the development and application of the Supreme Court's three-part test; identifies inconsistencies and problems in interpretations of the Establishment Clause.

120. Cowen, Lindsey. "Public Support for Private Higher Education--The Current Status and Possible Implications." In *Higher Education: The Law and Constructive Change*, pp. 40-48. Edited by D. Parker Young. Athens, GA: University of Georgia Center for Continuing Education, 1976.

Outlines current policies of both the states and the national government with respect to funding private institutions (including those that are church-related); reviews cases; points to controls that accompany aid; asks if that is what colleges want.

121. Curley, John R. "The Politics of Federal Aid to Education." Paper presented at the 69th Annual Meeting of School Business Officials. Phoenix, AZ. October 2-6, 1983.

Describes how interest groups organize and act to influence United States policy on aid to education, including aid to church-related institutions of higher education.

122. Davidow, Robert P. "Governmental Aid to Church-Affiliated Colleges: An Analysis of a Possible Answer to a Constitutional Question." *North Dakota Law Review* 43 (1967): 659-89.

Discusses and evaluates the *Horace Mann League of the U.S.* v. *Board of Public Works* (no. 102); cites possible effects on federal programs of aid to higher education; concludes that the confusion in this case owes as much to the U.S. Supreme Court's earlier decisions as to the Maryland supreme court; finds the line that the Maryland court has drawn is reasonably calculated to preserve the religious freedom protected by the First Amendment's establishment and free exercise clauses.

123.   Department of Health, Education and Welfare. "Memorandum on the Impact of the First Amendment to the Constitution upon Federal Aid to Education." *Georgetown Law Journal* 50 (1961): 349-96.

Defends the Department's proposals for federal aid to education in light of the history of judicial interpretations of the First Amendment; sets out the distinction between higher education and elementary and secondary education that was later followed by the Supreme Court.

124.   Dickmeyer, Nathan. *The Impact of Federal Student Assistance on Tuitions, Institutional Student Aid and Alumni Giving.* Washington, D.C.: National Commission on Student Financial Assistance, June 18, 1983.

Describes effects of federal student assistance on 338 colleges and universities; found that private colleges with increasing enrollments were more likely to hold tuitions down than those with decreasing enrollments and that for both public and private colleges increased federal funding was associated with increased institutionally funded student aid and higher administrative and instructional costs; also reports that federally funded student assistance was associated with decreased alumni giving at private colleges.

125.   Drinan, Robert F. "Does State Aid to Church-Related Colleges Constitute an Establishment of Religion?   Reflections on the Maryland College Cases." *Utah Law Review* 1967 (1967): 491-516.

Reviews the legislation at issue and the opinions in *Horace Mann League of the U.S.* v. *Board of Public Works* (no. 102); suggests the majority view is at odds with opinions of the U.S. Supreme Court; sees confusion in the Maryland court's definition of "secular"; after examining the relationship between the First Amendment's free exercise and establishment clauses, concludes the *Horace Mann* decision is ambiguous as a precedent and that it distorts the two guarantees of the First Amendment because it prefers an establishment of the secular and a denial of claims based on religious liberty and academic freedom.

126.   Drinan, Robert F. *Religion, the Courts, and Public Policy.* New York: McGraw-Hill, 1963.

Describes the program of the Kennedy administration for

securing aid for all colleges, including those that are church-related; summarizes the legal memorandum of the Department of Health, Education and Welfare (no. 053) in support of aid to sectarian colleges; describes the politics and process of the 1962 Congressional decision on aid to public and private colleges and universities.

127.   Durrant, Matthew B. "Accrediting Church-Related Schools: A First Amendment Analysis." *Journal of Law and Education* 14 (April 1985): 147-79.

Considers argument that accrediting functions of certain agencies constitute state action; analyzes the religion clauses of the First Amendment in light of this claim, concludes that conferring accredited status on church-related schools does not amount to impermissible aid to religion; concludes also that the regulations inhering in the accrediting process need not inhibit religious liberty if standards do not restrict religious functions of church-related schools.

128.   Dutile, Fernand N. and Edward McGlynn Gaffney. *State and Campus: State Regulation of Religiously Affiliated Higher Education.* Notre Dame, IN: University of Notre Dame Press, 1984.

Identifies issues in regulation by states of religiously-affiliated colleges and universities but also points to problems in the use of publicly funded facilities in Chapter 5, "Facilities," pp. 34-40; presents state-by-state breakdown in Chapters 9 through 58.

129.   "Editorial. Free Choice for College Students." *America*, 137, October 22, 1977, p. 257.

Lauds Supreme Court's affirmation of federal district court decisions in cases involving government-provided financial aid to students attending church-related colleges.

130.   Education Commission of the States. Task Force on State Policy and Independent Higher Education. "The States and the Private Sector." *AGB Reports* 19 (September-October 1977): 43-47.

Recommends that state policy makers look closely at precedents established by the Supreme Courts in its decisions concerning public aid to church related colleges; points out that sectarian purposes and pervasively sectarian institutions must be excluded from public support; concludes that the states need administrative machinery and criteria to make determinations of which purposes are sectarian and which institutions are pervasively sectarian.

131.   Egan, James P. "Private/Public Tuition Change: Does It Affect Private College SAT Admission Standards?" Paper presented at the

Annual Meeting of the Midwest Economics Association. St. Louis, MO. March, 1983.

Demonstrates that the rate of tuition change at private colleges relative to tuition change at public colleges adversely affected SAT percentile change at most private colleges; shows also that most change in SAT scores at private colleges was due to institutional characteristics, not to dual tuition policy of the states.

132.   Elliott, Edward C. and M. M. Chambers. *The Colleges and the Courts: Judicial Decisions Regarding Institutions of Higher Education in the United States.* New York: Carnegie Foundation for the Advancement of Teaching, 1936.

Recounts legislation and associated judicial decisions providing for aid to private institutions from 1804 until the early 1930s; lists cases; discusses legislation and decisions by regions of the United States. Continued by no. 042.

133.   Elliott, T. Michael. *Endangered Service. Independent Colleges, Public Policy and the First Amendment.* Nashville, TN: National Commission on United Methodist Higher Education, 1976.

Lists and discusses the public purposes served by private institutions; recommends ways of financing programs for private, church-related institutions without violating the First Amendment.

134.   "The Establishment Clause: Grants to Sectarian Colleges for Secular Purposes Held Unconstitutional." *New York University Law Review* 41 (November 1966): 983-88.

Summarizes and comments on the decision in *Horace Mann* v. *Board of Public Works* (no. 102); criticizes the court, arguing that withholding aid from church-related colleges would frustrate any overall program of aid to higher education; contends that government support for higher education must include funds for church-related institutions because government cannot otherwise meet demands for higher education without spending enormous amounts to provide for needed facilities.

135.   Farwell, E. D. "The Future of Church-Related Colleges: Implications of *Tilton* v. *Richardson.*" *Liberal Education* 58 (May 1972): 280-85.

Reports results of a mail questionnaire sent to 92 Protestant church-related colleges requesting information about the strength of denominational affiliation, the likely response of the affiliated church to guidelines jeopardizing federal and state institutional grants, and the degree to which federal grants were essential to survival; offers recommendations based on answers to the questionnaire.

136.   Fein, Bruce E. *Significant Decisions of the Supreme Court, 1970-71 Term.* Washington, DC: American Enterprise Institute, 1971.

Continues summarizes begun and reported in no. 86.

137.   Fenske, Robert H. and Joseph D. Boyd. "The Impact of State Financial Aid to Students on Choice of Public or Private or College." *College and University* 46 (Winter 1971): 98-107.

Reports that 24% of recipients of aid from the state (Illinois) would have attended a different college without that aid; suggests two impacts of state aid: (1) the demand on tax funds for tax-assisted institutions has been reduced; and (2) the diversion of large numbers of students from public to private colleges has contributed substantially to the economic and enrollment stability of private colleges.

138.   Fenske, Robert H., Joseph D. Boyd, and E. James Maxey. "State Financial Aid to Students: A Trend Analysis of Access and Choice of Public and Private Colleges." *College and University* 54 (Winter 1979): 139-55.

Reports that awards from the Illinois State Scholarship Commission expand access to higher education and foster students' choice of colleges, both public and private; argues that state grants help to maintain vitality of private institutions.

139.   Folger, John K. "Building Public Support for Private Higher Education." *Compact* 10 (Summer 1976): 5-9.

Makes case for supporting private higher education (though does not specifically refer to church-related colleges) on grounds that private institutions provide diversity, increased access to higher education, reduced state tax burdens, and competition for state-supported institutions; sees no threat to independence of private institutions from state aid.

140.   Ford, William D. "Constitutional Implications of Federal Aid to Higher Education." *Journal of Law and Education* 1 (October 1972): 513-40.

Discusses problems in funding higher education, the history of federal aid to higher education, the U.S. House of Representatives proposal for the Education Amendments of 1972; reviews *Tilton* v. *Richardson* (no. 211) and its impact on general assistance to higher education and the problems created for legislators by the decision.

141.   Foster, Marilyn K. *Public Policy and Independent Higher Education.* Washington, D.C.: National Association of Independent Colleges and Universities, 1983.

Sets out antecedents of public policy in aid of private higher education; considers the variety of policies in effect since 1974; makes case for a dual system of higher education; takes into account effect of public support on church-related colleges and on small towns and rural areas where many of these colleges are located.

142.   Foster, Wayne F. "Validity, Under State Constitution and Laws, of Issuance by State or State Agency of Revenue Bonds to Finance or Refinance Construction Projects at Private Religious-Affiliated Colleges or Universities." 95 ALR 3d 1000-006 (1979).

Cites and summarizes cases involving state and federal constitutional provisions affecting public funding of construction at church-related colleges and universities.

143.   Frieber, Laury M. "Americans United for Separation of Church and State v. H.E.W.: Standing to Sue under the Establishment Clause." *Hastings Law Journal* 32 (March 1981): 975-1012.

Examines the right of Americans United to sue when the government's action did not affect the plaintiffs directly; draws out implications of this case for the establishment clause of the First Amendment and for judicial practice more generally.

144.   Fruechtel, Warren Bosset. "Relation of the State to Higher Education in Pennsylvania, 1776-1874." Ph.D. dissertation. University of Pittsburgh, 1965.

Finds that church-state relationships, as well as private and public interests have been areas of conflict which, though not examined in depth, have presented fundamental problems in attempts to formulate state policy for higher education in Pennsylvania.

145.   Fuller, Edgar. "Does Higher Education Aid Violate Church-State Principle and Implement False Images of Private Colleges?" *The Nation's Schools* 69 (January 1962): 116, 118.

Outlines perceived threat to public higher education from a then-pending bill to aid private institutions; sees threat to separation of church and state at all levels if aid is given to church-related colleges.

146.   Gaffney, Edward McGlynn Jr. and Philip R. Moots. *Government and Campus: Federal Regulation of Religiously Affiliated Higher Education.* Notre Dame, IN: University of Notre Dame Press, 1982. ED 216 624.

Reports responses from 210 of 800 church-related institutions in analyzing problems that federal laws and regulations raise for colleges administering federally funded facilities; reviews judicial decisions and makes recommendations for changes in statutory and regulatory policy.

147. Gellhorn, Walter and R. Kent Greenawalt. "Public Support and the Sectarian University." *Fordham Law Review* 38 (1970): 395-438.

Sets out the authors' views of the extent to which (then) present law requires official differentiation between church-related and other institutions as a condition for public assistance; describes the probable, future development of the law.

148. Gellhorn, Walter and R. Kent Greenawalt. *The Sectarian College and the Public Purse: Fordham--A Case Study.* Dobbs Ferry, NY: Oceana Publications, 1970.

Presents a case study of an institution (Fordham University) that secularized itself in order to qualify for public funds; describes position of sectarian institutions under United States, New York, and other states' constitutions; describes changes (including becoming nondenominational) that a church-related institution could make in order to receive public funding.

149. Giannella, Donald A. "*Lemon* and *Tilton*: The Bitter and the Sweet of Church-State Entanglement." *Supreme Court Review* (1971): 147-200.

Summarizes case law previous to *Lemon* v. *Kurtzman* 403 (403 U.S. 602, 29 LEd 2d 745) and *Tilton* v. *Richardson* (no. 211); describes the facts in these two cases, then compares the two rulings, concentrating on the Court's "entanglement" arguments; draws out implications of these rulings for numerous forms of aid; concludes that the Court will continue to have trouble writing a persuasive policy on aid to religious schools.

150. Giannella, Donald A. "Religious Liberty, Nonestablishment and Doctrinal Developments." *Harvard Law Review* 81 (1968): 513-90.

Suggests why state aid should not be denied to church-related colleges and the conditions such an institution should be expected to meet consistent with protection against an establishment of religion and the denial of free exercise of religion.

151. Gibney, Mark P. "State Aid to Religious-Affiliated Schools: A Political Analysis." *William and Mary Law Review* 28 (Fall 1986): 119-53.

Considers *Tilton* v. *Richardson* (no. 211) in the context of other decisions regarding public aid to religious schools; finds constitutional law of permissible aid to religious educational institutions in a "shambles"; highlights shortcomings in institutional relationships between the Supreme Court and the states and between the Supreme Court and the lower courts; offers suggestions on how the Supreme Court might render more satisfactory decisions.

152.   Gilbertson, Eric R. "The Supreme Court and Academe: The Evolution of Constitutional Doctrines for Higher Education." Paper presented at the Annual Meeting for the Study of Higher Education, Chicago, IL. March 15-17, 1985. Pp. 97.

Offers a historical review of relevant cases and the development of constitutional doctrine concerning individual rights and the interests of private institutions of higher education.

153.   Gladieux, Lawrence and Thomas R. Wolanin. *Congress and the Colleges.* Lexington, MA: Heath, 1976.

Touches *passim* on federal aid to church-related colleges in presenting the background to and the steps involved in passage of the Education Amendments of 1972.

154.   Goodall, Leonard E., ed. *State Politics and Higher Education: A Book of Readings.* Dearborn, MI: LMG Associates, 1976.

Contains papers on state constitutional provisions affecting higher education and legislative control of colleges and universities.

155.   Grace, James L. "The Law and Private Colleges." In *Contemporary Legal Issues in Education*, pp. 179-94. Edited by M. A. McGhehey. Topeka, KS: National Organization on Legal Problems of Education, 1979.

Demonstrates that private colleges are subject to regulation and constitutional restraint if as recipients of public funding they engage in "state action."

156.   Greenawalt, R. Kent. "Constitutional Limits on Aid to Sectarian Universities." *Journal of College and University Law* 4 (Spring 1977): 177-86.

Places *Roemer* v. *Board of Public Works* (no. 189) in historical and legal contexts; draws out relevant historical principles; concludes that church-related institutions must forego some of their religious character to get federal funding only if these institutions are pervasively sectarian.

157.   Gregory, Dennis E. "Financial Assistance by States to Independent Institutions of Higher Education." *Journal of Educational Finance* 10 (Summer 1984): 50-63.

Sets out arguments for public aid to private higher education; outlines the constitutional issues; discusses *Tilton* v. *Richardson* (no. 211) and *Hunt* v. *McNair* (no. 107); examines state constitutional limits; describes kinds of aid granted; predicts

difficulties for private institutions in securing state aid as the
financial prospects of state governments decline, federal reductions
in educational aid occur, and costs at public institutions increase;
concludes that public aid for private institutions may survive given
the political attractiveness of tuition grants, the lobbying strength
of individual institutions, and the fact that states may find it less
expensive to support private institutions than to provide
educational services at public colleges and universities.

158.   Habecker, Eugene B. *The Constitutionality of Compulsory
       Attendance at Religious Exercises in Religious Institutions of Higher
       Education Which Are Recipients of State and Federal Financial
       Assistance*. August, 1980. Pp. 25.

       Reviews cases in the general category of church-state
       relationships; outlines the Supreme Court's threefold test of
       impermissible aid to religious institutions, using compulsory
       attendance at religious exercises as a possible case in point.

159.   Habecker, Eugene B. and John E. Brown III. "Government
       Financial Assistance, Religious Colleges, and the First Amendment:
       A Call for a New Constitutional Alliance." Paper presented at the
       Christian Legal Society's Freedom and Faith Institute. South
       Bend, IN. April 23-26, 1981. Pp. 30.

       Sets out a list of strategies a religious college could use to
       receive government aid, including trying to reverse earlier doctrines
       of church-state separation (arguing that secularism is a new religion
       and that this religion is taught in public institutions), and using
       tactic of getting aid for students rather than for the institution.

160.   Hahn, J. Victor. "Constitutional and Legal Considerations." In
       Church and College: A Vital Partnership. Vol. 3.
       Accountability-Keeping Faith with One Another, pp. 117-26.
       Sherman, TX: The Center for Program and Institutional Renewal:
       National Congress on Church-Related Colleges and Universities,
       1980.

       Provides the constitutional and legal background for public
       policy affecting church-related colleges, including public financial
       assistance; summarizes cases and governmental regulations;
       concludes that many state constitutions are more stringent than the
       U.S. Constitution.

161.   Hamilton, Bette Everett and Martin E. Laufer. *Aid to Higher
       Education: A Continuing Federal Dilemma*. Ann Arbor, MI: The
       University of Michigan Center for the Study of Higher Education,
       1975.

       Presents a concise history of national or federal aid to higher
       education from 1636 to 1972; touches *passim* on the church-state
       issues of the past and how these were resolved; argues that this

history reflects the instability of a changing political environment and a lack of consensus among political leaders; funding increases as the definitions of public welfare and national security become broader and more inclusive.

162.   Hartman, John H. "Government Assistance to Church-Sponsored Schools: *Tilton* v. *Richardson* and *Lemon* v. *Kurtzman*." *Syracuse Law Review* 23 (1972): 113-24.

Reviews and summarizes the decisions in *Tilton* v. *Richardson* (no. 211) and *Lemon* v. *Kurtzman* (403 U.S. 602, 29 L.Ed. 2d 745); relates these cases to precedents; argues that the Supreme Court's use of the entanglement test is improper because the test is too obscure.

163.   Hauptman, Arthur M. and Lawrence E. Gladieux. *Tax Breaks for College: Current and Proposed Tax Provisions That Help Families Meet College Costs.* Washington, DC: College Entrance Examination Board, 1984.

Describes tax policies affecting higher education, with emphasis on areas of the tax code that help families finance college costs; concludes that direct aid is more effective and more equitable than tax incentives.

164.   Hendrickson, Robert M. "Private Higher Education and the State: The Developing Interdependent Relationship." In "Current Legal Developments Affecting Education" (A Symposium), pp. 65-72. Edited by Robert H. Shaffer. *Viewpoints* 52 (September 1976): 1-79.

Argues that private and public sectors of higher education will continue to resolve social and value conflicts only if private institutions are independent organizations able to make decisions concerning goals, purposes and programs; posits that the financial crisis in   private education and the strengthening relationship between private higher education and the state could erode institutional autonomy; cites reasons for increasing contact between the private sector and state governments; concludes that the issue is not whether private institutions are to receive public funds but how they may do so while protecting their autonomy.

165.   Hendrickson, Robert M. with Dennis E. Gregory. "Higher Education." In *The Yearbook of School Law 1984*, pp. 278-318. Topeka, KS: National Organization on Legal Problems of Education, 1985.

Reports on student aid grants and on a U.S. District Court ruling on the unconstitutionality of the North Dakota tuition assistance grant program when used to give money to students attending Bible colleges.

166.   Hendrickson, Robert M., Robert M. Mangum, and Ronald Scott. *The State and Private Education: Interdependence and State Action.* 1977.

Explores relationships between private colleges and state governments; describes and analyzes Supreme Court decisions affecting these relationships.

167.   Herbst, Jurgen. *Legal History of American Colleges and Universities. Final Report.* Madison, WI: University of Wisconsin, 1977.

Explains the legal status of university and college corporations in one of fourteen sections; treats public universities, independent colleges, and proprietary professional schools in another.

168.   Hester, Richard L. "Church Support for Higher Education in America: Issues of Survival and Purposes." *Journal of Church and State* 20 (Autumn 1978): 451-67.

Observes course of and reasons for secularization of both public and private higher education; sets out reasons for continuing to support church-related institutions.

169.   Hodgkinson, Virginia Ann. *The Initial Impact of the Middle Income Student Assistance Act upon Undergraduate Student Aid Recipients at Independent Colleges and Universities.* Washington, DC: National Association of Independent Colleges and Universities, 1981.

Assesses impact of the Middle Income Student Assistance Act by comparing student aid recipients before and after passage of the Act; uses a national sample for 1978-79 through 1979-80.

170.   Hodgkinson, Virginia Ann and Julianne Still Thrift. *Recent Trends in Financial Aid to Students Attending Independent Colleges and Universities.* Washington, DC: National Institute of Independent Colleges and Universities, 1982.

Analyzes trend data for federal financial aid to students in private colleges and universities, based on a 1981-1982 survey of student aid recipients in a national sample of 122 schools having enrollment of greater than 500.

171.   Hollander, Patricia A. *Legal Handbook for Educators.* Boulder, CO: Westview Press, 1978.

Reviews relevant legislation, regulations, and judicial decisions involving funding and use of facilities in institutions of higher education in Chapter 7, "Funding and Facilities," pp. 183-98; places special emphasis on aid to church-related colleges and universities at pp. 191-96; concludes with recommendations to college and university development and academic officers.

172.   *Horace Mann League of the U.S.* v. *Board of Public Works.* 242 Md. 645, 220 A.2d 51 (1966). Cert. Denied, 358 U.S. 97 (1967).

Holds that state (Maryland) appropriations to three church-related colleges are constitutionally invalid on grounds that these colleges were religious institutions; finds that a grant to a fourth college was permissible because the college was not religious given its attenuated ties to a church; establishes distinction between "church-related" and "religiously oriented" institutions; constitutional restrictions on public aid apply to the latter but not to the former.

173.   Howard, A. E. Dick. *State Aid to Private Higher Education.* Charlottesville, VA: Michie, 1977.

Summarizes national and all fifty state aid programs; emphasizes state-church issues involved in these programs; gives legal analysis of state and federal constitutional law as well as the historical background for these provisions.

174.   Hudson, Edward G. "Church, State, and Education in Canada and the United States: A Study in Comparative Constitutional Law." *Les Cahiers du Droit* 21 (September 1980): 461-84.

Compares constitutional law in the United States and Canada with respect to public aid to sectarian institutions, with special attention to higher education at pp. 476-77.

175.   Hughes, Jerome W. "Future Relationships between State Legislatures and Higher Education." Paper presented a Seminar for State Leaders in Postsecondary Education, Tuscon, AZ, December, 1977.

Expresses concern for how and the extent to which state financial aid will affect private higher education.

176.   Hughes, John F. and Patricia Smith. *Policy Options for Federal Considerations.* Washington, DC: American Council on Education, Policy Analysis Office, 1976.

Reports conditions and needs of private institutions; suggests sets of policy options open to government should it wish to address those needs.

177.   *Hunt* v. *McNair.* 413 U.S. 734, 37 L.Ed. 2d 923 (1973).

Holds that the issuance of state (South Carolina) revenue bonds for the benefit of church-related colleges does not violate the establishment clause of the First Amendment because (1) the state had a secular purpose in issuing the bonds, (2) the recipient colleges' operations are not significantly oriented toward sectarian education, (3) the bond issue would not have the primary effect of advancing religion since none of the publicly funded facilities would be used for religious purposes, and (4) the state's ability to foreclose in case of default would not foster excessive entanglement of the state in religious affairs.

178.   Jellema, William W. *From Red to Black? The Financial Status of Private Colleges and Universities.* San Francisco: Jossey-Bass, 1973.

Reports survey of 544 private four-year institutions, including a representative number of church-related colleges; details financial problems of these institutions and how they propose to deal with them.

179.   Jencks, Christopher and David Riesman. *The Academic Revolution.* Garden City, NY: Doubleday, 1968.

Describes the financial imbalance between private (especially church-related) and public colleges, how it came about, and what private institutions were trying to do about it, in a section, "The Financing of Public and Private Colleges," in Chapter VI, at pp. 270-79.

180.   Jones, Harry W. "The Constitutional Status of Public Funds for Church-Related Schools." *Journal of Church and State* 6 (Winter 1964): 61-73.

Considers implications of then just-approved college aid bill by the U.S. Senate Labor and Public Welfare Committee; questions distinction between elementary and secondary schools on one hand and colleges on the other; places the college aid bill in a context of government aid to all kinds and levels of church schools.

181.   Kaplin, William A. *The Law of Higher Education: Legal Implications of Administrative Decision Making.* San Francisco: Jossey-Bass, 1978.

Summarizes the law and judicial decisions regarding public aid to church-related colleges and universities through *Roemer* v. *Board of Public Works* (no. 189) in Section 1.5, "Religion and the Public-Private Dichotomy," pp. 28-33; advises administrators of church-related schools to be sensitive to establishment clause issues.

182.   Kauper, Paul G. "Public Aid for Parochial Schools and Church Colleges: The *Lemon, DiCenso,* and *Tilton* Cases." *Arizona Law Review* 13 (1971): 567-94.

Analyzes *Lemon* v. *Kurtzman* and *DiCenso* v. *Robinson,* 403 U.S. 602, 29 L.Ed. 2d 745 and *Tilton* v. *Richardson* (no. 211); assesses the doctrinal significance of these cases; examines and summarizes the concrete effects of these cases on the freedom of government to aid church-related institutions.

183.   Kauper, Paul G. "Religion, Higher Education and the Constitution." *Alabama Law Review* 19 (Spring 1967): 275-97.

Suggests that the question of public aid to sectarian higher education did not become acute until passage of the Higher Education Facilities Act of 1963; summarizes the decision in *Horace Mann League of the U.S. v. Board of Public Works* (no. 102); finds ambiguities in earlier U.S. Supreme Court decisions led to uncertainties in this case.

184.   Kauper, Paul G. "Supreme Court and the Establishment Clause: Back to *Everson*?" *Case Western Reserve Law Review* 25 (Fall 1974): 107-29.

Examines *Hunt* v. *McNair* (no. 107) in the context of precedents set by the opinions in earlier cases; concludes that decisions in those cases reflect an overly broad interpretation of the First Amendment's establishment clause and disregard both the policy considerations favoring reduction of the financial burdens on religious schools as well as the competing demands of the free exercise and equal protection clauses.

185.   King, H. Spencer. "Federal Aid to Church Affiliated Colleges and Universities: Breaching the Wall?" *South Carolina Law Review* 19 (1967): 231-48.

Concludes, after reviewing the decision in *Horace Mann* (no. 102) in light of earlier decisions by the U.S. Supreme Court, that the constitutionality of aid to church-related colleges is still an open question; doubts that anyone could get standing to sue in order to challenge federal aid to sectarian colleges; finds it unlikely that aid will be altogether denied to church-related colleges given increasing enrollments and the implied demand for higher education.

186.   King, Lauriston R. *The Washington Lobbyists for Higher Education.* Lexington, MA: D. C. Heath, 1975.

Discusses positions of church-related colleges on public aid, pp. 66-68; describes organization and activities of interest groups representing church-related colleges, *passim*.

187.   King, Richard A. "The Crisis in Higher Education: Facing Reduction and Financial Exigency." Paper presented at the Annual Meeting of the American Educational Research Association. Los Angeles, CA. April, 1981.

Reports survey of presidents of 19 public and 35 private colleges on how these institutions were responding to financial exigency; compares retrenchment strategies.

188.   Kirby, James C., Jr. "Everson to Meek and Roemer: From Separation to Détente in Church-State Relations." *North Carolina Law Review* 55 (April 1977): 573-75.

Describes the background to *Meek* v. *Pittinger*, 421 U.S. 349, 44 L.Ed. 2d 217 and *Roemer* v. *Board of Public Works* (no. 189); summarizes the holdings in these cases, emphasizing their differences; concludes by trying to reconcile the apparent conflicts between holdings in these two cases.

189.   Kirkwood, John B. and David S. Mundel. "The Role of Tax Policy in Federal Support for Higher Education." *Law and Contemporary Problems* 39 (Autumn 1975): 117-55.

States in general and in detail what tax policy is, how it works, how it may be beneficial to higher education; does not deal specifically with church-related higher education but should serve as a reliable guide nevertheless.

190.   Koelsch, William A. "Should the 'Christian College' Survive?" *Soundings* 52 (Summer 1969): 218-32.

Sets out problems facing church-related colleges, argues that survival of these institutions depends on their leaders' capacity to adjust and to develop programs; reflects on work of Harvey Cox, Christopher Jencks and David Riesman (no. 109), and on the Danforth Foundation report on 800 colleges.

191.   Kramer, Donald T. "Supreme Court Cases Involving Establishment and Freedom of Religion Clauses of Federal Constitution." 37 L.Ed. 2d 1147-1221, Part III, Section 5(d), "Construction Grants or Assistance," pp. 1186-1187.

Summarizes, comments on *Tilton* v. *Richardson* (no. 211) and *Hunt* v. *McNair* (no. 107). (The 1986 Pocket Part, pp. 32-37, updates the commentary through *Roemer* v. *Board of Public Works*, [no. 189] at p. 35.)

192.   LaNoue, George R. "Church-State Relations in the Federal Policy Process." Ph.D. disseration. Yale University, 1966.

Shows, based on documentation of all important federal programs and an intensive study of the Peace Corps, that the participation of church agencies in federal agencies has resulted in greater benefits for private than for public institutions and for church-related private institutions than for private non-sectarian institutions; argues that church participation in federal programs is so extensive that the concept of separation of church and state is no longer empirically accurate; concludes that even though such participation is as extensive as it is, the government has stopped short of full-scale establishment of religion by limiting aid to certain church activities and by secularizing the activities that it does support.

193.   Lapati, Americo D. *Education and the Federal Government.* New York: Mason/Charter, 1975.

> Presents background for Supreme Court cases involving aid to church-related institutions of higher education; summarizes and comments on *Tilton* v. *Richardson* (no. 211) and *Hunt* v. *McNair* (no. 107), in Chapter 7, "Private and Religious Schools," pp. 150-96.

194.   Leavy, Edward N. and Eric Alan Raps. "The Judicial Double Standard for State Aid to Church-Affiliated Educational Institutions." *Journal of Church and State* 21 (Spring 1979): 209-22.

> Reviews *Roemer* v. *Board of Public Works* (no. 189), *Tilton* v. *Richardson* (no. 211), and *Hunt* v. *McNair* (no. 107); asserts that in these cases the Supreme Court applied its three-part test less rigorously than it customarily has in similar cases involving elementary and secondary education and that the Court has therefore set a double standard in dealing with public aid to religious schools.

195.   Levy, Daniel. "Private Versus Public Financing of Higher Education: U.S. Policy in Comparative Perspective." *Higher Education* 11 (November 1982): 607-28.

> Compares sources of funding and the institutional targets of that funding (including church-related institutions) in the United States with those in other countries; concludes that the United States is significantly different from other nations in the degree to which it depends on private financing of higher education.

196.   Lewis, Ronald J. "The Future of the Independent Sector of Higher Education: An Economic Appraisal." *College and University* 56 (Fall 1980): 66-75.

> Finds that relevant economic factors point to the demise of non-subsidized private sector of higher education, assuming steadily declining enrollment through 1990; concludes that it will take larger numbers of college-age people going to college or significant increases in endowment support from private or public sources to save private higher education.

197.   Lorenson, Frederick Hamilton. "The Evaluation and Implications of *Tilton* v. *Richardson*: The First United States Supreme Court Test of the Constitutionality of Federal Grants to Religious-Affiliated Colleges and Universities." Ph.D. dissertation. University of Connecticut, 1979.

> Traces development of *Tilton* v. *Richardson* (no. 211) from filing of the initial complaint in 1968 through the decision in 1971;

sets out implications for higher education generally; relates the decision to views of constitutional law scholars and to decisions in other cases.

198.   Loveless, William Alfred. "Federal Aid and the Church-Operated College: A Case Study." Ph.D. dissertation. University of Maryland, 1964.

Traces the history of attitudes in Seventh Day Adventism toward federal aid; compares denominational policy with practice in the church's colleges; reports extensive participation in federal assistance programs, in some cases in direct opposition to denominational policy; perceives adverse effects on religious freedom and goals of educational institutions should aid continue; also perceives adverse effects on educational missions should participation stop.

199.   Lowell, C. Stanley. *The Great Church-State Fraud.* Washington, DC: Robert B. Luce, Inc., 1973.

Recounts the passage of the Higher Education Facilities Act of 1963; gives history of similar policies; shows distribution of funds to church-related institutions; describes other forms of aid available to such schools; considers cases and legal issues involved in public aid to religious schools; sets out implications of such aid for public policy and for the institutions themselves, in Chapter 5, "Defense Does It: Helping the Church in Higher Education," pp. 85-108.

200.   Lowell, C. Stanley. "Will Churches Give Up Their Colleges? Can Colleges Survive Without Governmental Aid?" *Education Digest* 37 (October 1971): 24-25.

Predicts that churches will lose most of their colleges, if not by disassociation then by permeation of these schools by public purposes; describes how this happens and offers suggestions to church administrators on how to make the transitions required.

201.   MacLeod, Edward. "Federal Aid to Church-Related Colleges: Theological and Legal Arguments of Baptists as Separationists." *Journal of Church and State* 10 (Autumn 1968): 405-20.

Identifies and summarizes the views of two schools of thought on public aid to church-related colleges, the "transformationists," who would accept aid, and the "separationists," who would refuse; examines separationist views, looking for a theological base; questions whether such ideas were included in the First Amendment.

202.   Magill, Samuel H., ed. *The Contribution of the Church-Related College to the Public Good.* Washington, DC: Association of American Colleges, 1970.

Collects papers whose central task is to describe the loss to the public good were church-related colleges to be phased out to be substantially weakened.

203.   Malbin, Michael J. *Religion and Politics: The Intentions of the Authors of the First Amendment.* Washington, DC: American Enterprise Institute, 1978.

Asserts that the Supreme Court has misinterpreted the intentions of the framers of the First Amendment since 1947; argues that the framers supported aid to religion if it furthered a purpose government could lawfully pursue and so long as it did not discriminate in favor of some sects over others.

204.   Maltby, Gregory P. "Aid to Individuals versus Aid to Institutions: A Discussion of Basic Issues." *Notre Dame Journal of Education* 4 (Fall 1973): 258-67.

Examines assumptions used in arguments against voucher systems; favors aid to individuals over aid to institutions, though expresses preference for some institutional aid to continue.

205.   Manion, Maureen. "The Impact of State Aid on Sectarian Higher Education: The Case of New York State." *Review of Politics* 48 (Spring 1986): 264-88.

Describes how New York state administers aid to church-related colleges; reports that state standards of constitutionality are applied, rather than the standards developed by the U.S. Supreme Court in *Lemon* v. *Kurtzman* (403 U.S. 602, 29 L.Ed. 2d 745), *Tilton* v. *Richardson* (no. 211) and *Roemer* v. *Board of Public Works* (no. 189); notes strong tendencies toward secularization of colleges receiving aid; concludes by discussing some problems that may arise in the future.

206.   Manion, Maureen. "The Impact of State Aid upon Church-Related Higher Education in the State of New York: The First Amendment Issues." Ph.D. dissertation. State University of New York at Albany, 1982.

Examines the development and implementation of aid to colleges and universities against that background of U.S. Supreme Court decisions and the New York state constitution and relevant decisions by state courts; considers the extent to which state aid has influenced internal governance and academic programs of recipient and non-recipient church-related institutions; reports trends away from denomination control and diversity of programs.

207.   McCoy, Charles S. *The Church-Related College in American Society.* Washington, DC: Association of American Colleges, 1970.

Urges church-related colleges to keep denomination ties and

to counter state-supported higher education by educating middle-ability and disadvantaged students for social involvement.

208.   McCoy, Marilyn and D. Kent Halstead. *Higher Education Financing in the Fifty States: Interstate Comparisons, Fiscal Year 1982.* 4th edition. Boulder, CO; National Center for Higher Education Management Systems, 1984.

Presents data and narrative describing revenues (including those from public sources) and expenditures for specific types of public and private colleges and universities.

209.   McFarlane, William H. "Patterns of State Aid to Private Higher Education." *College and University Journal* 11 (May 1972): 19-21.

Proposes that the church-state issue is a primary reason why support of private higher education is effected through student aid rather than through direct support of institutions.

210.   McFarlane, William H. *State Support for Private Higher Education.* Atlanta: Southern Regional Education Board, 1969.

Examines issues related to restructuring of state systems of higher education, with special concern for the role of private colleges and universities; uses a variety of perspectives in considering these issues, including one that emphasizes legal and political considerations.

211.   McFarlane, William H., Jay L. Chronister, and A. E. Dick Howard. "State Aid for Virginia's Private Colleges?" *Journal of Law and Education* 2 (October 1973): 593-611.

Offers historical background to legislation providing limited aid to church-related colleges in Virginia; describes and analyzes court tests and judicial holdings; compares holdings of the Virginia Supreme Court with those made by the U.S. Supreme Court in *Tilton* v. *Richardson* (no. 195) and *Hunt* v. *McNair* (no. 107).

212.   McFarlane, William H., A. E. Dick Howard, and Jay L. Chronister. *State Financial Measures Involving the Private Sector of Higher Education.* Washington, DC: Association of American Colleges, 1974.

Examines the rationale for state aid to private institutions (including church-related ones); reviews constitutional considerations involved in state aid to private higher education; summarizes constitutional provisions in all 50 states.

213.   McFarlane, William H. and Charles L. Wheeler. *Legal and Political Issues of State Aid for Private Higher Education.* Atlanta: Southern Regional Education Board, 1971.

Asks what kinds and amounts of state support are possible

within existing legal and political constraints; reviews legislation and judicial decisions to ascertain legal limitations; considers survey data collected from educational and political leaders to determine political constraints; draws out implications of these findings and identifies potential problem areas.

214.   McGrath, Earl J. "The Independent Institutions of Higher Education in the Eighties." In *Private Higher Education: The Job Ahead*, Vol. 9, pp. 8-13. Rockford, IL: American Association of Presidents of Independent Colleges and Universities, 1981.

Treats the loss of individual and church support of church-related colleges because of increasing secularization; discusses the resulting loss of distinctiveness and the declining attractiveness of such institutions to students; finds that the colleges doing best are those with a clear religious commitment and strong denominational support; urges a clearer definition of purpose by church-related colleges; observes that student aid does not become "entangled in the prescriptions of the First Amendment."

215.   McKeefery, William, et al. *Patterns of Private-Public Relatedness: Five Institutional Histories and an Analysis.* Bridgeport, CT: University of Bridgeport, 1981.

Reports findings of five case studies illustrating a variety of individual differences among institutions; describes schools that developed a public connection, why and how they did it, what was achieved by doing so, and what the consequences were.

216.   McMahon, Linda. *Independent College Interest Group Influence on State Policy.* Washington, DC: National Institute of Independent Colleges and Universities, 1981.

Indicates that the chief factor in motivating states to help independent colleges and universities is the influence exercised by interest groups representing these institutions at the state level; reports that the amount of aid was also dependent on the strength of these interest groups.

217.   Miliken, Christine Topping. *A Guide to Tax Policy and Higher Education: An Analysis of Tuition Tax Credits, Tax Savings Plans, Vouchers and Independent Higher Education.* Tax Policy Papers: 1981, Issue 1. Washington, DC: National Association of Independent Colleges and Universities, 1981.

Details the policy implications of tuition tax credits, tax allowances, and vouchers for private colleges and universities; cites advantages and disadvantages of each.

218.   Miller, Arthur L. "Church Schools and the Church-State Issue." In *Church and State Under God*, pp. 322-62. Edited by Albert G. Huegli. St. Louis, MO: Concordia Publishing House, 1964.

Distinguishes between church-related higher education and church-run elementary and secondary schools; discusses forms of federal aid to nonpublic colleges and universities available since the end of World War II; suggests influences on curriculum such aid has had.

219. Minter, John. "Financial Conditions and Trends of Church-Related Colleges." In *Church and College: A Vital Partnership.* Vol. 3: *Accountability-Keeping Faith with One Another*, pp. 141-152. Sherman, TX: The Center for Program and Institutional Renewal: National Congress on Church-Related Colleges and Universities, 1980.

Shows income for church-related colleges from publicly supported student aid programs, government contracts, and government grants.

220. Moots, Philip R. "Legal Issues for Church-Related Colleges and Universities." In *Church and College: A Vital Partnership.* Vol. 3: *Accountability-Keeping Faith with One Another*, pp. 13-32. Sherman, TX: The Center for Program and Institutional Renewal: National Congress on Church-Related Colleges and Universities, 1980.

Argues that state constitutions and their interpretations are more likely to cause problems for aid to church-related institutions than the U.S. Constitution and the interpretations of federal courts; summarizes *Tilton* v. *Richardson* (no. 211) *Hunt* v. *McNair* (no. 107), and *Roemer* v. *Board of Public Works* (no. 189), concludes that the Supreme Court was trying to determine if the schools involved were practicing free academic inquiry or were only proselytizing; suggests that relationships between a church and a college receiving public aid are not the only factor the courts will consider and that these relationships are irrelevant if government gives aid to students; believes that the question of admissions of students all of one religion has been considered by the courts but that the degree of preference allowable has not yet been settled; considers religious use of government funded facilities and other government regulations based on public funding.

221. Moots, Philip R. and Edward McGlynn Gaffney, Jr. *Church and Campus: Government Regulation of Religiously Affiliated Higher Education.* Notre Dame, IN: Center for Constitutional Studies, Notre Dame Law School, 1979.

Asks two questions: (1) what legal problems arising from governmental regulations have religiously affiliated colleges experienced at least partially because of their religious affiliation; and (2) how might the relationship between government and these institutions be ameliorated; considers judicial decisions regarding public aid for facilities, *passim*.

222.   Moots, Philip R. and Edward McGlynn Gaffney, Jr. *Colleges and Sponsoring Religious Bodies: A Study of Policy Influence and Property Relationships.* Washington, DC: Association of Catholic Colleges and Universities and South Bend, IN: Center for Constitutional Studies, University of Notre Dame, 1978.

     Aims at delineating desirable relationships between colleges and their sponsoring religious bodies, including those relationships that would serve to maintain eligibility of the college and its students for support by federal and state financial aid programs.

223.   Moran, Gerald P. *Private Colleges: The Federal Tax System and Its Impact.* Toledo, OH: University of Toledo Center for the Study of Higher Education, 1977.

     Supports thesis that federal and state tax systems are rich and varied sources of increased indirect revenue for private education; discusses legal issues and judicial decisions, though with little emphasis on church-state issues.

224.   Morgan, Richard E. *The Supreme Court and Religion.* New York: Free Press, 1972.

     Gives immediate background to *Tilton* v. *Richardson* (no. 211); dissects the majority and dissenting opinions; shows that Chief Justice Burger drew all members of the Court to see the issues in terms of "his preferred category of entanglement," in section "Aid to Higher Education--*Tilton*," pp. 107-10.

225.   Mullaney, Mary. "Religious Discrimination and Higher Education: A Continuing Dilemma." *Notre Dame Lawyer* 52 (October 1976): 152-65.

     Reviews decisions in *Tilton* v. *Richardson* (no. 211), *Hunt* v. *McNair* (no. 107), and *Roemer* v. *Board of Public Works* (no. 189); examines questions of constitutionality of introducing considerations of religion into employment decisions of church-related colleges in light of these decisions.

226.   Murray, Michael A. "Defining the Higher Education Lobby." *Journal of Higher Education* 47 (January-February 1976): 70-92.

     Provides brief descriptions of organizations lobbying for higher education, including organizations representing church-related colleges and universities.

227.   National Commission on United Methodist Education. *Endangered Service: Independent Colleges, Public Policy and the First Amendment.* Nashville, TN: National Commission on United Methodist Education, 1976.

     Stresses the social benefits of private education and the

corresponding need for government to preserve diversity and autonomy within higher education; review judicial decisions and concludes that while the legal validity of aid to private institutions has been established, such aid has not yet become accepted public policy; emphasizes need for tax incentives, planning, and removal of excessive governmental regulation.

228.   Norton, James A. "State Relationships to the Private Sector." Paper presented at a Seminar for State Leaders in Postsecondary Education. St. Petersburg, FL. January, 1976.

Delineates relationships between state governments and private higher education, with emphasis on Ohio; furnishes examples of means by which a state may aid private institutions.

229.   O'Brien, J. Stephen and Richard S. Vacca. *The Supreme Court and the Religion-Education Controversy: A Tightrope to Entanglement.* Durham, NC: Moore Publishing Co., 1974.

Covers case law established in Supreme Court decisions on religion and education up to but not including *Roemer* v. *Board of Public Works* (no. 189); sets cases involving higher education with a more general context; points to contradictory holdings; sets out problems likely to arise as the Court and others try to follow these precedents.

230.   O'Grady, Joseph P. "Control of Church-Related Institutions of Higher Learning." *Journal of Higher Education* 40 (February 1969): 108-21.

Argues that if colleges separate from churches in order to survive, a basic shift in control will result, as will a movement of church-related colleges away from the church; but also asserts that other influences (secular movements of the last 500 years, departures from institutionalism, ecumenical developments, Vatican II) have been having the same effects.

231.   O'Hara, Julie Underwood. "State Aid to Denominational Higher Education: A First Amendment Problem." Ph.D. dissertation, University of Florida, 1984.

Outlines permissible criteria to be followed in granting aid to church-related higher education; reports amounts spent by states and the relation of these amounts to the strictness of those states' consititutional provisions.

232.   O'Hara, Julie Underwood. "State Aid to Sectarian Higher Education." *Journal of Law and Education* 14 (April 1985): 181-209.

Establishes a typology of state aid to church-related institutions of higher education; examines selected state programs for constitutional compliance; analyzes relevant cases; concludes that courts are more lenient with higher education than with elementary and secondary schools and that states therefore have wide latitude in developing programs; but reports that because state legislators are inattentive to legal restrictions, these programs may be vulnerable to constitutional attack.

233.   Olliver, James. "The Legal Status of State Aid for Non-public Colleges and Universities." Vols. I and II. Ph.D. dissertation. Florida State University, 1975.

Reports the legal status of state aid for non-public higher education for each of the 50 states through analysis of state constitutions, state and federal court rulings, operational programs, and opinions of state attorneys general; reviews *Tilton* v. *Richardson* (no. 211) and *Hunt* v. *McNair* (no. 107) and delineates the effects of these decisions on state aid to church-related colleges.

234.   Olliver, James. *The States and Independent Higher Education: Policies, Programs and Planning for the 1980s. A Research Report from the State-National Information Network.* Washington, DC: National Institute of Independent Colleges and Universities, 1982.

Describes types of state support and policy implications of funding options; sets out a history of policies of the 1960s and 1970s; gives overview of range and extent of support available to independent colleges and universities.

235.   Olson, Lawrence. *The Public Stake in Independent Higher Education.* Washington, DC: National Institute of Independent Colleges and Universities, 1982.

Defends public funding of private colleges and universities, citing contributions to the public good made by these institutions; considers implications of public aid for government and industry; states that independent schools cost taxpayers less than do public institutions.

236.   O'Neil, Robert M. *The Courts, Government and Higher Education.* New York: Committee for Economic Development, 1972.

Predicts continuing financial austerity for higher education accompanied by increasing demand for governmental support, which he believes will be met; concludes that private institutions can expect increasing control by government as public aid increases.

237.   Pattillo, Manning M. and Donald M. MacKenzie. *Church-Sponsored Higher Education in the United States.* Washington, DC: American Council on Education, 1966.

Paints a highly sympathetic picture of church-related colleges and their contributions to American life and culture; summarizes current status of enrollments, numbers of graduates, faculties, curricula, facilities, government aid, and educational results; considers major strengths and weaknesses; asks what the educational and religious roles of church-colleges should be; makes recommendations for future development and cites problems of increasing secularization as a concomitant of the increase in public funding.

238. Perkins, John A. and Daniel W. Wood. "Issues in Federal Aid to Education." In *The Federal Government and Higher Education*, pp. 140-75. Edited by Douglas M. Knight. Englewood Cliffs, NJ: Prentice-Hall, Inc., 1960.

Argues that the stalemate in federal funding of education results from the fact that no bill with aid to religious schools can pass and no bill without such aid can pass; suggests that a bill containing aid to church-related schools be passed and then adjudicated in order to learn what the Constitution will and will not permit.

239. Peterson, Walfred H. "The Thwarted Opportunity for Judicial Activism in Church-State Relations: Separation and Accommodation in Precarious Balance." *Journal of Church and State* 22 (Autumn 1980): 437-58.

Uses Guttman scale analysis to show how activist judges on the Supreme Court may be thwarted by judges advocating judicial restraint; uses cases involving public aid to church-related colleges (among others) as part of the data base.

240. Pettit, Lawrence Kay. "The Policy Process in Congress: Passing the Higher Education Academic Facilities Act of 1963." Ph.D. dissertation. University of Wisconsin, 1965.

Describes the passage of the act that was tested in subsequent Supreme Court cases; concludes that the bill passed because (among other reasons) agreement on the church-state issue was reached by making a plausible distinction between higher education, on the one hand, and elementary and secondary education on the other.

241. Pfeffer, Leo. "Aid to Parochial Schools: The Verge and Beyond." *Journal of Law and Education* 3 (January 1974): 115-21.

Summarizes holdings of the Supreme Court on aid to church-related colleges, with particular emphasis on *Tilton* v. *Richardson* (no. 211), at pp. 120-21.

242. Pfeffer, Leo. *Church, State and Freedom.* Revised Edition. Boston: Beacon Press, 1967.

Recounts passage of the Higher Education Facilities Act of

1963; summarizes the legal memorandum prepared by the Department of Health, Education and Welfare (no. 053) in support of aid to church-related colleges; comments critically on arguments used in this memorandum and by the Kennedy Administration generally to support funding of facilities at religious institutions of higher education.

243.   Pfeffer, Leo. *God, Caesar, and the Constitution: The Court As Referee of Church-State Confrontation.* Boston: Beacon Press, 1975.

Reviews and summarizes Supreme Court cases concerned with public aid to church-related colleges; distinguishes college aid cases from those based on aid to elementary and secondary schools, in section on "College Aid," pp. 292-97.

244.   Pfeffer, Leo. "A Momentous Year in Church and State: 1963." *Journal of Church and State* 6 (Winter 1964): 36-43.

Views portents of the Higher Education Facilities Act of 1963 in the context of earlier church-state relationships; sees threat of religious fragmentation and disintegration of the publicly supported educational system.

245.   Pfeffer, Leo. "Uneasy Trinity: Church, State, and Constitution." *Civil Liberties Review* 2 (Winter 1975): 138-61.

Summarizes Congressional legislation leading to *Tilton* v. *Richardson* (no. 211) and describes the holding in that case; places the conflict over public aid to church related institutions of higher education within the more general context of church-state relations.

246.   Pfinister, Allan O. "Development of the American System of Higher Education: The Two-Sector Theory." Paper presented at the Annual Meeting of the Association for the Study of Higher Education. Washington, DC. March 4-5, 1980.

Traces the evolution of the two-sector theory of public and private colleges from the colonial period to the present.

247.   Phillips, John D. "Policy Issues, the Federal Government, and Diversity." Paper presented at a Seminar for Leaders in Postsecondary Education. Orlando, FL. November, 1978.

Considers federal policy toward private higher education; argues that independent colleges are among the best places to learn the basic moral and educational heritage of the nation; says that state governments may exert too much control, that a free-choice marketplace is needed, and that government intervention may be necessary to prevent unfair competition by public colleges and universities.

248.   Phillips, John D. and James L. Chapman. "Point/Counterpoint:

Should Public Funds Be Used to Support Independent Colleges and Universities?" *Community and Junior College Journal* 55 (November 1984): 48-51.

Presents opposing points of view on public aid of private colleges; Phillips is in favor of such aid and cites the public service of private institutions in support of his position; Chapman is opposed to aiding private schools with public funds, claiming that a loss of autonomy accompanies public funding.

249.   Pope, Kenneth H. "Public Funds and Private Colleges." Speech, August 23, 1978.

Acknowledges the First and Fourteenth Amendments as barriers to public aid to sectarian institutions; cites problems in private colleges as the gap between tuition charged by private colleges and that collected by public institutions continues to grow.

250.   President's Task Force on Higher Education. *Priorities in Higher Education.* Washington, DC: Government Printing Office, 1970.

Recommends dependence on "increasing private support to sustain" private colleges that maintain "maximum institutional autonomy."

251.   "Private Colleges, State Aid, and the Establishment Clause." *Duke Law Journal* 1975 (September 1975): 976-98.

Traces the Supreme Court's treatment of the First Amendment establishment clause in relation to public aid to institutions of elementary, secondary, and higher education; examines several federal courts decisions in cases involving aid to church-related colleges; finds concepts of "pervasive sectarianism" and "excessive entanglement" elusive.

252.   "Public Payment of Tuition, Scholarships, Or the Like, As Respect to Sectarian Schools." 81 ALR 2d 1309-17.

Cites and summarizes case law on the constitutional validity of public funding of individual instruction in sectarian schools; Section 4, "Universities; advanced training," pp. 1314-15, concerns higher education; see 79-82 ALR 2d Later Case Service, p. 393-95 for cases to 1979; see Pocket Part, pp. 171-72 for cases to 1986.

253.   Rabineau, Louis. "State Policy and Postsecondary Education: The Relationship of the Independent and Public Sectors." Paper presented at a Seminar for Leaders in Postsecondary Education. Orlando, FL. November, 1978.

Outlines relationships between public and private sectors in higher education; states reasons for public aid to private institutions (public mission of private schools, diversity in institutions, tradition); describes means of aiding private institutions; calls for a reduction in state control.

254.   Radcliffe, Robert James.   "The Compromise of Mission in Church-Related Colleges."   Ph.D. dissertation.   Claremont Graduate School, 1982.

Reports examination of four representative schools' compromise on six different measures of mission in response to six factors, including one measuring financial struggle.

255.   Reinert, Paul C.   *To Turn the Tide.*   Englewood Cliffs, NJ: Prentice-Hall, Inc., 1972.

Describes the financial crisis in private higher education; sets out reasons for continuing private higher education; supports increased federal funding of private institutions.

256.   "Religious Purposes and Sectarian Instruction."   63A Am.Jur. 2d, Public Funds, Section 71.

Lists cases involving public aid to sectarian institutions and summarizes the general effects of the cases on laws governing the use of public funds.

257.   Rivlin, Alice M.   *The Role of the Federal Government in Financing Higher Education.*   Washington, DC: The Brookings Institution, 1961.

Discusses distinction between loans and grants and the differences between general aid and aid for particular programs in light of the church-state issue, as well as the effect this issue has had on the more general question of federal aid to higher education; sees aid to students as aid to their institutions.

258.   Robison, Joseph B.   "Summary and Analysis of the Maryland Court of Appeals' Decisions on State Aid to Church Colleges: *Horace Mann League* v. *Board of Public Works of Maryland.*"   *Journal of Church and State* 8 (Autumn 1966): 401-14.

Sets out the origins of the suit, describes the trial proceedings, and summarizes the court's opinion as well as the major points made in the dissenting opinion; draws out implications for future instances of direct and indirect public aid to church-related colleges.

259.   *Roemer* v. *Board of Public Works of Maryland.*   426 U.S. 736, 49 L.Ed. 2d 179 (1976).

Holds that the First Amendment establishment clause was not violated by a state (Maryland) statute (1) authorizing public funds for annual noncategorical grants to private colleges and (2) requiring that the funds conveyed not be used for sectarian purposes.

260. "The Sacred Wall Revisited-The Constitutionality of State Aid to
      Non-Public Education Following *Lemon* v. *Kurtzman* and *Tilton* v.
      Richardson." *Northwestern University Law Review* 67 (1972):
      118-45.

      Summarizes holdings in *Lemon* v. *Kurtzman* (403 U.S. 602,
      29 L.Ed. 2d 745) and *Tilton* v. *Richardson* (no. 211); discusses the
      effects of these decisions on a variety of forms of state aid; questions
      whether tax credit or parental reimbursement programs could
      withstand constitutional scrutiny.

261. Sauser, Robert W. "State Aid to Nonpublic Sectarian Colleges."
      Tennessee Law Review 44 (Winter 1977): 377-88.

      Summarizes cases through *Roemer* v. *Board of Public Works*
      (no. 189); suggests need for increased vigilance by the U.S.
      Supreme Court as pressures increase for public aid to
      church-related colleges; sees revival of the Court's entanglement test
      as an appropriate first step.

262. Scher, Richard K. "The State and Private Colleges and
      Universities: The Politics of Private Higher Education in New
      York." Ph.D. dissertation. Columbia University, 1972.

      Reports that the church-state issue was a primary deterrent
      to aid for private higher education in New York; finds that a
      student aid program was a compromise designed to circumvent
      state constitutional restrictions; suggests that the issue was also
      defused by other factors, including the willingness of the Catholic
      Church not to oppose aid to non-sectarian private institutions.

263. Schmarak, Barry. "Governmental Aid to Church-Related Colleges:
      Side-Stepping the 'Wall of Separation.'" *DePaul Law Review* 16
      (1967): 409-20.

      Traces the historical development of relationships between
      church and state; outlines the U.S. Supreme Court's interpretation
      of the First Amendment establishment clause; summarizes the
      decision in *Horace Mann League of the U.S* v. *Board of Public
      Works* (no. 102); sets out conditions in which courts appear to be
      willing to uphold aid to church related colleges.

264. Schmidtlein, Frank A. and Joseph J. Popovich, Jr. "Higher
      Education Finance Issues in a Period of Transition. Working
      Papers in Education Finance No. 3." Paper presented at the
      Postsecondary Education Finance Conference. Denver, CO.
      November 16-18, 1978.

      Sketches trends affecting the financing of higher education;
      considers changes in participation in higher education by

examination of several variables, including type of institution (public, private, church-related).

265.   Shulman, Carol. *State Aid to Private Higher Education.* Washington, DC: American Association for Higher Education, 1972.

Evaluates the claim of private institutions that they piovide diversity, allow innovation, and give students more attention than they receive at public institutions; offers reasons for extending public aid to private institutions; considers methods for providing such aid; asks whether student aid raises enrollment to the point where an institution's financial needs are met; considers problems associated with public aid for private institutions, including problems of constitutionality.

266.   Shulman, Carol. *Private Colleges: Present Conditions and Future Prospects.* Washington, DC: American Association for Higher Education, 1974. ED 098 888.

Reviews history of public aid to higher education from colonial times to the 20th century; summarizes state programs in effect in 1974; considers church-state questions in the context of problems and prospects of private higher education in general.

267.   Silber, John R. "Paying the Bill for College--The Private Sector and the Public Interest." *Atlantic* 235 (May 1975): 33-40.

Justifies public funding for private institutions by emphasizing the contribution to the public good that private institutions can and do make; stumps for tuition vouchers to take advantage of what private institutions can offer.

268.   Silberman, Ralph M. "Supreme Court's Views Regarding State Aid to Sectarian Schools under Establishment and Freedom of Religion Clauses of United States Constitution." 63 L.Ed. 2d 804-26.

Annotates *Committee for Public Education* v. *Regan* (444 U.S. 646, 63 L.Ed. 2d 94); discusses the constitutionality of grants to church-related colleges and sets this case in the general context of public aid to religious institutions.

269.   Sirico, Louis J., Jr. "The Secular Contribution of Religion to the Political Process: The First Amendment and School Aid." *Missouri Law Review* 50 (Spring 1985): 321-76.

Argues that religion makes a secular contribution to society and that increased attention to this contribution by courts would be desirable; applies this thesis to cases involving public aid to religious schools, including *Roemer* v. *Board of Public Works* (no. 189).

270.   Smith, Michael R. "Emerging Consequences of Financing Private

Colleges with Public Money." *Valparaiso University Law Review* 9 (Spring 1975): 561-610.

Presents a legal and policy analysis of government subsidies for private, church-related higher education; discusses *Tilton* v. *Richardson* (no. 211) and *Hunt* v. *McNair* (no. 107), as well as important state court decisions; considers a vast variety of means by which church-related colleges may be aided and how each of these will be affected by the decisions reviewed.

271.   Sorauf, Frank J. *The Wall of Separation: The Constitutional Politics of Church and State.* Princeton, NJ: Princeton University Press, 1976.

Details the origins, issues, sponsorship, and aftermath of cases raising issues of church-state separation from 1951 through mid-1971; places aid to church-related higher education within this broad context; relates decisions to the imperatives of the Constitution and the realities of American society.

272.   Stahmer, Harold. "Defining Religion: Federal Aid and Academic Freedom." In *Religion and the Public Order, 1963: An Annual Review of Church and State and of Religion, Law, and Society.* Edited by Donald R. Giannella. Chicago, IL: University of Chicago Press, 1964.

Says constitutionality of public aid to church-related colleges should be decided on the basis of free speech, an element of academic freedom, rather than on the basis of the First Amendment clauses.

273.   Stanford, Edward V. "The Relation of the Catholic College to Church and State." *The Catholic Educational Review* 60 (November 1962): 512-17.

Considers a church-related college as both a civil and a religious institution in which both the church and the state have an interest; sees the civil authority as the proper agency to set requirements for an educational institution; perceives the problem of dual control more seeming than real; believes that a federal agency may balk at making loans or grants to a church-related college unless the institution has a corporate identity separate from that of the religious community.

274.   Stokes, Anson Phelps. *Church and State in the United States.* 3 Vols. New York: Harper and Brothers, 1950.

Recounts the early history of higher education in the United States and of the role of churches in that history in section "The Development of Higher Education to Meet New Needs of the State," pp. 628-38, Vol. I; gives early history of state aid to church-related colleges, describes conflicts between supporters of public institutions and backers of private schools, and sums up the then (1950) present situation regarding state support for church-related colleges in section "Higher Education," pp. 616-25, Vol. II.

275.   Stokes, Anson Phelps and Leo Pfeffer. *Church and State in the United States.* New York: Harper and Row, 1964.

Updates Stokes' 1950 work; discusses the Higher Education Facilities Act of 1963, supplying details of the legislation restrictions, and background; sets out views of the Kennedy Administration on this legislation, and summarizes arguments of Congressional opponents, at pp. 445-46.

276.   Swomley, John M. *Religion, the State and the Schools.* New York: Pegasus Press, 1968.

Distinguishes (in "The Dilemma of Public Funds for Church Colleges," pp. 139-52) elementary and secondary schools from colleges and gives arguments for aiding church related higher education; supplies counter-arguments against each of his propositions in support of aid to sectarian colleges; recommends that church-related colleges that cannot get money from the church or other private sources give up their sectarian relationship before seeking public assistance; examines (in "Aid to Church Colleges," pp. 153-61) kinds of government funding and the impact of this money on church-related colleges; concludes that the United States has a church-state problem because there has been inadequate planning at all levels of government to meet the needs of people for education beyond high school; asserts that if local governments were to provide adequately for secular higher education, there would be no need for a public subsidy to church-related colleges.

277.   Tarr, G. Alan. *Judicial Impact and State Supreme Courts.* Lexington, MA: Lexington Books, 1977.

Reports variance in the responses of state supreme court judges to U.S. Supreme Court decisions on the establishment of religion; uses cases through *Tilton* v. *Richardson* (no. 211); tests several hypotheses to account for variance; concludes that the best hypothesis is one emphasizing the impact compliance with the Supreme Court's rulings would have on the state's levels of social and political peace and tranquility.

278.   Task Force of the National Council of Independent Colleges and Universities. *A National Policy for Private Higher Education.* Washington, DC: Association of American Colleges, 1974.

Argues that the private sector of higher education is important because it maintains diversity, sets standards, reinforces academic freedom, supports liberal learning, and relieves taxpayer burdens; offers evidence for the financial distress of private institutions; proposes a program of tuition offset grants, with alternative ways outlined for putting this program into effect.

279. Thomas, Norman C. "Public Subventions to Nonpublic Education: Values, the Courts, and Educational Policy." *Detroit College Law Review* 1976 (1976): 199-233.

Gives arguments for and against aid to church schools and describes the issues at stake in *Horace Mann League of the U.S.* v. *Board of Public Works* (no. 102) and *Tilton* v. *Richardson* (no. 211) in light of these arguments; sees the normal processes of pluralistic politics leading to a role for the federal government in enabling church-related colleges to secure aid for themselves and their students, subject only to a restriction that public money may not be used for religious purposes.

280. Tierney, Michael L. "The Impact of Financial Aid on Student Demand for Public/Private Higher Education." *Journal of Higher Education* 51 (September/October 1930): 527-45.

Concludes that provision of financial aid to students is an effective way to increase competition between public and private institutions.

281. *Tilton* v. *Richardson*. 403 U.S. 672, 29 L.Ed. 2d 790 (1971).

Holds that the Higher Education Facilities Act of 1963 was not unconstitutional since it had neither the intent nor the effect of promoting religion, except for that portion of the Act allowing for religious use of publicly funded facilities after twenty years.

282. "Tuition Tax Credit Issue." *Momentum*, 9, May, 1978, pp. 2-9.

Supports tax credits for those paying tuition to colleges and universities, church-related or not.

283. Underwood, James L. "Permissible Entanglement under the Establishment Clause." *Emory Law Journal* 25 (Winter 1976): 17-62.

Focuses on entanglement questions in *Hunt* v. *McNair* (no. 107) and *Meek* v. *Pittenger* (421 U.S. 349, 44 L.Ed. 2d 217); sees *Hunt* as reflective of a readiness to uphold non-financial assistance to church-related institutions and *Meek* as representative of an incompatible readiness to rule against such assistance; views the combined effect of these two rulings as confusing and inconsistent.

284. Valente, William D. "The Strange Case of Horace Mann." *National Catholic Educational Association Bulletin* 65 (May 1969): 11-17.

Describes the strategies used in filing *Horace Mann League of the U.S.* v. *Board of Public Works* (no. 102) in Maryland courts;

summarizes the opinion of the Maryland supreme court; discusses the earlier Maryland and other cases used as precedents; asserts that the decision has been misinterpreted; reviews holdings and the facts concerning each of the four colleges involved in the case; questions the use of *Horace Mann* as a precedent, even in Maryland; considers future prospects and the application of this case to church-related colleges in New York.

285.   Vasey, Vincent R. *"Roemer v. Board of Public Works of Maryland*: The Supreme Court's Evaluation of the Religious Mission of Catholic Colleges and Church Expectations." *Catholic Lawyer* 23 (Spring 1978): 108-17.

Provides background for and states the issues in *Roemer v. Board of Public Works* (no. 189); considers whether Catholic higher education is so devoid of religious content that it passes for secular education.

286.   Warshaw, Thayer S. *Religion, Education, and the Supreme Court.* Nashville, TN: Abingdon, 1979.

Summarizes and comments on the decisions in *Hunt v. McNair* (no. 107), *Tilton v. Richardson* (no. 211), and *Roemer v. Board of Public Works* (no. 211); relates these cases to other major decisions of the Supreme Court involving religion and education, both public and private.

287.   Webb, LaVar G. and Lenore Marema. "God and Mammon: At Brigham Young University: At Wheaton College." *Change* 9 (May 1977): 38-42.

Describes the problems of church-related colleges have in abiding by federal regulations; points to the potential loss of the religious character of such institutions in accepting federal support.

288.   Weber, Paul J. and Dennis A. Gilbert. *Private Churches and Public Money: Church-Government Fiscal Relations.* Westport, CT: Greenwood Press, 1981.

Uses economic principles relating to equity to develop a policy, called "fiscal neutrality," to be applied to church-state fiscal relationships, including the funding by the public of sectarian higher education; suggests this approach after determining that case law (as set out in *Tilton v. Richardson* [no. 211] and *Roemer v. Board of Public Works* [no. 189]) and public policy are inconsistent and lack a common rationale.

289.   Weber, Thomas J. "Supreme Court Upholds Direct Noncategorical Grants To Church-Affiliated Colleges." *Fordham Law Review* 45 (1977): 979-92.

Summarizes *Roemer v. Board of Public Works* (no. 189);

places the case in historical contexts; concludes that the U.S. Supreme Court has yet to arrive at a definitive standard which legislatures may follow in granting aid to church-related colleges.

290. Weeks, Kent M. "Religion and Independent Higher Education: The Constitutional Argument." In *Freedom and Education: Pierce v. Society of Sisters Reconsidered*, pp. 11-36. Edited by Donald P. Kommers and Michael J. Wahoske. Notre Dame, IN: Center for Civil Rights, University of Notre Dame, 1978.

Draws the economic and educational contexts for aid to church-related colleges; outlines the U. S. Supreme Court's interpretation of the First Amendment establishment clause and the Court's development of tests applicable to governmental action; describes the use of these tests in *Tilton* v. *Richardson* (no. 211), *Hunt* v. *McNair* (no. 107), and *Roemer* v. *Board of Public Works* (no. 189); summarizes current conditions, cites other court challenges, and discusses unresolved legal issues; concludes by indicating policy issues yet to be settled.

291. Wenberg, Stanley J. "Private Higher Education in America Today." *School and Society* 97 (November 1969): 439-41.

Defends public aid to private institutions, especially church-related ones, on grounds of diversity of opportunity and program and the need for private as well as public higher education.

292. West, Cameron P. "What the Nation's Private Colleges Perceive as the Implications for Their Future." Paper presented at a Seminar for Leaders in Postsecondary Education. Denver, CO. December, 1975.

Discusses problems of private institutions with emphasis on those in North Carolina; claims that private institutions serve a public purpose (by educating citizens and saving money for the state); suggests the development of portable scholarship programs to give students a choice of institutions to attend and to help private institutions meet their expenses.

293. Whelan, Charles M. "The Church, the College and the State: Changing Patterns of Relationship." *Liberal Education* 59 (May 1973): 217-22.

Sees church-related colleges as caught between the state and the church; describes problems faced by these colleges as constitutional, political, and ecclesiastical; offers suggestions on how to solve each kind of problem.

294. Whelan, Charles M. "School Aid Decisions." *America*, July 7, 1977, pp. 6-8.

Applauds the U.S. Supreme Court's decision in *Hunt* v.

McNair (no. 107); finds the decision "reassuring and particularly timely" in view of campaigns by the American Civil Liberties Union and Americans United for Separation of Church and State against aid to church-related colleges.

295.   Whelan, Charles M. "The School Aid Decisions." *America*, July 10, 1971, pp. 10-11.

Comments favorably on the Supreme Court's decision in *Tilton* v. *Richardson* (no. 211) and criticizes the Court for not going further in cases involving elementary and secondary education.

296.   Whelan, Charles M. "The School Aid Decisions: 'Not Dead But Sleeping.'" *America*, July 7, 1973, pp. 6-8.

Reviews the Supreme Court's holding in *Hunt* v. *McNair* (no. 107) sympathetically and calls for similar rulings in other cases on other issues.

297.   Whitehead, John S. *The Origins of the Public-Private Distinction in American Higher Education: A Story of Accidental Development.* New Haven: Yale University Institute for Social and Policy Studies, 1977.

Examines the historical development of public and private colleges and universities; suggests that financial support of both has been based on the need to train leaders and citizens and not on any inherent state or private interest in learning.

298.   Wilson, Charles H. Jr. "The School Aid Decisions: A Chronicle of Dashed Expectations." *Journal of Law and Education* 3 (January 1974): 101-06.

Reviews *Tilton* v. *Richardson* (no. 211) and *Hunt* v. *McNair* (no. 107) in the general context of public aid to religious educational institutions; points to problems state legislatures may have in deciding what they can and cannot do to help church-related colleges. (Mr. Wilson was counsel for the defendant Connecticut colleges in *Tilton*.)

299.   Wilson, Charles H. Jr. "*Tilton* v. *Finch*: The Connecticut Colleges Case." *Liberal Education* 56 (May 1970): 339-49.

Describes proceedings, parties, parties' legal positions, and implications for higher education of the contending legal theories on how the case should be decided (written while the case was still pending in federal district court; with the change in leadership of the Department of Health, Education and Welfare, this case became *Tilton* v. *Richardson* [no. 211] on appeal; Mr. Wilson was counsel for the defendant Connecticut colleges in *Tilton*).

300.   Wilson, Charles H. Jr. *Tilton v. Richardson: The Search for Sectarianism in Education.* Washington, DC: Association of

American Colleges, 1971.

Reviews relevant U.S. Supreme Court decisions up to *Tilton* v. *Richardson* (no. 211); analyzes the majority and dissenting opinions in this case; suggests what institutions can do and still remain on safe constitutional grounds. (Mr. Wilson was counsel for the defendant Connecticut colleges in *Tilton*.)

301.   Wood, Harry A. "Colleges and Universities." 15A Am.Jur. 2d, Colleges and Universities, Section 34.

Summarizes (at pp. 296-99) state constitutional provisions and state and federal judicial holdings on aid to church-related institutions; updated to 1986 in Pocket Part, p. 83.

302.   Wood, James E., Jr. "Religion and Education: A Continuing Dilemma." *Annals of the American Academy of Political and Social Science* 446 (November 1979): 63-77.

Summarizes holdings in *Tilton* v. *Richardson* (no. 211), *Hunt* v. *McNair* (no. 107), and *Roemer* v. *Board of Public Works* (no. 189); places these cases in the historical and legal contexts of church-state relations.

303.   Wood, James E., Jr. "Tuition Tax Credits for Nonpublic Schools?" *Journal of Church and State* 23 (Winter 1981): 5-14.

Expresses opposition to tuition tax credits for parochial schools and church-related colleges which are part of the religious mission of a church; argues that tuition tax credits imperil the separation of church and state.

304.   Young, D. Parker. "Legal Considerations Concerning Public Support for Private Higher Education." *Peabody Journal of Education* 49 (October 1971): 60-67.

Explains that legal considerations are the same for all types of public aid to private institutions: the aid must serve a public purpose, the grantor and the recipient must meet all requirements for due process and equal protection, and separation of church and state must be maintained.

305.   Young, D. Parker. "School Finance," Sec. 1.6. In *The Yearbook of Higher Education Law 1980*, pp. 12-14. Edited by D. Parker Young. Topeka, KS: National Organization on Legal Problems of Education, 1980.

Contrasts treatment of state tuition grants to students attending church-related colleges when challenged under the United States Constitution and when challenged under a state constitution.

306.   Yoxall, Rick. "First Amendment Restrictions on Aid to Parochial Schools." *Washburn Law Journal* 16 (1977): 469-78.

Reviews *Roemer* v. *Board of Public Works* (no. 189) and its precedents; concludes that permissible aid has expanded from aid to students and their parents for specific secular purposes to approval of direct subsidies for any secular purpose; argues that any further relaxation of constitutional restrictions would lead to direct funding of sectarian facilities, courses, and activities.

307.   Zimmerman, Mark. "State Aid to Students Attending Sectarian Schools Found Unconstitutional Due to 'Excessive Entanglement.'" *Cumberland-Samford Law Review* 4 (Winter 1974): 620-26.

Reports an advisory opinion of the Alabama supreme court on a pending bill that would grant aid to students attending church-related colleges; describes how the court reached the conclusion that such aid would lead to an "excessive entanglement."

308.   Zirkel, Perry A., ed. *A Digest of Supreme Court Decisions Affecting Education.* Bloomington, IN: Phi Delta Kappa, 1978.

Lists cases from 1859 to 1977, with emphasis on last 25 years; most cases listed affect education at levels kindergarten through high school, but a few cases on higher education are also listed.

309.   Zollinger, Richard A. "Governors and Higher Education: An Unstudied Relationship." Paper presented at the Annual Meeting of the Association for the Study of Higher Education. Chicago. March 15-17, 1985.

Reports 1984 survey data collected from 70 former governors from 40 states; states that these governors, regardless of party or region, were evenly split on state aid to private higher education.

310.   Zurkellen, Henry S. "The Role of the Federal Government in Higher Education." Paper presented at the Annual Meeting of the American Educational Studies Association. Atlanta, GA. November 9, 1985.

Traces the history of the federal government's role in higher education since colonial times; includes among other major topics a discussion of federal activities touching private institutions both secular and church-related.

CHAPTER 3
GOVERNMENT REGULATION OF CHURCH-AFFILIATED
COLLEGES AND UNIVERSITIES
Ralph D. Mawdsley

Preface

In discussing the broad topic of Government Regulation of Church-Affiliated Colleges and Universities, an attempt has been made to include a broad range of topics relevant to such institutions. Thus the reader will find books or articles addressing very particular or special religious problems, such as religious tax exemption, religious standards in employment and admissions, and ministerial status. In addition there are some items discussing the broad categories of private education or independent colleges and universities, such as applicability of Section 1983 or the Fourteenth Amendment, on the basis that much of the law applicable to religious private education in general is applicable to religious private education. Finally, there are materials of general interest to all education, irrespective of its religious or secular nature, such as land use, copyright, trademark, and most anti-discrimination legislation. From this broad spectrum of materials it is hoped the reader will have a better understanding of the kaleidoscope of problems faced by church-affiliated colleges and universities.

Law Cases

311.   *Bob Jones University* v. *United States.* 461 U.S. 574 (1983).

   Upholds the authority of the Internal Revenue Services to revoke the tax-exempt status of a university because of its discriminatory practices, even though those practices have a long-standing religious basis. Affirms that an established national public policy can be a compelling governmental interest for superseding a sincerely held religious belief.

312.   *Equal Employment Opportunity Commission* v. *Mississippi College.* 626 F.²ᵈ 477 (5th Cir. 1980).

   Interprets one of the religious exemptions of Title VII as to whether the College's failure to hire a female applicant was sex discrimination. Decides that EEOC has jurisdiction until the College presents convincing evidence that challenged employment practice results from discrimination on the basis of religion.

313.   *Equal Employment Opportunity Commission* v. *Southwestern Baptist*

Theological Seminary. F.²ᵈ 277 (5th Cir. 1981).

Determines that the Seminary does not have to complete EEOC's routine information EEO-6 form as to its faculty and administrative positions that are traditionally ecclesiastical or ministerial but must complete the form as to other administrative and support staff.

314.   *Grove City College* v. *Bell.* 465 U.S. 555 (1984).

Affirms the obligation of every higher education institution receiving Title IV federal funds to execute a nondiscrimination compliance form but interprets Title IX as program specific. Does not clarify whether program specificity applies also to Title VI, Rehabilitation Act of 1973, or the Age Discrimination Act of 1975.

315.   *Napolitano* v. *Princeton University Trustees.* 453 A.²ᵈ 263 (N.J. Super. Ct. App. Div. 1982).

Considers the legality of an institutional penalty, delay of one year in awarding diploma, for plagiarism violation in one academic course. Discusses important questions relevant to all nonpublic colleges and universities, especially the importance of University handbooks as part of the institution-student contract.

316.   *National Labor Relations Board* v. *Catholic Bishop.* 440 U.S. 490 (1979).

Rules on narrow statutory grounds that the NLRB does not have jurisdiction under the NLRA over Catholic archdiocese schools, including a seminary. Contains helpful dicta on possible Establishment Clause problems.

317.   *National Labor Relations Board* v. *Yeshiva University.* 444 U.S. 672 (1980).

Decides that faculty at defendant religious university are managerial employees and therefore exempt under the National Labor Relations Act from the jurisdiction of the NLRB. Rejects efforts by NLRB to impose the standard manager-worker model on the university and instead finds the managerial model in the faculty's inseparable alignment with the university through its governance authority. Includes an incisive 4 member dissent authored by Justice Brennan in which the modern university is perceived as more adversarial with administration looking to the faculty only for recommendations.

318.   *New Jersey State Board of Higher Education* v. *Board of Directors of Shelton College.* 448 A.²ᵈ 988 (N.J. 1982).

Represents the culmination of over a decade of litigation regarding state refusal to license Shelton College to confer baccalaureate degrees. Chronicles college's unsuccessful challenges to state authority under the Free Exercise and Establishment Clauses to prohibit issuance of degrees.

319.   *State ex rel. McLemore v. Clarksville School of Theology.* 636 S.W.²ᵈ 706 (Tenn. 1982).

Upholds an injunction prohibiting defendant school from offering degrees without first obtaining a state license. Rejects the school's argument that inability to award degrees violates the Religion Clauses by regulating its beliefs, practices or teaching for the reason that awarding degrees is a secular activity while the religious activity is training ministers.

320.   *Trustees of Dartmouth College v. Woodward.* 17 U.S. 518 (1819).

Recognizes the plenary authority of government to alter, enlarge or abolish its own public educational institutions but declares that private institutions obtain their authority from perpetual charters of incorporation and government attempts to assume control of such private colleges violates the Constitution's contract clause.

Books, Pamphlets and Monographs

321.   Ball, William B. *Litigation in Education: In Defense of Freedom.* Wichita, KS: Center for Independent Education, 1977.

Summarizes in a few pages significant legal and social policy problems with governmental efforts to regulate religious education, to control individual conscience in public education and to deny distributive justice in the use of tax funds. Is written in clear language by one of our country's premier constitutional lawyers representing religious education.

322.   Bird, Wendell R. "Exempt Organizations and Discriminations." *Tax-Exempt Organization.* Vol. 1. Paramus, NJ: Prentice-Hall, 1984, pp. 3295-3302.

Summarizes federal legislation prohibiting discrmination on the basis of gender, religion, age and handicap and how religious exempt organizations are affected.

323.   Brenenman, David W. and Chester E. Finn, Jr., eds. *Public Policy and Private Higher Education.* Washington, DC: The Brookings Institution, 1978.

Contains a series of well-researched and well-documented chapters, each written by authorities in their fields. Approaches the subject from the viewpoint of two propositions: either private colleges must be made more financially similar to public ones, or public colleges more like private; and coordination is needed in federal and state policies if a balanced system of higher education is to be preserved. Presents in clear fashion the differing federal and state perceptions toward the private-public dichotomy in higher education and how those differing perceptions affect government policies toward private education.

324.   Bromberg, Robert S. "Unrelated Business Income of Museums, Hospitals, Hospital Associations, and Universities." *Tax-Exempt Organizations.* Vol. 1. Paramus, NJ: Prentice-Hall, 1984, pp. 3488-3500.

Explores ways in which tax exempt colleges and universities can generate taxable income under the unrelated business income tax (UBIT) through rental or lease of their facilities, equipment and personnel.

325.   Civil Rights Act of 1984: Hearings on S. 2568 Before the Subcommittee on Constitution of the Senate Committee on the Judiciary, 98th Cong., 2d sess. (1984).

Contains a complete record of statements favoring and opposing amendment of Title IX, Title VI, the Age Discrimination Act of 1975 and Section 504 of the Rehabilitation Act of 1972 to clarify what constitutes a "program or activity" after the U.S. Supreme Court decision in *Grove City College* v. *Bell.* Of special interest are religious claims at pages 342-52.

326.   Curry, James E. *Public Regulation of the Religious Use of Land.* Charlottesville, VA: The Michie Co., 1964.

Approaches the subject of land use in textbook fashion without any use of case opinions. However, discusses important cases at sufficient length and intersperses the discussions with relevant comments from media publications and individuals of that time. Covers a general discussion of police power and a number of factors considered in balancing the claim of the religious institution for use of the property with governmental or public interests, such as: space, light, air and ease of access; fiscal consideration; protection of property values; protection of neighbors; traffic control; and discrimination.

327.   Dutile, Fernand N. and Edward McGlynn Gaffney, Jr. *State and Campus: State Regulation of Religiously Affiliated Higher Education.* Notre Dame, IN: University of Notre Dame Press, 1984.

Contains a state-by-state analysis of state regulations affecting religiously affiliated colleges and universities with a special "Overview" of important state policies. Addresses eight categories of state regulation: corporate status, state financial aid, personnel policies and practices, student admission and student discipline, use of publicly funded facilities, taxation, charitable solicitation and fund-raising, and miscellaneous provisions.

328. Gaffney, Edward McGlynn, Jr. and Philip C. Sorenson. *Ascending Liability in Religious and Other Nonprofit Organizations.* Atlanta, GA: Mercer University Press, 1984.

Reviews the law of ascending liability for nonprofit corporations and suggests procedures and structures to limit liability for organization acts. Includes an appendix with three denominational perspectives on ascending liability.

329. Gaffney, Edward McGlynn, Jr. and Philip R. Moots. *Government and Campus: Federal Regulation of Religiously-Affiliated Higher Education.* Notre Dame, IN: University of Notre Dame Press, 1982.

Begins with the results of studies revealing the increasing frequency of legal problems in church-related colleges and universities and the extent to which government subsidies and regulations have undercut religious commitment on some campuses. Explores the statutory exemption and exception available to religiously affiliated colleges under Title VII and judicial and EEOC decisions restricting the exemption and exception. Includes a discussion of alcoholism and drug addicts as handicapped persons and the nature of their protection under the Handicapped Act of 1973. Discusses tax problems of unrelated business income, and the college as an integrated auxiliary of a church for purposes of filing the detailed financial Form 990. Analyzes the extent of NLRB jurisdiction over religious schools against the protection of the First Amendment Religion clauses. Concludes with a pre-*Grove City College* Supreme Court decision analysis of Title IX and its impact on relationships among the sexes.

330. Gellhorn, Walter and R. Kent Greenawalt. *The Sectarian College and the Public Purse.* Dobbs Ferry, NY: Oceana Publications, Inc., 1970.

Reviews the history and organizational changes within one major Catholic institution, Fordham University, in order for that university to be eligible for state and federal funds available to non-sectarian colleges and universities. Would be of considerable assistance to any religious higher education institution as a blueprint in selecting areas to be reviewed in light of state and federal statutory and constitutional restrictions on reception of aid. Discusses such relevant topics as chapels on campus, prayer in the classroom, physical symbols of religion, religious garb, professional associations and publications.

331. Gumper, Lindell L. *Legal Issues in the Practice of Ministry.* Franklin Village, MI: Psychological Studies and Consultation Program, Inc., 1981.

Addresses the state statutory and common law problems encountered where persons performing in a ministerial capacity furnish advice to counselors. Considers such matters as duty of confidentiality, torts like negligence, malpractice, libel and slander, invasion of privacy, and what to expect at trial.

332.   Hammar, Richard R. *Pastor, Church and Law.* Springfield, MO: Gospel Publishing House, 1983.

Thorough discussion of legal areas pertinent to higher educational institutions that maintain a close church affiliation. Included are chapters on such matters as Privacy Act of 1974, taxation, social security and federal anti-discrimination statutes.

333.   Henzke, Leonard J. "Taxation on Churches, Ministers and Church Employees Under the Social Security Act." *Tax-Exempt Organizations.* Vol. 1. Paramus, NJ: Prentice-Hall, 1984, pp. 3681-685.

Explains the 1984 Tax Reform Act FICA exemption for churches and qualified church-controlled organizations. Also discusses the problems when persons identified as ministers are exempt under either FICA or SECA.

334.   Hobbs, Walter C., ed. *Government Regulations of Higher Education.* Cambridge, MA: Ballinger Publishing Co., 1978.

Discusses in a series of essays the regulatory problems experienced by all institutions of higher education either because they are employers or because they receive governmental assistance. The comments range from the ominous, "[as] the influence of regulatory procedures, programs, and techniques spreads throughout higher education, there may be fundamental changes not only in the way the university interacts with the outside world but also in the way it governs itself internally," (p. 48) to the optimistic, "it will do no good simply to rail at regulation; instead, higher education must learn to educate its regulators and to function effectively within the bureaucratic process" (p. 69).

335.   Jonsen, Richard W. *State Policy Issues Affecting Independent Higher Education.* Washington, DC: National Institute of Independent Colleges and Universities, 1980.

Reviews general state objectives for postsecondary education and the role intended for independent institutions in meeting them. Focuses on fiscal relationships between states and independent institutions on resource sharing, on adult education, on application of public policies to the nonpublic sector and on declining enrollments.

336.   Kaplan, Michel G. and Mark W. Cochran. "Unrelated Business Income Problems of Churches and Other Organizations."

Tax-Exempt Organizations. Paramus, NJ: Prentice-Hall, 1984, pp. 3649-664.

Details the source of taxable unrelated business income for religious organizations, how to compute and report the income for tax purposes and the effect such income might have on an organization's tax-exempt status.

337.   Mawdsley, Ralph D. and Steven Permuth. "Faculty Dismissal: Comparison of Public and Private Higher Education." In *School Law Update 1985*, pp. 138-61. Edited by Thomas N. Jones and Darel P. Semler. Topeka, KS: National Organization on Legal Problems of Education, 1985.

Compares public and private (including religious) higher educational institutions and the constitutional and contractual constraints on the termination of tenured and nontenured faculty members. Also includes a discussion of financial exigency as it applies to both kinds of institutions.

338.   Mawdsley, Ralph D. and Steven Permuth. *Legal Problems of Religious and Private Schools.* Topeka, KS: National Organization on Legal Problems of Education, 1983.

Comprehensive treatment of critical legal problems faced by all non-public educational institutions and especially religious higher education. Covers topics such as tort liability, government regulations, anti-discrimination legislation, governing board liability and copyright.

339.   Mawdsley, Ralph D. and Steven Permuth. "Private School's Tax Exempt Status and Application of Section 1983." In *School Law Update - Preventive School Law*, pp. 46-58. Edited by Thomas N. Jones and Darel P. Semler. Topeka, KS: National Organization on Legal Problems of Education, 1984.

Discusses the advantages of Section 1983 of the Civil Rights Act as a legal remedy against nonpublic institutions, and whether tax exemption would constitute "state action" under Section 1983, especially in light of *Bob Jones University* v. *U.S.*, where tax exemption was considered to be a form of government subsidy.

340.   McGrath, John J. *Church and State in American Law.* Milwaukee, WI: The Bruce Publishing Co., 1962.

Contains cases and other materials focusing solely on the constitutional rights of religious institutions and the rights of religious expression in public settings. Reviews in Chapter I the U.S. Supreme Court's limitation on resolving matters of religious doctrine, background information that may be helpful for church-controlled colleges or universities. Includes a very helpful appendix with some of the major American religious documents, such as the "Maryland Toleration Act" of 1649, "The Pennsylvania Charter of Privileges" of 1701 and Jefferson's "Bill for Establishing Religious Freedom."

341.   Moots, Philip R. *Ascending Liability: A Planning Memorandum.* Atlanta, GA: Mercer University Press, 1987.

Outlines a practical planning process to meet the challenges of ascending liability. Identifies useful steps to limit or prevent liability and suggests general procedures which will be functional for most institutions. Presents material in concise rather than definitive manner.

342.   Moots, Philip R. and Edward McGlynn Gaffney, Jr. *Church and Campus: Legal Issues in Religiously Affiliated Higher Education.* Notre Dame, IN: University of Notre Dame Press, 1979.

Covers general legal issues affecting religiously affiliated colleges and universities, including religious preference employment and ascending liability.

343.   Oaks, Dallin H. *Trust Doctrines in Church Controversies.* Atlanta, GA: Mercer University Press, 1984.

Examines the applicability of common law concepts of charitable trusts to controversies among members of a religious body and the government. Includes an analysis of the constitutional problems of applying the "implied trust" doctrine to church controversies.

344.   O'Neill, Joseph P. and Phillip M. Grier. *Financing In A Period of Retrenchment: A Primer For Small Colleges.* Washington, DC: National Association of College and University Attorneys, 1984.

Contains a wealth of practical advice for any small college on a variety of topics such as reorganization under Chapter 11 of the Bankruptcy Code, staff reduction and early retirement, college-financed student aid and managing real estate assets. Includes helpful bibliography at the end of each section for more detailed study.

345.   Peterson, Walfred H. *Thy Liberty in Law.* Nashville, TN: Broadman Press, 1978.

Proposes biblical themes that bring religious action into conflict with government and reviews key U.S. Supreme Court decisions supporting and prohibiting religious activity. Develops four theoretical bases for religious liberty in: God's authority over human authority, God's use of individuals and groups, propagation of the message through oral or written persuasion, and concern for the dignity of the believer when his conduct comes in conflict with legal or social standards.

346.   Richardson, Herbert, ed. *Constitutional Issues in the Case of Rev. Moon.* New York: The Edwin Mellen Press, 1984.

Contains copies of the 16 *amicus curiae* briefs presented to the U.S. Supreme Court on behalf of Sun Myung Moon from such diverse groups as the American Association of Christian Schools, The American Civil Liberties Union and the Church of Jesus Christ of Latter-Day Saints. Will be of interest to religious colleges and universities which are part of a hierarchical religious structure and which tend to have authority consolidated in one office or person.

347.   Rubenstien, I. H. *Law on Cults.* Chicago: The Ordain Press, 1981.

Explores a wide range of religious practices, such as fortune telling, faith healing and witchcraft, as they relate to common and statutory law. Addresses matters that may be of interest to certain religious institutions of higher education or to individuals within sectarian colleges and universities, such as the definition of a minister, use of mails to defraud, medical neglect of children and religious malpractice.

348.   *Rules and Standards For Licensing Non-Public Educational Institutions to Confer Degrees.* Chapel Hill, NC: University of North Carolina Press, 1974.

Documents licensing requirements in North Carolina based on legislative model proposed by the Education Commission of the States. Comprehensive identification of criteria and procedures required as minimum standards.

349.   Valente, William D. *Education Law, Public and Private.* 2 vols. St. Paul, MN: West Publishing Co., 1985.

Discusses in Volume 2 the most complete description in any book of the legal topics pertaining to private education. Includes discussion of such areas as legal structure, organization, rights of students, rights of professional personnel, anti-discrimination laws, tort liability and finance. Will be updated regularly with pocket parts.

350.   Weeks, Kent M. *A Legal Inventory For Independent Colleges and Universities.* Notre Dame, IN: Center for Constitutional Studies, 1981. (Please note Center for Constitutional Studies now located at Mercer University, Macon, GA.)

Contains in brief pamphlet form a checklist in question format for administrators of nonpublic higher education institutions. For example, under "Academic Administration," "Do policies specify who makes final decisions on matters of appointment, promotion, and tenure?" and under "Special Problems of Church-Related Colleges," "Has the institution and its related religious body developed a clear statement regarding matters of governance, finance and property ownership?" Each question has four possible responses: "not applicable," "reviewed and currently OK," "needs attention," and "consult counsel." Will not furnish answers to problems but will identify areas to be examined.

351.   Worth, B. J. *Income Tax Law for Ministers and Religious Workers*. Winona Lake, IN: Worth Tax Service, 1987.

Published annually and includes explanations of important tax matters such as professional expense deductions and housing allowances. Also includes sample filled-in forms and helpful checklists. Especially useful for employees of religious colleges and universities who claim ministerial status as a result of their teaching religious subjects.

352.   Yudof, Mark G., ed. *Legal Deskbook for Administrators of Independent Colleges and Universities*. Macon, GA: Mercer University Press, 1986.

Easily useable loose leaf book covering a number of topics important to religious colleges and universities, such as employment, students, physical facilities, taxation. Especially helpful is a separate chapter on church-related colleges and universities addressing issues of religious preference in admissions and hiring and establishing proper relationships between churches and institutions of higher education regarding use of property.

Periodicals

353.   Albert, James A. "Federal Investigation of Video Evangelism: The FCC Probes the PTL Club." *Oklahoma Law Review*. 33: 782-823 (1980).

Considers and rejects PTL arguments that the FCC does not have jurisdiction to investigate allegations of misleading or deceptive fund raising even though the television station investigated is an integral part of a larger religious ministry.

354.   Baer, Richard A. "Higher Education, The Church, and Environmental Values." *Natural Resources Journal* 17: 477-91 (1977).

Challenges the university and church to go beyond attacking the ugliness in the environment to planning creatively for a future where students are exposed to beauty, civic virtue and moral responsibility. Argues for a voucher system so all students can choose a setting for instruction.

355.   Bagni, Bruce N. "Discrimination in the Name of the Lord: A Critical Evaluation of Discrimination by Religious Organizations." *Columbia Law Review* 79: 1514-1549 (1979).

Examines the extent to which religious organizations should be permitted to practice discrimination otherwise prohibited by federal legislation. Presents an analytic framework for resolving the clash between claims of religious autonomy and principles of equal opportunity and equal access that would insulate only spiritual core matters, such as church membership or employment of clergy, from all government regulation.

356.   Beach, John A. "Fundamental Fairness In Search of a Legal Rationale In Private College Student Discipline and Expulsions." *The Journal of College and University Law* 2 (Fall 1974): 65-81.

Argues against convoluted judicial reasoning to attempt to find state action in private colleges for a student lawsuit. Proposes instead a public policy favoring fundamental fairness in the contractual relationship between student and private educational institutions, with a special concern for the adhesive nature of the contract.

357.   Bell, Sheila Trice and Martin F. Majestic. "Protection and Enforcement of College and University Trademarks." *Journal of College and University Law* 10 (1983-84): 63-77.

Emphasizes the importance to a college and university of its name, logo, and other institutional symbols as means of protecting the integrity of its educational service and as a source of revenue through licensing agreements. Reviews the requirements and procedures for trademark registration.

358.   Boland, Thomas R., Thomas E. Szykowny and Shawn M. Flahive. "Copyright Infringement-Video Cassettes on Campus." *West's Education Law Reporter* 23 (1985): 11-25.

Reviews the public performance rights of a copyright owner under the 1976 Copyright Act. Interprets display of videocassettes in dormitories, fraternities or sororities in light of the U.S. Supreme Court's *Sony* decision and the Copyright Act's fair use provisions. Discusses potential legal liability for a college or universities where students violate the Copyright Act in using videocassettes.

359.   Byers, David F. "Title VII and Sectarian Institutions of Higher Education: Congress Shall Make No Law Prohibiting the Free Exercise of Religion." *Cumberland Law Review* 14 (1983-84): 597-641.

Surveys religious employment cases involving Title VII and concludes that a proper constitutional construction requires no further review of a religious educational institution when its sincerely held religious belief is demonstrated.

360.   Capps, Kline and Carl H. Esbeck. "The Use of Government Funding and Taxing Power to Regulate Religious Schools." *Journal*

of Law and Education 4 (October 1985): 553-74.

Reviews efforts in Spain, France and Malta to regulate religious schools through licensure, faculty criteria and budget control. Compares the European experience to possible similar control through federal government funding and taxing power and questions whether the diverse character of religious schooling in the United States can be guaranteed by the First Amendment.

361.   Cassou, April Kestell and Robert F. Currau. "Secular Orthodoxy and Sacred Freedoms: Accreditation of Church-Related Law Schools." *The Journal of College and University Law* 11 (Winter 1984): 293-322.

Analyzes the current application of ABA Standard 211 and AALS Regulation 6.14 to Church-Related law schools from the perspective of possible First Amendment and antitrust law violations. Considers accrediting agencies to be performing public function. Concludes that a more insightful, analytical evaluation of the mission of religious law schools and an awareness of the secular orthodoxy being imposed would alleviate the hostile attitude of accrediting agencies.

362.   Durrant, Matthew B. "Accrediting Church-Related Schools: A First Amendment Analysis." *Journal of Law and Education* 14 (April 1985): 147-79.

Analyzes the problem of accreditation through several issues: whether the accrediting agency is engaged in state action; whether accreditation represents a form of state aid; and whether accreditation through imposition of standards and possible denial of accreditation represents an infringement of free exercise of religion.

363.   Echols, Robert M. and Steven F. Casey. "The Right To Counsel In Disciplinary Proceedings in Public and Private Educational Institutions." *Cumberland Law Review* 9 (1978-79): 751-66.

Discusses when the fair treatment aspect of due process would require legal counsel in a public educational institution and draws the comparison to the private sector which is currently free from such constitutional constraints.

364.   Fitzgerald, Joseph M. "Origin and Impact of Government Regulations." *The Catholic Lawyer* 24 (Winter 1978): 236-45.

Assails the judiciary's contribution to a religion of secular humanism through its interpretations of a wall of separation of church at odds with tradition and usage up to the *Everson* case.

365.   Friedland, Jerold A. "Constitutional Issues In Revoking Religious Tax Exemption: Church of Scientology of California v.

Commissioner." *University of Florida Law Review* 85 (1985): 565-89.

Argues that where there is evidence of IRS hostility toward a religious organization, IRS should be required to produce evidence that its audit was based on factors other than protected religious activity. Represents an application and extension of *Bob Jones University* v. *U.S.*

366. Gerstman, Leslie. "*Valley Forge Christian College* v. *Americans United for Separation of Church and State, Inc.*" *West's Education Law Reporter* 5 (1982): 339-49.

Critical discussion of U.S. Supreme Court decision upholding revocation of tax exempt status for a university with racial segregation rules. Analyzes the court's definition of "charitable contributions" and projects possible future legal problems from the Court's creation of an established public policy.

367. Godshall, Scott David. "Land Use Regulation and the Free Exercise Clause." *Columbia Law Review* 63 (1984-85): 404-29.

Argues for an exemption-centered inquiry into state or local land use laws by requiring the government to prove the strength of its interest before a court has to engage in the difficult task of measuring the importance of a particular practice to a religious group.

368. Greenawalt, R. Kent. "Constitutional Limits On Aid to Sectarian Universities." *The Journal of College and University Law* 4 (Spring 1977): 177-86.

Contains informative background to U.S. Supreme Court decision, *Roemer* v. *Board of Public Works of Maryland*, where state aid to sectarian universities was upheld. Discusses religious activities on Fordham University campus not considered to cause university to be "pervasively religious" and thus ineligible for aid under Establishment Clause.

369. Gregory, David L. "The First Amendment Religion Clauses and Labor and Employment Law in the Supreme Court, 1984 Term." *New York Law School Law Review* 31 (1986): 1-36.

Discusses, among other cases, *Alamo Foundation* v. *Secretary of Labor* where minimum wage section of Fair Labor Standards Act held by court to apply to employees engaged in commercial activities of religious foundation. Speculates but does not reach conclusion as to strength of free exercise claims where income would not be derived from commercial activities.

370. Grosch, Carla A. "Church-Related Schools and the Section 504 Mandate of Nondiscrimination In Employment on the Basis of

Handicap." *DePaul Law Review* 31 (1981-82): 69-113.

Argues persuasively that, following the reasoning in *NLRB* v. *Catholic Bishop*, the absence of any affirmatively expressed intention of Congress to include religious schools under Section 504 should mean they are excluded. Suggests the absence of establishment problems by excluding religious schools because of the schools' countervailing free exercise concerns.

371.   Habecker, Eugene B. "Students, Christian Colleges, and the Law: and the Walls Come Tumbling Down." *The Journal of College and University Law* 2 (Summer 1975): 369-86.

Explores the extent of federal interventions into religious colleges by considering the Privacy Act, Guaranteed Student Loan Program and Title IX. Proposes that *in loco parentis* model be replaced by a burden-bearing/confrontation model.

372.   Haskell, Anne Sanders. "The Church-State Controversy Redux: EEOC v. Mississippi College-A Case in Point." *Rutgers Law Review* 35 (1982-83): 361-88.

Suggests that the federal appeals court decision upholding the nonhiring of a female, if done for religious reasons, exceeds the legislative history of Title VII and the case law.

373.   Johnson, Edward A. and Kent M. Weeks. "To Save A College: Independent College Trustees and Decisions On Financial Exigency, Endowment Use, and Closure." *The Journal of College and University Law* 12 (Spring 1986): 455-88.

Chronicles the legal issues concerning the effects of financial crises on institutional decisions such as reduction in staff or school closures. Examines the standard of care for trustee decisions to lay off staff, close the institution or merge with another institution and reviews the *cy pres* doctrine where restricted gifts or endowment funds can no longer be used for the specific purposes for which they were given.

374.   Kegelman, Joan B. "Labor Law-Constitutional Law-Private University Faculty Excluded From NLRA Coverage Under Managerial Exemption-*NLRB* v. *Yeshiva University*, 100 S.Ct. 856 (1980)." *Seton Hall Law Review* 11 (1980-81): 287-98.

Reviews critically the *Yeshiva* decision and predicts circumvention of NLRA private university administration through transfer of enough academic issues to faculty recommendation making the faculty managerial personnel and thus excusing the university from an obligation to bargain with the faculty union.

375.   King, Harriet M. "The Voluntary Closing of a Private College: A Decision For the Board of Trustees?" *South Carolina Law Review*

32 (1980-81): 547-84.

Covers a wide range of legal questions related to closing a private college, including the necessity of court approval, distributions of assets under the charter or *cy pres*, standing to sue by those displeased with the closure decision and standard of care and personal liability of college trustees.

376. Kirby, Wendy T. "Federal Antitrust Issues Affecting Institutions of Higher Education: An Overview." *The Journal of College and University Law* 11 (Winter 1984): 345-76.

Discusses comprehensively areas affecting education that are covered or excluded under the Sherman, Clayton, Robinson Patman and Federal Trade Commission Acts. Of special interest are certain proprietary activities, such as offering textbooks, supplies, hospital and medical services, and their probable scrutiny under antitrust laws and then a possible antitrust law exemption for nonprofit institutions.

377. Kirk, Russell. "Shelton College and State Licensing of Religious Schools: An Educator's View of the Interface Between the Establishment and Free Exercise Clauses." *Law and Contemporary Problems* 44 (Spring 1981): 169-84.

Describes vividly the conflict between New Jersey and tiny Shelton College which refused to seek state licensure prior to granting degrees. Flows easily from a discussion of the neutrality principle under the establishment clause to philosophical concerns about the purpose and direction of American education.

378. Lacey, Linda J. "Gay Rights Coalition v. Georgetown University: Constitutional Values on a Collision Course." *Oregon Law Review* 64 (1986): 405-55.

Considers the difference between individual and institutional right to alleged free exercise rights in the context of a university that has received federal funds to construct buildings for secular education. Argues that prohibition of sexual preference discrimination is a compelling government interest and that courts must act aggressively to prevent powerful religious institutions from infringing on individual freedom.

379. Laycock, Douglas. "Civil Rights and Civil Liberties." *Chicago-Kent Law Review* 54 (1977): 390-435.

Contains section reviewing cases involving regulation of church labor relations in light of *NLRB* v. *Catholic Bishop*. Suggests four categories distinguishing among regulations that: increase the expense of operation; interfere with the way church activities are conducted; control who will perform church functions; and interfere with decisions to conduct the activity at all.

380.   Laycock, Douglas. "Towards a General Theory of the Religion Clauses: The Case of Church Labor Relations and the Right to Church Autonomy." *Columbia Law Review* 81 (1981): 1373-1417.

Presents a strong free exercise argument for church autonomy based not on claims of conscientious objection but on the right of organizations to develop religious doctrine. Would make the intensity of relationship between a church and its employees a barometer as to whether a church should be insulated from government regulation.

381.   Mawdsley, Ralph D. and Steven Permuth. "*Bob Jones University* v. *United States:* A Decision With Little Direction." *West's Education Law Reporter* 12 (1983): 1939-1051.

Discusses critically the U.S. Supreme Court decision upholding revocation of tax exempt status for a university with racial segregation rules. Analyzes the court's definition of "charitable contributions" and projects possible future legal problems from the Court's creation of an established public policy.

382.   Mawdsley, Ralph D. "God and the State: Freedom of Religious Universities to Hire and Fire." *West's Education Law Reporter* 36 (1987): 1093-1113.

Discusses in depth the leading employment litigation involving religious institutions especially under the Title VII religious exemptions. Addresses applicable statutory and constitutional provisions and identifies policy concerns on both sides of the issue. Concludes with some practical advice regarding the use of religious criteria for employment.

383.   Mawdsley, Ralph D. "Use of Videocassettes in the Classroom." *West's Education Law Reporter* 32 (1986): 1163-1172.

Analyzes use of videocassettes by teachers in face-to-face classroom teaching under Section 110 of the 1976 Copyright Act. Discusses interpretation of the 3 key legal terms, "ownership," "public performance," and "lawfully made." Considers the use of videocassettes secured from a number of different sources and where use would clearly be impermissible.

384.   McCarthy, Martha M. "The Developing Law Pertaining to Sexual Harassment." *West's Education Law Reporter* 36 (1987): 7-14.

Presents an overview of litigation pertaining to sexual harassment, with particular emphasis on recent Supreme Court action. Discusses various state and federal remedies available to aggrieved plaintiffs and the likelihood of success under those remedies. Focuses on the "hostile environment" claim upheld under Title VIII in the U.S. Supreme Court's decision in *Meritor Savings Bank* v. *Vinson*.

385.   McNally, Charla D. and Sue Sutherland. "Copyright Law and the Classroom: Photocopying, Videotaping and Fair Use." *Journal of Law and Education* 15 (Spring 1986): 229-36.

Summarizes the legal concept of fair use and provides direction for teacher conduct. Includes appendices regarding guidelines for Classroom Copying, Educational Uses of Music and Off-the Air Copying.

386.   Miller, Charles R. "Rendering Unto Caesar: Religious Publishers and The Public Benefit Rule." *University of Pennsylvania Law Review* 134 (January 1986): 433-568.

Reviews Third Circuit decision in *Presbyterian and Reformed Publishing Co.* v. *Commissioner* overruling IRS efforts to revoke tax exempt status because the company was nondenominational and not owned by a particular church and because the company had accumulated net profits over several years. Summarizes significant cases interpreting sec. 501(c)(3) requirements that a tax-exempt organization be"operated exclusively" for exempt purposes. Argues that after the *Bob Jones University* decision, tax-exempt status can be revoked where no public benefit can be proved.

387.   Mitchell, Susan B. "Civil Rights-Handicapped Discrimination-Private College Required to Provide Interpreter Services For Deaf Student Under Section 504 of the Rehabilitation Act of 1973." *Cumberland Law Review* 8 (1977-78): 977-89.

Reviews a leading case where teacher in private college summer program to earn recertification credits had private cause of action under Section 504 and was an "otherwise handicapped person" who could not be denied benefits of a program or activity receiving federal financial assistance.

388.   Nelson, Leonard J. III "Religious Discrimination, Christian Mission, and Legal Education: The Implications of the Oral Roberts University Accreditation Controversy." *Cumberland Law Review* 15 (1984-85): 663-701.

Presents persuasive argument supporting law schools with a religious mission and against the ability of accrediting agencies to monitor the philosophical orientation of schools. Views the ORU case as a watershed and discusses that case from the aspects of state action, Title VII and the Religion Clauses.

389.   Nordin, Virginia Davis and William Lloyd Turner. "Tax Exempt Status of Private Schools: Wright, Green and Bob Jones." *West's Education Law Reporter* 35 (1987): 329-49.

Examines an important governmental privilege, tax exemption, and its status where there is or may be racial discrimination. Presents 3 different standards enunciated by the

U.S. Supreme Court and attempts to resolve the apparent anomaly. Argues against the indirect use of the common law of charitable trusts to deny tax-exempt statutes in attacking discrimination admissions and suggests instead a direct attack under the Civil Rights Act of 1964.

390.   Note. "Financial Exigency As Cause for Termination of Tenured Faculty Members in Private Post Secondary Educational Institutions." *Iowa Law Review* 62 (1976-77): 481-521.

Analyzes termination of tenured faculty in light of contract law developed in litigation involving commercial contracts for lifetime employment. Suggests that a specific definition of financial exigency be stated and that a procedure be established to make certain exigency decisions are based on sound educational considerations.

391.   Read, George R. "Origin and Impact of Government Regulations." *The Catholic Lawyer* 24 (Winter 1978): 232-35.

Reviews the basic procedure in assisting regulatory agencies to produce regulations not harmful to religious organizations, from developing a good legislative history to establishing good contacts.

392.   Renahan, Kathryn R. "*Bob Jones University* v. *United States*-No Tax Exemptions For Racially Discriminatory Schools-Supreme Court Clarifies Thirteen-Year Policy Imbroglio." *The Journal of College and University Law* 11 (Summer 1984): 69-83.

Views favorably the U.S. Supreme Court opinion in *Bob Jones University* v. *U.S.* where revocation of tax exemption by the I.R.S. was upheld. Concludes that the Court accurately applied the law of charitable trusts, determined the existence of an established public policy against racial discrimination and interpreted the First Amendment religious clauses.

393.   Reynolds, Laurie. "Zoning the Church: The Police Power Versus The First Amendment." *Boston University Law Review* 64 (1984): 767-819.

Concludes that zoning ordinances may exclude religious uses if adequate alternative siting possibilities are provided and that judicial exemption of religious uses of land from religiously neutral land use regulation violates the establishment clause.

394.   Richardson, Elizabeth Cameron. "Applying Historic Preservation Ordinance to Church Property: Protecting the Past and Preserving the Constitution." *North Carolina Law Review* 63 (1984-85): 404-29.

Analyzes the free exercise, establishment and due process problems that can arise when permission is sought by owners of buildings used for religious purposes and designated as historic landmarks to alter the buildings and the conflict that can result with local or state land use agencies.

395. Schneebeck, Richard. "Constitutional Law-Religious Freedom and Public Land Use. *Welson* v. *Block*, 708 F²ᵈ 735 (D.C. Cir. 1983)." *Land and Water Review* 20 (1985): 109-19.

Discusses federal use of public lands in a manner inconsistent with religious worship of Indian tribes where the tribes lost because they could not prove a religious practice was being impaired and the practice could not be performed at another site. Has possible implication to a religious institution where a particular site may have religious significance.

396. Sciarrino, Alfred J. "*United States* v. *Sun Myung Moon:* Precedent for Tax Fraud Prosecution of Local Pastors?" *Southern Illinois University Law Journal* (1984): 237-81.

Reviews thoroughly the trial and appellate decisions and the arguments raised by the defendant and numerous *amici curiae*. Determines that the effect of Moon's criminal conviction was to disregard donor's intent under the law of trusts, to allow a jury to substitute its judgment of use of funds for the churches and to subject any religious organization where one person owns the religion or has a dominant role in its use to the possibility of IRS harassment. Raises the possibility that this case may affect church behavior if IRS enforcement of its regulations compels loss of some autonomy in church structure and spending practices by church leaders.

397. Silverman, Debra A. "Defining the Limits of Free Exercise: The Religion Clause Defenses in *United States* v. *Moon*." *Hastings Const. L. Quarterly* 2 (1984-85): 515-28.

Concurs with tax evasion conviction of Reverend Sun Myung Moon despite defendant's free exercise claim that church practice was to treat defendant as the church itself. Concludes that governmental interest in collecting revenue outweighs a church's right to allocate property however it chooses.

398. Simmons, Nancy L. "*Salem College and Academy* v. *Employment Division:* State Unemployment Tax and the Interdenominational School-The Lions Win Again." *Williamette Law Review* 21 (Fall 1985): 937-43.

Reviews Oregon Supreme Court decision interpreting its own state constitution making all private religious schools subject to the state's unemployment compensation laws.

399. Tewes, R. Scott. "Religion, Education and Government Regulation: Implications of *Bob Jones University* v. *United States*

For Congressional Decisionmaking." *South Carolina Law Review* 34 (1982-83): 885-930.

Discusses public policy arguments for denying tax exemption to racially segregated schools in light of the First, Fifth and Thirteenth amendments. Argues that denial of tax exemption would not further the state interest of eliminating discrimination; therefore such denial should be a violation of the free exercise clause.

400.   West, Ellis M. "The Free Exercise and the Internal Revenue Code's Restrictions On the Political Activity of Tax-Exempt Organizations." *Wake Forest Law Review* 21 (1986): 395-429.

Discusses problems that arise when religious organizations, which can include post secondary institutions, become actively involved in the political process. Analyzes the issues by explaining: the relevant Internal Revenue Code provisions; constitutional challenges in *Regan* v. *Taxation Without Representation* under free speech, free press, right to assemble and right to petition clauses; likelihood of future free exercise clause protection and the possibility of constitutional exemption from the Code of religious groups but not for secular groups.

401.   Whelan, Charles M. "Origin and Impact of Government Regulations." *The Catholic Lawyer* 24 (Winter 1978): 228-31.

Discusses the three fundamental arguments against government regulation of church affairs: church objection, constitutional objection, and public policy objection. Declares that no new applications of excessive entanglement be developed which decrease the church's contact with governmental agencies and political processes.

402.   White, Rebecca. "Wanted: A Strict Contractual Approach To the Private University/Student Relationship." *Kentucky Law Journal* 68 (1979-80): 439-56.

Argues that catalogues or handbooks relied upon by private universities to govern student conduct be viewed as contracts of adhesion with ambiguities resolved against the university.

403.   Wilson, Suzanne. "Bankruptcy-Private College May Withhold Transcripts From Students Whose Educational Loan Debts Were Discharged." *Howard Law Journal* 22 (1979): 155-64.

Discusses the special status of private colleges under the Bankruptcy Act in being able to continue demand for payment of delinquent accounts notwithstanding discharge in bankruptcy through control of issuance of official transcripts.   Somewhat outdated since current law has now altered the ability of private colleges to withhold transcripts.

CHAPTER 4
BAPTIST COLLEGES AND UNIVERSITIES
Jerry M. Self and Harold D. Germer*

Part I: Institutional Histories

A. American Baptist Related Colleges and Universities

404.   Africa, Philip A. *Keuka College: A History.* Valley Forge: PA: Judson Press, 1974.

405.   Armacost, George H., Ralph E. Hone, and Esther N. Mertens. *Whose Emblem Shines Afar: A Commemorative Account of the University of Redlands for the Years 1945-1982.* Redlands, CA: The University of Redlands, 1983.

406.   Bacoats, Inez. *Echoes From a Well-Spent Life: A Biography of John Alvin Bacoats and Eight Addresses.* Columbia, SC: State Printing Co., 1970.

407.   Baird, John. *A Leap of Faith: The First Twenty Years of Eastern College.* St. Davids, PA: Eastern College, 1972.

408.   Baird, John. *Great House.* St. Davids, PA: Eastern College, 1984.

409.   Baker, Noel Custer. *Description of a Private Liberal Arts College 1961-1970.* Ph.D. dissertation. Indiana University, 1972.

410.   Browne, Benjamin P. *Comrades in an Adventure of Faith.* Elgin, IL: Judson College, typewritten manuscript, n.d.

411.   Cady, John Frank. *The Centennial History of Franklin College.* Franklin, IN: Franklin College, 1934.

412.   Carter, Wilmoth A. *Shaw's Universe.* Raleigh, NC: Shaw University, 1973.

413.   *A Century of Service to Education and Religion, Virginia Union University 1865-1965.* Richmond, VA: Virginia Union University, 1965.

414.   *The First Half Century of Franklin College, Franklin, Indiana 1834-1884. Jubilee Exercises. June 5-12, 1884.* Cincinnati, OH: Journal and Messenger, 1884.

415.   Fisher, Miles Mark. *Virginia Union University, Some of Her*

Achievements. Richmond, VA: Virginia Union University, 1924.

416.   Goodsell, Charles T., and Willis F. Dunbar. *Centennial History of Kalamazoo College*. Kalamazoo, MI: Kalamazoo College, 1933.

417.   Griffin, Gail, Josephine Csete, Ruth Ann Moerdyk, and Cheryl Limer. *Emancipated Spirits: Portraits of Kalamazoo College Women*. Kalamazoo, MI: Kalamazoo College, 1983.

418.   Haworth, B. Smith. *Ottawa University: Its History and Its Spirit*. Lawrence, KS: The Allen Press, 1957.

419.   Hester, Hubert Inman. *Jewell Is Her Name*. Liberty, MO: William Jewell College, 1967.

420.   Hinkle, Marilyn. *On Such a Full Sea*. Kalamazoo, MI: Kalamazoo College, 1982.

421.   Holmes, Kenneth L. *Linfield's Hundred Years: A Centennial History of Linfield College, McMinnville, Oregon*. Portland, OR: Binfords and Mort, 1956.

422.   Jeschke, Reuben P. *A Decade of Growth: Historical Review of Events of Sioux Falls College, 1958-1968*. Sioux Falls, SD: Jeschke, 1968.

423.   Jeschke, Reuben P. *Dream of the Pioneers*. Sioux Falls, SD: Jeschke, 1958.

424.   Jeschke, Reuben P. *My Life and My Family*. Salem, OR: Jeschke, 1985.

425.   Jonasson, Jonas A. *Bricks Without Straw: The Story of Linfield College*. Caldwell, ID: Caxton Printers, 1938.

426.   *Kalamazoo College: A Sesquicentennial Portrait*. Kalamazoo, MI: Kalamazoo College, 1982.

427.   Martin, Andrew B. *Out of the Lean Years*. Merriam, KS: Allied Publishing Group, 1986.

428.   Mulder, Arnold. *The Kalamazoo College Story*. Kalamazoo, MI: Kalamazoo College, 1958.

429.   Nelson, Lawrence Emerson. *Redlands: Biography of a College*. Redlands, CA: University of Redlands, 1958.

430.   Simpson, Ervin Peter Young. *A History of Alderson-Broaddus College, 1812-1951*. Philippi, WV: Alderson-Broaddus College, 1983.

431.   Starks, J. J. *Lo These Many Years*. Columbia, SC: The State Co., 1983.

432.   Turner, Wallace B. *Colorado Women's College, 1888-1982: The*

Story of a Dream. Marceline, MO: Walsworth Publishing Company, 1982.

433. Williams, John and Howard L. Meredith. *Bacone Indian University.* Oklahoma City, OK: Western Heritage Books, Inc., 1980.

B. Southern Baptist Colleges and Universities

434. *A Guide to Historic William Jewell College and Clay County, Missouri.* Department of Public Relations of William Jewell College in collaboration with Clay County Missouri Historical Society, July 4, 1940.

435. Baker, Robert A. *Tell the Generations Following: A History of Southwestern Baptist Theological Seminary 1908-1983.* Nashville, TN: Broadman Press, 1982.

436. Camden, Aubrey H. *1909-1959 Fifty Years of Christian Education in a Baptist School: A Historical Record of Hargrave Military Academy Chatham, Virginia.* Lynchburg, VA: J. P. Bell Company, Inc. (N.D.)

437. Carr, Isaac Newton. *History of Carson-Newman College,* Vol. I. Jefferson City, TN: Carson-Newman College, 1959

A survey history, 1851-1959 with appendices containing important documents.

438. Cosby, Col. Joseph Hathaway. *From Ashes to Excellence 1950-1970.*

The story of the recovery of Hargrave Military Academy from the devastating fire of February 20, 1950, to the retirement of President Joseph H. Cosby on June 20, 1970, a period of twenty years of unparalleled growth.

439. Cuthbertson, William C. "DOC: The Life Work of H. I. Hester." Liberty, MO: William Jewell College, 1981.

440. Daniel, Robert Norman. *Furman University: A History.* Greenville, SC: Furman University, 1951.

441. Davis, John E. "Fifty Years at William Jewell." N.P., N.D.: 108 mimeographed pages.

442. Dedmond, Francis B. *Lengthened Shadows: A History of Gardner-Webb College 1907-1956.* Boiling Springs, NC: Gardner-Webb College, 1957.

443. Dowell, Spright. *A History of Mercer University 1833-1953.* Macon, GA: Mercer University, 1958.

444. Duff, Katharyn, Elizabeth A. Gatlin, Calvin C. Turpin, and

Charles R. Richardson. *Rupert N. Richardson: The Man and His Works.* Abilene, TX: Hardin-Simmons University, 1971.

445.   Flynn, Jean Martin. *A History of North Greenville Junior College.* Tigerville, SC: North Greenville Junior College, 1953.

446.   Gardner, Robert G. *On the Hill: The Story of Shorter College.* Rome, GA: Shorter College, 1972.

447.   Gardner, Robert, G. *Shorter and Rome, Partners.* Rome, GA: Shorter College, (N.D.).

448.   Grenga, Kathy Ann. *The Shorter College Baptist Student Union, 1940-75.* Rome, GA: Shorter College, 1975.

449.   Hamlett, Mayme Lucille. *To Noonday Bright: The Story of Southwest Baptist University 1878-1984.* Bolivar, MO: Southwest Baptist University, 1984.

450.   Harnage, Brenda A. *A History of Speech Activities at Carson-Newman from 1851 to 1945.* M.A. Thesis, University of North Carolina, 1972.

451.   Heilman, E. Bruce. "The Story of the University of Richmond." Address: 1979.

452.   Hester, Hubert Inman. *Jewell Is Her Name: A History of William Jewell College.* Liberty, MO: William Jewell College, 1967.

453.   Hester, Hubert Inman. *Jewell Is Her Name: A History of William Jewell College 1967-1979.* Liberty, MO: William Jewell College, 1979. Booklet, 37 pp.

454.   Hester, Hubert Inman. *Jewell: A 125th Anniversary History.* Liberty, MO: William Jewell College, 1975.

455.   Hester, Hubert Inman. *The Founding of Midwestern Baptist Theological Seminary.* Kansas City, MO: Midwestern Baptist Theological Seminary, 1964. Pamphlet, 20 pp.

456.   Hester, Hubert Inman. *They That Wait: History of Anderson College.* Anderson, SC: Anderson College, 1969.

457.   Higgins, George Lewis, Jr. "The Louisiana Baptist Convention and Christian Education, 1893-1956." Ed.D. dissertation. Oklahoma State University, 1971.

458.   Hoffmeyer, Oscar, Jr. *Louisiana College 75 Years: A Pictorial History.* Pineville, LA: Louisiana College, 1981.

459.   Johnson, Mary Lynch. *A History of Meredith College.* Second Edition. Raleigh, NC: Meredith College, 1956.

460.   Lawson, L. M. *Founding and Location of William Jewell College.* Reprint from Missouri Historical Society Collections Vol. 4 No. 3,

1914.

461. Littlejohn, Carrie U. *History of Carver School of Missions and Social Work.* Nashville, TN: Broadman Press, 1958.

462. Magruder, Edith Clysdale. *A Historical Study of the Educational Agencies of the Southern Baptist Convention 1845-1945.* New York, NY: Bureau of Publications, Teachers College, Columbia University, 1951.

463. McKnight, Edgar V. and Oscar Creech. *A History of Chowan College.* Murfreesboro, NC: Chowan College, 1964.

464. McLemore, Richard Aubrey. "A History of Mississippi Baptist 1780-1970." Jackson, MS: Mississippi Baptist Convention Board, 1971, pp. 346, 356.

465. McLemore, Richard Aubrey and Nannie Pitts McLemore. *History of Mississippi College.* Jackson, MS: Hederman Brothers, 1979.

466. McLeod, John Angus. *From These Stones: Mars Hill College, The First Hundred Years.* Mars Hill, NC: Mars Hill College, 1955.

467. McLeod, John Angus. *From These Stones: Mars Hill College 1856-1968.* Mars Hill, NC: Mars Hill College, 1968.

468. Murray, Lois Smith. *Baylor at Independence.* Waco, TX: Baylor University Press, 1972.

469. Owens, Uncle Jimmy. *Annals of O.B.U.* Shawnee, OK: The Bison Press, Oklahoma Baptist University, 1956. Published by the Historical Commission, Baptist General Convention of Oklahoma.

470. Pearce, J. Winston. *Campbell College: Big Miracle at Little Buies Creek, 1887-1974.* Nashville, TN: Broadman Press, 1976.

471. Pearce, J. Winston. *Campbell University: Big Miracle at Little Buies Creek,* Vol. 2. Nashville, TN: Broadman Press, 1985.

472. Ray, Willis J. *The Miracle of Grand Canyon College.* Paris, TX: Maxwell House of Printing, Inc., N.D.

473. Reid, Alfred Sandlin. *Furman University: Toward a New Identity 1925-1975.* Durham, NC: Duke University Press, 1976.

474. Richardson, Rupert Norval. *Famous Are Thy Halls: Hardin-Simmons University as I Have Known It.* Printed by Abilne Printing & Stationery Co. copyright, 1976. Second Edition with Autobiographical Sketches.

475. Robinson, R. L. *Memoirs of R. L. Robinson, President Emeritus.* Brewton Parker College: Copyright 1963.

476. Sample, Betty Jo. "A History of Louisiana College." M.A. thesis. Northwestern State University, 1969.

477.   Sanderfer, Inez Woodward. *Jefferson Davis Sanderfer: Christian Educator*. Nashville, TN: Broadman Press, N.D.

478.   Student League and Alumnae Association of Baylor College, Belton, Texas. *After Seventy-Five Years*. Refers to charter day, February 1, 1920, Baylor College's Diamond Jubilee.

479.   Sumrall, Robbie Neal. *A Light On A Hill: A History of Blue Mountain College*. Nashville, TN: The Benson Printing Company, 1947.

480.   Tardy, W. T. *Trials and Triumphs: An Autobiography*. Marshall, TX: Mrs. W. T. Tardy, Publisher. Edited by J. B. Cranfill, LL.D. Ch. XII "The College of Marshall," deals with the founding of East Texas Baptist College.

481.   Ward, Richard H. *History of Union University*. Jackson, TN: McCowat Mercer Press, 1975.

482.   Watson, Bert A. "Baylor University: A Military History." M.A. thesis. Baylor University, 1968.

483.   White, Michael A. *History of Baylor University*. Waco, TX: Texian Press, 1971.

Part II: General Works

484.   Adkins, Robert T. "Strategic Market Planning for Student Recruitment." *The Southern Baptist Educator*, December 1985-January 1986, pp. 3-9.

            Addresses problem of recruiting students from a diminishing pool of young people. Places responsibility for marketing strategies at the topic of institutional structure. Suggests techniques for the admissions office.

485.   Agee, Bob R. "Faculty Development: Pathway to Academic Vitality." *The Southern Baptist Educator*, February 1986, pp. 3-5.

            Describes faculty development as a planned process intended to improve professional skills. Proposes that ingredients of faculty development program include a definition of a standard of excellence, a willingness to make faculty development mandatory, and an appropriate committee for oversight of the program.

486.   Anders, Sarah Frances. "My Role In the Development of Christian Leaders." *The Southern Baptist Educator*, March 1978, p. 11.

487.   Anderson, Kelly Dennis. "The Contributions of Charles W. Barnes to the Development of the Baptist Student Union Work at the University of Alabama During 1940-74." Ed.D. dissertation. Southwestern Baptist Theological Seminary, 1983.

488.   Armstrong, Jerilynn Wood. "A Critical Evaluation of the Image

Texas Baptists Have of Their Eight Colleges and Universities."
M.A. thesis. North Texas State University, 1985.

489. Ashburn, Arnold Grayum. "An Analytical and Comparative Study of Course Offering Efficiency in Selected Texas Baptist Colleges and Universities, 1961, 1965." Ph.D. dissertation. University of Southern Mississippi, 1967.

490. Ashcraft, Charles H. "New Life in Old Structures-Christian Education." *The Southern Baptist Educator*, July 1972, p. 16.

491. Ashcraft, Robert Russell. "A Historical Study of Higher Education in the American Baptist Association." Ph.D. dissertation. East Texas State University, 1968.

492. Bargainer, James D. "Academic Computing and the Information Society." *The Southern Baptist Educator*, March-April 1984, pp. 6-7.

493. Barlow, Herman Zulch, Jr. "Leadership Effectiveness of Chief Executives in Southern Baptist Colleges and Universities." Ed.D. dissertation. University of Houston, 1985.

Describes management style of chief executive officers of selected Baptist institutions. Argues that future assessment of leadership style should include the perspectives of the chairs of the boards of trustees, chief executive officers, and vice presidents for academic affairs.

494. Basden, Edward Jeter. "The Programming of Religious Education in Southern Baptist Institutions of Higher Education, 1977-1978." Ed.D. dissertation. North Texas State University, 1978.

495. Bell, Bobby G. "Misplaced Concreteness." *The Southern Baptist Educator*, March 1983, pp. 3-5.

Deplores expressing crisis in higher education in fiscal terms. Contends financial solutions insufficient and views education as something other than a commodity. Calls for substantive planning.

496. Bell, John Michael. "A Study of the Self-Perceived Administrative Styles and Effectiveness of Senior Administrative Officials of Southern Baptist Senior Colleges and Universities." Ph.D. dissertation. The American University, 1981.

Reviews Baptist commitment to higher education historically.

497. Bell, Robert Galen. "Student Personnel Services in Four Year Coeducational Colleges and Universities of the Southern Baptist Convention." Ph.D. dissertation. University of Northern Colorado, 1973.

498. Blamires, Harry. "Implications of Christian Thought in

Contemporary Culture and Education." *The Southern Baptist Educator*, September 1978, p. 3.

499. Bolling, Landrum R. "Seedbed for Moral and Spiritual Values." *The Southern Baptist Educator*, January 1978, p. 12.

500. Bonniwell, Hilton T. "Distinctiveness of Christian Education." *The Southern Baptist Educator*, November 1966, p. 6.

501. Borders, George Randolph. "A Study of Student Involvement in the Governance of Southern Baptist Colleges and Universities." Ph.D. dissertation. University of Southern Mississippi, 1973.

502. Borders, George Randolph. "Weathering the Financial Aid Storm: One Possibility." *The Southern Baptist Educator*, September 1978, p. 12.

503. Bowman, Mary D. "The Distinctive Features of Christian Higher Education: An Uncommon Gift." *The Southern Baptist Educator*, January 1984, p. 7.

504. Brand, Paul W. "Feet on the Ground." *The Southern Baptist Educator*, September 1985, pp. 8-13.

Contrasts lecture and case study presentations to show the value of relating education to life experiences.

505. Brand, Paul W. "The Guru and the Disciple." *The Southern Baptist Educator*, September 1985, pp. 3-7.

Extracts from his experience as a physician in a teaching hospital in India a paradigm for teaching. Calls for a teacher-pupil relationship which displays the teacher as whole and fallible; for tutors or personal guides during the whole course of personal study; and for projects for tutors which become vehicles of interchange with students.

506. Brooks, Oscar S. "Some Ideals for a Christian College." *The Southern Baptist Educator*, December 1969, p. 6.

507. Brown, Jack Elliotte, Jr. "A Comparative Study of Student and Faculty Morale Determinants and Relationships in Southern Baptist Institutions of Higher Education." Ed.D. dissertation. Western Michigan University, 1981.

508. Brown, Robert W. "Church-Related Colleges...Rising to Fall?" *The Southern Baptist Educator*, July 1969, p. 12.

509. Bruster, Bill G. "A History of Oklahoma Baptist University With Special Reference to the Contribution of John Wesley Raley." Ph.D. dissertation. Southwestern Baptist Theological Seminary, 1972.

510. Bryan, Ralph T. "The Distinctive Features of Christian Higher

Education: The Truth Shall Make You Free." *The Southern Baptist Educator*, January 1984, p. 6.

511. Bryant, Gladys. "The Milk of Human Kindness." *The Southern Baptist Educator*, July 1982, pp. 12-13.

512. Cameron, Vernon Wayne. "The Development of Faculty Recruitment and Retention Guidelines for Departments of Music in Selected Universities and Colleges Supported by the Southern Baptist Convention." Ed.D. dissertation. The University of Alabama, 1978.

513. Campbell, Doak S. "The Crisis in Baptist Higher Education." *Review and Expositor*, Winter 1967, p. 31.

514. Campolo, Anthony. "The Challenge of Radical Christianity for the Christian College." *The Southern Baptist Educator*, July 1980, pp. 4-15.

Describes three types of Christian colleges: traditional denominationally-sponsored schools, sectarian schools, and radical Christian colleges. The types all compared and contrasted with a detailed treatment of what is necessary for radical Christianity to have a place on these campuses.

515. Carden, William R. "A University For All Seasons." *The Southern Baptist Educator*, November 1969, p. 3.

516. Carder, Clarence A. "A Study of Teacher Education in Southern Baptist Colleges and Universities." Ph.D. dissertation. The University of Tennessee, 1955.

517. Chamblee, James. "Values Oriented Education and The Fine Arts." *The Southern Baptist Educator*, January 1982, pp. 3, 12.

518. Chaney, Charles L. "Christian Higher Education: The Permanent and Paramount Tasks." *The Southern Baptist Educator*, May 1985, pp. 3-7.

Discovers the tasks of a Christian to demonstrate Christianity, to educate, and to be obedient to Jesus Christ. Obedience means to exhibit love in obedience to Christ's great command and to evangelize, thus obeying the great commission.

519. Clark, George Edmond. "English Programs in Southern Baptist Senior Colleges and Universities." Ph.D. dissertation. George Peabody College for Teachers, 1962.

520. Clark, Thomas D. "A History of Baptist Involvement in Higher Education." *Review and Expositor*, Winter 1967, p. 19.

521. Collmer, Robert G. "Walking in the Path of Those Stern Impassioned Feet." *The Southern Baptist Educator*, November 1984, pp. 3-5.

522.   Corts, Paul R. and John R. Prince, Jr. "MBO Planning in the Small
        College: Personnel, Programs, and Budgeting." *Cause/Effect* 3
        (September 1980): 22-27.

        Discusses application of management by objective concepts
        for planning and management in a small college.

523.   Curtis, Ben. "Chapel: What It Should Be." *The Southern Baptist
        Educator*, April 1987, pp. 3, 16.

524.   Davis, Cora Anne. "An Approach to Resolving Issues in the Work
        Place: A Study of Cognitive Styles as a Variable in the
        Person-Work Environment Fit of Social Work Majors Graduating
        from the Southern Baptist Theological Seminary, 1970-1980
        (Kentucky)." Ph.D. dissertation. University of Louisville, 1984.

        Did not find a significant relationship between the cognitive
        styles of the workers studied and their preferred work environment.

525.   Dawson, Jerry F. "Trustee, College Identified Together." *The
        Southern Baptist Educator*, May 1983, p. 4.

526.   Dean, Joseph O., Jr. "Lest We Forget: Reminders for The
        Christian College Community." *The Southern Baptist Educator*,
        January 1987, pp. 4-5.

527.   DeRooy, Joan. "Instructional Television: Expanding the
        Institution." *The Southern Baptist Educator*, March 1987, pp. 3-7.

528.   Dixon, B. Aldon. "Student Development: The Past, The Present
        and The Future." *The Southern Baptist Educator*, November 1982,
        pp. 6-9.

        Describes four concerns of student development: residence,
        services, activities, and retention.

529.   Du Charme, Robert. "Incorporating "High Tech" Into Liberal Arts
        Instruction." *The Southern Baptist Educator*, March 1984, pp. 8-9.

530.   Duncan, Pope A. "Being President of a Baptist College." *The
        Southern Baptist Educator*, January 1979, p. 3.

531.   Duncan, Pope A. "The Changing Role of the University in
        Contemporary Society." *Review and Expositor*, Summer 1972, p.
        293.

532.   Edwards, W. T., Jr. "Students On Today's Campus." *The Southern
        Baptist Educator*, September 1982, pp. 4-7, 9.

533.   Elrod, Ben M. "Functions of A Trustee In College Public
        Relations." *The Southern Baptist Educator*, May 1983, p. 5.

534.   Fan, Joyce. "Putting Hope Where It Belongs." *The Southern
        Baptist Educator*, January 1980, p. 3.

535. Fant, John F. "Legal Issues Facing Baptist Schools." *The Southern Baptist Educator*, November 1979, pp. 8-9.

536. Farthing, James P. "Critical Thinking, Values and Faith." *The Southern Baptist Educator*, December 1986, pp. 3-5.

537. Finley, Dean Nolan. "A Profile of Full-time Southern Baptist Campus Ministers on State College and University Campuses (Student Work)." Ed.D. dissertation. The Southern Baptist Theological Seminary, 1985.

538. Fisher, Ben C. *Duties and Responsibilities of College and University Trustees.* Raleigh, NC: North Carolina Board of Higher Education, 1969.

Encourages improved trustee understanding of duties and a more efficient discharge of responsibilities.

539. Fisher, Ben C. "Foundation to Student Government-College Problems." *The Southern Baptist Educator*, March 1977, p. 13.

540. Fisher, Ben C. "The Trustee and The Faculty: A Trustee Orientation To Faculty Relations." *The Southern Baptist Educator*, September 1980, pp. 4-7.

541. Fisher, Ben C. "Widening Scope of Trusteeship in Higher Education." *The Southern Baptist Educator*, March 1972, p. 7.

542. Garner, Donald W. "The Distinctive Features of Christian Higher Education: Baptist College vs. State University." *The Southern Baptist Educator*, January 1984, p. 8.

543. Garwood, Harry Crawford. "The Development of Religious Education in Southern Baptist Colleges and Universities With Special Reference to the Period Since 1900." Ph.D. dissertation. Yale University, 1934.

544. Genesh, Donald. "A Study of Bachelor of Career Arts Programs at Dallas Baptist College." Ed.D. dissertation. Nova University, 1976.

545. Glover, Willis B. "The Idea of a Christian College." *The Southern Baptist Educator*, April 1966, p. 3.

546. Godsey, R. Kirby. "Pious Intelligence: The Challenge of Church-Related Education." *The Southern Baptist Educator*, June 1987, pp. 3-5, 16.

547. Gonzalez, Martin. "An Appraisal of the Division of Business and Economics at Ouachita Baptist University Based on a Follow Up of the Graduates 1972-76." Ph.D. dissertation. The University of Mississippi, 1979.

548. Gooch, David. "The Responsibility of Christian Higher Education

for The Transmission of Values." *Search*, October 1973, p. 30.

549. Grant, Daniel R. "Moral Relativism and Christian Absolutes: Problems and Opportunities for The Christian College." *The Southern Baptist Educator*, July 1976, p. 5.

550. Grant, Daniel R. "The Responsibility of Christian Higher Education for The Transmission of Values." *Search*, October 1973, p. 28.

551. Grant, Daniel R. "The Significance of The McGrath Study of 49 Southern Baptist Colleges: Seeing Ourselves as Others See Us." *The Southern Baptist Educator*, July 1977, p. 5.

552. Greer, Thomas J. "Humanities and The Christian College." *The Southern Baptist Educator*, November 1985, pp. 3-5.

553. Grigson, Albert Clay. "A Critical Analysis of the Endowment Funds of the Denominational Colleges and Universities of Texas With Special Emphasis on Baptist Institutions." Ph.D. dissertation. University of Texas at Austin, 1967.

554. Grimes, Paul Edward. "The Administrative Preparation of Clergymen Serving as Administrators in Colleges and Universities of the Southern Baptist Denomination." Ed.D. dissertation. University of Missouri, 1976.

555. Guenther, James P. "The Right to Discriminate?" *The Southern Baptist Educator*, March 1980, pp. 3-5.

    Explains legal issues relating to hiring and firing practices of private institutions.

556. Guenther, James P. "The Student Versus the College." *The Southern Baptist Educator*, January-February 1983, pp. 3-5.

    Examines legal relationship between student and college with suggestions.

557. Hall, Eugene E. "Student Development-Today and Tomorrow." *The Southern Baptist Educator*, January 1979, p. 4.

    Declares student development programs should integrate students into environment, integrate the educational task, and evaluate the students' experience.

558. Hall, Eugene E. "The Liberal Arts College and Christian Higher Education." *The Southern Baptist Educator*, October 1977, p. 3.

559. Hall, Harriet Grant. "What Makes a Christian College Different?" *The Southern Baptist Educator*, September 1980, pp. 3, 16.

560. Hanle, Robert Vail. "A History of Higher Education Among the German Baptist Brethren: 1708-1908." Ph.D. dissertation.

University of Pennsylvania, 1974.

561.   Hardcastle, Donald L. "Computers in Higher Education." *The Southern Baptist Educator*, March 1984, pp. 3-5.

562.   Harper, James Clyde. "A Study of Alabama Baptist Higher Education and Fundamentalism, 1890-1930." Ph.D. dissertation. The University of Alabama, 1977.

563.   Harris, Fred E. "Reexamining the Christian View of the Student-Teacher Relationships." *The Southern Baptist Educator*, November 1976, p. 4.

564.   Heard, Gerry C. "Should I State My Position?" *The Southern Baptist Educator*, May 1981, pp. 3, 12.

        Asks whether professor should state a position on questions of value and concludes that sensitivity is required.

565.   Heard, Gerry C. "The Vocational Crisis: Answers to The Problem." *The Southern Baptist Educator*, May 1987, pp. 3-7.

        Provides answers to the perceived moral crisis including developing a meaningful concept of work, a greater sense of integrity in the practice of vocation, and a more authentic lifestyle in relation to work. The author carefully explains these concepts stating their implications for higher education.

566.   Heilman, E. Bruce. "Management of Church-Related Colleges." *The Southern Baptist Educator*, September 1976, p. 15.

567.   Hendrix, Gene Allen. "The Role of the Education Commission of the Mississippi Baptist Convention and the Coordination of Baptist Higher Education in Mississippi." Ed.D. dissertation. University of Mississippi, 1981.

        Reviews literature on church related higher education. Calls for clarity in mission statements.

568.   Henry, Will Wright, Jr. "The Inter Relationship Between the Tennessee Baptist Convention and Its Three Institutions of Higher Education (Church-Related, Perception)." Ph.D. dissertation. George Peabody College for Teachers of Vanderbilt University, 1984.

        Explores perceived relationships between the Tennessee Baptist Convention and its three institutions of higher education: Belmont College, Carson-Newman College, and Union University. Finds a close relationship between the three colleges and the sponsoring denomination; however, determines that financial support of the schools represents a sensitive issue.

569.   Hewlett, James Edwin, Jr. "The Development of Guidelines for an

Optimal Student Personnel Program for Colleges and Universities of the Southern Baptist Convention." Ph.D. dissertation. Florida State University, 1975.

570.   Hinson, E. Glenn. "Why Baptist Colleges?" *The Southern Baptist Educator*, May 1972, p. 3.

571.   Horne, Chevis F. "What Makes the Christian School Unique?" *The Southern Baptist Educator*, January 1973, p. 3.

572.   Jackson, James Larry. "An Analysis of Leisure Lifestyle of Students Attending Southwest Baptist University as Measured by a Leisure Inventory and Attitude Scale." Ph.D. dissertation. University of Missouri-Columbia, 1983.

573.   Jenkins, Ernest Alfred. "Higher Education in the American Baptist Convention--A Study of the Relationships Between the Board of Education of the American Baptist Convention and Affiliated Liberal Arts Colleges." Ph.D. dissertation. University of Chicago, 1968.

574.   Johnson, Elyot Wymberly. "Preparation of Church Educational Leadership in Baptist Higher Education." Ed.D. dissertation. University of Colorado at Boulder, 1964.

575.   Johnston, Ronald Leslie. "A Study of Non Traditional Education at Southern Baptist Universities, Colleges, and Junior Colleges." Ed.D. dissertation. East Texas State University, 1981.

Discovers thirty-nine non-traditional programs in Southern Baptist institutions.

576.   Jones, Glen Edward. "Faculty Development Practices in Southern Baptist Institutions of Higher Education in the United States." Ed.D. dissertation. Oklahoma State University, 1982.

Determines that there is a significant relationship between the size of an institution and the existence of a faculty development program.

577.   Keyser, Bernard D. "A History of Baptist Higher Education in the South to 1865." Ph.D. dissertation. The Southern Baptist Theological Seminary, 1956.

578.   Kingsley, Gordon. "The Liberal Arts: A Practical Christian Education?" *The Southern Baptist Educator*, March 1983, pp. 6-9.

Contends that a liberal education is not contradictory to a vocational education, is a relevant education, is practical, and provides excellent Christian learning.

579.   Kinlaw, Howard McConneral. "Richard Furman as a Leader in Baptist Higher Education." Ph.D. dissertation. George Peabody College for Teachers, 1960.

580. Kirkman, Ralph Everett. "A Plan of Christian Higher Education for Arkansas Baptists." Ed.D. dissertation. North Texas State University, 1957.

581. Kirksey, Howard. "A Value-Centered Central Curriculum." *The Southern Baptist Educator*, May 1978, p. 12.

582. Kruschurtz, Verlin. "The Significance of Christian Higher Education In the Life of Our Nation." *The Southern Baptist Educator*, March 1976, p. 9.

583. La Bouve, Michael Frank. "A Study of Undergraduate Student Recruiting Programs in Southern Baptist Colleges and Universities." Ph.D. dissertation. The Florida State University, 1971.

584. Landes, James H. "How Important Are Our Colleges?" *The Southern Baptist Educator*, January 1983, p. 18.

585. Lee, Douglas H. "Confronting the Beast: A Foundation for Accountability in Fund Raising for Baptist Colleges and Universities." *The Southern Baptist Educator*, July 1983, pp. 3-7.

Discusses accountability in fund raising suggesting that accountability must be planned.

586. Lee, William Rory. "Graduates and Non-Graduates Who are High-Risk Freshmen at Selected Southern Baptist Colleges." Ed.D. dissertation. The University of Mississippi, 1984.

Studies the differences and characteristics between the high risk freshmen who graduated as opposed to the high risk freshmen who fail to graduate. Describes at least six differences in characteristics.

587. Lewis, Judith Ann. "The Selection Process of Dramatic Literature for Production at Southern Baptist Colleges and Universities." Ed.D. dissertation. The University of Mississippi, 1983.

Surveys attitude and practices of drama directors and chief academic officers at forty-six Southern Baptist Colleges and Universities. Finds that the most important consideration reported by directors was availability of actors and facilities capabilities.

588. Lindsey, Jonathan. "Education Is a Commodity." *The Southern Baptist Educator*, March 1973, p. 5.

589. Losh, Paul T. "Religion in Northern Baptist-Related Colleges and Universities--A Study in Status and Tendencies." Ph.D. dissertation. University of Colorado, Boulder, 1948.

590. Lynn, Robert L. "The Baptist College Speaks to the Third Century." *The Southern Baptist Educator*, March 1976, p. 8.

591.   Lynn, Robert L. "Trustee Involvement in Institutional Public Relations." *The Southern Baptist Educator*, May 1983, p. 3.

592.   Martin, Theodore K. "Administration of the Instruction in Southern Baptist Colleges and Universities." Ph.D. dissertation. George Peabody College for Teachers, 1949.

593.   Martin, Warren Bryan. "The Leadership Most Needed Now." *The Southern Baptist Educator*, September 1986, pp. 4-9, 20.

Sets forth a concept of ideational leadership as opposed to managerial leadership. Limits focus to one area of leadership responsibility, that of reordering of basic values.

594.   McBeth, Leon. "History of Southern Baptist Higher Education, A Synopsis." *The Southern Baptist Educator*, March 1967, p. 3.

595.   McGrath, Earl J. "Financing the Church-Related Institution." *The Southern Baptist Educator*, September 1976, p. 15.

596.   McKinney, Rhea. "Christian Education: Putting the Learner in the Center." *Search*, October 1977, p. 36.

597.   McMillan, Ann. "Private Colleges Will Prevail." *The Southern Baptist Educator*, September 1984, p. 3.

598.   McRae, Donald Andrew. "Contemporary Southern Baptist Involvement With the State Regarding Higher Education." Ph.D. dissertation. New Orleans Baptist Theological Seminary, 1969.

599.   McWilliams, Warren. "To Be A Theologian On a Southern Baptist Campus." *The Southern Baptist Educator*, May 1985, pp. 8-10.

600.   Miller, Calvin. "Real Education - The Great Integration." *The Southern Baptist Educator*, September 1983, pp. 3-7.

Calls for an integration of the rational and the devotional for fully developed education.

601.   Miller, Calvin. "The Demon of Elitism." *The Southern Baptist Educator*, September 1983, pp. 8-12.

Demonstrates the value of simplicity in communicating profound values.

602.   Miller, Francis G. "Student Personnel Services in Southern Baptist Colleges and Universities." Ph.D. dissertation. University of Southern Mississippi, 1964.

603.   Moisan, Leonard J. "An Economic Impact Study of Liberty Baptist College on the Lynchburg Metropolitan Area." Unpublished, 1982.

Reports on Liberty Baptist College's impact on the Lynchburg area in the 1980 fiscal year. Study presented to the president and board of trustees of Liberty Baptist College.

604. Moore, Robert Wayne. "The Organized Programs of Student Activities and Student Attitudes Toward Them at Selected Southern Baptist Colleges and Universities." Ed.D. dissertation. The University of Mississippi, 1968.

605. Moots, Philip R. "Current Legal Problems For Church-Related Colleges." *The Southern Baptist Educator*, September 1978, p. 15.

606. Moots, Philip R. "Pressing Legal Issues Confronting Church-Related Colleges." *The Southern Baptist Educator*, July 1977, p. 9.

607. Moots, Philip R. and Edward McGlynn Gaffney, Jr. "Church and Campus: Legal Issues in Religiously Affiliated Higher Education." Notre Dame University, 1979.

Analyzes legal issues confronting religiously-affiliated colleges and other nonprofit institutions.

608. Musacchio, George. "The Distinctive Features of Christian Higher Education: A Biblical Foundation." *The Southern Baptist Educator*, January 1984, p. 4.

609. Neptune, William E. "On Being A Professor In A Baptist School." *The Southern Baptist Educator*, July 1980, pp. 3, 24.

610. Newell, Robert Mocell. "The Development, Implementation, and Evaluation of a Program of Guidance and Supervision for Church-Vocation Students at Houston Baptist University, Houston, Texas." D.Min. dissertation. The Southern Baptist Theological Seminary, 1974.

611. Nichols, Don, et al. "Religious Counseling at Public Community Colleges." Research report, 1977.

Surveys eight hundred and two public two year colleges determining that a large minority of the schools provides some sort of religious counseling for students.

612. Noonkester, J. Ralph. "Thirty-Four Years of Fall Beginnings." *The Southern Baptist Educator*, September 1986, p. 3.

613. Paine, J. H. E. "Scholarship: The Sheer Love of Learning." *The Southern Baptist Educator*, May 1985, p. 11.

614. Parrish, Tom Z. "Exodus From the Poverty Syndrome." *The Southern Baptist Educator*, July 1982, pp. 3-5.

Addresses the concern of higher costs and diminished support for Christian higher education. Argues that the determining factor in the future of private colleges will not be the high tuition cost, but the availability of student aid funds.

615.   Peterson, Hazel. "The Distinctive Features of Christian Higher Education: That 'Something Extra.'" *The Southern Baptist Educator*, January 1984, p. 3.

616.   Pope, Kenneth H. "Filling The Value Void." *The Southern Baptist Educator*, September 1981, pp. 3, 16.

617.   Price, Theron D. "Rationale of Baptist Higher Education." *Review and Expositor*, Winter 1967, p. 5.

618.   Rainsford, George N. "Encouragement for the Private College." *The Southern Baptist Educator*, September 1978, p. 9.

619.   Raley, Coleman Lavan. "Personality Traits of High-Academic Achievers at Oklahoma Baptist University, 1958-1959." Ed.D. dissertation. University of Oklahoma, 1960.

620.   Reddish, Mitchell G. "The Role of Religion In A Liberal Arts Curriculum." *The Southern Baptist Educator*, October 1985, pp. 3-5, 16.

621.   Reist, John S., Jr. "What's The Use? The Interrogative Mood of Christian Liberal Arts Education." *Perspectives in Religious Studies*, Spring 1978, p. 10.

622.   Rhea, Claude H. "'What' Is Christian Higher Education?" *The Southern Baptist Educator*, September 1982, p. 3.

623.   Richardson, Dennie Karl. "A Study of the Leadership Styles of the Chief Student Affairs Administrators of Southern Baptist Colleges and Universities." Ed.D. dissertation. North Texas State University, 1980.

624.   Rifkin, Paul Grant. "A Study of Religious Values of Southern Baptist College Students Enrolled at Selected Private Liberal Arts Colleges and Universities." Ph.D. dissertation. Florida State University, 1981.

         Demonstrates that Southern Baptist students in denominational colleges are more strongly influenced by their religion than non-denominational students.

625.   Robinson, Larry Ernest. "The Establishment of Managing Ministry by Objectives for the Baptist Student Union, Mercer University, Macon, Georgia." D.Min. dissertation. New Orleans Baptist Theological Seminary, 1982.

626.   Schrader, Gigi. "America's Schools-Destined To Doom?" *The Southern Baptist Educator*, November 1984, p. 6.

627.   Scott, Richard C. "Can Ethics Be Taught?" *The Southern Baptist Educator*, October 1984, p. 3.

628.   Seaton, Craig E. "The Christian College as a Source of Students for

Selected Theological Seminaries." Biola College, 1970.

Analyzes extent to which Christian colleges serve as a source of students for selected theological seminaries.

629.   Silver, Jane H. "An Analysis of the Words Incompetency and Immorality in Southern Baptist Colleges and Universities." Practicum report. Nova University, 1978.

Studies use of the terms incompetency and immorality to determine their use in reprimands and dismissals in Southern Baptist Colleges and Universities. Discovers that no studied institution had a printed definition of words used for reprimand or dismissal.

630.   Silver, Jane H. "Fifty Years of Southern Baptist Junior College Education 1927-1977: An Historical Analysis." Ed.D. dissertation. Nova University, 1979.

Traces the development of Southern Baptist Junior Colleges from 1927 to 1977. Accesses strengths and weaknesses of surviving junior colleges with recommendations.

631.   Sims, O. Suthern, Jr. "The Way It Was and Still Ought To Be." *The Southern Baptist Educator*, March 1985, pp. 3-7.

632.   Smiley, David L. "Redeeming the Christian Idea of the Liberal Education." *The Southern Baptist Educator*, January 1977, p. 9.

633.   Smith, Claudius Ray. "An Analysis of Men's Physical Education Programs in Texas Baptist Colleges and a Comparison of Physical Education Programs in Texas Baptist Colleges With Selected Texas State Colleges and Universities." Ed.D. dissertation. North Texas State University, 1970.

634.   Smith, Glen. "Speech and Theatre Education at Central College." *Journal of Communication Studies* 3 (October 1984): 25-27.

Reports on study of drama at an Arkansas Baptist school which concluded in 1950.

635.   Spears, Philip Yates. "A Critical Analysis of the Role of Southern Baptist Colleges and Universities in Decisions for Church-Related Vocations." Ed.D. dissertation. Southwestern Baptist Theological Seminary, 1982.

636.   St. Amant, C. Penrose. "Undergraduate Education in Historical Perspective." *The Southern Baptist Educator*, July 1984, pp. 3-15, 19.

Outlines history of American undergraduate education followed by an analysis of liberal arts education today. Finds that graduate school perspectives have stifled general, liberal arts education on the undergraduate level in large universities. Expresses concern that undergraduate education does not fare well in competition with the goals of research, professional training, and service to the community. Note that small liberal arts colleges are better equipped to provide sound undergraduate education.

637.   Taylor, James Rodney. "A Study of the Attitudes of Faculty Members at Selected Southern Baptist Colleges and Universities Toward Collective Bargaining in the Relationship to Specific Demographic Variables." Ed.D. dissertation. Florida State University, 1979.

638.   Theobald, Robert. "Meshing Old and New Visions." *The Southern Baptist Educator*, July 1986, pp. 3-10.

Proposes a model of servant leadership and all-win strategies for leadership at all levels. Outlines techniques for teaching positive attitudes toward current crises. Describes a problem/possibility focuser for group problem solving.

639.   Thomason, Tommy. "Freedom of the Student Press at Southern Baptist Colleges and Universities." Ed.D. dissertation. East Texas State University, 1984.

Argues that censorship and the potential for censorship are widely present in Southern Baptist Colleges and Universities.

640.   Thomason, Tommy. "Student Press Freedom at Southern Baptist Colleges." *The Southern Baptist Educator*, November 1985, pp. 6-7.

641.   Tilley, W. Clyde. "The Christian College as Change Agent." *The Southern Baptist Educator*, September 1979, p. 6.

642.   Tresch, John W., Jr. "Telling An Institution's Story." *The Southern Baptist Educator*, December 1985, pp. 6-9.

643.   Tresch, John W., Jr. "Values: Focal Point of Education." *The Southern Baptist Educator*, October 1984, p. 4.

644.   Turner, Paul Winston. "A Study of Attitudes and Selected Graduates of the Southern Baptist Theological Seminary Toward Ministry: 1950-1970." STD dissertation. The Southern Baptist Theological Seminary, 1972.

645.   Walker, Arthur L., Jr. "A Call to Excellence." *The Southern Baptist Educator*, April 1985, pp. 15-16.

646.   Walker, Arthur L., Jr. "A Humanities Renaissance." *The Southern Baptist Educator*, November 1980, p. 19.

Argues the strength of Christian education in linkages across disciplinary bounds, in exploring ethical issues, and in cross-cultural experiences.

647. Walker, Arthur L., Jr. "An Awareness of Differences." *The Southern Baptist Educator*, January 1987, pp. 13, 15.

Takes issue with Education Secretary William J. Bennett's view of college life as being limited to a few elite schools. Details the wealth of diversity in higher education.

648. Walker, Arthur L., Jr. "A New Beginning." *The Southern Baptist Educator*, September 1979, p. 15.

649. Walker, Arthur L., Jr. "An 'Old' Word for the Eighties." *The Southern Baptist Educator*, November 1979, p. 19.

Presents challenges of planning by visionary leaders.

650. Walker, Arthur L., Jr. "Back to the Past for the Future." *The Southern Baptist Educator*, April 1987, pp. 14-15.

651. Walker, Arthur L., Jr. "Baptist Colleges Fulfill Purpose." *The Southern Baptist Educator*, July 1986, pp. 18-19.

652. Walker, Arthur L., Jr. "Commitment to a Cause." *The Southern Baptist Educator*, May 1981, p. 11.

653. Walker, Arthur L., Jr. "Communications and the College." *The Southern Baptist Educator*, May 1984, pp. 15-16.

654. Walker, Arthur L., Jr. "Distinctives of Christian Leadership." *The Southern Baptist Educator*, January 1984, pp. 19-20.

655. Walker, Arthur L., Jr. "Don't Forget the Faculty." *The Southern Baptist Educator*, March 1985, pp. 15-16.

656. Walker, Arthur L., Jr. "Evaluating From Results." *The Southern Baptist Educator*, August 1984, pp. 23-24.

657. Walker, Arthur L., Jr. "Examining the System." *The Southern Baptist Educator*, January 1980, p. 15.

Assesses the use of examinations for grading and credit purposes.

658. Walker, Arthur L., Jr. "Facing the Desacralized Society." *The Southern Baptist Educator*, March 1979, p. 3.

Analyzes problems of value based education in a society which has denied its sources of ultimate value.

659. Walker, Arthur L., Jr. "Forecasting the Future." *The Southern Baptist Educator*, February 1985, pp. 15-16, 14.

660. Walker, Arthur L., Jr. "Keeping Our Students." *The Southern Baptist Educator*, July 1983, p. 19.

661. Walker, Arthur L., Jr. "Looking at Tuition Increases Realistically."

The Southern Baptist Educator, May 1987, pp. 15-16.

662.   Walker, Arthur L., Jr. "Meaning In the Information Society." *The Southern Baptist Educator*, May 1983, p. 19.

Declares the emphasis on meaning is the primary value of church-related educational institutions.

663.   Walker, Arthur L., Jr. "New 'Nontraditional' Approach. *The Southern Baptist Educator*, November 1981, p. 15.

664.   Walker, Arthur L., Jr. "Planning: Finding the Solution Before the Problem." *The Southern Baptist Educator*, September 1983, pp. 23-24.

665.   Walker, Arthur L., Jr. "Preserving Diversity." *The Southern Baptist Educator*, November 1983, pp. 19-20.

Expresses concern over loss of diversity within institutions of learning. Pleads for smaller schools to find and affirm distinctive contributions.

666.   Walker, Arthur L., Jr. "Redefining Independent Education." *The Southern Baptist Educator*, December 1984-January 1985, pp. 19-20.

Comments on the blurring of distinctions between public and private education financing. Both types of schools use similar fund-raising strategies.

667.   Walker, Arthur L., Jr. "Remaining (Somewhat) Optimistic." *The Southern Baptist Educator*, July 1980, p. 23.

668.   Walker, Arthur L., Jr. "Response to Facts of Existence." *The Southern Baptist Educator*, May 1980, p. 15.

Places the recruiting of students as a high priority in the face of a declining student population.

669.   Walker, Arthur L., Jr. "Rethinking Financial Aid." *The Southern Baptist Educator*, March 1982, pp. 15-16.

670.   Walker, Arthur L., Jr. "Self-Examination is a Must." *The Southern Baptist Educator*, July 1985, pp. 19-20.

671.   Walker, Arthur L., Jr. "State Schools Morally Neutral." *The Southern Baptist Educator*, August 1981, p. 15.

672.   Walker, Arthur L., Jr. "The Challenge of Distinctives." *The Southern Baptist Educator*, October 1984, pp. 15-16.

673.   Walker, Arthur L., Jr. "The Challenge of Recruiting." *The Southern Baptist Educator*, February 1987, pp. 15-16.

674.   Walker, Arthur L., Jr. "The Future in Perspective." *The Southern Baptist Educator*, March 1987, pp. 15-16.

675.   Walker, Arthur L., Jr. "The Quest for Ultimate Compatibility." *The Southern Baptist Educator*, November 1982, pp. 19-20.

676.   Walker, Arthur L., Jr. "The Value of Cooperation." *The Southern Baptist Educator*, May 1982, p. 11

677.   Walker, Arthur L., Jr. "Trusteeship." *The Southern Baptist Educator*, June 1987, pp. 14-15.

678.   Walker, Arthur L., Jr. "Trustees in Baptist Colleges." *The Southern Baptist Educator*, May 1982, pp. 3-4, 12.

679.   Walker, Arthur L., Jr. "Values Can Be Transmitted." *The Southern Baptist Educator*, December 1986, pp. 15-16.

        Contends that institutions and faculty members which avoid trivializing the powerful and revolutionary message of Christ can be an influence on the values of students.

680.   Walker, Arthur L., Jr. "Will Education Win the Race?" *The Southern Baptist Educator*, March 3, 1984, pp. 19-20.

        Indicates that trustees of Christian institutions have a responsibility to see that their policies produce an effective result. The Christian orientation of these institutions requires a sensitivity to persons.

681.   Walters, Terry. "Learning to Teach." *The Southern Baptist Educator*, November 1980, pp. 4-6.

682.   Ward, Richard H. "The Development of Baptist Higher Education in Tennessee." Ph.D. dissertation. George Peabody College for Teachers, 1954.

683.   Weaver, G. Norman. "Administrative Policies of Southern Baptist Senior Colleges and Universities: A Status Survey and Critique." Ph.D. dissertation. Southwestern Baptist Theological Seminary, 1961.

684.   Wee, David L. "Values in the Undergraduate Curriculum." *The Southern Baptist Educator*, September 1978, p. 17.

685.   Wheeler, Ed. "The Distinctive Features of Christian Higher Education: Confessions of An Undistinctive Christian Educator." *The Southern Baptist Educator*, January 1984, p. 5.

686.   Wood, Gary E. "Taxes and Independent Higher Education." *The Southern Baptist Educator*, March 1986, pp. 3-7.

        Describes investment charitable institutions have in high tax rates, that in high tax rates mean the cost of tax-exempt gifts are lower. Considers problems and potentials in tax reform.

687.   Wood, James E., Jr. "The Dilemma of The *Bakke* Decision." *The Southern Baptist Educator*, September 1978, p. 2.

688.   Wood, Ralph. "The Case for an Extrinsic Relation." *The Southern Baptist Educator*, October 1986, pp. 3-4, 9.

* Jerry M. Self compiled the entries for the Southern Baptists; Harold D. Germer compiled the American Baptist section.

CHAPTER 5
BIBLE COLLEGES
Virginia Lieson Brereton

689.   American Association of Bible Colleges. *Directory, 1985-86.*
        Wheaton, IL: American Association of Bible Colleges.

        Lists the colleges that are currently members of the
        accrediting association of Bible colleges.

690.   Behan, Warren Palmer. "An Introductory Survey of the Lay
        Training School Field." *Religious Education* 11 (1916): 47-52.

        Describes the missionary training schools that existed in
        1916, among which some of the Bible schools are included.

691.   "Bible Schools That Are True to the Faith." *The Sunday School
        Times* 72 (February 1, 1930): 63.

        Lists the schools considered safe in 1930 by the editors of a
        leading conservative evangelical periodical.

692.   Black, Robert E. *The Story of Johnson Bible College.* Kimberlin
        Heights, TN: Tennessee Valley Printing Co., 1951.

        Tells the history, from an insider's point of view, of the
        Johnson Bible College, established in 1892 by Ashley Johnson in
        Tennessee.

693.   Boon, Harold W. "The Development of the Bible College or
        Institute in the United States." Ph.D. dissertation. School of
        Education, New York University, 1960.

        Describes the curriculum of the "standard" Bible school and
        contains some information on the establishment of an accrediting
        agency of Bible schools.

694.   Bowman, Katherine Elizabeth. "Columbia Bible College: A Leader
        in a New Movement in Religious Education." M.A. thesis. School
        of Education, University of South Carolina, 1941.

        Describes the religious education curriculum, from an
        insider's perspective, of Columbia Bible College, Columbia, SC.

695.   Brackett, Charles H. "The History of Azusa College and the
        Friends." M.A. thesis. University of Southern California, 1967.

        Tells the history of an institution that began in the Los
        Angeles area in the late nineteenth century as a Bible school of a
        holiness wing of the Society of Friends.

696.   Breed, David R. "Bible Institutes of the United States." The
        Biblical Review 12 (1927): 372-78.

        Outlines the general characteristics of the Bible school
        movement during the twenties.

697.   Brereton, Virginia Lieson. "The Bible Schools and Conservative
        Higher Education, 1880-1940." In Making Higher Education
        Christian: The History and Mission of Evangelical Colleges in
        America. Edited by Joel Carpenter and Kenneth W. Shipps.
        Grand Rapids, MI: Eerdmans, 1987.

        Surveys the history of the Bible school movement and places
        it in the perspective of the rest of conservative evangelical higher
        education.

698.   Brereton, Virginia Lieson. "Protestant Fundamentalist Bible
        Schools, 1881-1940." Ph.D. dissertation. Columbia University,
        1981.

        Furnishes an outsider's analysis of the Bible school
        movement, its history, themes, and purposes.

699.   Brereton, Virginia Lieson. "The Public Schools Are Not Enough:
        the Bible and Private Schools." In The Bible in American
        Education, pp. 41-75. Edited by David L. Barr and Nicholas
        Piediscalzi. Philadelphia: Fortress Press; Chico, CA: Scholars
        Press, 1982.

        Treats the Bible school movement as the conservative
        evangelicals' response, paralleling that of Jews and Catholics, to the
        public education then available, which all three groups found
        unacceptably secular and inimical to their purposes.

700.   Cable, John H. A History of the Missionary Training Institute: The
        Pioneer Bible School of America. Harrisburg, PA: Christian
        Publications, 1933.

        Traces a history of what is now Nyack College, Nyack, NY,
        which is generally regarded as the first Bible school in the United
        States.

701.   Carpenter, Joel A. "The Renewal of American Fundamentalism,
        1930-1945." Ph.D. dissertation. Johns Hopkins University, 1984.

        Deals at some length with the subject of the Bible school as one of the vehicles for "renewal," especially with aspects of the history of Providence Bible Institute.

702.   Clark, Robert.   "Bible Institutes and Theological Seminaries," *Moody Bible Institute Monthly* 22 (March 1922): 259.

Describes the "popular" nature of Bible school education, open to all students, as contrasted with the exclusivism of the seminary.

703.   Cobb, William. "The West Point of Fundamentalism." *American Mercury* 16 (1929): 104-12.

Provides a hostile observer's description of Moody Bible Institute and its students' activities in the twenties.

704.   Cook, Harold R. "Preparing Tomorrow's Missionaries." Wheaton, IL: Accrediting Association of Bible Colleges, 1972.

Evaluates the Bible colleges' programs for preparing missionaries.

705.   De Remer, Bernard. *Moody Bible Institute: A Pictorial History*. Chicago: Moody Press, 1960.

Provides a rich visual picture of the history of Moody Bible Institute.

706.   Findlay, James F., Jr. *Dwight L. Moody: American Evangelist, 1837-1899*. Chicago: University of Chicago Press, 1969.

Describes the life of the founder of Moody Bible Institute, which reveals his purposes in establishing the school.

707.   Flood, Robert G. and Jerry B. Jenkins. *The Men Behind Moody*. Chicago: Moody Press, 1984.

Sketches the biographies of the leading figures in Moody Bible Institute history.

708.   Flood, Robert G. and Jerry B. Jenkins. *Teaching the Word, Reaching the World: Moody Bible Institute, the First 100 Years*. Chicago: Moody Press, 1985.

Retells the history of Moody Bible Institute on the occasion of its hundredth anniversary.

709.   Gaebelein, Frank. *Christian Education in a Democracy: The Report of the N.A.E. Committee*. New York: Oxford University Press, 1951.

Offers an appraisal of the goals and condition of the Bible school movement in the late forties and early fifties by a conservative evangelical educator much respected by his fellow religionists.

710.   Gangel, Kenneth. "The Bible College: Past, Present, and Future." *Christianity Today*, November 7, 1980, pp. 1324-26.

Discusses issues that Bible school educators face currently, partly as a result of their concern with accreditation.

711.   Gasper, Louis. "Fundamentalist Education, Scholarship, and Literature." In *The Fundamentalist Movement*. The Hague: Mouton and Co., 1963.

Sketches some of the general themes of the Bible school movement--one of the first attempts to do so.

712.   Getz, Gene A. *MBI: the History of Moody Bible Institute*. Chicago: Moody Bible Institute, 1969.

Traces the history of Moody Bible Institute, probably the most scholarly of the several histories of this institution.

713.   Gordon, A. J. "Short Cut Methods." *The Watchman*, November 7, 1889, p. 1.

Attempts to answer the critics of the earliest missionary training/Bible schools.

714.   Gordon, Ernest B. *Adoniram Judson Gordon: A Biography*. New York: Fleming H. Revell, 1896.

Traces the biography of the founder of Gordon College, a missionary training/Bible school in its early years.

715.   Gray, James M. *Synthetic Bible Studies*. Cleveland: F.M. Barton, 1900.

Sets forth a method of studying and teaching the Bible. Gray was a longtime leader of Moody Bible Institute, and his method widely influenced the teaching in Bible schools.

716.   Harkness, Robert. *Reuben Archer Torrey: The Man, His Message*. Chicago: The Bible Colportage Association, 1929.

Describes the life of one of the early leaders both of Moody Bible Institute and of the Bible Institute of Los Angeles.

717.   Henry, James O. "Black Oil and Souls to Win." *Biola Broadcaster*, December, 1973, pp. 4-28.

Provides a history of the Bible Institute of Los Angeles. Henry was a professor of history at Biola.

718. Henstock, Thomas F. "A History and Interpretation of the Curriculum of Central Bible Institute." M.A. thesis. Central Bible Institute, 1963.

     Traces the history of Central Bible Institute, an Assemblies of God institution in Springfield, MO.

719. Krivoshey, Robert Martin. "'Going Through the Eye of the Needle': The Life of Oilman Fundamentalist Lyman Stewart, 1840-1923." Ph.D. dissertation. University of Chicago, 1973.

     Explores the life of one of the founders--and chief early source of funds--for the Bible Institute of Los Angeles. Stewart also financed the publication of *The Fundamentals*.

720. Martin, Dorothy. *Moody Bible Institute: God's Power in Action.* Chicago: Moody Press, 1977.

     Sketches the history of Moody Bible Institute, a supplement to Getz and Flood.

721. Martin, Roger. *R. A. Torrey: Apostle of Certainty.* Murfreesboro, TN: Sword of the Lord Publishers, 1976.

     Recounts the life of one of the early leaders at Moody Bible Institute and Bible Institute of Los Angeles--a supplement to the information available in the Harkness biography.

722. Mathews, R. Arthur. *Towers Pointing Upward.* Columbia, SC: Columbia Bible College, 1973.

     Traces the history, in a celebratory vein, of the Columbia, SC Bible Institute.

723. McBirnie, William Stuart. "A Study of the Bible Institute Movement." D.R.E. dissertation. Southwestern Baptist Theological Seminary, 1952.

     Furnishes a list of Bible schools then in existence.

724. McKaig, Charles Donald. "The Educational Philosophy of A.B. Simpson, Founder of the Christian and Missionary Alliance." Ph.D. dissertation. School of Education, New York University, 1948.

     Describes the educational ideas of A. B. Simpson, founder of the Missionary Training Institute at Nyack, New York.

725. Metcalf, Edith E. *Letters to Dorothy.* Chicago: Fleming H. Revell Co., 1893.

     Provides a detailed view, in letters written by a student, into the early life at Moody Bible Institute.

726.   Miller, J. Melvin. "The Torch Held High: A History of Pacific Bible College of Azusa, California." M.A. thesis. Pacific Bible College, 1957.

Furnishes an insider's history of a Society of Friends Bible School, started in the 1890s in the Los Angeles area.

727.   "Missionary Training Colleges." *Christian Alliance*, May, 1888, p. 76.

Describes the training school movement just then beginning in the United States, out of which the Bible school movement evolved.

728.   "Missionary Training Schools--Do Baptists Need them? A Discussion." *Baptist Quarterly Review* 12 (January 1890): 69-100.

Discusses the advantages and disadvantages of the new missionary training schools, which some writers saw as competitors with the theological seminaries.

729.   Mostert, John. "The Bible College Today." *Accrediting Association of Bible Colleges Newsletter* 11 (1967): 5-14.

Evaluates the then-current situation in the Bible school movement.

730.   Mostert, John. "General Education in the Bible College." Wheaton, IL: American Association of Bible Schools, 1976.

Evaluates the Bible school curriculum. Mostert has been a leader in the accrediting agency.

731.   Mostert, John. "Preparing Bible College Students for Ministries in Christian Education." Wheaton, IL: American Association of Bible Schools, 1973.

Evaluates the Christian Education programs in Bible colleges accredited by the AABS.

732.   Nelson, Shirley. *The Last Year of the War.* New York, NY: Harper and Row, 1978.

Although a fictional work, this novel contains a sense of what it might have been like to be a Bible school student in the late forties, at an institution almost certainly modeled after Moody Bible Institute.

733.   Reed, Lenice. "The Bible Institute in America." M.A. thesis. Wheaton College, 1947.

Describes the origins of the Bible school movement, one of the first attempts to do so.

734. Reynhout, Hubert, Jr. "A Comparative Study of Bible Institute Curriculums." M.A. thesis. Department of Education, University of Michigan, 1947.

735. Ringenberg, William C. "The Bible College Movement." In *The Christian College: A History of Protestant Higher Education in America*, pp. 157-73. Grand Rapids, MI: Eerdmans, 1984.

   Gives a brief but informative history and description of the Bible school movement.

736. Robinson, Margaret Blake. *A Reporter at Moody's*. Chicago: The Bible Institute Colportage Association, 1900.

   Describes life--from a student's perspective--at Moody Bible Institute at the end of the nineteenth century; gives a glimpse into the experience and attitudes of women students there.

737. "Rock of Ages at the Edge of Old Town." *Midwest*, January 27, 1974, pp. 4-5, 8.

   Gives a view of Moody Bible Institute in the early seventies, as it appeared to a journalist.

738. Runyan, William M. *Dr. Gray at Moody Bible Institute*. New York: Oxford University Press, 1935.

   Traces the biography of the well-known Bible teacher and head of Moody Bible Institute during the first third of the twentieth century.

739. Russell, C. Allyn. "Adoniram Judson Gordon: Nineteenth-Century Fundamentalist." *American Baptist Quarterly* 4 (March 1985): 61-89.

   Sketches the life of the founder of Gordon College, which was a missionary training school and Bible school in the late nineteenth and early twentieth centuries.

740. Schlienz, C. F. *The Pilgrim Institution of St. Chrischona, near Basle, Switzerland.* London: John Farquhar Shaw, 1850.

   Furnishes a history and description of a European missionary training school. The European schools furnished models for American founders of such training schools.

741. Showers, Renald. "A History of Philadelphia College of the Bible." Th.M. thesis. Dallas Theological Seminary, 1962.

   Gives an insider's account of the history of Philadelphia College of the Bible, an institution which resulted from a merger between the Bible Institution of Pennsylvania and the Philadelphia School of the Bible (the latter founded by C. I. Scofield).

742.   Smith, Wilbur M. *Will H. Houghton: A Watchman on the Wall.* Grand Rapids, MI: Eerdmans Publishing Co., 1951.

Supplies a biography of the man who was president of Moody Bible Institute during the late thirties and the forties.

743.   Spence, G. H. "History of the Northwest Bible College." B.S. thesis. Minot State College, 1974.

Sketches a history of Northwest Bible College, an Assemblies of God institution in Minot, ND.

744.   Sweeting, George. "Bible Colleges and Institutes: Chronicling the Vision of a Century." *Christianity Today*, February 5, 1982, pp. 38-41.

Furnishes a perspective on the Bible school from the point of view of a president of Moody Bible Institute.

745.   Talbot, Carol. *For This Was I Born: the Captivating Story of Louis T. Talbot.* Chicago: Moody Press, 1977.

Furnishes a biography, by his wife, of an early leader of the Bible Institute of Los Angeles.

746.   Thompson, A. E. *A. B. Simpson: His Life and Work.* Harrisburg, PA: Christian Publications, 1960.

Tells the life of the founder of the Missionary Training Institute (now Nyack College), generally considered the first Bible school in the United States.

747.   "The Training and Sending Forth of Workers." *Christian and Missionary Alliance*, April 30, 1897, p. 419.

Provides an early statement of the importance and necessity of training missionary workers in new institutions outside the college-seminary orbit.

748.   Torrey, Reuben A. *The Importance and Value of Proper Bible Study: How Properly to Study and Interpret the Bible.* New York: George H. Doran Co., 1921.

Furnishes an exposition of how to study or teach the Bible. Torrey was a leading early Bible school educator.

749.   Trollinger, William Vance, Jr. "One Response to Modernity: Northwestern Bible School and the Fundamentalist Empire of William Bell Riley." Ph.D. dissertation. University of Wisconsin, 1984.

Provides a history of the Northwestern Bible School, founded by a foremost leader of twenties and thirties fundamentalism.

Shows how the school developed as a spearhead for the fundamentalist organizations in Minneapolis and the state of Minnesota.

750. Wiersbe, Warren W. *William Culbertson, A Man of God.* Chicago: Moody Press, 1974.

Gives the life story of the president of Moody Bible Institute during the fifties and sixties.

751. Williams, Robert and Marilyn Miller. *Chartered for His Glory: Biola University, 1908-1983.* La Mirada, CA: Association Students of Biola University, 1983.

Gives a history of the Bible Institute of Los Angeles.

752. Witmer, Safara. *The Bible College Story: Education with Dimensions.* Manhasset, NY: Channel Press, 1962.

Describes the Bible school movement. It focuses mostly on the early sixties, but also contains some history. Witmer was a leader in the accrediting association of Bible schools, started in the late forties.

753. Wood, Nathan R. *A School of Christ.* Boston: Gordon College of Theology and Missions, 1953.

Provides a history of Gordon College, which began as the Boston Missionary Training School in 1892. Wood was the institution's longtime president.

CHAPTER 6
CATHOLIC COLLEGES AND UNIVERSITIES
Mary A. Grant

Part I: Institutional Histories

754. Ahern, Patrick Henry. *The Catholic University of America 1887-1896: The Rectorship of John V. Keane.* Washington, DC: The Catholic University of American Press, 1949.

   Relates the story of the administration of the first rector of the Catholic University of America during a period of controversy, growth and expansion of American Catholicism.

755. Angelo, Mark V. *The History of St. Bonaventure University.* St. Bonaventure, NY: Franciscan Institute, 1961.

756. Arthur, David Joseph. "The University of Notre Dame, 1919-1933: An Administrative History." Ph.D. dissertation. University of Michigan, 1973.

   Explores the university's extensive growth during this time and includes the development of Notre Dame's football team under Coach Knute Rockne.

757. Barry, Colman J. *The Catholic University of America 1903-1909: The Rectorship of Denis J. O'Connell.* Washington, DC: The Catholic University of America Press, 1950.

758. Barry, Colman J. *Worship and Work; St. John's Abbey and University, 1856-1956.* Collegeville, MN: St. John's Abbey, 1956.

759. Bennish, Lee J. *Continuity and Change; Xavier University 1831-1981.* Chicago: Loyola University Press, 1981.

760. Bowler, Mary Mariella. "A History of Catholic Colleges for Women in the United States of America." Washington, DC: Ph.D. dissertation. Catholic University of America, 1933.

761. Brady, Charles A. *The First Hundred Years: Canisius College, 1870-1970.* Buffalo, NY: Canisius College, 1970.

762. Breslin, Richard David. "The Development of Villanova Since Its Inception As a University in 1953." Ph.D. dissertation. Catholic University of America, 1969.

763.   Callahan, Generosa. *Mother Angelique Ayres, Dreamer and Builder of Our Lady of the Lake University.* Austin, TX: Jenkins Publishing Company, 1981.

Gives a brief account of the first American born superior general of the Sisters of Divine Providence and dean of Our Lady of the Lake University from 1913 to 1960.

764.   Cameron, Mary David. *The College of Notre Dame of Maryland, 1895-1945.* New York: Declan X. McMullen, 1947.

Tells the story of the first fifty years of the oldest American Catholic college for women.

765.   Cassidy, Francis Patrick. "Catholic College Foundations and Development in the United States, 1677-1850." Ph.D. dissertation. Catholic University of America, 1924.

766.   Covert, James T. *A Point of Pride: The University of Portland Story.* Portland, OR: University of Portland Press, 1976.

767.   Curley, Thomas E., Jr. "Robert I. Gannon, President of Fordham University 1936-49: A Jesuit Educator." Ph.D. dissertation. New York University, 1974.

Examines the educational leadership of Father Gannon who established Fordham as a strong university with restored accreditations.

768.   Daley, John M. *Georgetown University: Origin and Early Years.* Washington, DC: Georgetown University Press, 1957.

Relates the history of the beginnings of the first Catholic college in the United States, established in 1789 as the "Academy of George Town, Potowmack River, Maryland" and opened November 22, 1791.

769.   Deferrari, Roy J. *Memoirs of the Catholic University of America 1918-1960.* Boston: St. Paul Editions, 1962.

770.   Dixon, Blase. "The Catholic University of America, 1909-1928: The Rectorship of Thomas Joseph Ryan." Ph.D. dissertation. Catholic University of America, 1972.

771.   Dixon, Henry William. "An Historical Survey of Jesuit Higher Education in the United States with Particular Reference to the Objectives of Education." Ed.D. dissertation. Arizona State University, 1974.

772.   Donaghy, Thomas J. *Conceived In Crisis: A History of La Salle College, 1863-1965.* Philadelphia: La Salle College, 1966.

773.   Dunn, Edward T. "A Gymnasium in Buffalo: The Early Years of Canisius College." *Urban Education* 18 (January 1984): 426-37.

774.   Durkin, Joseph T. *Georgetown University: First in the Nation's Capital.* Garden City, NY: Doubleday & Company, Inc., 1964.

775.   Ellis, John Tracy. *The Formative Years of the Catholic University of America.* Washington, DC: American Catholic Historical Association, 1946.

        Studies the years from the post-Civil War days when the American hierarchy first began to think of a university to its formal opening in November 1889.

776.   Engelmeyer, Bridget Marie. "A Maryland First." *Maryland Historical Magazine* 78 (Fall 1983): 186-204.

777.   Erbacher, Sebastian A. "Catholic Higher Education for Men in the United States, 1850-1866." Ph.D. dissertation. Catholic University of America, 1931.

778.   Faherty, William B. *Better the Dream, Saint Louis: University and Community 1818-1968.* St. Louis, MO: Saint Louis University, 1968.

779.   Faherty, William B. "Nativism and Midwestern Education: The Experience of Saint Louis University, 1832-1856." *History of Education Quarterly* 8 (Winter 1968): 447-58.

        Describes the open hostility and the events that caused the withdrawal of the medical college affiliated with Saint Louis University, the first university west of the Mississippi.

780.   Flahive, Robert F. "Cardinal Stritch College." Ph.D. dissertation. Marquette University, 1973.

781.   Freitag, Alfred J. *College With a Cause; A History of Concordia Teachers College.* River Forest, IL: Concordia Teachers College, 1964.

782.   Friel, Mary E. "History of Emmanuel College 1919-1974." Ph.D. dissertation. Boston College, 1980.

        Explores the beginnings, growth and development of the first Catholic college for women in New England.

783.   Frost, John Edward. *The Crowned Hilltop: Boston College in Its Hundredth Year.* New York: Hawthorne Press, 1962.

784.   Hamilton, Raphael. *The Story of Marquette University: An Object Lesson in the Development of Catholic Higher Education.* Milwaukee, WI: Marquette University Press, 1953.

785.   Harney, Thomas E. *Canisius College: The First Nine Years, 1870-1879.* New York: Vantage Press, Inc., 1971.

786.   Hilliard, Annie P. Toler. "An Investigation of Selected Events and

Forces That Contributed to the Growth and Development of Trinity College, Washington, D.C. from 1897 to 1982." Ed.D. dissertation. The George Washington University, 1984.

787.   Hogan, Peter E. *The Catholic University of America, 1896-1903: The Rectorship of Thomas J. Conaty*. Washington, DC: Catholic University of America Press, 1949.

788.   Holland, Dorothy Garesche. "Maryville - The First Hundred Years." *Missouri Historical Society Bulletin* 29 (April 1973): 145-62.

789.   Kearney, Anna Rose. "James A. Burns, C.S.C. - Educator." Ph.D. dissertation. University of Notre Dame, 1975.

Examines the contributions of Father Burns to Catholic education, particularly to Notre Dame University where he became President in 1919, and reorganized the academic structure of the university.

790.   Kelley, William Frederick. *The Jesuit Order and Higher Education in the United States, 1788-1966*. Milwaukee, WI: Wisconsin Jesuit Province, 1966.

791.   Kujawa, Rose Marie. "Madonna College: Its History of Higher Education, 1937-1977." Ph.D. dissertation. Wayne State University, 1979.

792.   Lukacs, John. *A Sketch of the History of Chestnut Hill College, 1924-1974*. Philadelphia: Chestnut Hill College, 1975.

793.   McCarthy, Abigail. "A Luminous Minority." *Current Issues in Catholic Higher Education* 5 (Winter 1985): 7-10.

Records historical information on Catholic women's colleges and reviews the current scene.

794.   McKevitt, Gerald. *The University of Santa Clara: A History 1851-1977*. Stanford, CA: Stanford University Press, 1979.

795.   McKey, Joseph P. *History of Niagara University; Seminary of Our Lady of Angels 1856-1931*. Niagara County, NY: Niagara University, 1931.

796.   Meagher, Walter J. and William J. Grattan. *The Spires of Fenwick: A History of the College of the Holy Cross 1843-1963*. New York: Vantage Press, 1966.

797.   Morrison, Betty L. "A History of Our Lady of Holy Cross College, New Orleans, Louisiana." Ph.D. dissertation. The Louisiana State University and Agricultural and Mechanical College, 1976.

798.   Peterman, Thomas J. "History of St. Mary's College, Wilmington, Delaware, 1847-1867." *Records of the American Catholic Historical*

Society of Philadelphia 77 (March-December 1966): 131-74.

799.   Power, Edward J. *Catholic Higher Education in America: A History.* New York: Appleton-Century-Crofts, 1972.

800.   Schlereth, Thomas J. *The University of Notre Dame: A Portrait of Its History and Campus.* Notre Dame, IN: University of Notre Dame Press, 1976.

801.   Schoenberg, Wilfred P. *Gonzaga University: Seventy-five Years, 1887-1962.* Spokane, WA: Gonzaga University, 1963.

802.   Shaw, Richard. *John Dubois: Founding Father. The Life and Times of the Founder of Mount St. Mary's College, Emmitsburg; Superior of the Sisters of Charity; and Third Bishop of the Diocese of New York.* Yonkers, NY: United States Catholic Historical Society; Emmitsburg, MD: Mount St. Mary's College, 1983.

803.   Tares, Thomas Frances. "Ecumenical Action: A History of Springfield College in Illinois, 1929-1969." Ph.D. dissertation. Saint Louis University, 1972.

804.   Troutman, R. Dwight. "Hazard Yet Forward: A History of Seton Hill College." Ph.D. dissertation. University of Pittsburgh, 1978.

        Includes an account of Catholic education in the pre-Revolutionary War period, and of the life of Saint Elizabeth Seton.

805.   Varga, Nicholas. "Rejoining the American Educational Mainstream: Loyola College, 1890-1931 as a Case Study." *Records of the American Catholic Historical Society of Philadelphia* 96 (March-December 1986): 67-82.

806.   Vosper, James Michael. "A History of Selected Factors in the Development of Creighton University." Ph.D. dissertation. University of Nebraska, Lincoln, 1976.

807.   White, Raymond Joseph. "The Effects of Internal Goals and External Pressures on the Development of a Catholic Liberal Arts College." Ph.D. dissertation. University of California, Berkeley, 1981.

        Examines the historical development of Saint Mary's College of California.

808.   Willis, H. Warren. "The Reorganization of the Catholic University of America During the Rectorship of James H. Ryan, 1928-1935." Ph.D. dissertation. Catholic University of America, 1971.

809.   Witt, Michael John. "The Devolution of Christian Brothers College: 1900-1931." Ph.D. dissertation. Saint Louis University, 1980.

Part II: General Works

810.   "Academic Freedom and Tenure: Seton Hall University (New Jersey)." *Academe* 71 (May-June 1985): 28-36.

Presents the case of a priest faculty member whose tenure was terminated upon his refusal to be transferred and his resignation from the priesthood. The central issue was whether or not the termination of tenure was permissible under the 1940 *Statement of Principles on Academic Freedom and Tenure* without the university administration giving a statement of cause for dismissal, and without offering an appropriate hearing before a duly constituted faculty body.

811.   Antone, M. Therese. "Governance of Catholic Colleges Sponsored By Religious Communities: A Case Study." Ed.D. dissertation. Harvard University, 1980.

Reviews in Part I the corporate structure of colleges and the process of laicization of boards of Catholic colleges in the United States. Studies in Part II the case of a Catholic college that restructured the governance model twice. Advises the necessity to research state laws governing a college before revising any bylaws and to consider the legal consequences of formal structural links between a college and a religious body.

812.   Beauregard, Erving E. "An Archbishop, A University, and Academic Freedom." *Records of the American Catholic Historical Society of Philadelphia* 93 (March-December 1982): 25-39.

Examines the confrontation over academic freedom at the University of Dayton during 1966-1967, involving members of the Philosophy department. Describes the conflict beginning with the accusation of subversion of Church doctrine by one faculty member against another, the escalation to formal review by the university and the appointment of a fact-finding committee by the Archbishop of Cincinnati.

813.   Berbusse, Edward J. "The Catholic College vs. Academic Freedom." *Homiletic & Pastoral Review* 86 (August-September 1986): 11-20.

Believes that the modern Catholic college has capitulated either to the modernist dogma of academic freedoms or has become confused in its purpose mixing commitment to the Church with belief that academic freedom is the ultimate value in any academic institution.

814.   Bernardin, Joseph Cardinal. "Address to the National Catholic Student Coalition." *Current Issues in Catholic Higher Education* 6 (Summer 1985): 35-38.

Exhorts Catholic college students to prepare now to be leaders of tomorrow approaching social issues with a comprehensive moral vision or "constant ethic" of life. Highlights two things they can do: contribute to public opinion and serve their neighbor.

815.   Berquist, Marcus R. and Thomas E. Dillon. "The Great-Books Curriculum at a Reforming Catholic College." *Journal of General Education* 32 (Summer 1980): 123-34.

Describes the curriculum of Thomas Aquinas College, a Catholic liberal arts college in Santa Paula, California, founded in 1971. Uses the "Great Books" instead of textbooks to understand the truth about reality, not as an end in itself. Includes in the curriculum a comprehensive introduction to theology, philosophy, mathematics, grammar, and experimental science. Stresses the fact that it is a Catholic college, not a liberal arts college that happens to be Catholic.

816.   Boisson, George Edward. "An Investigation of Faculty Receptivity to an Undergraduate Curriculum Innovation Within Their Own University." Ed.D. dissertation. University of San Francisco, 1983.

Surveys the faculty of Arts and Sciences to determine the levels of acceptance of an innovative four-year undergraduate program at St. Ignatius Institute of the University of San Francisco. Explains the innovative components of the program: a structured curriculum with emphasis on the classics, a student community designed in the Catholic tradition, and the operation of two overseas campuses.

817.   Byrne, Patrick H. *Paradigms of Justice and Love.* Presented at the Annual Meeting of the Manhattan College Conference on Education for Justice and Peace (Bronx, NY, June 14, 1981).

Examines the philosophy behind the Boston College Pulse Program which attempts to integrate theory and practice. Explains the off-campus field projects which have a social action-social service orientation in coordination with a specially designed course.

818.   Calderone, Joseph Daniel. "An American Catholic Model of Higher   Education   Administration."   Ed.D.   dissertation. Northeastern University, 1982.

Compiles a practical manual for those administering a Catholic college with strong emphasis on the post-Vatican II Catholic teachings on social justice. Recommends a First Among Equals model of administration rather than the Hierarchical or Chief Executive model.

819.   "Catholic College and University Presidents Respond to Proposed Vatican Schema." *Origins* 15 (April 10, 1986): 697, 699-704.

Synthesizes the responses from 110 presidents on the proposed schema for a pontifical document on Catholic universities. Expresses satisfaction with some parts of the schema but strongly criticizes other sections, and urges that the final document "will be pastoral in tone rather than juridical, and the rich diversity that exists among Catholic universities will be appreciated and strengthened."

820.   Channing, Rhoda K. and John C. Stalker, eds. *Boston College Libraries: Systems, Services, Resources.* Chestnut Hill, MA: Boston College, 1982.

Updates the faculty and administrative personnel on the impact of automation and resource sharing on the Boston College library system. Emphasizes the evolution of systems and services to aid faculty in teaching and research.

821.   Cody, Frank J. "University of Detroit: Education in the City." *Current Issues in Catholic Higher Education* 6 (Winter 1986): 28-33.

Relates how after a twenty year controversy between the community and the university over the closure of the block that fringes the institution, the City Council agreed in 1984 to the closing. Tells how the community and university have effected a partnership and explores some of the ways the University impacts on the city of Detroit.

822.   Coffman, Ralph J. "The Hilaire Belloc Collection at Boston College." *Catholic Library World* 56 (July/August 1984): 32-36.

Describes the archives at Boston College comprising Belloc's extensive correspondence with publishers, family and friends, as well as the Belloc Manuscript Archive and Belloc's Working Library, one of the most complete bibliographical repositories of a literary figure of the twentieth century.

823.   Connolly, Mary Kennedy. "The Anomaly of Catholic Higher Education for Women." Ed.D. dissertation. Columbia University Teachers College, 1976.

Examines four Catholic institutions of higher learning founded for women: St. Joseph College, Emmitsburg, Maryland; St. Mary-of-the-Woods, near Terre Haute, Indiana; Manhattanville, founded as the Academy of the Sacred Heart in New York; and Mount St. Vincent, New York.

824.   Cosmos, Spencer. "Community Involvement at the Catholic University of America." *Current Issues in Catholic Higher Education* 6 (Winter 1986): 9-12.

Looks at the variety and content of programs at CUA that show the thrust toward community service resulting from the university's sense of social responsibility.

825.   Curran, Charles E. "Academic Freedom: The Catholic University and Catholic Theology." *Academe* 66 (April 1980): 126-35.

Explores the meaning of academic freedom and discusses it as related both to *Sapientia Christiana*, the apostolic constitution on norms for ecclesiastical universities and faculties, and to the new code of canon law.

826.   Deferrari, Roy J. *The Philosophy of Catholic Higher Education.* Washington, DC: The Catholic University of America Press, 1947.

Discusses the questions presented at the Workshop of 1947 held at the Catholic University of America: What makes a Catholic college Catholic? How can the social and religious life on the campus of a Catholic college be made dynamic and a force contributing to the aims of every Catholic institution of higher learning?

827.   Dellapenna, Joseph W. *The Impacts of the Federal Government on Villanova University. A Self Study.* Villanova, PA: Villanova University, 1977.

Describes the results of a self-study conducted by Villanova University on government policies affecting the university, including federal reporting requirements, national labor policy and state coordination. Finds the financial aid office most affected but not significantly since the regulations came some time after major changes in society as a whole.

828.   Dougherty, Jude P., Desmond Fitzgerald, Thomas Langan, and Kenneth Schmitz. "The Secularization of Western Culture and the Catholic College and University." *Current Issues in Catholic Higher Education* 2 (Summer 1981): 7-23.

Examines a study of philosophy programs in Catholic colleges and universities prepared for the American Philosophical Society in 1979. Describes three challenges affecting the Catholic college and university: secularization, rapid social change, and the furthering of the Catholic intellectual and spiritual tradition. Calls for reassessment and planning to meet these challenges.

829.   Drinan, Robert F. "The Challenge to Catholic Educators in the Maryland College Case." *NCEA Bulletin* 63 (May 1967): 3-7.

Analyzes the Maryland decision of November 15, 1966 which held that the "no-establishment" clause of the first amendment renders unconstitutional grants for clearly secular purposes to church-sponsored colleges when these colleges have a pervasive religious orientation. Covers the history and nature of the Maryland grants to private colleges, the tests of constitutionality employed by the majority opinion, and the implications of the ruling.

830.   Earley, Margaret and Joel Read. "Identity and Quest: Their Interrelationship at Alverno College." *Current Issues in Catholic Higher Education* 5 (Winter 1985): 11-15.

Describes a radical approach to the communication of values and the measurement of outcomes, and how students move through a series of levels as they develop valuing abilities.

831.   Ellis, John Tracy. "The Catholic Liberal Arts College: Has It a Future?" *Current Issues in Catholic Higher Education* 3 (Winter 1983): 3-9.

Recalls some of the roots of the Catholic liberal arts college and says that they must be reaffirmed. Keynotes the contributions a Catholic liberal arts college can make to society, and is optimistic about the future.

832.   Evans, John Whitney. *The Newman Movement: Roman Catholics in American Higher Education, 1883-1971.* Notre Dame, IN: University of Notre Dame Press, 1980.

Traces the history of the Newman Movement which endeavors to serve the pastoral needs of Catholic students enrolled in secular colleges and universities.

833.   Fanelli, Joseph Peter. "Sexual Attitudes and Behavior of Catholic College Students Attending a Catholic Campus: An Exploratory Study of Some Critical Issues Facing the Catholic Church." Ph.D. dissertation. Syracuse University, 1980.

Researches the degree of association between religious measures and sexual attitudes and behavior among eight hundred students randomly selected from the college directory of an upstate New York college. Concludes that while religiosity exerts some influence on sexual attitudes and behaviors, there is a low relationship between religion and sexual behavior.

834.   Fichter, Joseph H. "Academic Responsibility on the Believing Campus." *Social Thought* IX (Spring 1983): 33-45.

Discusses the question of whether a Catholic university can maintain a middle ground that shares both religiosity and secularity. Asserts that maintaining academic excellence while professing strong religious faith no longer is thwarted by church officials, ridiculed by academic colleagues or limited by state and federal law.

835.   Fitz, Raymond L. *Linking Faith and Justice: Reflections On Institutional Conditions and Educating for Justice.* Presented at a conference entitled: "Education for Justice: A Conference for the

College and University Community." University of Notre Dame, June 28, 1981.

Develops two ideas for promoting justice education within the Catholic university: experimental learning for justice's sake, and its promotion within the campus community; and exploration of conditions for institutionalizing program centers that promote justice and justice education.

836.   Fitzgerald, Paul A. *The Governance of Jesuit Colleges in the United States, 1920-1970.* Notre Dame, IN: University of Notre Dame Press, 1984.

Focuses on the changes undergone by twenty-eight Jesuit institutions during this fifty year period and tells how the Jesuits reaffirmed their commitment to higher education. Discusses the restructuring of the Jesuit Educational Association in the 60's with new directions in governance.

837.   Fitzpatrick, M. Fenton Joseph. *The Problem of Nursing Education: Articulation.* Gwynedd Valley, PA: Gwynedd-Mercy College, 1981.

Reviews the development of diploma, BS, and Associate degree nursing programs at Gwynedd-Mercy College. Explains the theoretical framework and design of the nursing curricula, focusing on the articulation of program content and goals.

838.   Flaherty, Etienne, and John D'Espinosa. "A New Language Program: Using Native Speakers." *Improving College and University Teaching* 30 (Fall 1982): 175-78.

Reviews the restructured core curriculum at Saint Anselm College which includes an interdisciplinary humanities program and incorporates a foreign language sequence using native speakers in weekly informal conversation sessions.

839.   Fox, Marie. "Changes in Relationships Between Governing Boards of Catholic Colleges and Universities and Their Sponsoring Religious Bodies." Ph.D. dissertation. The Florida State University, 1974.

Examines the areas of changes in board composition, structure, and powers, and the results of these changes. Finds significantly altered relationships between boards and sponsoring religious bodies (SRB). Discovers that most major board changes occurred in 1969, and that advantages of board changes were perceived to outweigh the disadvantages.

840.   Gallin, Alice. "Academic Freedom at Church-Related Institutions." *Academe* 72 (January-February 1986): 48-49.

Discusses problem areas for Catholic colleges and universities in safeguarding academic freedom. Asserts that they will not abdicate their responsibility to maintain the freedom of academic enterprise.

841.   Gallin, Alice. "Catholic Universities Facing New Cultures." *Seminarium* 25 (April 1985): 304-14.

Cites the Vatican II document *Gaudium et Spes* (The Church in the Modern World) summoning to an openness and appreciation of all cultures. Identifies the new cultures emerging and exhorts Catholic colleges and universities in the United States to respond to these new cultures. Outlines efforts already being made in American higher education.

842.   Gallin, Alice. "Sponsorship as Partnership." *Current Issues in Catholic Higher Education* 4 (Winter 1984): 7-10.

Discusses the change today in the relationship between the founding group and the Catholic college or university. Suggests that the term "sponsoring religious body" or "SRB" is no longer viable and "RFG" or "religious founding group" should be used. Gives six elements to be considered in recognizing the reality of a partnership rather than a sponsorship between the RFG and the college or university.

843.   Galvin, James Michael. "Secularizing Trends in Roman Catholic Colleges and Universities, 1960-1970." Ed.D. dissertation. Indiana University, 1971.

Finds that during the 1960-1970 decade Roman Catholic colleges and universities became more like their nondenominational counterparts, but no patterns developed to indicate that some types of institutions had become more secularized than other types. Reports the least apparent change was in degrees of Catholicity among full and part-time students, and the greatest degrees of change towards secularization occurred at policy-making administrative and faculty levels.

844.   Ganss, George E. *The Jesuit Educational Tradition and Saint Louis University*. St. Louis, MO: Institute of Jesuit Sources, 1969.

Analyzes Ignatius of Loyola's thoughts on education and sets the University into the context of Jesuit educational theory.

845.   Gatto, Louis C. "The Catholic College Presidency - A Study." *Current Issues in Catholic Higher Education* 2 (Summer 1981): 24-30.

Gives the results of a study by the Association of Catholic Colleges and Universities in 1979-1980, of all Presidents of the ACCU membership. Includes in the survey sections on professional preparation, presidential selection process, administrative achievements, and relationships with the sponsoring religious body (SRB). Finds little to distinguish lay and religious responses, though more religious presidents than lay reported negative experiences regarding SRB associations.

846.   Gleason, Philip. "The Curriculum of the Old-Time Catholic College: A Student's View." *Records of the American Catholic Historical Society of Philadelphia* 88 (March-December 1977): 101-22.

Provides a close-up view of the academic life of a philosophy student during his last year at Holy Cross College, Worcester, Massachusetts, 1848-1849. Describes the formal curriculum and the personal reading of James A. Healy who kept a detailed diary of that year, later became a priest, and eventually the second bishop of Portland, Maine.

847.   Glynn, Edward. "The Jesuits in Jersey City: Saint Peter's College." *Current Issues in Catholic Higher Education* 6 (Winter 1986): 13-14.

Describes the Public Policy program, an annual Youth Education Seminar, and other programs that serve both the College and the City.

848.   Greeley, Andrew M. *From Backwater to Mainstream; a Profile of Catholic Higher Education.* With a commentary by David Riesman. New York: McGraw-Hill Book Company, 1969.

Studies 350 Catholic colleges and universities and discovers their diversity. Concludes that most of them will survive but there is concern for the Catholic colleges and universities to be part of the mainstream of American higher education without losing their unique character and vision.

849.   Greeley, Andrew M., with the assistance of William Van Cleve and Grace Ann Carroll. *The Changing Catholic College.* Chicago: Aldine Publishing Company, 1967.

Investigates why some Catholic colleges are changing rapidly while others are slower to move from the traditional. Studies the system of relationships within thirty-six Catholic colleges and discovers there is not just self-improvement but self-transformation with the intent of preserving a uniquely religious character.

850.   Greenburg, S. Thomas. "The Problem of Identity in Catholic Higher Education: The Statement of the Question." In *Why Should the Catholic University Survive? A Study of the Character and Commitment of Catholic Higher Education,* pp. 13-26. Edited by George A. Kelly. New York: St. John's University Press, 1974.

Examines the results of research in the areas of: the role of theology, the role of the theologian, the role of the magisterium, and the subject of academic freedom in the Catholic institution of higher learning.

851.   Griffin, Kevin J. "A History of Teacher Education in the Seven Colleges Conducted by the American Christian Brothers." Ph.D. dissertation. St. Louis University, 1976.

Discusses the basic influences in the development of the teacher education program in the following colleges: Manhattan College, Bronx, NY; La Salle College, Philadelphia, PA; St. Mary's College, Winona, MN; Lewis University, Lockport, IL; Christian Brothers College, Memphis, TN; College of Santa Fe, Sante Fe, NM; and St. Mary's College, Moraga, CA. Notes the strong tradition of teacher training and reviews recommendations that emerge from the study.

852.   Grisez, Germain. "American Catholic Higher Education: The Experience Evaluated." In *Why Should the Catholic University Survive? A Study of the Character and Commitment of Catholic Higher Education*, pp. 41-55. Edited by George A. Kelly. New York: St. John's University Press, 1974.

Reflects on the criticisms of Catholic colleges of the late 1950s and early 1960s, recounts the changes that took place between 1962-1972, and considers the essential characteristics of the Catholic university as formulated in the document, "The Catholic University in the Modern World," drawn up by the delegates of the Catholic Universities of the World, who met in Rome, November 20-29, 1972.

853.   Grusczynski, Mary Lauriana. *Belief in a Catholic College. Madonna College as a Catholic College.* Livonia, MI: Madonna College, 1985.

Assesses the character and commitment of Madonna College using empirical studies, eccelsiastical documents and statements on the mission and role of Catholic institutions of higher learning as a frame of reference.

854.   Gunti, Frederick Walter. "Academic Freedom and Church-Related Schools." In *Academic Freedom as an Operative Principle for the Catholic Theologian*, pp. 79-101. S.T.D. dissertation. The Catholic University of America, 1969.

Addresses the controversy concerning the viability of academic freedom in church-related institutions of higher learning. Presents expressed opinions related to the American Association of University Professors (AAUP) 1915 and 1940 *Statement of Principles on Academic Freedom and Tenure.*

855.   Hasenstab, Robert Leroy. "The Determinants of Board

Restructuring in Catholic Higher Education in the United States."
Ph.D. dissertation. St. Louis University, 1971.

Explores six major causes for board restructuring which is
defined as the addition of lay trustees to previously all religious
governing boards. Gives the determinants as the need to seek lay
expertise, a sense of moral obligation to share in a partnership with
the community it serves, a need to provide financial resources and
business acumen, a need to distinguish the operations of the
institution from the sponsoring group, a need for separate
stewardship and accountability, and the need to improve
educational quality of the institution.

856.   Hassel, David J. *City of Wisdom: A Christian Vision of the
American University.* Chicago: Loyola University Press, 1983.

Unfolds a vision of an ideal Christian university by
integrating basic concepts of a Christian university with the
understandings of Christian university life. Sees the Christian faith
of the religious founding group imbuing the life of the college or
university without undermining its autonomy or its competence in
secular wisdom.

857.   Hassenger, Robert, ed. *The Shape of Catholic Higher Education.*
Chicago: The University of Chicago Press, 1967.

Examines in eleven independently written chapters Catholic
undergraduate education at the time of new activism and revolution
on the college campus.

858.   Hauser, Richard J. "Creighton University: Still Catholic and
Jesuit." *Lumen Vitae* 40 (1985): 286-93.

Reflects on the religious dimension of a Catholic university
centering on the factors that contribute to a positive Christian
atmosphere: the liturgical life, study of theology, community service
program and the counseling program.

859.   Henle, Robert J. "The Pluralism of North America and the
Catholic University of Today." In *The Catholic University
Instrument of Cultural Pluralism to the Service of Church and
Society (Thematic Report)* XII General Assembly of the
International Federation of Catholic Universities, 1979, pp. 22-79.
Paris, France: Permanent Secretariate, 1979.

Reports on the pluralism of North American society and the
Catholic university within that pluralistic society; the diversity of
the American educational system and the diversity in Catholic
higher education. Believes that the new and future Catholic
university should be more pluralistic because of a broader Catholic
perspective, and should be more Catholic in its pluralism.
Delivered at the XII General Assembly held at Porto Alegre, Brazil,

August 21-24, 1978.

860.   Henriot, Peter J. "University Education For the Year 2000: Toward a Humane and Sustainable Future." *Current Issues in Catholic Higher Education* 1 (Winter 1981): 31-39.

Recognizes problems but speaks with hope of a humane future which emphasizes the dimensions of justice and survival for everyone. Challenges universities to address the future so that students are prepared for this kind of world.

861.   Henry, Edward L. "Sponsor/Partnership of Catholic Higher Education: The President as Middleman." *Current Issues in Catholic Higher Education* 4 (Winter 1984): 22-27.

Analyzes the transition and change in Catholic colleges and the impact on sponsoring religious bodies. Explains the role of president and the relationship between SRBs and laity in operating the college.

862.   Hesburgh, Theodore M. "Preparing for the Millennium." *Current Issues in Catholic Higher Education* 3 (Winter 1983): 10-14.

Addresses the 1980 final report of the Carnegie Council on Policy Studies in Higher Education, *Three Thousand Futures.* Reviews the hard choices the individual university and college must make during the next two decades, choices concerning quality, balance, integrity, adaptation, dynamism, effective use of resources, financing, leadership, the private sector and basic research.

863.   Hesburgh, Theodore M. "The College Presidency: Life Between a Rock and a Hard Place." *Change* 11 (May-June 1979): 43-47.

Gives advice on being a college president, gleaned from his own twenty-five years experience as president of Notre Dame University. Reflects on some basic characteristics needed: personal and moral courage, an educationally sound vision of the institution, concern that students are being educated for tomorrow, and being human.

864.   Hesburgh, Theodore M. *The Hesburgh Papers: Higher Values in Higher Education.* Kansas City, KS: Andrews and McMeel, Inc., 1979.

Focuses on Catholic or Christian higher education and the importance of values in that education because wisdom is more than knowledge. Includes sections on the contemporary Catholic and Christian university; special concerns in higher education in modern America; the years of campus crisis; and the future: church, education, world.

865.   Hesburgh, Theodore M. "The Vatican and American Catholic Higher Education." *America*, 155, November 1, 1986, pp. 247-53.

Relates the background story leading to the document on the Catholic university in the modern world, promulgated in 1973, and speaks about the proposed schema of the Congregation on Catholic Education addressed to Catholic colleges and universities. Declares that most of the Catholic colleges and universities in the United States "are far more Catholic than the pontifical universities throughout the world." Believes the dilemma for the best Catholic universities is being asked to choose between being real universities and being really Catholic, when they are already both.

866.   Hesburgh, Theodore M. "The Vision of a Great Catholic University." *Catholic Mind* LXVI (February 1968): 42-54.

Answers critics of the idea of a Catholic university and defines what a great Catholic university should be.

867.   Hruby, Norbert J. *A Survival Kit For Invisible Colleges.* 2nd ed. Boulder, CO: National Center for Higher Education Management Systems, 1980.

Reports the self-study of Aquinas College, Grand Rapids, Michigan, resulting in new ideas for development, implementation of a number of programs and an accreditation report. Presents in the first edition, the detailed steps that the college took to remain viable in the seventies, and gives in the second edition, an account of the institution's determination to provide new and needed services to its community as a means of survival.

868.   Hunt, John F. and Terrence R. Connelly, with Charles E. Curran, Robert E. Hunt and Robert K. Webb. "The Inquiry: Newer Dimensions of Academic Freedom in Catholic Universities." In *The Responsibility of Dissent: The Church and Academic Freedom*, pp. 113-128. New York: Sheed and Ward, Inc., 1969.

Discusses the declarations and understandings since Vatican II of academic freedom as a necessary characteristic of a distinctively Catholic university.

869.   Ingram, Richard T. "Trusteeship in the Church-Related College in the '80s." *Current Issues in Catholic Higher Education* 2 (Summer 1981): 32-37.

Explores the responsibilities of the governing board, the role of the president, how to improve trustee selection, and discusses some hypotheses on the future of trusteeship. Believes that trustees are ready to react responsibly to the needs of church-related higher education as never before.

870.   Johnson, David M. "Graduate Education in Catholic Colleges and Universities: A Report on the ACCU Survey of Graduate Programs." *Current Issues in Catholic Higher Education* 3 (Summer

1982): 4-39.

Presents statistical results from the 91 responses received from surveys sent to 113 Catholic colleges and universities. Summarizes data for postbaccalaureate degree programs excepting professional legal or medical degrees.

871.   Johnson, David M. and the Advisory Council on Justice Education. "Programs in Peace and Justice Education: Report on ACCU's Pilot Programs." *Current Issues in Catholic Higher Education* 2 (Winter 1981): 3-10.

Provides an overview of the experiences of seven Catholic institutions that implemented pilot projects in peace and justice education, and includes a chart outlining the programs by college. Covers the areas of program focus, curricular initiative, experiential learning, other educational programming, spirituality, and governance.

872.   Kaasa, Harris, et al. *Humanism: A Christian Perspective.* National Endowment for Humanities (NEH), 1981.

Presents the report on a program to revitalize the humanistic tradition according to the Christian dimension of each of four cooperating midwest colleges: St. John's University, Collegeville, MN; The College of St. Catherine, St. Paul, MN; Luther College in Iowa and St. Olaf College, Northfield, MN. Describes special features including new courses in Christian humanism, joint activities, faculty seminars and the preparation of publications. Explains specific challenges that affect each of the four colleges.

873.   Kampwerth, Virginia Jane. "Catholic Higher Education's Role in Helping Individuals Deal With the Developments of Biotechnology." Ph.D. dissertation. Saint Louis University, 1983.

Gives philosophical analysis of idealism, materialism, pragmatism, and Christianity. Shows how they affect attitudes regarding human life and underscores the responsibility of Catholic higher education to include the Christian point of view in the public form where decisions are made regarding the application of biotechnology on a societal and individual level.

874.   Kelly, Dorothy Ann. "The College of New Rochelle and Its School of New Resources." *Current Issues in Catholic Higher Education* 6 (Winter 1986): 26-27.

Describes a school that is a pioneer in adult higher education, focusing on a respect for the adult student's experience and featuring Travel/Study courses, "Telecourses," "Exit" seminars, Independent Study and Prior Learning Portfolios.

875.   Kelly, George A. "The Battle for the Catholic Campus." In *The*

Battle for the American Church, pp. 59-97. Garden City, NY: Doubleday and Company, Inc., 1979.

Capsulates the development of American Catholic universities and colleges, focusing on Catholic intellectual revival, academic freedom and the essential characteristics of a Catholic university.

876.   Klein, Mary Ellen. "Sister Madeleva Wolff, C.S.C., Saint Mary's College, Notre Dame, Indiana: A Study of Presidential Leadership 1934-1961." Ph.D. dissertation. Kent State University, 1983.

Develops a profile of the effective educational leadership characteristics evidenced in Sister Madeleva's twenty-seven years as president of St. Mary's College, one of the first American Catholic colleges for women.

877.   Kraetzer, Mary C., et al. *Design and Implementation of Multi-Strategy, Collegewide Program of Evaluation and Planning: The Mercy College Self-Study Project.* Presented at the Evaluation Research Society/The Evaluation Network, San Francisco, CA, October 13, 1984.

Considers the rationale, strategies, methods, and evaluation instruments used in the self-study project of Mercy College in Westchester County, New York.

878.   Kriss, M. Elise. "The Goals of Franciscan Higher Education in the United States: Trustee, Administrator, and Faculty Perceptions (Institutional Goals)." Ph.D. dissertation. Saint Louis University, 1984.

Shows that three goal areas receiving top priority in the study remained preferred future priorities: academic development, ethical/moral orientation, and community of faith.

879.   LaMagdeleine, Donald Robert. "The Changing American Catholic University." Ph.D. dissertation. Loyola University of Chicago, 1984.

Examines religion as a key factor in the development of Catholic higher education in the United States and its continuing influence on the organizational processes of the Catholic university. Analyzes Loyola University's changes from a denominational institution and studies its new corporate identity.

880.   Lanagan, Margaret Ann. "The Distribution of Catholic Campus Ministers' Time Among Work Components Established by the United States Catholic Conference and the National Catholic Educational Association." Ph.D. dissertation. The American University, 1979.

Finds that campus ministers spend one-half of their time in spiritual/pastoral activities and the rest in organizational and personal/professional activities. Concludes that Catholic campus ministers do meet the guidelines suggested by U.S. Catholic Conference and NCEA.

881.   "Land O'Lakes Statement: The Nature of the Contemporary University." In *The Catholic University: A Modern Appraisal*, pp. 336-41.   Edited by Neil G. McCluskey.   Notre Dame, IN: University of Notre Dame Press, 1970.

Articulates the consensus of a group of North American leaders in Catholic higher education concerning the modern identity of a Catholic university. Asserts that institutional autonomy and academic freedom are essential conditions for Catholic universities as well as for all universities. Was adopted at an invitational seminar held in Land O'Lakes, Wisconsin, July 20-23, 1967, and was a basis for dialogue at the Congress of Catholic Universities held in Rome, April 25 to May 1, 1969.

882.   Laverty, Mary Louise. "Presidents' Perceptions of Student Trustee Influence on Governing Board Decisions in Catholic Higher Education in America."   Ph.D. dissertation.   Indiana University, 1984.

Finds an increase of student participation on governing boards over thirteen years, and that student affairs issues have been influenced by students more than any other board issue. Indicates students perceive that they have greater influence on governing boards than presidents report. Suggest students may gain greater influence by utilizing formal channels of input to the board.

883.   Le Febre, Joseph and Patrick Miederhoff. "Description of a Skills Oriented Health Ethics Program." *American Journal of Pharmaceutical Education* 48 (Summer 1984): 163-65.

Attempts to develop critical thinking in the College of Pharmacy at Xavier University of Louisiana by requiring students to find and define solutions to ethical dilemmas by applying and refining ethical theory.

884.   Lewis, Lionel S. and Philip G. Altbach. "Secularism and Survival: An Academic Portrait." *Liberal Education* 68 (Fall 1982): 167-80.

Surveys the faculty in seven western New York State colleges with a Roman Catholic tradition. Focuses on the teaching population and what it thinks about work and leisure, teaching and research. Finds that the two larger institutions, Canisius College and St. Bonaventure University, retain formal ties to their sponsoring religious orders; the five smaller institutions, Daemen College, D'Youville College, Medaille College, Nazareth College, and Saint John Fisher College are formally independent of Roman

Catholic sponsorship.

885.   Loughran, James N. "A New Curriculum Can Make a Difference."
         Current Issues in Catholic Higher Education 5 (Winter 1985): 16-22.

         Describes the revision in the Fall of 1980, of Fordham
         College's curriculum from a loose, "distribution requirements" one
         to a more structured core curriculum. Explains the structures and
         strategies, the effects of the revision, and the keys to success.
         Claims a radically transformed college.

886.   Lux, M. Janet. *Total-System Design: Planning, Delivering, and
         Sharing Instruction Oriented to Professional Practice and Human
         Values.* Omaha, NE: Creighton University, 1981.

         Describes a four-year project at Creighton University using
         Total-System (STD) principles to produce a medical technology
         major within a program study leading to a B.S.M.T. degree.

887.   Lyons, Robert S., Jr. "La Salle University: Urban Partner."
         Current Issues in Catholic Higher Education 6 (Winter 1986):
         15-19.

         Discusses different kinds of outreach programs such as the
         Campus Boulevard Corporation involving eleven neighborhood
         institutions, and the University's Urban Studies and Community
         Service Center which established Communiversity, an outreach
         effort providing a variety of non-credit courses to neighborhood
         residents on campus and to senior citizens in other Philadelphia
         facilities.

888.   MacEoin, Gary. "Notre Dame's Father Hesburgh." *Change* 8
         (February 1976): 46-51, 70.

         Gives an account and impressions of Notre Dame's
         internationally recognized college president. Reviews his
         philosophy, accomplishments and personal style.

889.   Mallonee, Barbara C. and John R. Breihan. *Writing Across the
         Curriculum Phase Two: Beyond the Workshop Empirical Rhetoric
         at Loyola.* Paper presented at the Annual Meeting of the
         Conference on College Composition and Communication (35th,
         New York, NY, March 29-31, 1984).

         Describes the program, "Empirical Rhetoric," developed at
         Loyola College in Maryland, and supported by the National
         Endowment for the Humanities (NEH). Involves a joint effort
         between writing specialists and teachers of content subjects.

890.   Maloney, Edward Francis. "A Study of the Religious Orientation
         of Catholic Colleges and Universities in New York State From 1962
         to 1972." Ph.D. dissertation. New York University, 1974.

Explains results of the study: Boards of Trustees expanded through addition of Catholic and non-Catholic lay persons; more Catholic and non-Catholic lay persons added to staff, and 11% growth in the percentage of non-Catholic students; theology and philosophy requirements cut in half; 15 of the 25 colleges studied became coeducational; more freedom with respect to attendance at religious services and discipline in general.

891.   Manier, Edward and John W. Houck, eds. *Academic Freedom and the Catholic University.* Notre Dame, IN: Fides Publishers, Inc., 1967.

Records the papers presented at a symposium held at the University of Notre Dame, April 22 and 23, 1966. Considers those concerned with the foundation and basic structural expression of academic freedom, and those related to topical issues such as academic freedom of members of religious orders. Gives the text of the three documents from the American Association of University Professors concerning academic freedom and faculty participation in university government.

892.   Markham, Elizabeth M. "The Catholic Women's Colleges: A Challenge." *Catholic Mind* 78 (October 1980): 26-33.

Calls upon religious women educators in Catholic women's colleges to reaffirm their commitment to higher education and to bring to it the resources of their professional expertise and religious experience, and their determination to improve the quality of life for society and the individual.

893.   McBride, Alfred. "The Value Neutral Catholic College." *Momentum*, 11, May 1980, pp. 5, 31-34.

Believes that a clue to Catholic identity can be found in moral and ethical challenge. Recommends that Catholic higher education engage students in the moral issues of our time and create a value environment that produces a literate graduate possessing the capacity to make a moral judgment.

894.   McCluskey, Neil G., ed. *The Catholic University: A Modern Appraisal.* Notre Dame, IN: University of Notre Dame Press, 1970.

Confronts the meaning of the Catholic University and its reason for being in the modern world.

895.   McInnes, William. "The Catholic College: Model for Justice." *Current Issues in Catholic Higher Education* 1 (Winter 1981): 30-33.

Declares the necessity to demonstrate justice in actions as well as in mission statements. Describes the premises of justice reflecting on how a collegiate community can measure its commitment to justice.

896.   McWilliams, Perry.   "Uncovering the Ostrich's Head: Global
        Studies at St. Edward's University."   *Current Issues in Catholic
        Higher Education* 5 (Summer 1984): 16-20.

        Relates the events leading to the "Global Studies" program
        at St. Edward's University in Austin, Texas, the response to
        problems encountered, and a new focus that heightened interest in
        the international studies program.

897.   Meighan, Cecilia.   "Nativism and Catholic Higher Education,
        1840-1860."   Ed.D. dissertation.   Columbia University, Teachers
        College, 1972.

        Examines the effect of the pressures of anti-Catholic bigotry
        on two Catholic institutions during the twenty year period
        preceding the Civil War -- St. Louis University and the College of
        the Holy Cross.   Contends that effects of nativism had far greater
        import on the development of the Catholic Church, creating a
        ghetto mentality which had a long range impact on the growth of
        Catholic colleges.

898.   Merritt, Edward Herter.   "The Character of an Undergraduate
        College: A Study of Organizational Stability and Transition."
        Ed.D. dissertation.   Columbia University, Teachers College, 1980.

        Defines the essential character of Ignatius Loyola College,
        tracing its elements from the fall of 1965 to spring of 1978 during
        which time its formal designation of "Catholic" changed to
        "independent."

899.   Miner, Lynn E.   "Research Administration in Jesuit Colleges and
        Universities."   *Journal of the Society of Research Administrators* 13
        (Winter 1982): 35-43.

        Summarizes results from 25 responses to a survey
        questionnaire sent to 28 Jesuit institutions.   Discusses the findings
        that cover six major categories: background information,
        administrative organization, useful periodicals, useful reference
        tools, computer applications and research environment.

900.   "Ministry of Faculty in the Catholic College/University."
        Occasional Papers on Catholic Higher Education III (Winter 1977).

        Compiles various papers that focus on the ministry of faculty
        and considers the teaching of science, theology, economics,
        philosophy, and sociology in Catholic institutions.

901.   Morris, Barbara Louise.   "To Define a Catholic University: The
        1965 Crisis at St. John's."   Ed.D. dissertation.   Columbia
        University, Teachers College, 1977.

Analyzes the confrontation between the administration and faculty members at St. John's University, New York, which resulted from non-renewal of contracts of thirty-three members of the faculty and suspension from classroom activities of twenty-two of them. Studies the central issue concerning the existence, definition, role and purpose of Catholic higher education.

902. Murphy, John F. "The Colleges Sponsored by a Diocese." *Current Issues in Catholic Higher Education* 4 (Winter 1984): 11-14.

Summarizes the principal findings from a questionnaire sent to the presidents of colleges and universities that are diocesan sponsored. Concludes that the most successful feel a responsibility to the local Church and its people; the local Church involved with higher education prompts more interest in intellectual life; support comes from the parish that has pride in the college; and the institution knows its mission is to be a truly Catholic college.

903. Murphy, John F., et al. *The Future of Catholic Higher Education. Proceedings of a Panel Discussion, Meeting of Foundations and Donors Interested in Catholic Activities (June 24-25, 1980).* Washington, DC: Association of Catholic Colleges and Universities, 1980.

Presents the addresses of five panelists: "Catholic Higher Education - An Overview," "Education in the 80s," "Research and Graduate Studies in Catholic Universities: Present and Future Prospects," "A Bishop Looks at the Contemporary Catholic College/University," and "The Catholic Universities As an International Community."

904. National Conference of Catholic Bishops. "Catholic Higher Education and the Pastoral Mission of the Church." *Catholic Mind* 79 (April 1981): 50-64.

Presents the pastoral letter on higher education issued by the American Catholic hierarchy during their November 10-13, 1980 meeting in Washington, DC. Reaffirms the intellectual importance of Catholic colleges and universities in the modern world and expects them to continue to manifest their Catholic identity and mission.

905. Nelson, Leonard J., III. "God and Man in the Catholic Law School." *The Catholic Lawyer* 26 (Spring 1981): 127-46.

Gives an historical perspective of Catholic law schools in the United States and describes a progressive secularization that has become part of the Catholic law schools. A few schools are cited as unusual since they still offer distinctively Catholic courses in their curricula.

906. Neusse, C. Joseph. "Assessing Catholic Purpose in American

Catholic Higher Education." *Social Thought* VII (Summer 1981): 35-51.

Notes the relevance of Catholic purpose with respect to Catholic institutions internally and with respect to the problems these institutions face in American society. Explains the aspects that give perspective to Catholic purpose in higher education and declares that it will not be achieved without retention of Catholic identity.

907.   O'Brien, David J. "The Catholic College As Responsible Critic." *Current Issues in Catholic Higher Education* 2 (Winter 1982): 29-36.

Addresses the Catholic institution's responsibility to be committed to justice and peace, and to the dignity of the human person.

908.   O'Brien, David J. "Education for Justice: Concern, Commitment and Career." *Current Issues in Catholic Higher Education* 5 (Winter 1985): 23-30.

Reminds the Catholic academic community that transforming the world cannot be relegated to the abstract or utopian. Offers specific proposals for a course of action.

909.   O'Keefe, Mary Daniel. "Factors Affecting the Growth of Adult Degree Programs in Catholic Women's Colleges (Continuing Education)." Ph.D. dissertation. Boston College, 1984.

Investigates case studies of colleges attracting high adult enrollment -- the College of Notre Dame (MD), the College of Mount St. Joseph (OH) and Marymount (NY).

910.   Parente, William J. "Are Catholic Colleges Still Catholic?" *Current Issues in Catholic Higher Education* 6 (Summer 1985): 29-34.

Focuses on the role of the Catholic colleges in the conserving, the transmitting, and the improvement of the Catholic tradition. Develops five aspects of Catholic higher education -- curriculum, course contents, faculty, institutional service to the Church, and institutional ethos. Contends that Catholic colleges are indeed Catholic.

911.   Pellegrino, Edmund D. "Catholic Colleges and Universities: Options for Survival." *Hospital Progress* 61 (February 1980): 41-49, 60.

Presents three choices open to American Catholic higher education: 1) develop academic excellence divorced from religious origins; 2) retreat from higher education; or 3) address the task of supporting first rank universities that are Catholic and part of the international Church. Argues that only the third alternative is morally, socially and historically defensible.

912. Pellegrino, Edmund D. "Professional Studies and Catholic Universities: The Consecration of Expertise." *Social Thought* IX (Spring 1983): 23-31.

Maintains that professional education is intrinsic to the mission of Catholic universities in the modern world, and that in re-assessment of what the Catholic university is, and the relevance of professional studies must be included. States the moral obligation to retain and expand them, and to imbue them with the Catholic intellectual tradition.

913. Poirier, Therese I. and Mitchell L. Borke. "An Integrated Approach to Teaching Biochemistry for Pharmacy Students." *American Journal of Pharmaceutical Education* 46 (Summer 1982): 151-54.

Describes a course at Duquesne University integrating biochemistry lectures, clinical applications lectures, and laboratory sessions to make it more relevant to students' perceived needs.

914. Ratterman, P. H. *The Emerging Catholic University. With a Commentary on the "Joint Statement on the Rights and Freedoms of Students."* New York: Fordham University Press, 1968.

Discusses the changes on Catholic campuses and the developments in Catholic academe. Gives in its entirety the text of the document on rights and freedoms of students and evaluates it as a primary part of the changes taking place.

915. Reinert, Paul C. *The Urban Catholic University.* New York: Sheed and Ward, 1970.

Reflects on the nature of the Catholic college and university and the changes in the American urban university during the 60s.

916. "Report of the ACCU Task Force on the Future of Catholic Higher Education." *Current Issues in Catholic Higher Education* 7 (Summer 1986): 4-34.

Articulates a vision of the future based on realistic information and reaffirms a commitment to the purpose and mission of the Catholic colleges and universities.

917. "Report of the ACCU Task Forces on Campus Community Behavior." *Current Issues in Catholic Higher Education* 2 (Winter 1982): 6-28.

Presents reports from Minnesota and Indiana task forces of the American Catholic Colleges and Universities that indicate the ways that the Catholic identity is reflected in the campus life and atmosphere.

918.   Rewak, William J. "Commentary On Bishops' Pastoral Letter On Catholic Education." *Current Issues in Catholic Higher Education* 2 (Summer 1981): 3-6.

Explains the main points covered in the American Catholic Bishops' first pastoral letter on Catholic higher education approved in November 1980. Regards it as a blueprint for the '80s, encouraging examination of curriculum, adherence to academic standards, and growth of young people in mature commitment.

919.   Reynolds, Thomas Edward. "Developing Programs in Social Justice Education: Case Studies at Catholic Colleges in California." Ph.D. dissertation. University of California, Los Angeles, 1985.

Examines the development, organization and operation of the curricular and extracurricular efforts to expose student and faculty to values and societal issues from a contemporary Catholic perspective. Recommends a common program model for social justice education be adopted by Catholic colleges.

920.   Riesman, David. "Reflections on Catholic Colleges, Especially Jesuit Institutions." *Journal of General Education* 34 (Summer 1982): 106-19.

Discusses the differences between private religious and secular colleges focusing on the moral tone, faculty commitment, and student and parent expectations.

921.   Russell, Virginia. "A Vision Which Makes a Difference: Internationalizing the Catholic College and University in the 1980s." *Current Issues in Catholic Higher Education* 5 (Summer 1984): 3-7.

Addresses the challenge to Catholic institutions of higher education to develop a Christian ethos on campus that will move to a realization of the "universality" of the Church, and to provide an educational experience that will help students to become responsible citizens not only of the United States, but of the world community."

922.   Rypkema, Sally A. "Aquinas College, Good Neighbor." *Current Issues in Catholic Higher Education* 6 (Winter 1986): 23-25.

Outlines ways the college responds to the needs and concerns of its neighbors: Eastown Project, Community Action and Volunteers of Aquinas (CAVA), and Social Action Committee (SAC).

923.   Sagaria, Mary Ann D., et al. *Studying the Impact of College on Students: Project Development and Recommendations for Conducting Research. An Action Research Project for Ohio Dominican College.* Ohio State University, 1985.

Describes the development process used to design the graduate survey and a pilot test at Ohio Dominican College, as well as guidelines for implementing the research.

924. Salvaterra, David Lee. "The Apostolate of the Intellect: Development and Diffusion of an Academic Ethos Among American Catholics in the Early Twentieth Century." Ph.D. dissertation. University of Notre Dame, 1983.

Examines how intellectual and cultural changes in America during the first half of the twentieth century affected Catholic culture. Describes the work of Catholic educators and educational groups to rouse Catholics to an interest and consciousness of the need for scholarship and research, and for the professionalization of their educational efforts.

925. Sause, Robert B. and Salvatore M. Barcia. "Computer Assisted Instruction in Pharmaceutical Calculations." *American Journal of Pharmaceutical Education* 45 (February 1981): 41-47.

Reports the planning, design and construction of a computer-assisted instructional program at St. John's University College of Pharmacy and Allied Health Professions, New York. Concentrates on problem solving.

926. Savage, Mary. *General Education at Albertus Magnus College.* New Haven, CT: Albertus Magnus College, 1982.

Describes an alternative program for freshmen, an interdisciplinary student-centered introduction to general education, composed of two parts taken concurrently: a year-long seminar in thought and expression, and a sequence of four courses in particular disciplines.

927. Savage, Thomas J. "The Board's Role in Maintaining Institutional Identity." *Current Issues in Catholic Higher Education* 4 (Winter 1984): 3-6.

Urges trustees to carry out their role and discusses five recommendations to assist them in effectively fulfilling this role.

928. Scherrel, Rita Anne. "A National Study of Catholic Students Entering Colleges: Their Abilities, Aspirations and Attitudes As Compared to Other Students and As Determinants of Catholic College Choice." Ph.D. dissertation. University of California, Los Angeles, 1980.

Studies the students who go to Catholic colleges and compares them with Jews and traditional Protestants. Finds that Catholic colleges attract college students with strong Catholic identification, and that attitudes toward family life, involvement with the community and political affairs are associated with going to Catholic institutions, as are aspirations toward medicine, law and nursing.

929.   Schlaver, David Edward. "The Notre Dame Ethos. Student Life in a Catholic Residential University." (Volumes I and II.) Ph.D. dissertation. The University of Michigan, 1979.

Tells the story of student life at Notre Dame in two parts - The Historical period (1842-1960) and the Modern period (1960-1979). Emphasizes the sixties, the decade of change, giving special attention to the role of faculty, evolution of new administrative structures, changes in attitude on the part of and about students, and the development of the residence-hall system.

930.   Seaton, Jean Robarts. "The Impact of Changing Sex Roles on Higher Education For Women: The Case of Ursuline College." Ph.D. dissertation. Case Western Reserve University, 1982.

Explores the purposes of higher education for women and how women have been effected by their changing roles at each period of American history. Shows how a small Catholic women's college has maintained its central mission while adapting to changing times.

931.   Stamm, Martin J. "Emerging Corporate Models of Governance in Contemporary American Higher Education." *Current Issues in Catholic Higher Education* 2 (Summer 1981): 38-45.

Examines the current corporate governance structures which provide the basis for participation of lay leaders on boards of trustees of Catholic higher education. Investigates three basic corporation governance systems forming eight fundamental governance models.

932.   Stamm, Martin J. "The Laicization of Corporate Governance of Twentieth Century American Catholic Higher Education." *Records of the American Catholic Historical Society of Philadelphia* 94 (March-December 1983): 81-99.

Chronicles the growth and development of the role of the laity in the governance structures of the Catholic college and university. Analyzes the number of laicized boards at various time intervals, the proportion of the national lay trustee population in relation to the total national trustee population, and lay trustee voting on each board. Finds the lay presence on a Catholic institutional governing board minimal in the twentieth century until the Vatican II Council in 1962 when laicization grew into a major development.

933.   Stanford, Edward V. *A Guide to Catholic College Administration.* Westminster, MD: The Newman Press, 1965.

Deals with the practical problems of administration as found in the Catholic college of liberal arts and sciences. Gives a general picture of the role of Religious Communities in conducting Catholic colleges during the 60s.

934.   Steinkrauss, Philip J., and M. Rosaria Kranz. *Quality Assurance in Higher Education: An Outline Adaptable to Small Colleges Offerings On and Off-Campus Programs.* Joliet, IL: College of St. Francis, 1981.

Describes the Quality Assurance Program (QAP), its open systems approach and its three phases of the structure, process, and outcomes.

935.   Stemmer, Paul M., Jr., et al. *Implementation of Computer Based Education by a Small College.* Detroit, MI: Mercy College, 1983.

Describes a computer-assisted instruction (CAI) program funded with a comprehensive assistance to undergraduate science education (CAUSE) grant.

936.   Sullivan, William J. "Seattle University and the City: An Interwoven Fabric." *Current Issues in Catholic Higher Education* 6 (Winter 1986): 20-22.

Explains the university's partnership with business to the benefit of the city and the institution, and the graduate programs that portray the association between the city and the university.

937.   Thornton, James William. "A Study to Determine the Effects of Collective Bargaining Elections on Faculty Participation in Institutional Governance in Roman Catholic Related Four-Year Institutions of Higher Education." Ph.D. dissertation. University of Oregon, 1981.

Surveys Catholic institutions that have had a collective bargaining election since a research study that was done by the American Association of Professors in 1970. Shows no evidence that collective bargaining diminishes or embraces faculty participation in institutional decision making.

938.   Tripole, Martin R. "Why Teach Theology to a Catholic College Student Today?" *Horizons (College Theology Society)* 6 (Fall 1979): 265-76.

Explores the problems of teaching theology to college students and demonstrates two major patterns of teaching theology; the first, a general religious experience approach, and the second, an emphasis on the person of Jesus Christ and the history of the Christian tradition.

939.   *The University in a Developing World Society; A Commemorative Volume.* Notre Dame, IN: University of Notre Dame, 1968.

Celebrates the one hundred and twenty-fifth anniversary of the University of Notre Dame, 1842-1967, with four papers presented at an academic symposium, dealing with a certain aspect of the University's role in a developing world society: the responsibility of the University to the inmost man; the University as a fountainhead of knowledge; the University and the life of the student; and the vision of a great Catholic University in today's world.

940.   Vasey, Vincent R. *"Roemer* v. *Board of Public Works, Maryland*: The Supreme Court's Evaluation of the Religious Mission of Catholic Colleges and Church Expectations.*"* *Catholic Lawyer* 23 (Spring 1978): 108-17.

Upholds a Maryland statute allowing subsidies to church-affiliated colleges. Explains that the plurality and dissenting opinions agreed that the distinction between the mission of Catholic higher education and that of secular colleges has become blurred enough that state aid to the Catholic institutions does not violate the first amendment.

941.   Walsh, Stephen. *"*New Wine in Old Jars? New Focus for the Catholic University.*"* *Momentum*, 13, February 1982, pp. 20-22.

Describes special programs at St. Edward's University, Austin, Texas, which address the special educational needs of the migrant farmworker students. Tells the story of Jose who has earned a bachelor's degree in business administration because of these programs.

942.   Ward, Leo. *"*Crashing the Philosophers' Gate.*"* *Modern Age* 23 (Spring 1979): 154-57.

Expresses personal thoughts on joining the American Philosophical Association in the 30s at a time when most Catholic philosophers earned higher education degrees only at Catholic institutions. Gives the background of the separatist position, and the development since mid-century of dialogue between Catholic philosophers and secular philosophers.

943.   Waring, Richard Wayne. *"*A Study of the Fiscal and Personnel Resources of Catholic Colleges Founded by Women Religious (Contributed Services, Financial Support, Congregations, Founding Group, Living Endowment). Ph.D. dissertation. The University of Toledo, 1985.

Summarizes data received from 46 of 65 Catholic colleges surveyed. Indicates that in 1973-74 sisters provided 19.9 percent of total educational and general expenditures, and that mandatory transfers and programs will have decreased by 1989-90 to 7.2 percent. Recommends that boards of trustees and superiors of religious congregations develop written plans for future cash gifts and contributed service gifts, and consider long-range planning to replace the living endowment of sisters.

944.   Yanikoski, Richard A. "De Paul University, Urban by Design." *Current Issues in Higher Education* 6 (Winter 1986): 5-8.

Describes the many diverse programs and public services provided by the university to meet the needs of students from varied backgrounds and those of Chicago's citizens outside the campus.

945.   Yeager, Douglas M. and M. Daniel Henry. "Cooperative Planning Between NCR Corporation and the University of Dayton." *Planning for Higher Education* 12 (Winter 1984): 6-13.

Includes the NCR Executive Development Program and describes how the chief planning officers and public relations officers of the City of Dayton, the University of Dayton, and NCR Corporation meet regularly to share concerns.

946.   Zimmer, Agatho. "Catholic Higher Education." In *Changing Concepts of Higher Education in America Since 1700*, pp. 96-121. Ph.D. dissertation. The Catholic University of America, 1938.

Explains the trends, curriculum and commitments of Catholic higher education in the United States from 1700 to the 1930s. Summarizes the principal factors in the changes taking place in the social order and urges Catholic educators to apply principles of Catholic living to these social situations.

CHAPTER 7
CHRISTIAN CHURCH (DISCIPLES OF CHRIST)
COLLEGES AND UNIVERSITIES
D. Duane Cummins

Part I: Institutional Histories

947.   Adams, Harold. *The History of Eureka College 1855-1892.* Eureka, IL: Eureka College, 1982.

948.   Blanchard, Charles. *History of Drake University.* Des Moines, IA: Drake University, 1931.

949.   Burns, Lee. "The Beginnings of Butler College." *Butler Alumnae Quarterly* (April 1926). 3-12.

950.   Campbell, Clarice T. and Oscar Allan Rogers, Jr. *Mississippi: The View From Tougaloo.* Jackson, MS: University of Mississippi Press, 1979.

951.   Carty, James W., Jr. *The Gresham Years.* Bethany, WV: Bethany College, 1970.

952.   Chapman, Charles C. *C. C. Chapman: The Career of a Creative Californian.* Los Angeles, CA: Anderson, Ritchie & Simon, 1976.

953.   Clippinger, Frank W. *The Drury Story.* Springfield, MO: Drury College, 1982.

954.   Dickinson, Elmita. *A History of Eureka College.* Eureka, IL: Christian Publishing Co., 1894.

955.   Giovannoli, Harry. *Kentucky Female Orphan School.* Midway, KY: Midway College, 1930.

956.   Green, F. M. *History of Hiram College: 1850-1900.* Cleveland, OH: Hubbell Printing, 1901.

957.   Hale, Allean. *Petticoat Pioneer: Christian College Story 1851-1951.* Columbia, MO: Columbia College, 1956.

958.   Hall, Colby. *History of Texas Christian University.* Fort Worth, TX: Texas Christian University Press, 1947.

959.   Hamlin, Griffith A. *In Faith & History: The Story of William Woods College.* St. Louis, MO: Bethany Press, 1965.

960. Hamlin, Griffith A. *William Woods College: The Cutlip Years: 1960-1980*. Fulton, MO: Bethany Press, 1965.

961. Jennings, Walter W. *Transylvania: Pioneer University of the West*. New York, NY: Pageant Press, 1955.

962. Lee, George R. *Culver-Stockton College: The First 130 Years*. Canton, MO: Culver-Stockton College, 1984.

963. Marshall, Frank and Martin Powell. *Phillips University's First Fifty Years*. 3 Volumes. Enid, OK: Phillips University Press, 1957-1967.

964. Moomaw, Leon A. *History of Cotner University*. Lincoln, NE: Christian Church in Nebraska, 1916.

965. Moore, Jerome A. *Texas Christian University: A Hundred Years of History*. Fort Worth, TX: T.C.U. Press, 1974.

966. Osborn, Ronald. *Ely Von Zollars*. St. Louis, MO: Christian Board of Publication, 1947.

967. Peters, George L. *Dreams Come True: The Story of Culver-Stockton College*. Canton, MO: Culver-Stockton College, 1941.

968. Ritchey, Charles. *Drake University Through 75 Years*. Des Moines, IA: Drake University, 1956.

969. Shaw, Henry K. "The Founding of Butler University 1847-1855." *Indiana Magazine of History* 58 (September 1962): 233-63.

970. Stevenson, Dwight E. "The Bacon College Story 1836-1865." *The College of the Bible Quarterly* 39 (October 1962): 7-56.

971. Stevenson, Dwight E. *Lexington Theological Seminary*. St. Louis, MO: Bethany Press, 1964.

972. Taylor, Clifford. "Jarvis Christian College." Bachelor of Divinity thesis. Texas Christian University, 1948.

973. Trendley, Mary B. *Prelude to the Future: The First Hundred Years of Hiram College*. New York, NY: Associated Press, 1950.

974. Wake, Orville. "A History of Lynchburg College 1903-1953." Ph.D. dissertation. University of Virginia, 1957.

975. Ware, C. C. *A History of Atlantic Christian College*. Wilson, NC: Atlantic Christian College, 1956.

976. Woolery, W. K. *Bethany Years*. Huntington, WV: Standard Publishing, 1941.

977. Wright, John D., Jr. *Transylvania: Pioneer University of the West*. Lexington, KY: Transylvania University Press, 1975.

Essay

This body of literature is authored, for the most part, by graduates, long-time professors and close friends of the institutions, all of whom render sympathetic treatments of their subject schools. They are generally chronological studies, researched from college newspapers, catalogues, yearbooks and reminiscences, divided either by presidential administrations or by decades, providing very interesting stories with a minimum of analysis and few scholarly trappings. Clear exceptions to this general statement are the works of Wright, Warren, Clippinger and Campbell. Their histories are tied into the socio-economic themes of American history, carefully researched and documented from a wide range of sources. They are models of institutional history. An outstanding example of educational biography is *Ely Von Zollars* by Ronald Osborn. Thoroughly researched and eminently readable, it is an excellent scholarly treatment of a person who served as president of three Disciples institutions -- Texas Christian University, Hiram College, and Phillips University.

Part II: Analytical Studies of Disciples Colleges

Books

978.   Cummins, D. Duane. *The Disciples Colleges: A History.* St. Louis, MO: Christian Board of Publication, 1987.

979.   Gresham, Perry E. *Campbell and the Colleges.* Nashville, TN: The Disciples of Christ Historical Society, 1973.

980.   Gresham, Perry E. *The Sage of Bethany.* St. Louis, MO: Bethany Press, 1960.

981.   McCormick, Thomas R. *Campus Ministry and the Coming Age.* St. Louis, MO: Christian Board of Publication, 1987.

982.   Reeves, Floyd and Russell, John. *College Organization and Administration.* Indianapolis, IN: Board of Higher Education, 1929.

Articles

983.   Carpenter, G. T. "Our Colleges." *Christian Quarterly Review* 4 (July 1885): 372-82.

984.   Cummins, D. Duane. "The Preacher and the Promoter." *Discipliana* 44 (Winter 1984): 3-14.

985.   Cummins, D. Duane. "Black disciples and Higher Education." *Discipliana* 47 (Spring 1987): 3-10.

986.   Eminhizer, Earl E. "Alexander Campbell on Moral and Quality Education -- Some New Light." *The Iliff Review* 51 (Spring 1984): 284-92.

987.   Forrest, Albertina A. "Status of Education Among Disciples." *The New Christian Quarterly* 5 (October 1896): 401-16.

988.   Gresham, Perry E. "Proud Heritage." *West Virginia History* 15 (January 1954): 99-117.

989.   Osborn, Ronald. "Divinity's Need of the Humanities." *Encounter* 46 (Summer 1985): 193-212.

Essay

Two early attempts at analysis include a brief article by G. T. Carpenter which is essentially an editorial caution against founding too many colleges which Disciples could not financially sustain; and the article by Albertina Forrest which is a ground-breaking study in statistical research on Disciples colleges. Forrest provided data on endowments, operating costs, tuition income, professional salaries, libraries and a variety of other subjects within the life of the college during the 1890's. The most significant study by Disciples was the 1929 publication of *College Organization and Administration* by Reeves and Russell. The book was a pioneer study in the field of quantitative measurements for institutional analysis and became widely used as a text in higher education classes in graduate schools placing Disciples among the protest leaders in quantitative evaluation of institutions.

Finally, the recent (1987) writing by D. Duane Cummins is the first comprehensive history of Disciples colleges ever written. It is set in the religious, social and educational context of American History and provides substantial analytical data on Disciples colleges as well as church-related higher education in America.

Part III: Statistical Surveys and Reports

990.   Cummins Institutional Survey, Summer 1985.

991.   Cummins, D. Duane, et al. *Higher Education Evaluation Task Force Report.* Christian Church (Disciples of Christ), June 1976.

992.   Division of Higher Education Congregational Survey, January 1986.

993.   Division of Higher Education Statistical Research and Institutional Reports, 1978 through 1986.

994.   Lofton-Cummins College Curriculum Survey, Summer 1986.

995.   Rosner-Cummins Student and Pastor Survey, Fall 1985.

996.   Schroeder-Cummins Faculty Degrees Survey, Spring 1986.

997.   Spencer, Claude. Unpublished list of colleges, Disciples of Christ Historical Society, 1964.

Essay

Disciples are in the process of building a modern data base on their higher education ministry. All of the professional surveys have been published within the past decade and the great majority within the last two years. It is a very current data base revealing trends in college selection among church youth, factors influencing those decisions, demographic configurations and church youth, analysis of Disciples colleges curriculum designs and characteristics of Disciples college faculties. The data is drawn from professionally prepared survey instruments circulated among a carefully selected and representative group of 835 Disciples congregations, from audits, HEGIS reports and various other institutional reports prepared by the colleges. Collectively, the data are extremely useful for projecting with reasonable accuracy the nature of the institutions and the church educational ministry for the coming age.

Part IV: Disserations

998.   Bennett, Rolla J. "History of the Grounding of Education Institutions by the Disciples of Christ in Virginia and West Virginia." Ph.D. dissertation. University of Pittsburgh, 1932.

999.   Edwards, Arthur B. "Alexander Campbell's Philosophy of Education." M.A. thesis. East Tennessee State College, 1960.

1000.   Ferre, Gustave. "A Concept of Higher Education and its Relation to the Christian Faith as Evidenced in the Writing of Alexander Campbell." Ph.D. dissertation. Vanderbilt University, 1958.

1001.   Flowers, Ronald B. "The Bible Chair Movement in the Disciples of Christ Tradition: Attempts to Teach Religion in State Universities." Ph.D. dissertation. University of Iowa, 1967.

1002.   Hamlin, Griffith A. "The Origin and Development of the Board of Higher Education of the Christian Church (Disciples of Christ)." M.A. thesis. Southern Illinois University, 1968.

1003.   Lewis, Elmer Clifford. "A History of Secondary and Higher Education in Negro Schools Related to the Disciples of Christ." Ph.D. dissertation. University of Pittsburgh, 1957.

1004.   Morrison, John. "Alexander Campbell and Moral Education." Ph.D. dissertation. Stanford University, 1967.

1005.   Shaw, Henry K. "Alexander Campbell -- Educator." M.A. thesis. University of Akron, 1942.

CHAPTER 8
CHURCH OF CHRIST COLLEGES AND UNIVERSITIES
Robert E. Hooper,
Howard White, Raymond Muncy, Marsha Harper,
Winnie Bell and Marie Byers

1006.   Altman, Ted Max. "Contributions of George Benson to Christian Education." Ed.D. dissertation. North Texas State University, 1971.

This study is a biographical analysis of George S. Benson, the second president of Harding College. Besides his presidency, the study emphasizes Benson's role as a missionary to China during the 1920s and the 1930s. Special notice is given to Benson's dedication to the National Education Program at Harding College.

1007.   Atteberry, James L. *The Story of Harding College*. Searcy, AR: privately published, 1966.

Describes the early years of Harding College prior to moving to Searcy, Arkansas. The various chapters give the author's impressions of Harding College as it developed until 1966. It is not an attempt to give a thorough and definitive history of the school.

1008.   Bannister, Mickey Dean. "Changes in Religious Emphasis Among Selected Colleges Associated with the Church of Christ." Ed.D. dissertation. Oklahoma State University, 1985.

A study of David Lipscomb College, Pepperdine University, and Oklahoma Christian College to identify changes in religious emphasis. The author notes a major difference between Lipscomb and Oklahoma Christian on the one hand, and Pepperdine on the other. The two former schools are perceived as being "defenders of the faith" while Pepperdine is seen as a "free Christian College." This major difference determines the religious emphasis of the schools.

1009.   Banowsky, William S. *The Mirror of A Movement: Churches of Christ as Seen Through the Abilene Christian College Lectureship.* Dallas: Christian Publishing Company, 1965.

Because of the autonomous nature of churches of Christ, there is no formal method of exchanging ideas or giving direction to the fellowship. The college lectureship has somewhat filled this gap.

The book analyzes the types of speeches given, why they are given, and the impact of these ideas on churches of Christ.

1010.   Beeman, W. O. *Oklahoma Christian College: Dream to Reality.* Delight, AR: Gospel Light Publishing Company, 1970.

Chronicles the early failures of Christian education among churches of Christ in Oklahoma and the new attempt in Bartlesville when Central Christian College opened in 1949. Beginning as a junior college, the Board of Directors moved the school to Oklahoma City in 1958. The school moved to senior college status, gaining accreditation in 1966.

1011.   Boles, Leo Lipscomb and J. E. Choate. *I'll Stand on the Rock: A Biography of H. Leo Boles.* Nashville: Gospel Advocate Company, 1965.

A study of a former president of David Lipscomb College. Boles was an outstanding preacher and educator within churches of Christ. He was president of the school when it changed its name from Nashville Bible School to David Lipscomb College.

1012.   Cosgrove, Owen Glen. "The Administration of Don Heath Morris at Abilene Christian College." Ph.D. dissertation. North Texas State University, 1976.

The scope of the study includes background material on Don Morris and then an analysis of his administration as president of Abilene Christian College. Since Morris was president of the school during the growth years of the school, knowing his ideas on the purposes of the college, faculty growth, fiscal policies, academic freedom, racial integration, and morality are important for the future of the school.

1013.   Croom, A. S. *The Early History of Harding College.* Searcy, AR: privately published, 1954.

Attempts to give an alternate story of some of the early years of Harding College, especially as it involved Arkansas Christian College. The author is interested in correcting errors in Norvel Young's account of Harding in his *The History of Christian Colleges* published in 1949.

1014.   Evans, Jack. "The History of Southwestern Christian College, Terrell, Texas." M.A. thesis. Texas Western College, 1963.

Describes and chronicles the development of education among black churches of Christ culminating in the formation of Southwestern Christian College in 1950. In addition to a general history, the thesis deals with the struggle for accreditation and financing. Evans is currently president of the college.

1015.   Evans, Warren Donald. "Educational Expenditures Within Liberal

Arts Colleges and Colleges Maintained by Members of the Church of Christ." Ed.D. dissertation. Pennsylvania State University, 1963.

This study analyzes expenditures toward various activities in colleges operated by members of churches of Christ in the areas of internal distribution of expenditures, for long-range planning, and as a means to indicate to prospective donors the greatest needs of the college. The author compares the colleges within the fellowship of churches of Christ with schools listed in the *Sixty College Studies*. The dissertation indicates a number of conclusions based broadly on a need to study expenditures in order to better facilitate a better day-by-day operation of the schools and to be able to project with some accuracy the future.

1016.   Gresham, Perry E. *Campbell and the Colleges*. Nashville, TN: The Disciples of Christ Historical Society, 1973.

Analyzes the impact of Alexander Campbell on education within the broad scope of Disciples of Christ (Christian Church), Independent Christian churches, and churches of Christ. With the establishment of Bethany College in 1841, Campbell set in motion the establishment of numerous colleges in all segments of the American Restoration Movement.

1017.   Harris, Jim. *Schools of Preaching: An Evaluation of Ministerial Preparation*. Fort Worth: Star Bible Publications, Inc., 1984.

Analyzes and evaluates schools of preaching among churches of Christ. Using a questionnaire, a sampling of graduates from four schools of preaching responded to the impact the schools had upon them during their first year in the ministry. The study revealed two suggestions: (1) incorporate an internship requirement for graduation, and (2) if at all possible, the school of preaching graduate should continue his education beyond the two years required in most such schools.

1018.   Hooper, Robert E. *A Call to Remember: Chapters in Nashville Restoration History*. Nashville: Gospel Advocate Company, 1978.

A series of essays that focus on David Lipscomb and the school that bears his name. The chapter, "David Lipscomb College: A Reminder of the Restoration Movement," relates the various buildings on the campus to leaders in the more conservative direction of the Restoration Movement, the churches of Christ.

1019.   Hooper, Robert E. "The Political and Educational Ideas of David Lipscomb." Ph.D. dissertation. George Peabody College, 1965.

An analysis of David Lipscomb's views on education, showing how his views have had a major impact on higher education among churches of Christ. His emphasis on Bible training for all students without a seminary-type education for preachers was important for churches of Christ. Discusses the 1891 founding of the Nashville Bible School, now David Lipscomb College.

1020.   Hooper, Robert E. and Jim Turner. *Willard Collins: The People Person.* Nashville: 20th Century Christian, 1986.

A biography of the fourteenth president of David Lipscomb College. His strength as a "people person" can be seen in the more than twenty years he served as vice-president of the school prior to accepting the presidency in 1977. His administration witnessed considerable physical growth and an increased endowment of nearly $20,000,000.

1021.   Larsen, Dale Russell. "A History of York College, 1890-1966." Ed.D. dissertation. Teachers College, University of Nebraska, 1966.

This study of York College is historical in nature, beginning with its founding in 1890 until 1966. The school, a junior college, has had several sponsorships in its history. In 1956 members of churches of Christ began operation of the school. The college is rather unique among churches of Christ since it operates on a campus that restricts the use of the campus to ensure a continuation of York College.

1022.   Lawton, Eugene. "A Six Point Followup Study of the Graduates of Southwestern Christian College, Terrell, Texas from 1952-1957." M.A. thesis. Pepperdine University, 1959.

An analysis of the graduates of Southwestern Christian College graduates from 1952-1957 in the following aspects: (1) occupational standing, (2) economic development, (3) home ownership, (4) marital relationships, (5) religious involvement, and (6) educational advancement. The author used questionnaires to obtain his information.

1023.   Maddox, Douglas Pat. "A Financial Analysis of Church of Christ Related Institutions Based on Enrollment and Costs." Ph.D. dissertation. Texas Tech University, 1982.

An analysis of the financial problems of private colleges and universities in general, but more specifically of colleges and universities related to churches of Christ. The study includes sixteen two- and four-year schools. The schools should pay particular attention to resource management.

1024.   Morris, Don H. "Add-Ran and Its Heirs." *Restoration Quarterly* 16 (Summer-Fall 1973): 260-72.

Describes Add-Ran College's place in the development of

Christian education among those associated with the Restoration Movement. The division involving instrumental music is worship centered at Add-Ran College and the Clark family. The school moved to Waco and then to Forth Worth where it is today known as Texas Christian University. In 1910 members of churches of Christ organized Thorp Springs Christian College, now extinct, on the property of the old Add-Ran College.

1025.   Morris, Don H. and Max Leach. *Like Stars Shining Brightly: The Personal Story of Abilene Christian College.* Abilene, TX: Abilene Christian College Press, 1953.

A personal story of Abilene Christian College as told by men who were students, teachers, and administrators during the school's formative years. The last two chapters tell of Don Morris' presidential administration until 1953.

1026.   Muncy, Raymond L. *Searcy, Arkansas: A Frontier Town Grows up with America.* Searcy, AR: Harding Press, 1976.

A history of a small, rural Arkansas city where Harding University is located. Although there are no chapters specifically on Harding University, the book chronicles the relationship of the town and the university.

1027.   Nichols, James Don. "A History of Harding College, 1924-1984." Ed.D. dissertation. University of Arkansas, 1985.

The purpose of this study is to trace the historical circumstances surrounding the establishment, growth, and development of Harding College from 1924 to 1984. The study is organized around the three presidential administrations of the college.

1028.   Pittman, Samuel Parker. *Lipscomb's Golden Heritage: 1891-1941.* Nashville: Associated Ladies for Lipscomb, 1983.

A reprint of a history of the Nashville Bible School and David Lipscomb College that appeared in the 1941 edition of the *Backlog*, the school's yearbook. It is the best published history of the first fifty years of Lipscomb's history. Pittman was a long-time member of the faculty.

1029.   Powell, James Marvin and Mary Nelle Hardeman Powers. *N. B. H.: A Biography of Nicholas Brodie Hardeman.* Nashville: Gospel Advocate Company, 1964.

A biography of N. B. Hardeman that develops his relationship to the school that bears his name. Written in part by Hardeman's daughter, it is very sympathetic to him. Of special interest is the chapter, "F. H. C. -- Other Facets." It emphasizes the economic situation of the school during the 1930s.

1030.   Royce, Nyal D. "A Study of the Environment of Harding College as perceived by its Students and Faculty and as Anticipated by Entering Students." Ed.D. dissertation. Memphis State University, 1969.

A study of an 800 student sample composed of sub-groups of men and women incoming students, sophomores, juniors, and seniors to measure certain features of Harding College and to define the consequent presses which its students felt. These presses were to be related to institutional goals, to study the effectiveness of programs in implementing institutional objectives. Areas of congruence and dissonance between students and administration were sought in order to detect areas of foment and unrest.

1031.   Rushford, Jerry, ed. Text by Howard A. White. *Crest of A Golden Wave: A Pictorial History of Pepperdine University, 1937-1987.* Malibu, CA: Pepperdine University, 1987.

A pictorial history on the celebration of the university's fiftieth anniversary. The volume does not pretend to be a comprehensive or definitive history of the university. It deals with fifty years of progress of the school that began as George Pepperdine College in 1937.

1032.   Scobey, James E., ed. *Franklin College and Its Influences.* Nashville: McQuiddy Printing Company, 1906.

Includes a number of essays by graduates of Franklin College giving their assessment of the school. Franklin College was founded by Tolbert Fanning, a leader in the southern Restoration Movement. David Lipscomb, an 1849 graduate, contributed to the book.

1033.   Sears, Lloyd Cline. *For Freedom: The Biography of John Nelson Armstrong.* Austin, TX: Sweet Publishing Company, 1969.

A sympathetic investigation of the life of J. N. Armstrong, long-time president of Harding College. Armstrong had been a student at the Nashville Bible School under David Lipscomb and James A. Harding. The book chronicles the struggles of Cordell and Harper Christian colleges in Oklahoma prior to Armstrong's move to Arkansas.

1034.   Sears, Lloyd Cline. *What is Your Life?: An Autobiography.* Dallas: Temple Publishing Company, 1979.

The author and subject of this study served as dean of Harding College through the difficult years of the 1930s when the school moved to Searcy, Arkansas. He continued in this capacity during the growth years of the 1940s and the 1950s. The story of Harding College cannot be known without understanding the place of Dean Sears.

1035.   Thompson, Robert Edward. "An Analysis of Fund-raising Methods used by Church of Christ-related Four-year Colleges in the United States of America." Ed.D. dissertation. George Peabody College of Vanderbilt University, 1983.

The study focuses on eight four-year church of Christ-related colleges. These schools have little information concerning their development programs. Planning giving is not a major emphasis of the schools. To implement better planning giving, the development officers should be well trained through continuing education. Furthermore, schools would do well to add more well-trained development personnel as this has been shown to raise the level of giving in private schools.

1036.   Varner, Cleddy Louie. "The Development of an Undergraduate Recreation Curriculum for Abilene Christian University." Ed.D. dissertation. University of Northern Colorado, 1980.

The development of a recreation curriculum for Abilene Christian University is the focus of this study. Two goals are stated: (1) better trained municipal directors, and (2) more well-rounded youth ministers for churches of Christ. Based on a survey, the author urges better training in supervision of recreational programs and a restructured program in youth ministry.

1037.   West, Earl. "James A. Harding and Christian Education." *Restoration Quarterly* 24 (Spring 1981): 65-79.

Analyzes James A. Harding's philosophy of life by showing how his faith in God influenced his understanding of Christian education. A strong believer in God s providence, he believed God would care for him in all circumstances. Hence he would not accept remuneration for teaching the bible in the Nashville Bible School.

1038.   Young, M. Norvel. *A History of Christian Colleges Established and Controlled by Members of the Churches of Christ.* Kansas City, MO: Old Paths Book Club, 1949.

An overview of colleges operated by members of churches of Christ. The study relates present-day schools to the historic roots of the American Restoration Movement, including Alexander Campbell's Bethany College. It does not include a number of schools begun since 1949.

1039.   Youngs, Bill. *Faith was His Fortune: The Life Story of George Pepperdine.* No publication date. Probably published in 1976.

Describes the impact of George Pepperdine in the business world as the founder of the Western Auto Supply Company. Chapters thirty-one through thirty-four deal with Pepperdine's involvement in the school that would bear his name.

CHAPTER 9
CHURCH OF JESUS CHRIST OF LATTER-DAY SAINTS
COLLEGES AND UNIVERSITIES
Robert J. Matthews

1040.   "A Catalogue of Theses and Dissertations Concerning The Church
         of Jesus Christ of Latter-Day Saints, Mormonism and Utah."
         Compiled by the College of Religious Instruction, Brigham Young
         University (BYU), Provo, UT, 1971.

              Provides a more complete and more doctrinely oriented
         listing of theses and dissertations than the previous source with
         approximately 6,000 entries.

1041.   "A Collection of Abstracts of Theses and Dissertations" available
         from Seminaries and Institutes of Religion, BYU, Provo, UT.

              Provides the interested scholar with references to many
         theses and dissertations written by Mormon students related to
         Latter-day Saint educational thought and/or various phenomena
         associated with educational practice. Included are 151 entries with
         abstracts of 1-4 pp. Does not list the institution at which the work
         was completed (most were conducted at BYU).

1042.   Brigham Young University: The First One Hundred Years.
         Wilkinson, Ernest L. (Editor, all volumes), Arrington, Leonard J.
         (Associate Editor vols. 3 and 4), and Hafen, Bruce C. (Associate
         Editor vol. 4) 4 Volumes. Provo: BYU Press, 1975--vols. 1 & 2,
         1976--vols. 3 & 4.

              Presents a four volume, officially commissioned history of
         BYU for its centennial celebration in 1975. In its more than 2800
         pages with 48 appendices and 75n pages of topic index, the
         development of the university from a struggling frontier school to
         the largest private university in the nation is chronicled. The first
         volume covers the events from the founding of the Brigham Young
         Academy which evolved into Brigham Young University to the
         1920s when the first buildings were built on "Temple Hill," the
         present site of the university. The second volume takes the story
         from the 1920s to the 1950s when the tremendous growth of the
         student body was accompanied by a very rapid growth in the
         physical plant. The third volume covers most of the Wilkinson
         years during which the institution matured into a full-fledged
         university. The fourth volume covers the presidency of Dallin H.

Oaks. The account includes the struggles, financial and ideological, as well as the successes. Programs, presentations, people and events which shaped the institution are all portrayed.

1043.   *Charge to Religious Educators.* Compiled by the Church Educational System and published by The Church of Jesus Christ of Latter-day Saints, Salt Lake City, UT, 1982, available through the Church Distribution Center order number PTS10739.

Presents in a 155 page anthology 26 addresses given by General Authorities of the Church. These articles outline the objectives, purposes and ideals of the Church Educational System with particular emphasis on the teacher of religious instruction. Because all undergraduate students at Brigham Young University are required to enroll in a religion course each semester, religious instruction is a central part of the experience of a BYU student. Of particular importance to BYU research are "The Charted Course of the Church in Education," J. Reuben Clark, Jr., "The Mantle is Far, Far Greater than the Intellect," Boyd K. Packer, and "The Gospel Teacher and His Message," Ezra Taft Benson.

1044.   Clark, J. Reuben, Jr. "The Charted Course of the Church in Education." *Improvement Era* 41 (September 1938): 520-21.

Establishes the course for the future of the educational system of the Church. This often cited address by President Clark of the First Presidency of The Church of Jesus Christ of Latter-day Saints reiterates the basis of all of the Church's educational efforts to teach and testify of the truth of the Gospel of Jesus Christ, outlines the spiritual nature of students, and presents the needed professional and personal characteristics of teachers.

1045.   *Doctrine and Covenants.* Salt Lake City, UT: The Church of Jesus Christ of Latter-day Saints, 1981.

Contains three hundred pages with 138 sections (chapters), viewed as revelation by the members of The Church of Jesus Christ of Latter-day Saints. Several sections provide insights into the importance of education in the theology of the church. Section 88 describes the nature of the laws governing the universe, and enjoins leaders to teach. The "curriculum" is defined. The means for teaching was a "School of the Prophets," the first school developed within the theological structure of the church. Other sections of particular interest include 93 from which the university's motto comes, "The Glory of God is Intelligence," and 109.

1046.   Holland, Jeffrey R. "A 'Notion' at Risk." An address given by the current president of BYU at the National Press Club, Washington, DC, on March 22, 1984. Printed as a pamphlet by the BYU Press, Provo, UT.

Points to the omission from all the various reports on the

present state of education (public and higher) in the US of reference to the moral and civic (read "civilizing") values of education. The president reaffirms BYU's stand that at BYU students will receive instruction in moral and civic matters.

1047.   Holland, Jeffrey R. "The Mission of Brigham Young University." A statement in the official catalog of Brigham Young University, first published in November, 1981, Provo, UT.

Presents in a one page mission statement the purpose of Brigham Young University. The four major educational goals revolve around the general mission of BYU: "to assist individuals in their quest for perfection and eternal life."

1048.   Kimball, Spencer W. "BYU's Second Century" in Edward L. Kimball, ed., *The Teachings of Spencer W. Kimball -- Twelfth President of The Church of Jesus Christ of Latter-day Saints*. Salt Lake City, UT: Bookcraft, 1982.

Notes the double heritage of the faculty of BYU to combine secular "scholarly research" with "the vital and revealed truths that have been sent to us from heaven." In developing this "bilingualism" in scholarship and quality teaching, it is stressed that BYU "will never surrender its spiritual character to a sole concern for scholarship."

1049.   Kimball, Spencer W. "Education for Eternity" in Edward L. Kimball, Ed., *The Teachings of Spencer W. Kimball -- Twelfth President of The Church of Jesus Christ of Latter-day Saints*. Salt Lake City, UT: Bookcraft, 1982.

Sketches a vision of the purpose and potential of BYU. Originally given as a speech to the faculty of BYU in 1967, the purpose of the university is to educate not only the whole man, but the eternal man. The charge is given to blend the secular with the spiritual, but in the mix, character is higher than intellect.

1050.   Kimball, Spencer W. "Installation of and Charge to the President." Given at the inaugural of President Jeffrey R. Holland, Nov. 14, 1980, Provo, UT.

Charges the new president to create an "educational Mt. Everest" which will educate for eternity as well as for time, be a bastion against false ideologies, give rise to great artists and scholars, continue in its excellent teaching, inspire its students to service and overcome all obstacles in pursuit of its goals. "Remain a unique university in all the world!" In the process of time BYU will become the fully recognized university of the Lord about which the prophets have spoken.

1051.   Oaks, Dallin H. "Challenges to BYU in the Eighties." A commencement address given August 15, 1980.

Presents several significant challenges which the university faces in the 1980s. These included: enrollment pressures, financial problems, government regulations, effective use of resources, boldness in goals and reason and revelation.

1052.   Riddle, Chauncey C. "A BYU for Zion." *Brigham Young University Studies* 16 (Summer 1976): 485-500.

Describes six factors which would help qualify the university to be part of a "Zion society." These include dependence upon the savior, morality, concern for the poor, emphasis on doing, careful distinction between being intelligent and being intellectual, and no priestcraft.

1053.   Smith, Joseph--History: Extracts from the History of Joseph Smith, the Prophet. *The Pearl of Great Price.* Salt Lake City, UT: The Church of Jesus Christ of Latter-day Saints, 1981.

Presents a brief historical account of the establishment of The Church of Jesus Christ of Latter-day Saints which explains the sense of mission which characterizes the church. The need for an understanding of languages, cultures, and other general education disciplines is founded on the evangelical base established in this account.

1054.   Waterstradt, Jean Anne, ed. *They Gladly Taught: Ten BYU Professors.* 2 vols. Provo, UT: BYU, the Emeritus Club, 1986, 1987.

Presents a partial record of the contributions of "remarkable professors to whom the present university family is indebted." Each of the teachers featured in these volumes is commemorated in two essays: a biographical sketch and a reminiscence by a former student. Several academic disciplines are represented.

1055.   Wilkinson, Ernest L. "The Return of Full Value." *Brigham Young University Bulletin* 56 (1959): 1-20.

Speaking to the faculty, the university president outlined the requirements for acceptable performance of the faculty in teaching. In this speech a proposal was made to place on the entrance to the campus the slogan, "Enter to Learn, Go Forth to Serve."

1056.   Wilkinson, Ernest L. "The Unique Role of BYU Among Universities of America." An address given to the student body at Brigham Young University, February 5, 1970, Provo, UT.

Presents the theme that many of the great universities in America began with deep ties to Christian churches. Over the decades they have severed their ties with the church and become secular in outlook and teaching. Brigham Young University is directed by a Board of Trustees which involves the leadership of The Church of Jesus Christ of Latter-day Saints.

1057. Wilkinson, Ernest L. and W. Cleon Skousen. *Brigham Young University: A School of Destiny.* Provo, UT: BYU Press, 1976.

This one volume history of tne first one hundred years of Brigham Young University's existence was commissioned by the president of BYU, Dallin H. Oaks and the Board of Trustees. In its 895 pages and 42 chapters the various administrations of the university are related and the major decisions, programs and controversies which marked the first one hundred years are portrayed. The early financial crises, the ideological crisis of the early 20th century, the rapid growth during the post-war years and the academic consolidation of the 1970's are described. In addition, information concerning aspects of student life during several of the critical periods in the history of the institution. A 22 page topic index helps the reader find particular information about issues, persons or programs.

1058. Baugher, A. C. "A Challenge ... Understanding and Supporting an Adequate Program of Christian Higher Education in the Church of the Brethren in the Years Ahead." *Brethren Life and Thought* 3 (1958): 18-34.

Surveys trends of higher education in the United States in general, outlines a Christian philosophy of education, and makes recommendations for Brethren higher education.

1059. Bittenger, Emmert F. "Marking One Hundred Years of Brethren Higher Education." *Brethren Life and Thought* 25 (1980): 71-82.

Points to a trend in the past century for Brethren colleges to become gradually freer from church control, and suggests that a curbing of the secularization will result only from a conscious effort for church and college to strengthen their ties.

1060. Bowman, Paul Haynes. *Brethren Education in the Southeast.* Bridgewater, VA: Bridgewater College, 1956.

Traces the efforts of Brethren to found various preparatory schools from Maryland to Alabama, and shows how those efforts culminated in the establishment of Bridgewater College. Discusses attempts at providing secondary education beginning in 1858 at Cedar Grove Academy in Broadway, Virginia and ending with the closing of Daleville Academy in Daleville, Virginia in 1933.

1061. Boyers, Auburn A. "Changing Conceptions of Education in the Church of the Brethren." Ph.D. dissertation. University of Pittsburgh, 1968.

Summarizes the controversy over education that has been an integral part of Brethren history. Discusses how the historical Brethren attitudes toward education affected efforts to establish schools.

1062. Ellis, Charles C. *Juniata College: The History of Seventy Years.* Elgin, IL: Brethren Publishing House, 1947.

Written by a President Emeritus, this book recounts the first seventy years of Juniata College from 1876-1946.

1063.   Emmert, David. *Reminiscences of Juniata College: Quarter Century 1876-1901*. Harrisburg, PA: Mt. Pleasant Printery, 1901.

      David Emmert, a student and later a teacher at Juniata College, relates his memories of the first twenty-five years of the school's life.

1064.   Fasnacht, Harold D. "A Philosophy of Higher Education for the Church of the Brethren." *Brethren Life and Thought* 3 (1958): 4-17.

      Challenges the denomination to be closely involved with its colleges, and the colleges to be clear about their purpose.

1065.   *Fifty Years of Educational Endeavor: Bridgewater College, 1880-1930, Daleville College 1890-1930*. Staunton, VA: McClure Company, 1930.

      A tribute written by alumni, this volume recounts the separate histories of Bridgewater College (1880-1924) and Dalville College (1890-1924), and then of their combined story (1924-1930) after merging.

1066.   Flory, John S. "A History of Education in the Church of the Brethren." In *Educational Blue Book and Dictionary*, pp. 21-104. Edited by W. Arthur Cable and Homer F. Sanger. Elgin, IL: The General Education Board of the Church of the Brethren, 1923.

      Discusses the course of Brethren education beginning with ardent support of schools in the 1700's, followed by a period of opposition to education, then a revival of interest in education in the late 1800's. Describes the academies (high school level) that were established beginning in 1852 which paved the way for Brethren colleges.

1067.   Frantz, Ira H., ed. *Manchester College: The First Seventy-five years*. Elgin, IL: The Brethren Press, 1964.

      Written on the occasion of the seventy-fifth anniversary of the Manchester College, this book traces the school's history through 1963. It is compiled by a group of eight Manchester College alumni.

1068.   Hanle, Robert Vail. "A History of Higher Education among the German Baptist Brethren: 1708-1908."   Ph.D. dissertation. University of Pennsylvania, 1974.

      Traces Brethren efforts to provide education at elementary, secondary and higher levels from 1708 to 1908. Focuses on the effect that Brethren attitudes toward education had on educational endeavors.

1069. Holsinger, H. R. *Holsinger's History of the Tunkers and the Brethren Church.* Lathrop, CA: Pacific Press Publishing, 1901.

Gives a brief description of McPherson College, Plattsburg College, Bridgewater College, North Manchester College and Huntingdon Normal College.

1070. "How Big will our Colleges Get?" *Messenger.* January 7, 1965, p. 17.

Challenges Church of the Brethren related colleges to plan how to meet the exploding student population.

1071. Kaylor, Earl C. "Selling the Brethren on the Normal." *Messenger.* May 1976, pp. 20-24.

Lauds early Brethren pioneers in higher education, specifically at the Huntingdon Normal School, which later became Juniata College.

1072. Kaylor, Earl C. *Truth Sets Free: Juniata Independent College in Pennsylvania, Founded by the Brethren, 1876.* Cranbury, NJ: A. S. Barnes and Co., 1977.

Relates the story of the first one hundred years of Juniata College, from 1876 to 1976.

1073. Lauderdale, Kerby. "The Church, Education, and the Christian College." *Brethren Life and Thought* 16 (1971): 21-28.

Examines the relationship between the Church of the Brethren and its colleges.

1074. Lehman, James H. *Beyond Anything Foreseen: A Study of the History of Higher Education in the Church of the Brethren.* Prepared for the Conference on Higher Education and the Church of the Brethren at Earlham College. Richmond, IN: 1976.

Focuses mainly on the development of Brethren colleges, mentioning the earlier schools of academy (high school) level that helped to prepare the way.

1075. Mallott, Floyd E. *Studies in Brethren History.* Elgin, IL: Brethren Publishing House, 1954. Reprinted 1980, pp. 198-219.

The pertinent chapters in this account of Brethren History are: 22) "The Struggle for Brethren Schools," 23) "An Appraisal of Brethren Schools," and 24) "Other Ventures in Education."

1076. Miller, Howard. *The Record of the Faithful: For the Use of the Brethren.* Lewisburg, PA: J. R. Cornelius, 1882.

Gives a short sketch of each of the Brethren schools in

existence when the volume was published: Huntingdon Normal College, Ashland College, Mt. Morris College, and Virginia Normal School.

1077.   Muir, Gladdys E. *LaVerne College: Seventy-five Years of Service.* LaVerne, CA: Preston Printing, 1967.

Commemorates the first seventy-five years of LaVerne College, from 1891-1948. The author was a teacher at LaVerne for thirty-two years.

1078.   Noffsinger, John S. *A Program for Higher Education in the Church of the Brethren.* New York: Columbia University, 1925.

Gives a brief history of the three eras of Brethren educational activities: 1) Colonial (1708-1778); 2) Wilderness (1778-1850); and 3) Liberalization (1850-present); then focuses primarily on the establishment of colleges.

1079.   Schlosser, Ralph W. *History of Elizabethtown College 1899-1970.* Elizabethtown, PA: Sowers Printing Co., 1971.

Tells the history of the first seventy-five years of the life of Elizabethtown College. It is written by Ralph Schlosser who was related to the college since 1905 as student, professor, and president.

1080.   Schwalm, V. F. "Brethren Teachers in Brethren Colleges." *Gospel Messenger*, April 24, 1956, pp. 14-15.

Presents the results of a survey about teachers in Brethren Colleges, comparing the educational preparation and fields of study between the Brethren and non-Brethren teachers.

1081.   Sharp, S. Z. *The Educational History of the Church of the Brethren.* Elgin, IL: Brethren Publishing House, 1923.

Begins in 1860 with a history of Brethren education from 1708; then gives a short sketch of each of the Brethren educational institutions established between 1860 and 1923, including both secondary and college levels.

1082.   Shoup, William J. *Ammi-My People.* West Alexandria, OH: William Shoup, 1905.

This Brethren author intends to articulate true doctrine. His position on the subject of high schools and colleges is that they are dangerous because education makes people high-minded and leads them away from the simplicity of the gospel.

1083.   *Two Centuries of the Church of the Brethren.* Elgin, IL: Brethren Publishing House, 1908, pp. 307-39.

This book of bicentennial addresses at the Annual

Conference held at Des Moines, Iowa on June 3-11, 1908 includes an address by S. Z. Sharp entitled "Early Educational Activities," and one by John S. Flory entitled "Present Educational Activities." Sharp traces the history of Brethren educational endeavors, while Flory challenges the existing schools to raise their educational standards (pp. 307-39).

1084.　Wayland, John W. *Bridgewater College: Its Past and Present.* Elgin, IL: Brethren Publishing House, 1905.

Written by a group of alumni, this book was intended both to preserve the history of the first twenty-five years of Bridgewater College and also to raise money for the Alumni Scholarship Endowment Fund.

1085.　Winger, Otho. *Memories of Manchester.* Elgin, IL: The Brethren Press, 1940.

Otho Winger, president of Manchester College for thirty years (1911-1941), recounts his memories at the end of his term of office.

Archival holdings are located at the following college libraries:

Bethany Theological Seminary, Oak Brook, IL　60521

Bridgewater College, Bridgewater, VA　22812

Elizabethtown College, Elizabethtown, PA　17022

Juniata College, Huntingdon, PA　16652

Manchester College, North Manchester, IN　46962

McPherson College, McPherson, KS　67460

University of LaVerne, LaVerne, CA　91650

CHAPTER 11

CHURCH OF THE NAZARENE COLLEGES AND UNIVERSITIES
Harold Raser

1086.   Atwood, Alvin Ray. "A Study of Personnel Services Available in Colleges of the Church of the Nazarene in the United States With Certain Recommendations for Improvement." Ph.D. dissertation. East Texas State University, 1970.

Examines student personnel services in Nazarene colleges in order to evaluate their effectiveness, and the degree of coordination of such services among the various colleges. Also compares these to similar services in other private and public colleges. Makes twenty recommendations for improving student services.

1087.   Cameron, James R. *Eastern Nazarene College: The First Fifty Years, 1900-1950*. Kansas City, MO: Nazarene Publishing House, 1968.

Chronicles the development of one of the colleges of the Church of the Nazarene (now located in Wollaston, MA) from its beginning as Pentecostal Collegiate Institute and Bible Training School (1901) to a fully-accredited liberal arts institution bulging with World War II G.I. enrollment. Devotes considerable attention to the evolution of educational policy in both the college and denomination and to the relationship between college and church.

1088.   Cole, Harper Leroy, Jr. "A Study of the Governance Style of A.B. Mackey, President of Trevecca Nazarene College, 1936-1963." Ed.D. thesis. Oklahoma State University, 1978.

Analyzes the "governance style" of a college president whose long-term of service (touching four different decades) significantly shaped the institution (Trevecca Nazarene College, Nashville, TN). Examines his relationship to administrative processes, educational programming, physical facilities, finances, faculty, students, other administrators, alumni, and the public. Finds that Mackey used a different "style" with different groups and recommends a governance model based upon these findings.

1089.   Knott, James Proctor. *History of Pasadena College*. Pasadena, CA: Pasadena College, 1960.

Narrates the story of this California college (now Point Loma

Nazarene College, San Diego) from its 1902 appearance as Pacific Bible College through various threats to its existence, to accreditation and steady growth by 1960. Includes numerous lists of faculty members and administrators over the years.

1090. Lewis, Richard Joseph. "An Environmental Assessment of Self-Concept Development at Trevecca Nazarene College." Ed.D. dissertation. Southern Baptist Theological Seminary, 1978.

Identifies elements in the environment of Trevecca Nazarene College which facilitate the integration of student self-concept. On the basis of a four year longitudinal study of freshmen entering in 1972, measures changes in self-concept development which appear to be due to the college environment.

1091. Ludwig, Sylvester Theodore. "The Rise, Development and Present Status of the Educational Institutions of the Church of the Nazarene in the United States." M.A. dissertation. University of Wichita, 1932.

Surveys at a quite early date in the history of the Church of the Nazarene the events which led to the founding of its colleges (seven at the time). Also describes the growth of an "educational consciousness" in the church and the educational facilities of the schools at the time. Seeks to "call attention of the church leaders to some of the outstanding needs confronting our educational institutions" and to "bring together information that may be used throughout the church for emphasizing the importance of maintaining adequate educational support."

1092. McClain, Carl S. *I Remember: My Fifty Seven Years at Olivet Nazarene College.* Kansas City, MO: Pedestal Press, 1983.

Describes the history of a midwestern Nazarene college (now Olivet Nazarene University, Kankakee, IL) from the very personal angle of one who was involved as student, teacher, and dean between 1915 and 1972.

1093. McConnel, Leona Bellew. "A History of the Town and College of Bethany, Oklahoma." M.A. thesis. University of Oklahoma, 1935.

Sketches the beginning of Bethany Nazarene College (now Southern Nazarene University, Bethany, OK) and the Nazarene congregation and town which grew up with it. Draws parallels between the community and other experiments in close town-church-school interrelationship such as that at Oberlin, OH in the nineteenth century.

1094. Meyering, Chester. "Values of Nazarene Seniors in Higher Educational Institutions." Ed.D. dissertation. University of Denver, 1966.

Investigates differences in values between seniors in Nazarene colleges and Nazarene-affiliated seniors in public colleges. The main finding is significantly higher scores on the Religious Value of the Allport-Vernon-Lindsey *Study of Values* instrument by seniors in Nazarene colleges. Concludes that this difference is largely, though not totally fostered by the "nature of the total campus experience" available in Nazarene colleges.

1095.   Munro, Bertha. *The Years Teach: Remembrances to Bless.* Kansas City, MO: Beacon Hill Press of Kansas City, 1970.

Observes Eastern Nazarene College, its development over five decades, its students and leaders from the perspective of one who served as academic dean for thirty-eight years.

1096.   Parrott, Roger Lee. "A Comparison of Faculty Member's Reported Professional Activities and the Workload Desires of College Presidents for Faculty Members in Five Liberal Arts Colleges of the Church of the Nazarene." Ph.D. dissertation. University of Maryland, 1979.

Applies a "faculty activity analysis" to time-use reports by faculty members at five colleges. The results are compared to questionnaires obtained from the colleges' presidents. The results indicate that faculty members spend more time on public service, administration, and committee work, and less on instruction and student services than desired by the presidents. Further, finds that prior to the study neither group was fully aware of the percentage of time faculty members gave to their various responsibilities. Recommends adjustments in faculty teaching loads and non-instructional responsibilities to achieve a better balance between them.

1097.   Perry, Ralph Edward. "A Study of the Objectives in Higher Education of the Six Liberal Arts Colleges of the Church of the Nazarene." Ph.D. dissertation. Bradley University, 1952.

Surveys the educational objectives, the means for achieving them, and the extent of their achievement in Nazarene colleges based upon analysis of official institutional statements and questionnaire data collected from faculty, administrators, students, alumni, and governing boards. Finds significant agreement on objectives among the various groups, among the various colleges, and between the colleges and the denomination. Concludes that results are mixed in actually achieving these objectives, however. Recommends development of systematic means for better evaluating and facilitating the achievements of educational objectives.

1098.   Ray, Roy Fremont. "The Church of the Nazarene and Its Colleges." Th.D. dissertation. Central Baptist Theological Seminary, 1958.

Attempts a comprehensive survey of the service rendered to the denomination by its colleges over its first fifty years of existence. Assuming the purpose of the colleges to be providing clerical and lay leadership for work in the church through training students in the "definite spiritual environment of the church," it concludes from questionnaire data that this purpose has been accomplished.

1099.   Rice, George. "The History of Eastern Nazarene College." B.D. thesis. Nazarene Theological Seminary, 1952.

Describes the first fifty-two years of a Nazarene college situated near Boston which serves the Northeastern U.S.

1100.   Robinson, Kenneth. "Educational Development in the Church of the Nazarene." B.D. thesis. Nazarene Theological Seminary, 1948.

Presents a brief historical sketch of eight Nazarene colleges (six in the U.S., one in Canada, and one in the British Isles) and Nazarene Theological Seminary, Kansas City, MO.

1101.   Slifer, Kenneth B. "Relative Importance of Selected Factors Influencing Choice of College Among College Freshmen Affiliated with The Church of the Nazarene." Ed.D. dissertation. Auburn University, 1973.

Examines the factors influencing the choice of colleges by students who are Nazarene. Finds family environment (as reflected in religious devotion, family ritual, and ideas about college) to be the most important factor. Makes recommendations for maximizing this through local church congregations and through student recruitment.

1102.   Spindle, Oran Randall. "An Analysis of Higher Education in the Church of the Nazarene 1945-1978." Ed.D. thesis. Oklahoma State University, 1981.

Charts the development of higher education in the Church of the Nazarene after World War II against the background of change in American higher education generally during the same period. Also provides a brief profile of Nazarene higher education prior to 1945. Analyzing a variety of data, concludes that Nazarene higher education has evidenced a "growing trend toward educational pluralism" in the post-World II period, growing out of upward social mobility, conflict between pietism and intellectualism, and professionalization of faculty at Nazarene schools. Contains twenty-three appendices on finances, enrollment, curriculum, etc.

1103.   Spittal, David James. "The Image of Olivet Nazarene College as Perceived by Selected Institutional Reference Groups." Ed.D. dissertation. Ball State University, 1975.

Examines and compares the perceived images of a Nazarene college as reported by groups of administrators, trustees, faculty, students, alumni, parents, and prospective students. Finds that the images communicated to various "publics" are quite distinct, vary considerably from group to group, and are often unrelated to the actual environment of the institution.

1104.   Stallings, R. Wayne. "Building Church Support For a Church Related College." D. Min. project. United Theological Seminary, 1982.

Sets forth a program developed around a theological rationale for Christian higher education to help the constituency of Mount Vernon Nazarene College (Mount Vernon, OH) become aware that the work of the college is essential to the overall mission of the church. Describes and evaluates the results of the program as it was implemented in local churches through college student outreach groups (i.e., student musical groups).

1105.   Wynkoop, Mildred Bangs. *The Trevecca Story*. Nashville, TN: Trevecca Press, 1976.

Tells a typical story of a college's growth from small beginnings as Pentecostal Literary and Bible Training School (1901) to a fully accredited liberal arts college of the Church of the Nazarene serving the Southeast region of the U.S. Offers some pointed observations on the leadership style of various administrators, administration-trustee relations, and debates within the school over the nature of "Christian higher education" during these years.

CHAPTER 12
EPISCOPAL COLLEGES AND UNIVERSITIES
Arthur Ben and Elizabeth N. Chitty
with Clark W. Dimond III

ACKNOWLEDGMENTS

The following individuals contributed material for this chapter: Alvin W. Skardon and Oliver B. Smalls, College of Charleston. Laura Frances Parrish, College of William and Mary. Paul R. Palmer, Columbia University. Minor Myers, Jr., Hobart College. Thomas B. Greenslade, Kenyon College. Diane McBride, Nashotah House. Jacqueline S. Painter, Norwich University. Christine L. Thomson, St. Mary's College, Raleigh. Ralph S. Emerick, Trinity College. Marchita J. Phifer, Voorhees College.

INTRODUCTION

As a national entity, the Episcopal Church has never started a college, though dioceses, parishes, bishops, and other clergy, and groups of Episcopalians have been responsible for founding or supporting 70 colleges considered to have had an Episcopal Church relationship. General Convention, the church's ruling body with its two parts, the House of Bishops and the House of Deputies, has officially authorized the beginning of only one educational institution, the General Theological Seminary in New York, established in 1822. National budget support authorized by General Convention for education at the college level has been restricted to overseas missionary enterprises and to historically black institutions, first through the American Church Institute and now direct to Saint Augustine's, Raleigh NC, Saint Paul's, Lawrenceville, VA, and Voorhees, Denmark, SC.

Colleges called "Episcopal Church related" by themselves or others have been founded in various ways. Here are some examples: by Anglicans, clergy and lay, before the Revolution (William and Mary, Columbia University), by a single diocese (Lehigh), by a group of dioceses (University of the South), by an Episcopal bishop (Kenyon, Hobart, Bard), by an Episcopal clergyman (Saint Paul's, Lawrenceville, Saint Augustine's, Raleigh), or combinations of these groups or persons. Some have "joined the Episcopal Church" (Voorhees, Shimer) after being established under other auspices, and others have "left the church" (Fort Valley, Saint Philip's, San Antonio) when governmental or other secular sponsorship seemed more likely to assure survival.

The General Convention in the 1890's established a "Church University Board of Regents," but these regents did not have any ruling power over the college. The Board was an effort to secure support for them. In 1919 the Christian Education Department of the national church had a division concerned with "Church College," but the main thrust of the national church in campus ministry became the establishment of denominational centers on campuses throughout the country. The Church Society of College Work was concerned with the work of this ministry more than with "church college." An informal relationship began in 1947 among four Episcopal colleges for mutual promotion and encouragement had evolved by 1962 into the Association of Episcopal Colleges, which now includes seven U.S. colleges and two overseas in Liberia and the Philippines.

SOURCES

Every Episcopal diocese must by canon publish every year a Journal of the Proceedings of its Diocesan Convention, and it is in these annual volumes that accounts of many Episcopal colleges, however transitory, may be found. For example, the 200-year-old Diocese of Connecticut would have published over 200 journals. The most complete files of diocesan journals are located in the Episcopal Church Archives, Austin, TX, and the library of the General Theological Seminary, New York City. The Journals of General Conventions might also from time to time contain references to Episcopal colleges, whose presidents are entitled to seat and voice (but no vote) in convention. Diocesan histories and biographies of Episcopalians involved in the colleges are other fruitful sources. In the Manuscript Cage of the Library of General Theological Seminary and in the Archives of the University of the South, Sewanee, TN, are folders with the bibliography and references on each college considered to have an Episcopal Church relationship.

Part I: Institutional Histories

Colleges now or formerly related to the Episcopal Church
(*Currently postsecondary and related to the Episcopal Church)

1106.   All Saints' College, Vicksburg, MS (1909)

         Junior college discontinued 1961; currently preparatory.

1107.   Turner, Mary Ellen.   Manuscript material, 1977.   All Saints' College.

1108.   Bard College (formerly Saint Stephen's), Annandale-on-Hudson, NY (1860)

         Associated with Columbia University 1928-1944.

1109.   Bell, Bernard Iddings. *Crisis in Education.* New York: Whittlesey House, 1949.

1110.   Fairbairn, Henry A. *The College Warden.* New York: Whittaker, 1899.

1111.   Hopson, George B. *Reminiscences of Saint Stephen's College.* New York: Gorham, 1910.

1112. Kline, Reamer. *Education for the Common Good: A History of Bard College -- the First 100 Years (1860-1960).* Annandale-on-Hudson, NY: Bard College, 1982.

1113. Bethany, Missionary College of the Sisters of, Topeka, KS (1861)

    Closed in 1928.

1114. Giles, F. W. *Thirty Years in Topeka: A Historical Sketch.* Topeka, KS: Geo. W. Crane & Co., 1886.

1115. King, James L., ed. and comp. *History of Shawnee County, Kansas, and Representative Citizens.* Chicago: Richmond and Arnold, 1905.

1116. McClintock, Helen Isis. "The Episcopal Female Seminary." In *Bulletin of the Shawnee County Historical Society* (December 1963): 60-63.

1117. Taylor, Blanche Mercer. *Plenteous Harvest. The Episcopal Church in Kansas 1837-1972.* Topeka, KS: Diocese of Kansas, 1973.

1118. Bristol College, Bristol, PA

    A "manual labor" college 1833-1837.

1119. Packard, Joseph. *Recollections of a Long Life.* Washington, D.C.: Byron S. Adams, 1902.

1120. Burlington College, Burlington, NJ (1846)

    Burlington Colleges trustees still operate two preparatory schools on college site.

1121. Schermerhorn, William E. *History of Burlington, New Jersey.* Burlington: Enterprise Publishing Co., 1927.

1122. Shaw, Helen Louise. *The First Hundred Years of St. Mary's Hall on the Delaware, 1837-1937.* Yardley, PA: Cook Printers, 1936.

1123. Charleston, College of, Charleston, SC

    Episcopalians influential in early years; now municipal institution.

1124. Chitty, Arthur Ben. "College of Charleston: Episcopal Claims Questioned, 1785--." *Historical Magazine of the Protestant Episcopal Church* 37 (December 1968): 413-16.

1125. Easterby, J. H. *A History of the College of Charleston.* Charleston, SC: College of Charleston, 1935.

1126. Eckelberry, R. H. *The History of the Municipal University in the United States.* Washington, D.C.: U.S. Government Printing Office, 1932.

1127.   Colorado School of Mines, Golden, CO

A part of Jarvis Hall, an Episcopal college, 1870-1874. Became a Territorial institution in 1874.

1128.   Breck, Allen duPont. *The Episcopal Church in Colorado. 1860-1963.* Denver: Big Mountain Press, 1963.

1129.   Hafen, Leroy R. *Colorado: The Story of a Western Commonwealth.* Denver: Arms Press, 1933.

1130.   Hoyt, Mary E. "Short History of the Colorado School of Mines." *Mines Magazine,* 1949.

1131.   Columbia University (King's College) New York, NY

Anglicans influential in founding; Episcopal influence continued until 1950s.

1132.   Amringe, J. H., et al. *A History of Columbia University, 1754-1904.* New York: Columbia University Press, 1904.

1133.   Coon, Horace. *Columbia: Colossus on the Hudson.* New York: E. P. Dutton, 1947.

1134.   Humphrey, David C. *From King's College to Columbia University, 1846-1900.* New York: Columbia University Press, 1976.

1135.   Keppel, Frederick Paul. *Columbia.* London: Oxford University Press, 1914.

1136.   Miner, Dwight C., ed. *A History of Columbia College on Morningside.* New York: Columbia University Press, 1954.

1137.   Patterson, Robert Leyburne. *The Secularization of Two Anglican Colleges in the U.S., Columbia and Trinity.* Evanston, IL: Institute for Christian Learning, 1958.

1138.   Robson, John William, ed. *A Guide to Columbia University with Some Account of Its History and Traditions.* New York: Columbia University Press, 1937.

1139.   Episcopal Academy of Connecticut, Cheshire, CT

1140.   Weaver, Glenn. "America's First 'Junior College': The Episcopal Academy of Connecticut." *Connecticut Historical Society Bulletin* 27 (January 1962): 11-21.

1141.   Fort Valley College, Ft. Valley, GA

Affiliated with American Church Institute for Negroes 1919-1939, then merged with state college system.

1142.   Malone, Henry Thompson. *The Episcopal Church in Georgia, 1733-1957.* Atlanta: The Protestant Episcopal Church in the

Diocese of Atlanta, 1960.

1143. Griswold College, Davenport, IA

Founded by the Diocese of Iowa

1144. Chitty, Arthur Ben. "Griswold College, 1859-1897, Davenport, Iowa." *Historical Magazine of the Protestant Episcopal Church* 37 (March 1968): 73-75.

1145. Phelan, Mary Kay. "Heritage of a Dream. History of Trinity Cathedral, Davenport, Iowa." Unpublished MS, Cathedral Archives.

1146. White, Greenough. *An Apostle of the Western Church. A Memoir of the Right Reverend Jackson Kemper.* New York: Thomas Whittaker, 1900.

1147. Henrico College, Henrico, VA

First college projected for colonies in North America

1148. Brewer, Clifton H. *A History of Religious Education in the Episcopal Church to 1835.* New Haven: Yale University Press, 1924.

1149. Burton, Lewis W. *Annals of Henrico Parish.* Josiah S. Moore, ed. Richmond, VA: Williams Printing Co., 1904.

1150. Lund, Robert H. "Henrico and Its Colleges." *William and Mary College Quarterly Historical Magazine* 18 (October 1938): 453-98.

1151. McCartney, Martha W. "The Ancient City of Henrico." Chesterfield, VA: Chesterfield County Office of News and Information Services, 1984.

1152. Hobart College, Geneva, NY*

Hobart College, an Episcopal institution, is coordinate with William Smith College, a non-sectarian woman's college.

1153. William Smith College, a non-sectarian woman's college.

1154. Brown, Alan W. "Education for Christian Freedom." *The College Tower* (May 1949). Geneva: Hobart and William Smith Colleges.

1155. Brown, Alan W. *Hobart College: Oldest Episcopal College in U.S.A.* New York: Newcomen Society in North America, 1956.

1156. *Centers of Light and Learning.* Geneva: Hobart and William Smith Colleges, [n.d.].

1157. Eddy, William A. "Hobart College and the Church." *Living Church*, March 23, 1938, pp. 364-66.

1158.   Hale, Benjamin. *The Gray Years*. Geneva: Hobart and William Smith Colleges, 1959.

1159.   Smith, Warren Hunting. *Hobart and William Smith: The History of Two Colleges*. Geneva, NY: Hobart and William Smith Colleges, 1972.

1160.   Turk, Milton Haight. *Hobart: The Story of a Hundred Years, 1822-1922*. Geneva, NY: Hobart College, 1922.

1161.   Jarvis Hall, Golden and Denver, CO (See Colorado School of Mines)

1162.   Jubilee College, Robin's Nest, IL

         Operated 1839-1862 by Episcopal Church

1163.   Althoff, Shirley. "Old English Faire." *St. Louis Globe-Democrat*, September 14, 1975, pp. 5-11.

1164.   Moss, Julia. "Diary, 1838-1896." Microfilm, Archives of the University of the South, Sewanee, TN.

1165.   Swartzbaugh, Constance H. *The Episcopal Church, Fulton County, IL 1835-1959*. Canton, IL: Episcopal Book Fund, [n.d.].

1166.   Kemper College, St. Louis, MO

         Operated by the Episcopal Church from 1837-1845.

1167.   Meyer, Janice R. "Kemper College: Forgotten Dream." *St. Louis County Journal*, December 16, 1978.

1168.   Rehkopf, Charles F. "Beginnings of the Episcopal Church in Missouri." *Historical Magazine of the Protestant Episcopal Church* 29 (March 1955): 49-65.

1169.   Rehkopf, Charles F. "The Episcopate of Bishop Hawks." *Bulletin of the Missouri Historical Society* (July 1957): 367-80.

1170.   Richardson, Jack. "Kemper College of Missouri." *Historical Magazine of the Protestant Episcopal Church* 30 (January 1961): 111-26.

1171.   Skardon, Alvin W. "William Augustus Muhlenberg: Pioneer Urban Church Leader." Ph.D. dissertation. Ohio State University, 1960.

1172.   Kenyon College, Gambier, OH (1824)

1173.   Bodine, William B. *The Kenyon Book*. Gambier, OH: Kenyon College, 1890.

1174.   Greenslade, Thomas Boardman. *Kenyon College -- Its Third Half-Century*. Gambier, OH: Kenyon College, 1975.

1175.   Smythe, George F. *History of the Diocese of Ohio until the Year 1918.* Cleveland, OH: Diocese of Ohio, 1931.

1176.   Smythe, George F. *Kenyon College -- Its First Century.* New Haven, Yale University Press, 1924.

1177.   Lambeth College, Kittanning, PA (1868)

           Operated 10 years. Charter still in force.

1178.   Beers, J. H. *Armstrong County, Pennsylvania, Her People, Past and Present.* 2 vols. Chicago: J. H. Beers & Co., 1914.

1179.   Wickersham, James Pyle. *A History of Education in Pennsylvania.* Lancaster, PA: Inquirer Pub. Co., 1886.

1180.   Lehigh University, Bethlehem, PA (1865)

           Established by the Diocese of Pennsylvania

1181.   Bowen, Catherine Drinker. "A History of Lehigh University." *Lehigh Alumni Bulletin,* 1924.

1182.   Miller, Jonathan W. *History of the Diocese of Central Pennsylvania (1871-1909) and the Diocese of Harrisburg (1904-1909),* Vol. II. Frackville, PA: (The author), 1909.

1183.   Nashotah House, Nashotah, WI

           College department ceased 1933.   Now an Episcopal theological school.

1184.   Blackburn, Imri. *Nashotah House: A History of Seventy-five Years.* [n.p.], 1960.

1185.   Cooper, Frank M. *An Annotated Calendar of Papers for the Study of the History of Nashotah House.* [n.p.], 1972.

1186.   Orth, William E. *Materials for the History of Nashotah House.* [n.p.], 1974.

1187.   Nebraska College, Nebraska City, NE

           Operated 1861-1885.

1188.   Barnds, William J. "The Episcopal Church in Nebraska since 1875." *Historical Magazine of the Protestant Episcopal Church* 33 (September 1964): 185-223.

1189.   Caldwell, Howard Walter. *Education in Nebraska.* Washington, D.C.: U.S. Bureau of Education, 1902.

1190.   Norwich University, Northfield, VT

           Episcopal connection approximately 1850-1875.

1191.   Ellis, William Arba. ed., *Norwich University, Her History, Her Graduates, Her Roll of Honor.* 3 vols. Montpelier, VT: The Capital City Press, 1911.

1192.   Goddard, Merritt Elton. *A History of Norwich, Vermont.* Hanover, NH: Dartmouth Press, 1905.

1193.   Guinn, Robert Darius. *The History of Norwich University, 1912-1965.* Vol. 4. Burlington, VT: George Little Press, [n.d.].

1194.   Harmon, Ernest Nason. *Norwich University, Its Founder and His Ideals.* New York: Newcomen Society in North America, 1951.

1195.   Juckett, J. Walter. *In Retrospect.* Burlington, VT: George Little Press, 1982.

1196.   Reeves, Ira Louis. *Military Education in the United States.* Burlington, VT: Free Press Printing Co., 1914.

1197.   White, Homer. *History of Norwich University.* Northfield, VT: C. N. Whitemarsh, Printer, 1891.

1198.   Okolona College, Okolona, MS

         Affiliated with the American Church Institute for Negroes 1921-1965.

1199.   Burger, Nash K., ed. *Inventory of the Church Archives of Mississippi -- Protestant Episcopal Church, Diocese of Mississippi.* Mississippi Historical Records Survey Project, Works Progress Administration, 1940.

1200.   Caution, Tollie L. "The Protestant Episcopal Church: Policies and Rationale upon which Support of Its Negro Colleges is Predicated." *Journal of Negro Education* 29 (Summer 1960): 274-83.

1201.   Philadelphia, College of (later University of Pennsylvania)

         Episcopal influence ended in 1791, following American Revolution.

1202.   Brewer, Clifton H. *History of Religious Education in the Episcopal Church to 1835.* New Haven: Yale University Press, 1924.

1203.   Bridenbaugh, Carl and Jessica Bridenbaugh. *Rebels and Gentlemen: Philadelphia in the Age of Franklin.* New York: Oxford University Press, 1962.

1204.   Cheney, Edward Potts. *A History of the University of Pennsylvania.* Philadelphia: University of Philadelphia Press, 1940.

1205.   Labares, Leonard, ed. *The Papers of Benjamin Franklin.* New Haven: Yale University Press, 1959-.

1206.   Meyerson, Martin, and Dilys Peglar Winegrad. *Gladly Learn and*

Gladly Teach: Franklin and His Heirs at the University of Pennsylvania, 1740-1976. Philadelphia, PA: University of Pennsylvania Press, 1978.

1207.   Racine College, Racine, WI

An Episcopal College from founding until it closed in 1933.

1208.   Chitty, Arthur Ben. "Racine College, Racine, Wisconsin, 1852-1933." *Historical Magazine of the Protestant Episcopal Church* 37 (June 1968): 135-38.

1209.   Croft, Sydney H. "A Hundred Years of Racine College and DeKoven Foundation." *Wisconsin Magazine of History* 35 (Summer 1952): 250-56.

1210.   DeKoven, James A. *Twenty-Five Years of the Work of Racine College. A sermon preached on Re-Union Day, June 26, 1877.* In DeKoven Foundation papers, Racine, WI.

1211.   Gailor, Thomas F. *Some Memories.* Kingsport, TN: Kingsport Press, 1938.

1212.   Welles, E. R., G. D. Gillespie, and W. E. McLaren. *A Great Church University for the West and Northwest.* 1876.

1213.   Saint Andrew's College, Jackson, MS

Operated just prior to Civil War

1214.   Burger, Nash K. "Battle Hill and Saint Andrew's College." *Journal of Mississippi History* 4 (April 1942): 84-89

1215.   Burger, Nash K. "William Mercer Green." *Historical Magazine of the Protestant Episcopal Church* 19 (December 1950): 340-54.

1216.   Mayes, Edward. *History of Education in Mississippi.* Washington, DC: U.S. Bureau of Education, 1899.

1217.   Saint Augustine, Missionary College of, Benicia, CA

Opened in 1867, closed in 1889.

1218.   Carroon, Robert G. "Frontier Churchman: James Lloyd Breck." *Living Church*, March 28, 1976.

Bancroft Library, University of California at Berkeley, has catalogues and other papers of the college.

1219.   Saint Augustine's College, Raleigh, NC*

Throughout its continuing career an Episcopal college.

1220.   Boykin, James H. "Saint Augustine's College, 1938-1958." Typescript, Saint Augustine's College, Raleigh, NC.

1221.   Brewer, H. Peers. "The Protestant Episcopal Freedman's Commission, 1865-1878." *Historical Magazine of the Protestant Episcopal Church* 26 (December 1957): 361-81.

1222.   Chitty, Arthur Ben. "Saint Augustine's College, Raleigh, North Carolina." *Historical Magazine of the Protestant Episcopal Church* 35 (September 1966): 207-20.

1223.   Chitty, Arthur Ben. "Saint Augustine's College: An Account of Its One Hundred Years of Service, Learning and Growth." *Faculty Research Journal, Saint Augustine's College*, February 1967, pp. 1-11.

1224.   Halliburton, Cecil D. *A History of Saint Augustine's College, 1867-1937.* Raleigh, NC: Saint Augustine's College, 1937.

1225.   Hayden, John Carlton. "After the War: The Mission and Growth of the Episcopal Church Among Blacks in the South, 1865-1877." *Historical Magazine of the Protestant Episcopal Church* 42 (December 1973): 403-27.

1226.   Saint James College, Fountain Rock, Hagerstown, MD

         College work from 1843 to 1864; now a preparatory school.

1227.   Harrison, Hall. "The College of Saint James (1843-1864)." In Berhard C. Steiner, *History of Education in Maryland*, pp. 258-60. (Washington, DC: 1894.)

1228.   McLachlan, James. *American Boarding Schools.* New York: Charles Scribner's Sons, 1970.

1229.   Skardon, Alvin W. "William Augustus Muhlenberg: Pioneer Urban Church Leader." Ph.D. dissertation. University of Chicago, 1960.

1230.   Saint John's College, Annapolis, MD (From King William's Academy)

         Anglican connection primarily with King William's Academy.

1231.   Tilghman, Tench Francis. *The Early History of Saint John's College in Annapolis, Maryland.* Annapolis: Saint John's College Press, 1984.

1232.   Saint John the Evangelist, College of, Denver and Greeley, CO

         Grew out of Jarvis Hall, Golden and Denver, operating between 1879 and 1937.

1233.   Breck, Allen duPont. *The Episcopal Church in Colorado, 1860-1963.* Denver: Big Mountain Press, 1963.

1234.   Saint Mary's College, Dallas, TX

By 1900 offered a four-year program leading to a B.A. degree.

1235.   Enstam, Elizabeth York. "Saint Mary's College: A Modern Education for Women." *Heritage News*, Dallas County Heritage Society, Fall 1986.

1236.   Moore, Gerald. *The Diocese of Dallas, 1895-1952.* Dallas: 1952.

1237.   Saint Mary's Junior College, Raleigh, NC*

Under Episcopal auspices from its beginning in 1842.

1238.   Salley, Katherine Bates, ed. *Life at Saint Mary's.* Chapel Hill: University of North Carolina Press, 1942.

1239.   Stoops, Martha. *The Heritage: The Education of Women at Saint Mary's College, 1842-1982.* Raleigh, NC: Saint Mary's College, 1984.

1240.   Saint Paul's College, College Point (Flushing), NY

Degrees awarded by Saint James College, MD.

1241.   Brewer, Clifton H. *A History of Religious Education in the Episcopal Church to 1835.* New Haven: Yale University Press, 1924.

1242.   Skardon, Alvin W. "William Augustus Muhlenberg: Pioneer Urban Church Leader." Ph.D. dissertation. University of Chicago, 1960.

1243.   Woolverton, John F. "Muhlenberg and Saint Paul's College." *Historical Magazine of the Protestant Episcopal Church* 29 (September 1960): 192-218.

1244.   Saint Paul's College, Lawrenceville, VA

Under Episcopal auspices from its beginning in 1888.

1245.   Chitty, Arthur Ben. "Saint Paul's College, Lawrenceville, Virginia. A Brief History." Lawrenceville, VA: Saint Paul's College, 1983.

1246.   Edmonds, Helen G. "A Movement in Negro Education for Fifty Years under the Influence of the Episcopal Church." M.A. thesis. Ohio State University, 1938.

1247.   Hayden, John Carlton. "Reading, Religion and Racism: The Mission of the Episcopal Church to Blacks in Virginia, 1865-1877." Ph.D. dissertation. Howard University, 1972.

1248.   Jones, Thomas Hardy E. "An Historical Study of the Curricular Development of Saint Paul's Polytechnic Institute, Lawrenceville, VA." M.A. thesis. Atlanta University, 1950.

1249.   Russell, James Solomon. *Adventure in Faith: An Autobiographical Study of Saint Paul Normal and Industrial School, Lawrenceville, VA.* New York: Morehouse Publishing Co., 1936.

1250.   Russell, Ulysses W. "James Solomon Russell -- Priest, Educator, and Humanitarian." M.A. thesis. Virginia State College, 1962.

1251.   Thurman, Frances Ashton. "The History of Saint Paul's College, Lawrenceville, Virginia, 1888-1959." Ph.D. dissertation. Howard University, 1978.

1252.   Saint Paul's College, Palmyra, MO

1253.   Mackey, Katherine Wainwright. "Story of Saint Paul's College." Unpublished, 1983. Archives, Diocese of Missouri, St. Louis.

1254.   Schuyler, Montgomery. *History of the Diocese of Missouri.* 1890.

1255.   Saint Paul's College, Texas (Anderson, Austin, Hempstead, Brenham)

         Between 1852 and 1870 the Diocese of Texas made several attempts to operate a college known as Saint Paul's, finally abandoning the effort.

1256.   Brown, Lawrence L. "Alexander Gregg." *Historical Magazine of the Protestant Episcopal Church* 28 (December 1959): 306-23.

1257.   Brown, Lawrence L. *The Episcopal Church in Texas, 1838-1874; from Its Foundation to the Division of the Diocese.* Austin, TX: Church Historical Society, 1963.

1258.   Murphy, DuBose. *A Short History of the Protestant Episcopal Church in Texas.* Dallas, TX: Turner Co., 1935.

1259.   Nall, Mabel D. "History of the Educational Activity of the Protestant Episcopal Church in the Diocese of Texas." M.A. thesis. University of Texas, 1935.

1260.   Saint Philip's College, San Antonio, TX

         Became a public junior college in 1942.

1261.   "Artemesia Bowden." In *Who's Who in Colored America.* Fleming-Burckel, 1950.

1262.   Chitty, Arthur Ben. *In Memoriam Edward Girard Bowden, 1881-1963, Tribute to a Family.* Raleigh, NC: Saint Augustine's College, [?1981].

1263.   Troup, C. V. "Artemesia Bowden." In *Distinguished Negro Georgians.* Royal Publishing Co., [n.d.].

1264.   Shelby College, Shelbyville, KY

Episcopal Theological Seminary in Kentucky operated under Shelby College charter today.

1265.   Swinford, Frances Keller, and Rebecca Smith Lee. *The Great Elm Tree, Heritage of the Episcopal Diocese of Lexington.* Lexington, KY: Faith House Press, 1969.

1266.   Shimer College, Mt. Carroll and Waukegan, IL

Episcopalian from 1959 to 1973. Previously associated with the University of Chicago.

1267.   Gatch, Milton McC. "Universities Societas Magistrorum Discipulorum Shimer College and Mediaeval Education." *Anglican Theological Review* 48 (April 1966): 3-14.

1268.   Goodspeed, Thomas W. *A History of the University of Chicago.* Chicago: University of Chicago Press, 1916.

1269.   Jencks, Christopher, and David Riesman. "Shimer College." *Phi Delta Kappan* 47 (April 1966): 415-20.

1270.   "Shimer Joins the Church." *Forth Magazine* 125 (February 1960): 20-22, 25-26.

1271.   South, University of the, Sewanee, TN

Operated by 28 dioceses in South and Southwest.

1272.   Armentrout, Donald S. *The Quest for the Informed Priest: A History of the School of Theology* [of the University of the South]. Sewanee, TN: University of the South, 1979.

1273.   Chitty, Arthur Ben. *Reconstruction at Sewanee: The Founding of the University of the South and its First Administration, 1857-1872.* Sewanee, TN: University Press, 1954.

1274.   Chitty, Arthur Ben. *Sewanee Sampler.* Sewanee, TN: The Historiographer, 1978.

1275.   Dudney, Rainsford Fairbanks Glass, Helen A. Petry, and Elizabeth N. Chitty, eds. *Centennial Report of the Registrar of the University of the South.* Sewanee, TN: University of the South, 1959.

1276.   Fairbanks, George Rainsford. *History of the University of the South.* Jacksonville, FL: H. and W. B. Drew, 1905.

1277.   Green, Ely. Edited by Arthur Ben and Elizabeth N. Chitty. *Men Who Made Sewanee.* Sewanee, TN: University Press, 1932 and 1981.

1278.   Petry, Helen A., Elizabeth N. Chitty, and Mary Crockett Hunt, eds. *Centennial Alumni Directory.* Sewanee, TN: Sewanee Alumni News (1954-1962).

1279.	Trinity College, Hartford, CT (began as Washington College)

Founded by the Episcopal Church, with which the Trinity College Chapel is still associated.

1280.	Episcopal Church, Diocese of Connecticut. *Journal of the Annual Convention... 1835... with Documents Relating to Washington College and the Church Scholarship Society.* Middletown, CT: Stark, 1835.

1281.	Lockwood, Theodore D. *Trinity College: 150 Years of Quality Education.* New York: Newcomen Society in North America, 1974.

1282.	Steiner, Bernard Christian. *The History of Education in Connecticut.* Washington, D.C.: Government Printing Office, 1893.

1283.	Weaver, Glenn. *The History of Trinity College.* Hartford, CT: Trinity College Press, 1967.

1284.	Voorhees College, Denmark, SC

Association with Episcopal Church began in 1924.

1285.	Blanton, Robert J. *Story of Voorhees College from 1897 to 1982.* Denmark, SC: Alumni Association, Voorhees College, 1983.

1286.	Coleman, J. F. B. *Tuskegee to Voorhees, the Booker T. Washington Idea Projected by Elizabeth Evelyn Wright.* Columbia, SC: 1922.

1287.	Jabs, Albert Emil. "Voorhees College." Ph.D. dissertation. University of South Carolina, 1982.

1288.	Mooris, J. Kenneth. *Elizabeth Evelyn Wright 1872-1906. Founder of Voorhees College.* Sewanee, TN: University of the South, 1983.

1289.	Voorhees, Oscar M. *Ralph and Elizabeth Rodman Voorhees, A Tribute.* New York: Tribute Press, 1927.

1290.	Washington College, Chestertown, MD

Founded by Episcopalians

1291.	Goodfellow, Guy F. "200 Years: An Address Commemorating the 200th Anniversary of the Convention of 1780, 8 November 1980, at Washington College." *Historical Magazine of the Protestant Episcopal Church* 57 (September 1982): 229-40.

1292.	Noble, T. A. Fraser. "William Smith and the Colonial Scottish Connection." *Historical Magazine of the Protestant Episcopal Church* 51 (September 1982): 241-50.

1293.	William and Mary, College of

Founded by Anglicans

1294.   Goodwin, Mary R. M. *The College of William and Mary.* Williamsburg, VA: The Colonial Williamsburg Foundation, 1967.

1295.   Goodwin, Mary R. M. *William and Mary College Historical Notes.* 3 vols. Williamsburg, VA: The Colonial Williamsburg Foundation, 1954.

1296.   Osborne, Ruby Orders. "The College of William and Mary in Virginia, 1800-1827." Ed.D. dissertation. College of William and Mary, 1981.

1297.   Randolph, J. W. *The History of the College of William and Mary.* Richmond, VA: J. W. Randolph, 1874.

1298.   Smith, Russell T. "Distinctive Traditions at the College of William and Mary and Their Influence on the Modernization of the College, 1865-1919." Ed.D. dissertation. College of William and Mary, 1980.

1299.   Tyler, Lyon G. *A Few Facts from the Records of William and Mary College.* New York: G. P. Putnam's Sons, 1890.

1300.   Tyler, Lyon G. *The College of William and Mary in Virginia: Its History and Work, 1693-1907.* Richmond, VA: Whittet and Shepperson, 1907.

1301.   *Vital Facts: A Chronology of the College of William and Mary.* Williamsburg, VA: College of William and Mary, 1976.

1302.   Voorhees, Oscar M. *The History of Phi Beta Kappa.* New York: Crown Publishers, 1945.

1303.   Worthington College, Worthington, OH

         For a short time under the influence of Bishop Philander Chase.

1304.   Baker, Wallace J. *Bishops of Ohio 1819-1968.* Painesville, OH: Diocese of Ohio, 1968.

1305.   Salomon, Richard G. "Saint John's Parish, Worthington and the Beginning of The Episcopal Church in Ohio." *Ohio Historical Quarterly* 64 (January 1955): 55-76.

1306.   York College, York, PA

         Given to the Diocese of Pennsylvania 1873, closed in 1880's. There is now a four-year college in York by the name of the early college.

Other Episcopal Colleges

In the Episcopal college collection at the General Theological Seminary, New York, and the Archives of the University of the South, Sewanee, TN, may be found short manuscript accounts of the Episcopal Church. These unpublished manuscripts were compiled by Arthur Ben Chitty, as follows: Andalusia College, Bucks County, PA; Buckner College, Witcherville, AR; Daniel Baker College, Brownwood, TX; DeVaux College, Niagara Falls, NY: Rose Gates College, Okolona, MS; Saint Mark's College, Grand Rapids, MI; Saint Timothy's College, Catonsville, MD.

In the same repositories are notes, including bibliographic references, on these colleges with a relationship to the Episcopal Church, collected by Arthur Ben Chitty: Bethesda College, Savannah, GA; Canterbury College, Danville, IN; Cosmopolitan University, Irvington-on-Hudson, NY: Fairmont College, Monteagle, TN; Floriday Diocesan College, Auburndale, FL; Florida Episcopal College, DeLand, FL; Hoffman St. Mary's College, Mason, TN; Keble College, Pass Christian, MS; Madison College, Madison County, TN; Margaret College, Versailles, KY; Nativity College, Bridgeport, CT; Ravenscroft College, Columbia, TN; Saint Helen's Hall, Portland, OR; St. John's College, Spartanburg, SC; Saint Paul's College, Fairfield, CT; Saint Paul's College, New Orleans, LA; Saint Thomas College, Tampa, FL; Saint James College, Shelbyville, KY: Tuller College, Tucson, AZ; Washington College, Tacoma, WA; and Wharton College, Austin, TX.

Part II: General Works

1307.   American Church Institute for Negroes. *Acknowledgement of an Honest Debt: Negro Education.* New York: National Council of the Protestant Episcopal Church, 1925.

          Covers industrial high school, divinity school, junior college, training school for nurses, summer schools, and farmers' conferences operated by the Episcopal church.

1308.   Association of Episcopal Colleges, Inc. "Constitution and Bylaws. Revised 1972." "Certificate of Incorporation." 1962. Mimeographed. New York: The Association of Episcopal College, Episcopal Church Center, New York, NY.

          Begun as the Episcopal Church College Foundation in 1961, the names was changed to the Foundation for Episcopal Colleges in 1962, the Fund for Episcopal College, Inc., in 1965, and the Association of Episcopal College, Inc., its present designation, in 1965.

1309.   Booz, Allen and Hamilton Management Consultants. "A Study of the Association of Episcopal Colleges, Phase I. Summary of Existing College-Church Relationships and Considerations for Future College-Church Relationships." Mimeographed. Association of Episcopal Colleges, Episcopal Church Center, New York, NY, 1969.

Compares the status of nine relatively small, residential, liberal arts, autonomous institutions in regard to academic standards, financial status, location and type of student body. Diversity characterizes these factors. Thus church relationship varies greatly in strength and influence among them, and is primarily traditional and historical for most of the better endowed institutions.

1310.   Brewer, Clifton H. *A History of Religious Education in the Episcopal Church to 1835.* New Haven, CT: Yale University Press, 1924.

Describes exact relationship of colleges to the Anglican and Episcopal Churches in colonial and later periods.

1311.   Brewer, H. Peers. *The Protestant Episcopal Freedman's Commission, 1865-1878.*

Saint Augustine's College was founded in this period.

1312.   Brewton, John E. *A Survey of Educational Institutions Sponsored by the American Church Institute for Negroes.* Nashville, TN: George Peabody College for Teachers, 1946.

The A.C.I. sponsored schools and colleges for blacks in several Southern states.

1313.   Carter, John Paul. "Episcopal Schools." In *Religious Schools in America*, pp. 135-42. Edited by Thomas C. Hunt, James C. Carper, and Charles R. Kniker. New York and London: Garland Publishing Co., 1986.

Bibliographical references include the early history of the Anglican Church in education, at the college level as well as in schools. Particularly useful for notes on places where Episcopal source material may be found.

1314.   Caution, Tollie L. "The Protestant Episcopal Church Policies and Rationale Upon Which Support of Its Negro Colleges is Based." *The Journal of Negro Education* 29 (Summer 1960): 274-83.

Relates the role of the American Church Institute with which Dr. Caution was associated for many years.

1315.   Chitty, Arthur Ben. *The Episcopal Church in Education.* Cincinnati, OH: Forward Movement Publication, 1976.

Gives a brief history of Episcopal efforts in education and includes a list of 70 colleges -- opened, unopened, living and dead -- since 1620. A bi-centennial publication.

1316.   Cross, Wilford A. "The Church College." *Living Church*, March

9, 1952.

Divides colleges into three categories: 1) those strictly under the Episcopal Church; 2) those affiliated with the church; and 3) those making no pretension to a church connection. "At what precise point the line of demarcation should be drawn is, of course, a question on which good men are bound to differ."

1317.   DeMille, George E. "The Church Founds Colleges." *Living Church*, November 5, 1967, pp. 12-13.

Gives an overview of the thrust of Anglicans and later Episcopalians in higher education in U.S.A.

1318.   *Episcopal Church Annual: 1987.* Wilton, CT: Morehouse-Barlow Co., 1987.

Yearly publication provides listings of "church colleges and universities," with data about each, as well as listings of parishes, dioceses and church officials. This publication is successor to the Living Church Annual, Whittaker's Churchman's Almanac, and other church directories.

1319.   *Episcopal Clerical Directory.*   New York: Church Hymnal Corporation, 1987.

Published every two years, this directory and its predecessors, Stowe's Clerical Directory and Lloyd's Clerical Directory (1898-1913) contain biographies of all ordained persons in the Episcopal Church. These are principal sources for founders, professors and presidents of Episcopal colleges, especially those of more than 50 years ago.

1320.   Fisher, Sydney George. *Church Colleges: Their History, Position and Importance, with Some Account of the Church Schools.* Philadelphia: Printed by George Buchanan and Co., 1895.

Surveys colleges then existing and reports on the Church University Board of Regents, created in 1889 by General convention to promote education under the auspices of the church and to receive and distribute benefactions that may be entrusted to it. The board was to do what the Board of Missions had done for that work, "to localize and concentrate and intensify interest in" Episcopal colleges. The regents did not control any colleges but had a scholarship distribution program for them. [The board was discontinued in 1898.]

1321.   Gailor, Thomas F. *The Christian Church and Education.* [Bedell Lectures, Kenyon College, 1909.] New York: Thomas Whittaker, Inc., 1910.

Cites four characteristics of the Episcopal Church as marks

of its special fitness for educational work: freedom, historicity, sacramental view of nature, and its Prayer Book service. This graduate, chaplain, professor, vice-chancellor [president] and chancellor of Episcopal colleges explores the *laissez faire* policy of the church in regard to its institutions of higher learning.

1322. Godbold, Albea. *The Church College of the Old South.* Durham, NC: Duke University Press, 1944.

Episcopalians historically believed in education but lacked sufficient membership and wealth to support church colleges successfully.

1323. Hines, John E. *Episcopal Colleges: A Case for Church Relationship in Education.* New York: The Newcomen Society in North America, 1968.

Gives a two-fold justification for Episcopal Church-sponsored education: an openness to Truth and demonstratable concern for students as persons, a concern stemming from a basic religious commitment which both undergirds and pervades the institution and its practices. He was Presiding Bishop at the time of the address.

1324. Holland, Albert E. "A New Venture in Educational Cooperation." *Living Church,* November 5, 1967.

Traces the founding and growth of the Association of Episcopal Colleges.

1325. *Journal of the Proceedings of the Bishops, Clergy and Laity of the Protestant Episcopal Church in the United States of America, 1892, 1895, 1898.* Printed for the Convention, 1893, 1896, 1899.

Contains the three reports of the Church University Board of Regents which was dissolved in 1898. While the board had been urged to commit itself to the "founding of a central university under the auspices of the ecclesiastical authorities, or at least, officially allied to its specific worship and doctrine," lack of finances prevented. It was succeeded by a voluntary "Association for Promoting the Interests of Church Schools, Colleges and Seminaries."

1326. Klein, Walter C., Chairman. "Final Report to the Presiding Bishop, and Board of Directors of the American Church Institute, Regarding the American Church Institute and Its Relationship with Its Affiliated Colleges." May, 1967. Mimeographed. Archives, Historical Collections of the Episcopal Church, Austin, TX.

The American Church Institute, the channel through which the church assisted its predominantly black institutions was discontinued and aid given directly to its colleges.

1327.   Kline, Reamer. "Church-Related Colleges." In *The Episcopal Church and Education*, pp. 102-17. Edited by Kendig B. Cully. New York: Morehouse-Barlow Co., 1966.

Surveys all aspects of Episcopal Church interest in education from Sunday Schools to theological education. Concludes that Episcopal church-related colleges seem to be in a favorable position by virtue of their considerable experience in resting the religious case upon unostentatious, sincere, personal example, upon freedom of choice, and upon both the visible and the intangible manifestations of 'the beauty of holiness.'

1328.   Lindsay, John V. "Education: Diversity, Freedom, Excellence." *Living Church*, November 5, 1967, pp. 2-3.

Discusses private vs. public and religious vs. secular systems.

1329.   McGrady, Edward. "Biology." In *Religious Perspectives in College Teaching*. Edited by Hoxie N. Fairchild. New York: Ronald Press, Co., 1952.

This professor and president of an Episcopal college speaks in favor of a church college having "religion woven into the entire fabric of education instead of isolated in little fragements delivered to a relatively small clientele" as in secular colleges.

1330.   McGrath, Earl J. *The Predominantly Negro Colleges and Universities in Transition.* New York: For the Institute of Higher Education, by the Bureau of Publications for Teachers College, Columbia University, 1965.

Includes Okolona, St. Augustines's, St. Paul's, and Voorhees in its general survey of admissions, students' costs, curriculum, facilities, etc. Lack of an index makes it difficult to relate his findings to specific colleges.

1331.   Micou, Paul. *The Church at Work in College and University.* Milwaukee, Wi: Morehouse, 1919.

Published for the National Student Council of the Episcopal Church and devoted mainly to student work on secular and other campuses, with a chapter devoted to "Church colleges." Micou defined an Episcopal college "as an educational institution giving the standard work for a bachelor's degree, which maintains the worship of the Protestant Episcopal Church and in which the Church through Bishops ex officio, or through other trustees, has an effective voice in the control of the academic and temporal affairs of the college." His 1919 definition of church relationship with its emphasis on control is less applicable in 1987.

1332.   Micou, Paul. *The Church's Inquiry into Student Religious Life.* In collaboration with LeRoy S. Burroughs [and others]. New York:

National Council, Protestant Episcopal Church, Department of Religious Education, 1923.

1333.   Morehouse, Clifford P. "The Colleges of the Church." *Living Church*, November 5, 1967, pp. 6, 14.

Identifies qualities of Episcopal colleges: openness to new truth, tradition of excellence, high regard for educated clergy and laity. An Episcopal college seeks sound learning in an atmosphere of faith in God, rather than ecclesiastical authority, and an almost limitless capability of mental and spiritual maturity. The church does not dictate curriculum or limit pursuit of knowledge. An episcopal college does not inhibit free inquiry or stultify intellectual curiosity, place religion and science in opposition, substitute authority for freedom or impose religious or social conformity.

1334.   O'Connor, Brian R., Jr. "A Descriptive Survey of Colleges in the United States belonging to the Association of Episcopal College." Ph.D. dissertation. University of Denver, 1969.

Surveys the current operating procedures and standards, especially in the academic, financial and administrative areas, of the nine institutions in the U.S.A. which in 1969 were members of the Association of Episcopal colleges. Defines an Episcopal College as one that states in its catalogue or some other official publication that it is in some manner affiliated with the Episcopal Church, and that the Episcopal Church, in its Annual, or some other official publication, acknowledges its support of the college.

1335.   Parsonage, Robert Rue, ed. *Church-Related Higher Education, Perceptions and Perspectives.* Valley Forge, PA: Judson Press, 1978.

Includes a statement on 20 papers produced by a Colloquium on educational curriculum sponsored by the Associations of Episcopal Colleges and Episcopal Schools in 1974. Colloquium 20-20, according to John Paul Carter's "White Paper," sought to develop a new epistemological base which would make possible the development of a human-centered education which would be, at the same time, transcultural, multilingual, ecumenical, and global -- and necessary for survival in the 21st century.

1336.   Patillo, Manning M., and Donald M. MacKenzie. *Church-Sponsored Higher Education in the United States.* Report of the Danforth Commission. Washington, D.C.: American Council on Education, 1966.

States factors which enter into institutional relationships with religious bodies, no two of which are exactly the same, including institutional history, church policy, financial considerations, the influence of strong personalities, and other factors. The book assesses the relationship at that time of specific

Episcopal colleges in Institutions may be church-related through a board of control nominated or elected by a Church-body; or through ownership or financial support by a religious body; or through acceptance by the institution of denominational standards or use of denominational name; or through an institutional statement of purpose linked to a particular denomination or reflecting religious orientation; or by having Church membership a factor in selection of faculty and administrative personnel.

1337.   Potter, Eliphalet Nott [advocate and general secretary]. *Church University Board of Regents. Opinions of Educators and Others.* With Material Collected by the Advocate-Regent. Geneva, NY: Press of W. H. Humphrey, 1892.

Lists colleges at that time and formerly connected with the Episcopal Church. Contains statements by Endicott Peabody of Groton and others, urging the establishment of an Episcopal Church University.

1338.   Schock, Amy. "The Episcopal Colleges: A Vital Part of the Church's Ministry." *Living Church*, April 18, 1982, pp. 8-9.

The Episcopal colleges remain dedicated to value-centered education, for the particular gift of Anglicanism is to encourage intellectual freedom while nurturing Christain faith.

1339.   Snavely, Guy E. *The Church and the Four-Year College, An Appraisal of Their Relations.* New York: Harper and Brothers, 1955.

Gives brief notice of several Episcopal colleges, under "other church colleges," but main attention given to other denominations.

1340.   Tewksbury, Donald G. *The Founding of American Colleges and Universities before the Civil War, with Particular Reference to the Religious Influences Bearing Upon the College Movement.* New York: Teachers College, Columbia University, 1932; reprinted by Archon Books, 1955.

Names 11 Episcopal colleges. By a one-time president of Bard College and dean at Columbia University.

1341.   Tiffany, Charles C. *A History of the Protestant Episcopal Church in the United States of America.* New York: Charles Scribner's Sons, 1916.

Lists 9 Episcopal colleges and 15 seminaries, discussing the status of church-relationship to each as of 1895.

1342.   Woolverton, John F. *Colonial Anglicanism in North America.* Detroit, MI: Wayne State University Press, 1984.

Considers the College of Philadelphia, King's College

[Columbia], and the College of William and Mary to have been Episcopal colleges, and describes their relationship to the Church of England in the colonies prior to the American Revolution.

1343. Yanagahira, Hikaru. "Some Educational Attitudes of the Protestant Episcopal Church in America: A Historical Study of the Attitudes of the Church and Churchmen Toward the Founding and Maintaining of Colleges and Schools Under Their Influence Before 1900." Ph.D. disseration. Columbia University, 1958. Ann Arbor, MI: University Microfilms, 1958.

Concludes that the traditional pattern of decentralization in the Episcopal Church in part led to the breaking away of many Episcopal colleges from the church, and that the desire for freedom from even implied control of the church overrode the need for financial support from the church, even though the church rarely placed itself in the role of controlling the college.

CHAPTER 13
FOURSQUARE GOSPEL CHURCH COLLEGES AND UNIVERSITIES
John C. Holmes

1344.   Brown, Daniel Alan. "A Comparative Analysis of Bible College Quality." Ph.D. dissertation. University of California at Los Angeles, 1982.

Argues that Bible colleges attract more conservative students than do other colleges. Claims that Bible college students are more satisfied with their colleges because of a sense of warmth and community. Bible college students are similar in beliefs, are willing to travel far to attend, are older than 18 as freshmen (84%), and are more likely to be married than students in the liberal arts college. Bible colleges surveyed had few minority students (less than five percent). The students choose a Bible College because of a special program offered or the influence of an attendee. In spite of low selectivity level, the author contends that Bible colleges have a representative cross section of academic abilities. Asserts that Bible colleges are weak in teaching English communication skills. As professional schools, they offer little or no science, mathematics and fine arts. They do provide for a specific need, however, in the evangelical community.

1345.   Mosher, Craig E. "Free Methodist Educational Institutions as Perceived by Selected Constituents." Ph.D. dissertation. Southern Illinois University-Carbondale, 1983.

Analyzes perceptions of readers of Free Methodist periodicals. Finds a low level of knowledge about the colleges. Argues that those who had an adequate knowledge had a favorable image and valued the academic reputation of the schools. Points out that respondents were supportive of Christian environment in spite of the costs.

1346.   Newby, John M. "Perceptions of Graduates Regarding Selected Aspects of Spring Arbor College Program with Implications for Teacher Education." Ph.D. dissertation. Michigan State University, 1972.

Finds that graduates were relatively satisfied with academic preparation. Asserts that the faculty was very influential in choice of major (73% of the students decided on major after enrolling) and students' understanding of Christian perspective. Claims that the teacher education program was considered average and that respondent graduates had a high interest in the college.

1347.   Smith, Roderick J. "An Analysis of the Transition from the Junior College Program to that of a Four-year Liberal Arts Institution at Spring Arbor College." Ed.D. dissertation. Michigan State University, 1961.

Analyzes the needed ingredients for a junior college to become a four-year college. Cites how the "problem identifiers" were ascertained and then the actual problems are listed. Recommends master plan, use of problem identifiers, modernized techniques of teaching and long-range help for the faculty.

1348.   Stevens, W. Richard. "The Church and Colleges Face the Future." *Light and Life*, April 24, 1979, pp. 6-8.

Reviews the history of the Free Methodist Church, its commitment to Christian colleges quoting three early bishops: B. T. Roberts, Wilson T. Hogue and Leslie R. Marston. Notes the need for a dynamic balance between the personal and social aspects of the Christian gospel and how this balance is maintained in the Free Methodist college. Calls for 1) a commitment to trust between the denominational constituency and the colleges; 2) high quality academics; 3) program that prepare laity for effective churchmanship; 4) active college recruitment of denominational young people; 5) scholarships for Free Methodist students; and 6) churches should utilize the resources and expertise of the colleges.

CHAPTER 15
FRIENDS, RELIGIOUS SOCIETY OF COLLEGES
Clayton Farraday

1349.   Ahmad, Nesar, ed. *Common Vision* 1986 *Longitude 360*.
Huntington, NY: Friends World College, 1986.

Offers views on major strategies for social change evolving in
Asia, Africa and Europe. This is the first issue of *Common Vision*,
an annual academic journal which will exemplify the Friends World
College educational philosophy by examining from varied
perspectives global issues which both underlie important current
events and are likely to effect the human condition decisively over
the long term future.

1350.   Bickley, William Phillips. "Education as Reformation: An
examination of Orthodox Quakers' Formation of the Haverford
School Association and Founding of Haverford School, 1815-1840."
Ed.D. dissertation. Graduate School of Education, Harvard
University, 1983.

Discusses the founding of the Haverford School (Haverford
College). Orthodox Quakers were responding to what they viewed
as the dissolution of their religious community. It was their attempt
to use an educational institution to reform their community. The
School is examined as a response to conflict, schism, and
disintegration of the American Quaker community.

1351.   Brinton, Howard H. *Quaker Education in Theory and Practice.*
Wallingford, PA: Pendle Hill Publications, Pamphlet #9, 1969.

Discusses how the clear-cut philosophy of education planned
by the Society of Friends was based solidly on its religious faith and
practice. This book attempts to show that these principles grow out
of a special type of community which has a pattern of living
somewhat differently from that of the world around it. This pattern
seeks to propagate in the world the divine-human and inter-human
relationships developed within itself.

1352.   Cooper, Charles W. *Whittier Independent College in California.*
Los Angeles, CA: The Ward Richie Press, 1967.

Tells the story of a Quaker college founded to give an air of
decency to real estate development in southern California growing

from a symbol for the community into an excellent liberal arts college. The college no longer "stands for" truth and learning: it now is able to make them available. All became possible through the tenacious dreaming of the founding fathers backed up by the generous benefactions of today's fostering fathers.

1353.   Cooper, Wilmer. *The ESR Story - A Quaker Dream Come True*. Richmond, IN: Earlham School of Religion, 1985.

Contains an interpretive history of The Earlham School of Religion from its inception in 1960. It is an "inside story" written by a man who has been on the school's faculty for its entire existence and who served as its first dean. Especially important in the book is the presentation of the concerns for American Quakerism that gave rise to the only accredited Quaker Seminary in the United States. Chapters include "The Need and Vision for a Quaker Seminary," "The School in its Maturing Years," and "A Glimpse into the Life of ESR." The appendices offer a thorough outline of the care taken to insure that a Friends Graduate School of the Ministry possessed features distinctive in theological education which were also in keeping with the character of Quakerism.

1354.   Earlham College, "Program of Community Dynamics" Reports 1958-1960. Richmond, IN: Earlham College Bulletin, Fall, 1958.

Contains three related accounts of the Program of Community Dynamics: "Training of Community Educators," "the Community Dynamics Experiment," and "Historical Summary of Projects." From 1947 to 1960 Earlham has pioneered in projects giving persistent concern to the community town and gown problems, recreation, alleviating of racial tensions locally and to achievement of greater social justice. Graduates and undergraduates joined in negotiating with mature adults, planned and worked with them and participated in evaluation of results in each project.

1355.   Elliott, Charles J. *Whittier College, the First Century on a Poet Campus: a Pictorial Remembrance*. Redondo Beach, CA: Legends Press, 1986.

Contains the exciting story of the founding and growth of one of southern California's most prominent independent liberal arts colleges. Herein is the tale of how a college and a town survived though most other towns' colleges of the area founded during the 1880 boom disappeared quickly. Settlers came to the Quaker community for peace and citrus growing and insisted upon the blessings of higher education for their children and grandchildren.

1356.   Gilbert, Dorothy Lloyd. *Guilford A Quaker College*. Greensboro, NC: Guilford College, 1937.

Relates the story of a liberal arts college founded as New Garden Boarding School for Quaker boys and girls, the first school for coeducation in North Carolina. This is an intricate account of the life and development of the institution and emphasizing the place and influence of many men and women by name who were actively associated with the college. Herein is the strong leadership of the presidents of Guilford, particularly Lewis Lyndon Hobbs.

1357.   Gillespie, Maralyn Orbison. *Swarthmore Remembered.* Swarthmore, PA: Swarthmore College, 1964.

Contains a casual and informal account of what thirty-nine alumni (spanning sixty years of Swarthmore history) say stands out in memory about their college experiences. What strikes the reader most aside from deep affection is the continuity of certain themes: dedication to academic excellence, influence of the Quaker traditions, freedom of inquiry, respect for the individual, close relations between students and faculty.

1358.   Hole, Helen G. *Things Civil and Useful, A Personal View of Quaker Education.* Richmond, IN: Friends United Press, 1978.

Contains essays that demonstrate that Quaker schools and colleges can no longer even pretend to be principally of service to Quaker families. The schools and colleges have, therefore, an extraordinary challenge which they are meeting in diverse ways and degrees. Their staffs and students constitute the largest bodies of non-Friends gathered daily under Quaker influence anywhere in the world.

1359.   Jones, Elizabeth, ed. *Joys and Risks in Teaching Young Children.* Pasadena, CA: Pacific Oaks College, 1978.

Provides for teachers as learners in nursery/kindergarten/primary programs at Pacific Oaks, with emphasis on clarifying goals of the open classroom and dealing with built-in risks. Included is the emergent curriculum, dealing with feelings, the teacher's role as authority, developing social consciousness, children's use of bad language, the invisible child and a follow-up study.

1360.   Jones, Rufus M. *Haverford College. A History and an Interpretation.* New York, NY: The Macmillan Co., 1933.

Describes the development of the Quaker College with particular emphasis on many people who have been a part of the institution through the years: the founders, many interesting faculty and administrators and alumni. Chapters on cricket, intercollegiate sports, growth of science, drama and music in the curriculum, and the World War I period pressures give particular insight to the college.

1361. Jones, Rufus M. *Rethinking Quaker Principles*. Wallingford, PA: Pendle Hill Pamphlet #8, 1940.

Contains the story of the origin of the Society of Friends in the midst of the philosophical and theological upheavals in the early and mid 17th century in England. As the Society develops Rufus Jones explains the pitfalls and the urge to maintain its basic traits: sincerity, simplicity, spiritual nurture, and sacredness of human life. Quaker philosophy of life is a vivid experience, an experiment with patience and endurance to exhibit a way of life which implements this high estimate of man's divine possibilities.

1362. Kelly, Robert L. *Eight Friends Colleges: Earlham College, Friends University, Guilford College, Pacific College, Penn College, Whittier College, Wilmington College, with Sidelights from Other Institutions*. New York, NY: Association of American Colleges, Council of Church Boards of Education, 1933.

Contains information from a study to determine values and characteristics which may be unique to Friends Colleges.

1363. Kenworthy, Leonard S. *Quakerism--A Study Guide on the Religious Society of Friends*. Dublin, IN: Prinit Press, 1981.

Presents a textbook approach to studying about Quakers. History, philosophy, practices and procedures are explained. There are test questions at the end of each chapter.

1364. *Longitude 360 Degrees. Friends World College 1965-1985*. Huntington, NY: Friends World College, 1985.

Relates the highlights of the first two decades of a college that was unquestionably an experiment. The college was founded to respond to the challenges confronting education in the 1960's, namely to equip young people for a world terribly divided and totally interdependent. Study programs are initiated at the Long Island base and spread to 75 countries throughout the world.

1365. Mather, Eleanor Price. *Pendle Hill: A Quaker Experiment in Education and Community*. Wallingford, PA: Pendle Hill, 1980.

Tells the story of the Quaker Center's first fifty years, of its aims and policies, of the problems which beset such an enterprise, and the people who have passed through its portals and by their services made Pendle Hill possible. It is an experiment in adult education. No category in American education fits it precisely. It has been called an ashram, a Quaker monastery, and a school for prophets.

1366. McVickar, Polly. "Imagination: Key to Human Potential." Pasadena, CA: Pacific Oaks College, 1982.

Explores ways to encourage and su;, ort the thrust of imagination and creative exploration in the arts - in young children, and their teachers and parents from a Pacific Oaks/NAEYC conference.

1367.   Meigs, Cornelia. *What Makes a College? A History of Bryn Mawr College.* New York, NY: The Macmillan Company, 1956.

Contains an insider's history of Bryn Mawr College. Between 1932 and 1950, Cornelia Meigs, AB '08, was on the English Department faculty, until 1973 Professor Emeritus and College Historian. Meigs wrote eloquently about the Founder, Trustees, Directors, Administrators, Faculty and Alumnae -- many of whom she knew -- recording the College's growth during each new presidency. What made Bryn Mawr? A Quaker origin, graduate education, self government, and academic freedom.

1368.   Murphy, Carol R. "The Roots of Pendle Hill." Wallingford, PA: Pendle Hill Pamphlet #223, 1979.

Relates the founding of Pendle Hill and the planning for the unusual program for study based on the four aspects of Henry Hodgkin, the first director: "A Haven of Rest, A School of the Prophets, A Laboratory of Ideas, A Fellowship round Christ." Woodbrooke in England and the Woolman School in suburban Philadelphia are the forerunners. Pendle Hill has continued to fulfill the vision that it do something different from what other Friends colleges are doing and what is being done in existing graduate schools.

1369.   Osborne, Byron L. *The Malone Story. The Dream of Two Quaker Young People.* Newton, KS: United Printing Inc., 1970.

Contains the story of the development of a strongly Christian liberal arts college which had its beginnings as the Friends Bible Institute and Training School. The college aims to help students to be efficient workers in their line of Christian service to which God has called them and to pull together in Christian context their college experiences. Leaders of the College have felt and demonstrated their belief in the power of God to direct them and their work in the founding, the funding, the building of a faculty and the development of curriculum. "Expect great things from God; attempt great things for God."

1370.   Pickard, Gene. "An Evaluation and Revision of the Mission Program at Friends Bible College." D.Miss. dissertation. Trinity Evangelical Seminary, Deerfield, IL, 1986.

1371.   Read, James M. "The Making of Sensible Men." New York, NY: The Newcomb Society in North America, 1967.

Relates the speech by Dr. Read, President of Wilmington

College, telling about the approaches to its students and dedication of its faculty and administration. Making students capable and sensible is the essence of a liberal arts education.

1372.   Reeve, Juliet. *Friends University, the Growth of an Idea.* Wichita, KS: Wichita Eagle Press, 1948.

Presents the character of the founders and supporters of the college which became the character of the institution: sincerity, devotion, Christian love, service on the campus and wherever the graduates settle characterize the school. It is the story of a grass roots territory and a grass roots college.

1373.   Simpson, Catherine R. "Women at Bryn Mawr." In *Women on Campus: the Unfinished Liberation*, pp. 174-94. New York: Change Magazine, 1975.

Tells the frustrations, concerns, ideas, enjoyment of women in a woman's college.

1374.   Souders, Floyd and Norman Souders. *Friends University 1898-1973.* Wichita, KS: Friends University, 1974.

Contains a history of the growth and development of the University from its beginning in the fields of Kansas under the care of the Kansas Yearly Meeting. There is a liberal arts program presented under the influence of the Quaker Church providing instruction, research, community services, and related activities continuing to create a Christian atmosphere in a time of radically changing values.

1375.   Swarthmore College Faculty. *An Adventure in Education: Swarthmore College under Frank Aydelotte.* New York, NY: The Macmillan Co., 1941.

Contains the record of an experiment in higher education. The ideas underlying it are making their way and producing similar enterprises in scores of other institutions of higher education. The plan arousing the most interest is the system of honors instruction. Students meet with the professor in a seminar period once or twice a week for discussions and reading papers during the junior and senior years. Final examinations are given by outside professors at the end of the senior year.

1376.   Thornburg, Opal. *Earlham: The Story of the College, 1847-1962.* Richmond, IN: Earlham College Press, 1963.

Develops the life of the college as an educational institution with a devotion to academic excellence, and a concern for spiritual values and high social concern. Its faults and failures are honestly recorded as its works to uphold the ideal of a Christian college making a joint witness for vigorous scientific scholarship and open seeking for a spiritual center to life.

1377. "Two-and-a-Half Centuries of Quaker Education." *The Friend* (Phila.), Vol. 113 (1939), No. 9, pp. 153-60; No. 10, pp. 171-75.

Presents a series of five lectures on Quaker education. The first three by Henry Cadbury, Wilmot Jones, and William Comfort emphasize the historical background, the problems of today, and the future of Quaker education.

1378. Walton, Richard J. *Swarthmore College, An Informal History.* Swarthmore, PA: Swarthmore College, 1986.

Summarizes the conclusions of previous scholars and expands their research on understanding present day Swarthmore: how it grew from a parochial Quaker college to an institution looked to by many for leadership in demonstrating how powerful an instrument for education a small liberal arts college can be. It also contains the themes that define the college: concern for academic excellence, influence of the values of the Religious Society of Friends, a sense of caring shown in respect for individual and social justice, freedom of inquiry and critical self examination and testing of objectives.

1379. Watson, S. Arthur. *Penn College: A product and a producer.* Oskaloosa, IA: William Penn College, 1971.

Tells the story of the making of the college as a strong institution for developing education within the Quaker philosophy and producing students deeply concerned about the Quaker way of life not only on the campus but in the world around them as they become citizens of communities.

1380.   Bonis, Constantine. *Anthe eis tous Helleno-amerikanous* (Bouquet of Flowers to the Greek-Americans). Athens, n. p., 1960.

The author discusses Greek-American institutions and especially Hellenic College, for the Greek public. The book includes several speeches on various topics, especially on the future of Greek education in America.

1381.   Bonis, Constantine. *To Neon "Athenaion" Hetoi to Hellenikon Orthodoxon Panepestimion en Brookline, Mass.* (The New "Athenaion," that is, the Hellenic Orthodox University in Brookline, Mass.). New York: Argonantes Press, 1963, p. 19.

The present publication is devoted to the discussion of the Hellenic University, its curricula, function and administration as seen by a visiting Greek University professor at Brookline. He sees this institution as the center for study and research of Orthodox theology, Greek philosophy and language.

1382.   Bosse, Raymond. "Hellenic is in the Forefront on Hyman Development and Aging." *Koinonia* (the Magazine of Hellenic College and Holy Cross Greek Orthodox School of Theology), 3, Summer 1981, pp. 2-3.

This article discusses the human development program at Hellenic College and the grant awarded by the National Institute of Aging for Professor Bosse to research retirement and health in the United States.

1383.   Cavarnos, John P. "Hirysis Hellenikon Panepistimiou eis ten Amerike" (Establishment of a Greek University in America). *Nea Hestia* (Athens), Christmas 1955, pp. 23-27.

The present article discusses the plans for a Hellenic University in America. He gives fourteen reasons for the need of such a college in the United States.

1384.   Hatziemmanuel, Emmanuel. "HE AKADEMIA TOY HAGIOY BASILEIOY" (Saint Basil's Academy). *Krikos Greek Review*, 67-68, July-August 1956, pp. 46-51.

The author in this article describes the Teacher's College in Garrison, New York before it was moved and incorporated with the Hellenic College in Brookline, Mass. Describes the curriculum. The Teacher's College for women emphasized Orthodox theological studies and the Greek language. The author also gives budgetary and financial data of the College.

1385.   Kehayes, William S. "Holy Cross and the Eighties." *Koinonia*, 3, Spring 1980, p. 9.

This article discusses the mission of Hellenic College to educate young people in a Christian Orthodox environment and Greek heritage preparing them for ministry and teaching vocations.

1386.   Langer, William D. "The Hellenic University of America." *The Congressional Record.* 86th Congress, 1st Session. (Reprinted), p. 4.

This article focuses on the many contributions Greece has made to civilization and the significance of a Greek-American educational institution for America. It extols its location being in Boston, the Athens of America.

1387.   "Learning Greek at Hellenic." *Koinonia*, 2, Autumn 1979, p. 10.

This article discusses the effectiveness of the Summer Greek Language Program at Hellenic College.

1388.   Vaporis, Nomokos M. "Hellenic - the only Orthodox Christian College." *Koinonia*, 1, Winter 1978, p. 4.

This article focuses on the importance of Hellenic College as the only Orthodox Christian college in the world that is fully accredited. Its purpose is the transmission of Greek culture and the Greek Orthodox tradition in this country.

CHAPTER 17

INDEPENDENT CHRISTIAN COLLEGES AND UNIVERSITIES
William C. Ringenberg

Most Christian colleges are denominational in affiliation, and most independent colleges are not avowedly Christian. Therefore the category of "Independent Christian colleges and universities" is not a large one. I have seen it identified as such very infrequently. One major source that does recognize it is Manning M. Pattillo and Donald M. Mackenzie, *Church Sponsored Higher Education in the United States* (Washington, 1966), p. 249. Pattillo and Mackenzie found only fifteen independent Christian colleges; my list is longer, but nevertheless supports the impression that there are not many contemporary colleges and universities that are both continuing Christian in philosophical orientation and independent of denominational ties in governance.

Of the colleges that do fit this category, few are old or research-oriented. Many came into existence within the last century, partly, at least, in reaction to the growing secularization in higher education in general. Until about 1880, of course, almost all American colleges and universities were Christian in nature, whether denominational or state controlled. Independent Christian colleges tend to be teaching colleges that do not place major emphasis upon research, even that devoted to the recording of their own past. Some schools have no definitive history, even of article-length.

The sources cited in this bibliographical essay are of three types. The first are philosophical and general and recognize that the independent Christian colleges have much in common with the orthodox Protestant denominational institutions and that many of the most important sources describe their common world views and educational record. The second group identifies representative institutional histories and biographies of characteristic liberal arts institutions and leaders. The third section describes specialized institutions or colleges serving specialized constituencies, namely the Bible colleges and the fundamentalist liberal arts colleges.

Part I. General and Philosophical Studies

1389.   Askew, Thomas A.   *The Small College: A Bibliographic Handbook*. Washington, D.C.: Council for the Advancement of Small Colleges, 1972.

Lists with annotation the best literature published through 1971 on most aspects of the small, mostly Christian, liberal arts college movement.

1390. Berk, Harold W. "The Christian College Consortium in Social Context." Ph.D. dissertation. University of Toledo, 1974.

Provides a historical record of the founding period and early years of a noteworthy consortium of some of the leading evangelical colleges, half of whom are independent.

1391. Briggs, Kenneth. "Evangelical Colleges Reborn." *New York Times Magazine*, 14 December 1980, pp. 140-54.

Recognizes and describes the increasing quality and prosperity of the contemporary evangelical colleges.

1392. Buttrick, George Arthur. *Biblical Thought and the Secular University*. Baton Rouge: Louisiana State University Press, 1960.

Gives one of the best and most effective critiques of the secularistic philosophy in higher education.

1393. Ferre, N. F. S. "Church-Related Colleges and a Mature Faith." *Religious Education* 54 (March 1959): 149-55.

States, supports, and explains the purpose of the Christian college--particularly the liberal Protestant college--at its best. This is an excellent statement.

1394. Hill, Alfred T. *The Small College Meets the Challenge*. New York: McGraw-Hill, 1959.

Presents a history of the early years of the Council of Independent Colleges (later renamed the Council for the Advancement of Small Colleges) which came into existence in 1955 to assist small independent colleges in achieving regional accreditation.

1395. Holmes, Arthur F. *All Truth is God's Truth*. Grand Rapids, MI: Eerdmans, 1977.

Suggests in title and develops in narrative a basic concept in the educational philosophy of the evangelical colleges, namely the unity and sacredness of all truth.

1396. Holmes, Arthur F., *The Idea of a Christian College*. Grand Rapids, MI: Eerdmans, 1975.

Presents the case for the undergraduate Christian liberal arts college. This concise general study describes the theological foundations, the commitment to faith/learning integration and values education, and the emphasis upon collegiality in such institutions. It is recognized by many of the personnel at the institutions which it describes as being the best book of its type.

1397. King, L. A. "A Fable About a Slanted Education." *Eternity*,

August 1978, pp. 22-25.

Discusses creatively the difficulties of maintaining academic freedom in both Christian colleges and secular universities, suggesting that it may be a larger problem in the latter.

1398.   Nelsen, Frank C. "Evangelical Living and Learning Centers: A Proposal." *Christianity Today*, 24 May 1974, pp. 7-8.

Calls for "satellite" Christian colleges that would operate as private institutions adjacent to large public universities. These Christian colleges would provide housing, religious support services, and limited instruction in Biblical studies, philosophy, and apologetics for its students who would maintain their primary enrollment with the university.

1399.   Pace, C. Robert. *Education and Evangelism*. New York: McGraw-Hill, 1972.

Identifies and compares the several types of Protestant colleges, including those with varying degrees of commitment to a traditional church connection and varying degrees of commitment to traditional Protestant beliefs. Pace finds the evangelical and fundamentalist colleges to be the most distinctive and facing the most secure futures.

1400.   Pattillo, Manning M. and Donald M. MacKenzie. *Church Sponsored Higher Education in the United States*. Washington, DC: American Council on Education, 1966.

Documents and assesses in comprehensive manner the status and goals of church-related higher education. This Danforth Foundation study is one of the most important and authoritative studies in all of the literature of American higher education. It identifies secularization as the most significant problem in Christian higher education in the mid-twentieth century period.

1401.   Ringenberg, William C. *The Christian College: A History of Protestant Higher Education in America*. Grand Rapids, MI: Eerdmans, 1984.

Traces the record of that changing body of American Protestant colleges which at any given time wished to be known as avowedly Christian in educational philosophy.

1402.   Trueblood, D. Elton. "The Redemption of the College." In *A Philosopher's Way*, pp. 105-25. Edited by Elizabeth Newby. Nashville, TN: Broadman Press, 1978.

Analyzes the historic uniqueness of the Christian college in American culture, laments its recent reduction in vision and vigor, and suggests a plan of action for its renewal.

1403.   Wolterstorff, Nicholas P. *Christian Liberal Arts Education: Report of the Calvin College Curriculum Study Committee.* Grand Rapids, MI: Eerdmans and Calvin College, 1970.

Serves as a model--as did St. Olaf's Henry Hong, ed. *Integration in the Christian Liberal Arts College* (Northfield, MN, 1956), earlier--for curriculum studies in many Christian liberal arts colleges. Its emphases upon the historical and philosophical background of Christian learning, much more than specific curricular proposals for a specific institution, explains its broad usefulness.

Part II. Institutional Studies of Characteristic Liberal Arts Colleges

1404.   Askew, Thomas A. "The Liberal Arts College Encounters Intellectual Change: A Comparative Study of Education at Knox and Wheaton College." Ph.D. dissertation. Northwestern University, 1969.

Compares with the better known John Barnard, *From Evangelism to Progressivism at Oberlin College, 1866-1917* (Columbus, 1969), as an able, detailed case study of the secularization process in higher education. Askew shows that while Knox and Wheaton both developed as little Midwestern Harvards in the Congregational tradition and while each was led early in its history by social reformer Jonathan Blanchard as president, they demonstrate differing responses to the turn-of-the-century intellectual forces.

1405.   Bechtel, Paul M. *Wheaton College: A Heritage Remembered, 1860-1984.* Wheaton, IL: Harold Shaw Publishers, 1984.

Replaces the more limited W. Wyeth Willard, *Fire on the Prairie* as the modern record of what in some ways is the most elite evangelical college in America. Bechtel, professor of English emeritus at Wheaton, has written a competent and comprehensive history.

1406.   Bryan, William Jennings. *The Last Message of William Jennings Bryan.* Dayton, TN: The Bryan Memorial University Association, 1929.

Calls for Christians in every state to establish colleges that employ only instructors who pledge to remain faithful to a conservative interpretation of the Bible.

1407.   Godsey, Helen and Townsend. *Flight of the Phoenix: The School of the Ozarks.* Point Lookout, MD: School of the Ozarks Press, 1984.

Tells the history of the first seventy-five years of one of the most significant and long-lasting of the manual labor, "work-as-you-learn" colleges for poor youth. This is an informal but comprehensive record by two retired School of the Ozarks administrators.

1408.   Harrell, David Edwin Jr., *Oral Roberts: An American Life.* Bloomington, IN: Indiana University Press, 1985.

Provides a first-rate and balanced account of a major historical figure who founded the most significant independent Christian college to come into existence during the second half of the twentieth century. This definitive biography gives significant attention to Oral Roberts University, much more so than does Robert's autobiography, *The Call* (Old Tappan, NJ, 1971).

1409.   Hilberry, Conrad. "Wheaton College." In *Struggle and Promise: A Future for Colleges*, pp. 17-45. Edited by Morris Keaton and Conrad Hilberry. New York: McGraw-Hill, 1969.

Presents an unusually objective, insightful, and readable profile of Wheaton College as it existed in the mid-1960's. For those not familiar with evangelical Protestantism and the evangelical college, it is a good introduction to the character of such institutions.

1410.   Kane, Harnett T. *Miracle in the Mountains.* Garden City, NY: Doubleday, 1956.

Written in the light, breezy style of a popular novel, this biography of Martha Berry focuses upon her forty-year work in founding (1902) and developing Berry College (GA), which in many respects became the Berea College (see Peck and Smith, *Berea's First 125 Years*, below) of the southernmost Appalachian region.

1411.   Kennedy, Ralph C., Jr. and Thomas Rothrock. *John Brown of Arkansas.* Siloam Springs, AK: John Brown University Press, 1966.

Tells the life story of the early-twentieth century evangelist-turned-college founder. It gives major attention to the interdenominational institution that began as another manual training school for poor youth and continues to give significant emphasis to a vocational curriculum.

1412.   Kilby, Clyde S., *Minority of One: The Biography of Jonathan Blanchard.* Grand Rapids, MI: Eerdmans, 1959.

Tells with skill and grace the life story of an important figure in American higher education. A first-rate biography by an important organizer of the major C.S. Lewis collection at Wheaton College.

1413.   LeTourneàu, R. G. *Mover of Men and Mountains.* Chicago: Moody Press, 1972.

Relates in an autobiographical manner the life of this major inventor, manufacturer, and contractor in the field of heavy-duty earth-moving equipment, who used his financial resources to support many missions programs and the Christian technical institute now know as LeTourneau College. This reissue of the original 1960 Prentice-Hall hardcover edition contains some new material added by Nels E. Stjernstrom, however, like the original version it gives little emphasis to the college.

1414. Miller, J. Melvin. "The Torch Held High: A History of Pacific Bible College of Azusa, California." A. M. Thesis. Pacific Bible College, 1957.

Describes the early history of one of the first Bible institutes on the West Coast. This first history of what is now Azusa College traces its interdenominational Holiness and Bible college origins.

1415. Peck, Elizabeth S. and Emily Ann Smith, *Berea's First 125 Years*. Lexington: University Press of Kentucky, 1982.

Updates Peck's centennial history, *Berea's First Century, 1855-1955* (Lexington, 1955) with Smith's chapter on the last twenty-five years adding to the length of the book by one-third. This book is important because the college which it describes is unique. Berea began as an anti-slavery school in a slave state; it pioneered as an interracial Southern college; it survives as the longest lasting "manual labor" college; and it serves as a prime example of an educational institution serving the needs and promoting the culture of its geographic region, which in Berea's case means the upper Southern Appalachian area. Also see Parker E. Liechtenstein, "Berea College," in *Struggle and Promise: A Future for Private Colleges*, ed. Conrad Hilberry and Morris Keeton (New York, 1969), pp. 47-70.

1416. Reade, Thaddeus C. *Samuel Morris*. Upland, IN: Taylor University Press, 1921 edition.

Influenced as well as recorded history. This booklet biography made Morris one of the most publicized turn-of-the-century American college students. By the 1920's this biography of the Nigerian native, who studied at Taylor University during its Fort Wayne, Indiana years, had sold over 200,000 copies.

1417. Ringenberg, William C. *Taylor University: The First 125 Years*. Grand Rapids, MI: Eerdmans, 1973.

Records the history of one of the oldest of the now independent Christian colleges. Like Asbury College in Kentucky it previously held strong ties with the Holiness-wing of Methodism.

1418. Wesche, Percival A. *Henry Clay Morrison: Crusader Saint*.

Wilmore, KY: Asbury Theological Seminary, 1963.

Traces the record in evangelism and education of one of the best known leaders of the Southern Methodist Holiness movement during the first half of the twentieth century. Wesche's biography of the twenty year president of Asbury is essentially his earlier doctoral dissertation at the University of Oklahoma.

1419.   Williams, Earl R. "John Brown University: Its Founding and Founders." Ed. D. dissertation. University of Arkansas, 1971.

Emphasizes the influence of Evangelist John Brown on his school from its founding until his death. It places the college in the context of the manual labor movement in higher education.

1420.   Wood, Nathan R. *A School of Christ*. Boston: Gordon College of Theology and Missions, 1953.

Continues as the traditional but now outdated history of the best recognized evangelical college in New England.

1421.   Zopfi, David Noel. "Forward Through Faith: The Founding of William Jennings Bryan Memorial University." History Seminar Thesis. Bryan College, 1979.

Summarizes clearly the events leading from the Tennessee Butler Act and the famous Scopes Trial of 1925 in Dayton, Tennessee involving lawyers Clarence Darrow and William J. Bryan through the planning for the founding and the early years of Bryan College in the same town where the trial took place. This article-length essay should be supplemented with Jess W. Lasley, "The History of Bryan College," Ph.D. dissertation, Baylor University, 1960.

Part III. Bible Colleges and Fundamentalist Liberal Arts Colleges

1422.   Brereton, Virginia Lieson. "Education and Evangelism: Protestant Fundamentalist Bible Schools." Ph.D. dissertation. Columbia University, 1981.

Presents the findings and views of the most widely recognized "outside" historian of the Bible college movement.

1423.   Boon, Harold W. "The Development of the Bible College or Institute in the United States and Canada Since 1880." Ph.D. dissertation. New York University, 1950.

Presents--along with William S. McBirnie, Jr., "A Study of the Bible Institute Movement," Ph.D. dissertation, Southwestern Baptist Theological Seminary, 1952--one of the best early histories of the Bible college movement.

1424.   Dobson, Ed, Ed Hindson, and Jerry Falwell. *The Fundamentalist*

Phenomenon. Garden City, NY: Doubleday, 1981.

Explains the fundamentalist tradition as taught and promoted at one of its most rapidly growing institutions, Falwell's Liberty Baptist College (now Liberty University).

1425. Ellison, Roger C. "A Foundation Study of the Development of Tennessee Temple Schools." Ph.D. dissertation. Bob Jones University, 1973.

Narrates the history of one of the most significant of the many Bible colleges and fundamentalist colleges to be founded by a local church in the twentieth century.

1426. Findlay, James F., Jr. "Moody, 'Gapmen,' and the Gospel: The Early Days of Moody Bible Institute." *Church History* (September 1962): 322-35.

Describes and analyzes the role of Dwight L. Moody in the planning for the founding of Moody Bible Institute.

1427. Gerig, Jared F. *Wine of God's Own Planting: A History of Fort Wayne Bible College.* Fort Wayne, IN: Fort Wayne Bible College, 1980.

Stands as the first full-length history of what by the 1960's had become one of the leading Bible colleges. This inside account by a long time instructor and president is complemented by William C. Ringenberg, "A Brief History of Fort Wayne Bible College," *Mennonite Quarterly Review*, April 1980, pp. 135-55.

1428. Getz, Gene A. *MBI: The Story of Moody Bible Institute.* Chicago: Moody Bible Institute, 1969.

Presents a sympathetic yet able account of the most significant Bible institute/college. This is the standard full-length history of Moody, a school which on one hand is something of an anachronism in that nearly all, if not all of the other older, well-established Bible institutes have for many years now operated as Bible colleges with general education core curricula. Ironically, however, in many other ways (e.g., breadth of Bible curriculum; size of student body, faculty and staff, and alumni; financial base; extent of auxiliary programs; and historic and current influence) Moody clearly continues as the leader in the Bible institute/college movement.

1429. Johnson, R. K. *Builder of Bridges.* Greenville, SC: Bob Jones University Press, 1982 edition.

Tells with sympathy the life story of the man who, with Oral Roberts, has been one of the most significant of the many twentieth-century evangelists to found independent Christian colleges.

1430.   King, Larry. "The Buckle on the Bible Belt." *Harper's Magazine*, June 1966, pp. 51-58.

Presents smartly and in an engaging manner the foibles of Bob Jones University; it is less good at demonstrating an understanding of them. It is similar in content and tone to Robert G. Sherrill, "Bob Jones University: New Curricula for Bigotry," *Nation*, 29 March 1965, pp. 326-33.

1431.   McKaig, Charles Donald. "The Educational Philosophy of A. B. Simpson." Ph.D. dissertation. New York University, 1948.

Relates the ideas of the most important early Bible school theoretician.

1432.   Witmer, Safara, *The Bible College Story: Education with Dimension.* New York: Channel Press, 1962.

Remains, despite its age, the single best introduction to the history and philosophy of the Bible College movement. In the mid-twentieth century the author was the recognized leader of the movement.

1433.   Wright, Melton. *Fortress of Faith: The Story of Bob Jones University.* Grand Rapids, MI: Eerdmans, 1960.

Presents in a sympathetic manner the only full-length history of the best-known fundamentalist college. Wright focuses upon the role of the Jones family.

CHAPTER 18
JEWISH COLLEGES AND UNIVERSITIES
Harold Wechsler

1434. Ben-Horin, Meir. "Scholar's Opinions': Documents in the History of the Dropsie College." In *Salo Wittmayer Baron Jubilee Volume on the Occasion of His Eightieth Birthday*, pp. 167-208. English Section, v. 1 Jerusalem, Israel: American Academy for Jewish Research, 1974.

Reprints letters from eleven American scholars elicited by Cyrus Adler and the Dropsie College Trustees, on the educational mission of the proposed Dropsie College. Themes discussed include the future of *Wissenchaft des Judentums*, the science of Judaism, in America, the relationship of Jewish scholarship in secular environments to theological education, and the range of subjects appropriate for investigation in an institution of higher Jewish learning.

1435. Dushkin, Alexander M. with the assistance of Nathan Greenbaum. *Comparative Study of the Jewish Teacher Training Schools in the Diaspora*. Jerusalem, Israel: Institute of Contemporary Jewry, Hebrew University, 1970.

Examines 78 Jewish teacher training schools, including American institutions, and offers statistical tables and analyses. Includes substantial demographic information on the teachers they educate, as well as information on the institutions.

1436. Dushkin, Alexander M. *Living Bridges*. Jerusalem, Israel: Keter Publishing House, 1975.

Offers reminiscences of the founding and early development of the Chicago College of Jewish Studies as a teacher-training and adult education institution by its first director (Chapter 4). Discusses the Chicago Board of Jewish Education under whose auspices the College was established.

1437. Haron, Miriam. "Towards a History of Spertus College of Judaica." Unpublished manuscript, 1986. Available from Spertus College of Judaica, 618 S. Michigan Avenue, Chicago, IL, 60606.

Discusses the College's history from its founding as the College of Jewish studies by the Chicago Board of Jewish Education through its maturation as an independent, multi-faceted institution. Traces the evolution of the institution's mission (general and professional education, establishment of important museum and library collections), faculty recruitment and retention, academic recognition (independence from the BJE was the price of accreditation), the relationship between the College and the area's other Jewish and secular institutions (it acted as the "Jewish Studies department" for many local colleges and universities), and financial and administrative problems.

1438.   Hartstein, Jacob I. "Yeshiva University." *American Jewish Yearbook* 50 (1948-1949): 73-84.

Stresses the continuity of the Yeshiva ideal and its compatibility with collegiate and university ideals as the institution evolved from an Orthodox Jewish seminary (the Rabbi Isaac Elchanan Theological Seminary) into a full university, the only one of the major rabbinical seminaries to do so. (The other seminaries are Hebrew Union College [Reform] and Jewish Theological Seminary of America [Conservative] and the Reconstructionist Rabbinical College [Reconstructionist].) Provides a short chronicle of this evolution.

1439.   Janowsky, Oscar, ed. *The Education of American Jewish Teachers.* Boston: Beacon Press, 1967.

Includes chapters by E. Silberschiag, "Accreditation of Hebrew Teachers Colleges," Walter Ackerman, "A Profile of Hebrew Teachers Colleges," and Samuel Dinin, "The Curricula of the Hebrew Teachers Colleges." Contains information about faculty salaries of Hebrew teachers colleges, and the presence of Israelis in the teaching force.

1440.   Klaperman, Gilbert. *The Story of Yeshiva Univeristy.* New York: Macmillan, 1969.

Offers a comprehensive history of Yeshiva University from its origins as the Rabbi Isaac Ilchanan Seminary through the 1960s. Contains chapter-length descriptions of the founding of Yeshiva College and of the rise of a full-scale university after World War II. Emphasizes the role of two presidents: Bernard Revel and Samuel Belkin.

1441.   Klaperman, Gilbert. "Yeshiva University: Seventy-five Years in Retrospect." *American Jewish Historical Quarterly* 54 (September and December 1964): 5-50 and 198-201.

Emphasizes the founding of the Rabbi Isaac Elchanan Seminary, out of which Yeshiva University emerged, and the decision to embark upon creation of a secular college (Yeshiva College) under Jewish auspices during the 1920s.

1442.   Loren, Morris Jacob. "Hebrew Higher Educational Institutions in
           the United States 1830-1975." Ph.D. thesis. Wayne State
           University, 1976.

                  Discusses twelve institutions of higher Jewish education,
           selected for their denominational affiliation, their historical
           importance, or their uniqueness. Concludes that rabbinical and
           teacher education were the primary reasons for founding these
           institutions and that teacher-training was the first offering to
           augment religious instruction, that most collegiate schools began on
           the sub-collegiate level and most suffered financial problems, and
           that although Hebrew and Talmudic studies were central subjects,
           most schools offered increased amounts of secular studies, often as
           a response to student demand.

1443.   Margolis, Isidor. *Jewish Teacher Training Schools in the United
           States.* New York: National Council for Torah Education of
           Mizrachi-Hapoel/Hamizrachi, 1964.

                  Includes historical accounts of Gratz College, the Teachers
           Institute of the Jewish Theological Seminary of America, the
           Teachers Institute of Yeshiva University, the Hebrew Teachers
           College of Boston, the Herzliah Hebrew Teachers Institute in New
           York, and the College of Jewish Studies in Chicago. Discusses
           enrollments (or rather the lack thereof) and the resultant shortage
           in trained teachers in Jewish subjects.

1444.   Neuman, Abraham A. "The Dropsie College for Hebrew and
           Cognate Learning-Basic Principles and Objectives." *The
           Seventy-Fifth Anniversary Volume of the Jewish Quarterly Review*
           (Philadelphia: The Jewish Quarterly Review, 1967), 18-46.

                  Traces Dropsie College's origins to the 19th century
           European *Wissenschaft des Judentums* movement and to Moses
           Dropsie's interest in a scientific basis for religious ecumenism.
           Stresses the institution's academic, non-sectarian approach to
           religious studies, its emphasis on subjects not generally offered in
           American academic institutions, and its role as a world center for
           Jewish learning after the destruction of European Jewry. Includes
           departmental histories and descriptions, illustrating dual
           approaches based on scientific investigation and on the Jewish
           experience.

1445.   Ohles, John F. and Shirley N. Ohles, eds. *Private Colleges and
           Universities.* 2 vols. Westport, CT: Greenwood Press, 1982.

                  Includes brief historical articles on Baltimore Hebrew
           College, p. 83, Cleveland College of Jewish Studies, p. 264, Dropsie
           University, p. 377, Hebrew College, p. 536, and Spertus College of
           Judaica, p. 1436. Also includes articles on Jewish seminaries,
           including Hebrew Theological College, p. 537, Hebrew Union
           College, p. 538, and Jewish Theological Seminary of America, p.

602.

1446.   Parzan, Herbert. "New Data on the Formation of Dropsie College."
         Jewish Social Studies 28 (July 1966): 131-47.

         Discusses the selection of Cyrus Adler, then at the
Smithsonian, as Dropsie's first president, the decision not to
proceed with creation of a department of Jewish education, and the
negotiations with Ahad Ha'am for a professorship. Adler's choice
over Israel Friedlander of the Jewish Theological Seminary of
America's faculty was based upon decisions that Dropsie would be
"non-sectarian," that is, it would not embrace the Conservative
Judaism of most of its founders to the exclusion of the other Jewish
movements, that it would confine itself to advanced Jewish
scholarship while refraining from work in Jewish religious
education.   Clarification of institutional mission led Dropsie's
authorities not to pursue the possibility of a faculty appointment
of Ahad Ha-Am, Zionist and man of letters.

1447.   Passow, Isidore D. and Samuel T. Lachs, eds.   *Gratz College
         Anniversary Volume: On the Occasion of the 75th Anniversary of the
         Founding of the College 1895-1970.*   Philadelphia: Gratz College,
         1971.

         Includes papers on American Jewish education, and provides
information on the evolution of Gratz College in Philadelphia, a
teacher-training institution.

1448.   Rothkoff, Aaron.   *Bernard Revel: Builder of American Jewish
         Orthodoxy.* Philadelphia: Jewish Publication Society of America,
         1972.

         Discusses Bernard Revel's life and especially his presidency
of Yeshiva College in the context of Orthodox Jewry's status in the
early twentieth century.   Discusses his role in Yeshiva's transition
from a seminary to a multi-divisional college, in opposing a
projected merger with the Jewish Theological Seminary of America,
in confronting Orthodox criticisms of his actions, in maintaining
contact with the rabbis graduated by the institution, and in seeing
the College through the economic problems resulting from the
Depression.

1449.   Sachar, Abram L.   "The Jewish Component of Brandeis
         University." In *Go and Study: Essays and Studies in Honor of
         Alfred Jospe*, pp. 29-43. Edited by Rachel Jospe and Samuel Z.
         Fishman. Washington, DC: B'nai B'rith Hillel Foundations, 1980.

         Discusses the ways in which Jewish-founded Brandeis
University, although not sponsored by a single Jewish denomination
or singularly concerned with Judaic content, exhibits a Jewish
component. Lists the students' and faculty's social conscience, the
Department of Judaic Studies' strength, the American Jewish

Historical Society's movement to the Waltham, Massachusetts campus, and the closeness of its ties to Israel. Concludes that "the Jewishness of Brandeis was in its climate, not its orientation."

1450.   Sherwin, Byron. "Go and Study: A New Curricular Model for Higher Jewish Education in the United States." Unpublished manuscript, 1987. Available from Spertus College of Judaica, 618 S. Michigan Avenue, Chicago, IL, 60606.

Offers a comprehensive discussion of higher Jewish learning in America, its evolution and contemporary status in various institutional settings, but with special emphasis on colleges of Judaica. Special attention is devoted to the emergence of bureaus of Jewish education and the concomitant evolution of Hebrew teachers colleges, to the changing missions of such institutions and to the curricular implications of such changes. The manuscript contains a detailed history of Spertus College of Judaica, Chicago, Illinois (especially chapter seven); and offers proposals for curricular reform in the context of that institution's history, the current national movement for curricular reform, general trends in Jewish education, and the resources available to that institution.

CHAPTER 19
LUTHERAN COLLEGES AND UNIVERSITIES
Richard W. Solberg and Jon Diefenthaler

Part I: Institutional Histories

1451. Albers, James W. *From Centennial to Golden Anniversary: The History of Valparaiso University from 1959-1975.* Valparaiso, IN: Valparaiso University, 1976.

Provides an account of the recent history of Valparaiso University, updating Strietelmeier's centennial history, published in 1959, and also listed in this catalog. Offers insights into the years of the university's rapid growth and the academic and social stress of the late '60s and early '70s. Includes enrollment data, 1959-75.

1452. Bergendoff, Conrad. *Augustana: A Profession of Faith.* Rock Island, IL: Augustana College Library, 1969.

Recounts the origin and development of the initial Swedish Lutheran college and seminary from its founding in 1860 to 1948. Emphasizes the intimate interaction of faith and learning as essential in the higher education enterprise.

1453. Bosse, Richard C. "Origins of Lutheran Higher Education in Ohio." Ph.D. dissertation. Ohio State University, 1969.

Describes the emergence of Capital University and Wittenberg College as expressions of the linguistic and confessional conflict between English-speaking "American" Lutherans and strongly confessional German-speaking "Old Lutherans" in Ohio in the 1840's and 1850's. Contains a valuable comparison of Capital's strictly pre-theological and classical curriculum and the more liberal offerings at Wittenberg before 1900. Includes extensive bibliography.

1454. Bredemeier, Herbert G. *Concordia College, Fort Wayne, 1839-1957.* Fort Wayne, IN: Fort Wayne Public Library, 1978.

Gives a personalized account of the pioneer "gymnasium" of the Lutheran Church-Missouri Synod during the formation of the Missouri system for preparation of clergy and teachers. Contains biographical sketches of its presidents and leading professors and descriptions of student life and academic programs.

1455.   Breidenbaugh, E. S., ed.   *The Pennsylvania College Book,*
         1832-1882. Philadelphia: Lutheran Publication Society, 1882.

         Contains biographical and historical essays and documents
         detailing the first half-century of Gettysburg College, the oldest
         Lutheran college in America.   Includes personal records of
         individual students and alumni and lists of patrons and trustees.

1456.   Brown, Dorothy Ann.   *We Sing to Thee: A Story about Clifton*
         College. Waco, TX: Texian Press, 1974.

         Provides an informal pictorial account of a Norwegian
         Lutheran junior college, merged in 1954 with Texas Lutheran
         College.

1457.   Calman, Alvin R.   *Upsala College: The Early Years.* New York:
         Vantage Press, 1983.

         Describes a Swedish Lutheran college in New Jersey, from its
         founding in 1893 to 1924.   Based largely on memoirs of founders
         and early faculty.

1458.   Chrislock, Carl.   *From Fjord to Freeway.*   Minneapolis, MN:
         Augsburg College, 1969.

         Recounts the history of Augsburg College and Seminary
         from its founding in 1869.   Analyzes the concept of a unified
         theological educational system articulated by Georg Sverdrup,
         eminent Norwegian-American theologian and president of
         Augsburg.   Describes Augsburg's modern development into a
         socially conscious urban liberal arts college.

1459.   Clark, William S. and Arthur H. Wilson. *The Story of Susquehanna*
         University. Selinsgrove, PA: Susquehanna University Press, 1958.

         Offers insight into the early Lutheran effort to provide
         practical preparation for missionary clergy on the frontier.
         Describes how the Missionary Institute, founded in 1858, became
         Susquehanna University in 1894, when a full baccalaureate
         curriculum was first offered.   Encompasses the history of the
         institution's first century, 1858-1958.

1460.   Dowie, James Iverne.   *Prairie Grass Dividing.*   Rock Island, IL:
         Augustana Historical Society, 1959.

         Furnishes an account of the Swedish Lutheran settlements
         in Nebraska and the important role of education in their
         development.   Describes the founding of Luther Academy at
         Wahoo, Nebraska, later to become Luther College, a two-year
         junior college, exemplifying the blending of ethnic and religious
         values in the Swedish-American culture.   Notes the merger of
         Luther with Midland College in Fremont, Nebraska, in 1962.

Contains an excellent bibliography.

1461. Dubbs, Joseph Henry. *History of Franklin and Marshall College.* Lancaster, PA: Franklin and Marshall College Alumni Association, 1903.

Contains the account of the founding of Franklin College in 1787 as a joint venture of the Lutheran and Reformed Churches. Describes the withdrawal of Lutheran participation in 1850 in favor of Gettysburg College, and Franklin's subsequent merger with Marshall College to become Franklin & Marshall College, related to the Reformed Church.

1462. Dunkelberger, Harold A. "Gettysburg College and the Lutheran Connection: An Open-Ended Story of a Proud Relationship." History Series No. 3, *The Gettysburg Bulletin*, December, 1975.

Describes the distinctive church relationship of Gettysburg College, an institution legally independent of the church, but strongly affirmative of its Lutheran identity.

1463. Eisenberg, William E. *The First Hundred Years: Roanoke College, 1842-1942.* Salem, VA: Roanoke College, 1942.

Presents an engaging account of Roanoke's first century, its Civil War experiences, and its pioneer ventures into international education and the education of native Americans. Offers insights into the problems of financial support for a church-related college with limited local church constituency. Appendix contains college charter, lists of faculty and trustees, and enrollment data.

1464. Evenson, George. *Adventuring for Christ.* Calgary, Alberta, Canada: The Foothills Lutheran Press, 1974.

Provides a general history of the Evangelical Lutheran Church of Canada. Contains several brief sections (pp. 73-79, 102-103, 186-189) dealing with the schools and colleges of the Lutheran church in Canada.

1465. Freitag, Alfred J. *College With a Cause: A History of Concordia Teachers College.* River Forest, IL: Concordia Teachers College, 1964.

Describes the emergence of the major institution of the Lutheran Church-Missouri Synod for the preparation of parochial school teachers. Contains an introductory description of the Missouri educational system, followed by sections dealing with the history of the school at its two successive locations in Addison and River Forest, Illinois.

1466. Gienapp, J. Henry & G. W. Mueller. *Concordia College Centennial Jubilee, 1881-1981.* Milwaukee, WI: Concordia College-Wisconsin, 1984.

Contains two brief informal histories of Concordia College in Milwaukee, (now Concordia College-Wisconsin, located in the Milwaukee suburb of Mequon), written in 1931 and 1981. Traces the school's development from a German-style "gymnasium" and junior college, almost exclusively for students desiring to study for the ministry, to a four-year college offering a variety of pre-professional programs. Includes enrollment data, pictures and biographical sketches of leading personalities.

1467.   Hansen, Thorvald. *We Laid Foundation Here: The Early History of Grand View College.* Des Moinnes, IA: Grand View College, 1972.

Describes the founding of the college and seminary of the Danish Lutherans who espoused the theological and educational tradition of Nicolai F. S. Grundtvig, Danish bishop and father of the Danish Folk School.

1468.   Harstad, Peter T. *Sigurd Christian Ylvisaker 1884-1959.* Mankato, MN: Bethany College, 1984.

Contains a chapter dealing with the founding and early history of the Bethany College, Mankato, Minnesota, junior college of the Evangelical Lutheran Synod, a conservative church body of Norwegian background.

1469.   Hefelbower, Samuel G. *The History of Gettysburg College, 1832-1932.* Gettysburg, PA: Gettysburg College, 1932.

Presents an account of the first century of the history of the oldest Lutheran college. Includes the text of the college charter, enrollment data, and a list of faculty.

1470.   Hegland, Georgina Dieson. *As It Was in the Beginning.* Northfield, MN: St. Olaf College Press, 1950.

Furnishes a personal account of early student life at St. Olaf College through the eyes of one of its first female students.

1471.   Heins, Henry Hardy. *Throughout All the Years: The Bicentennial Story of Hartwick in America, 1746-1946.* Oneonta, NY: Hartwick College, 1946.

Describes the founding of the first Lutheran theological seminary in 1797 by the executors of the estate of the Reverend John Christopher Hartwick. Recounts subsequent history of the Hartwick institutions through 200 years. Includes a reprint of the Hartwick will and a list of faculty from 1797 to 1941.

1472.   Hekhuis, Mary. *California Lutheran College: The First Quarter Century.* Thousand Oaks, CA: California Lutheran College, 1985.

Presents an informal pictorial history of the first permanent Lutheran liberal arts college in California, established in 1959 through the cooperative efforts of five Lutheran church bodies.

1473.   Henry, Gordon C., ed. *Newberry College, 1856-1976.* Newberry, SC: Newberry College, 1976.

Contains a brief summary of significant developments in the history of Newberry College in South Carolina from 1856 to 1976.

1474.   Hickman, Lillian. "The History of Midland College." M.A. thesis. University of Oregon, 1949.

Recounts the early history of Midland College, founded in 1883 by the Board of Education of the General Synod, the first college established by a board of education of any Lutheran church body. Notes that the school was first located in Atchison, Kansas, to serve English-speaking Lutheran settlers on the Great Plains, and that it offered a four-year liberal arts curriculum from its beginning. Describes the subsequent relocation of the college in Fremont, Nebraska, in 1919, in response to anti-German community tension during World War I.

1475.   Johnson, Roy H. *The History of Thiel College.* Philadelphia: Torrance & Co., 1974.

Describes the founding and subsequent development of Thiel College in western Pennsylvania in 1866, the first Lutheran institution of collegiate rank to adopt co-education. Contains appendix with complete list of faculty, 1866 to 1974.

1476.   Kinnison, William. *Wittenberg: A Concise History.* Springfield, OH: Wittenberg University, 1976.

Presents a brief interpretive account of the origin and growth of Wittenberg University, with emphasis upon the educational ideas of its leaders. Includes an appendix containing a complete chronological directory of Wittenberg faculty from 1845 to 1977.

1477.   Kowalke, Erwin E. *Centennial Story: Northwestern College, 1865-1965.* Watertown, WI: Northwestern College, 1965.

Recounts the founding and history of the pre-theological college of the Wisconsin Synod.

1478.   Larsen, Karen. *Laur. Larsen, Pioneer College President.* Northfield, MN: Norwegian American Historical Assn., 1936.

Views the founding and early history of Luther College, Decorah, Iowa, through the long and distinguished career of its founding president. Written by Larsen's daughter, herself a historian. Provides insights into the Norwegian-American culture as well as the character of academic life.

1479.   Lentz, Harold H. *A History of Wittenberg College.* Columbus, OH: The Wittenberg Press, 1946.

Describes the founding of a college on the New England model, in a conscious effort to interpret the Lutheran tradition in American terms. Traces its history as a liberal arts college with an associated theological seminary, through its first century, 1845 to 1945.

1480.   Lentz, Harold H. *The Miracle of Carthage: History of Carthage College, 1847-1947.* Kenosha, WI: Carthage College, 1975.

Traces the development of a frontier academy in Illinois, founded in 1847 to prepare English-speaking clergy, through several stages and relocations, including an early but ill-starred experiment as a small university, to its emergence as a liberal arts college in Carthage, Illinois, and a final migration to a new campus in Kenosha, Wisconsin.

1481.   Lindquist, Emory. *Bethany in Kansas.* Lindsborg, KS: Bethany College, 1975.

Describes the educational aspirations of Swedish Lutherans in central Kansas, and their expression through a strong tradition sponsored by Bethany College in music and the fine arts.

1482.   Lindquist, Emory. *Smoky Valley People.* Rock Island, IL: Augustana Book Concern, 1953.

Furnishes a cultural history of the Swedish-American community of Lindsborg, Kansas, which gave birth to Bethany College. Emphasizes the role of ethnic and religious factors in the growth of the college and the community.

1483.   Lund, Doniver A. *Gustavus Adolphus College: A Centennial History.* St. Peter, MN: Gustavus Adolphus College Press, 1963.

Describes the pattern of institutional development characteristic of Gustavus Adolphus College and many other midwestern Scandinavian Lutheran colleges, beginning as schools to assist immigrants in gaining basic skills, but growing to become academies and eventually liberal arts colleges.

1484.   Markley, Mary E. *Some Chapters on the History of Higher Education for Lutheran Women.* Philadelphia: Board of Education, United Lutheran Church in America, 1923.

Provides brief vignettes of many of the no-longer-surviving seminaries and colleges for women founded under Lutheran auspices between 1850 and 1910, mostly in Maryland, Virginia, and the Carolinas, but also in Pennsylvania, Ohio, and Illinois.

1485.   McCauley, J. William. "Elizabeth College and Related Lutheran

Schools." Privately published, 1901. In Archives of the North Carolina Synod, Lutheran Church in America, Salisbury, NC.

Contains a brief history of Elizabeth College, a degree-granting Lutheran college for women, founded in Charlotte, North Carolina, in 1897, later moved to Salem, Virginia, and closed in 1921.

1486.   Meyer, Carl S. *From Log Cabin to Luther Tower.* St. Louis, MO: Concordia Publishing House, 1965.

Furnishes a comprehensive history of Concordia Theological Seminary, as it progressed from its beginnings as a grammar school and "gymnasium" in 1839 to a full-fledged seminary, attended by the majority of clergy educated by the Missouri Synod. Points out that for several years following 1939 the Seminary also awarded the B.A. degree after the completion of two years of theological study and the fulfillment of prescribed baccalaureate requirements.

1487.   Nauss, Allen H. "Concordia College, Portland, Oregon." *Concordia Historical Institute Quarterly*, 25 (January 1953): 175-78; 26 (April, July, October 1953, January 1954): 17-35, 77-94, 119-30, 169-84; 27 (April 1954): 34-40.

Relates circumstances of the founding of Concordia College in Portland, Oregon, as a "pro-gymnasium" in 1905 and its progressive designation as a "gymnasium" and junior college of the Missouri Synod system.

1488.   Nelson, David T. *Luther College 1861-1961.* Decorah, IA: Luther College Press, 1961.

Describes the founding of Luther College as the classical pre-theological school of the immigrant Norwegian Synod and its later development as a coeducational liberal arts college. Provides insights into the linguistic and cultural transition from Norwegian to English.

1489.   Norris, Jeff. "Lenoir College: Its Founding and First Ten Years." Unpublished typescript in Lenoir Rhyne College Library.

Describes the conflict within the Tennessee Synod in 1889-1891 that led to the establishing of Lenoir College, and relates the history of its first decade.

1490.   Ochsenford, S. E., ed. *Muhlenberg College.* Allentown, PA: Muhlenberg College, 1892.

Includes an historical account of the first 25 years of the college, followed by biographical essays on all presidents, faculty, and alumni, and data on all students, 1867-1892.

1491.   Oppendahl, Richard A. "Waldorf College: First Fifty Years."

M.A. thesis, University of South Dakota, 1956.

Describes founding and early history of a Norwegian Lutheran academy, later developing as a junior college. Provides example of institutional ownership and governance by an association of pastors and lay persons.

1492.   Ottersberg, Gerhard. *Wartburg College, 1852-1952.* Waverly, IA: Waverly Publishing Co., 1952.

Describes the establishment of an institution exclusively designed for the preparation of pastors and parochial school teachers, and its gradual transition to the liberal arts and general teacher training. Illustrates the effect of the accreditation movement in early 20th century in hastening the transition.

1493.   Ottersberg, Gerhard. *Wartburg College, 1952-1977.* Waverly, IA: Wartburg College, 1977.

Updates the centennial history, describing recent developments in the growth of the college.

1494.   Overn, Oswald B. *History of Concordia College.* St. Paul, MN: Concordia College, 1967.

Illustrates the expansion of the Missouri Synod system of pre-theological education and its gradual broadening to include teacher preparation, co-education, and general and professional higher education for the laity.

1495.   Owens, David B. *These Hundred Years: The Centennial History of Capital University.* Columbus, OH: Capital University, 1950.

Describes an early unsuccessful attempt to establish the German university structure in America, the subsequent focus of the school upon a strongly classical German language oriented pre-theological curriculum, and its eventual emergence as a modern American liberal arts college.

1496.   Peterson, Peter L. *A Place Called Dana.* Blair, NE: Dana College, 1984.

Describes origin and development of Trinity Lutheran Seminary, Blair, NE, the theological school of the Danish Lutheran pietists, and the emergence of their preparatory school in 1899 as Dana College. Recounts the history of the college as representative of Danish-American culture.

1497.   Rolfsrud, Erling N. *Cobber Chronicle.* 2nd ed. Moorhead, MN: Concordia College, 1976.

Presents an informal illustrated history of the college established in 1891 by Norwegian immigrants in the Red River

Valley. Provides a major example of the initiative and consistent support of an institution of higher learning by a local church constituency.

1498. Schnackenberg, Walter C. "The Development of Norwegian Lutheran Schools in the Pacific Northwest from 1890 to 1920." Ph.D. dissertation. The State College of Washington, 1950.

Describes the several efforts of Norwegian Lutherans to establish academies and colleges in the Pacific Northwest, largely unsuccessful because of rivalry among competing Lutheran church bodies.

1499. Schnackenberg, Walter C. *The Lamp and the Cross*. Tacoma, WA: Pacific Lutheran University Press, 1965.

Based upon Schnackenberg's dissertation, relates the emergence of Pacific Lutheran University as a liberal arts college and small university with broad church support.

1500. Schroeder, Mortan A. *A Time to Remember: An Informal History of Dr. Martin Luther College*. New Ulm, MN: Dr. Martin Luther College, 1984.

Relates the story of the teacher training institution of the Wisconsin Synod from its founding in 1884.

1501. Shaw, Joseph. *History of St. Olaf College*. Northfield, MN: St. Olaf College Press, 1984.

Furnishes a comprehensive treatment of the history of one of the strongest Norwegian Lutheran colleges, from its beginning as an academy. Stresses the close church relationship of the college and its primary commitment to liberal arts education.

1502. Simon, Martin P. "College on the Cornfield." Ed.D. dissertation. University of Oregon, 1953.

Describes the establishment in 1893 of Concordia Teachers College in Seward, Nebraska, as the second teacher-preparation institution of the Missouri Synod. Provides insight into the rapid expansion of the synod's teacher education program in response to the growth of parochial schools in the early 20th Century.

1503. Sneen, Donald. *Through Trials and Triumphs: The History of Augustana College*. Sioux Falls, SD: Center for Western Studies, 1985.

Describes the migration of an institution founded by Norwegians and Swedes in Chicago in 1860, that followed westward-moving Norwegian settlers into Wisconsin, Iowa, and eventually into South Dakota. Provides insights into the role played by ethnic and ecclesiastical factors in Lutheran college history.

1504. Statius, Arnold. "Suomi College and Seminary." In *The Finns in North America: A Social Symposium*, pp. 91-123. Edited by Ralph J. Jalkanen. East Lansing, MI: Michigan State University Press, 1969.

Traces the educational efforts of Finnish Lutheran immigrants in northern Michigan to establish an academy that developed into a junior college and seminary. Notes the pervasive emphasis on Finnish ethnic identity and language.

1505. Steinberg, Alan G. *We Will Remember: Concordia College, The First Century*. Bronxville, NY: Concordia College, 1981.

Presents an illustrated history of the Missouri Synod's eastern seaboard college. Describes the special role played by a local educational association in supporting the college.

1506. Stoeppelwerth, H. J. "History of St. John's College, Winfield, Kansas." *Concordia Historical Institute Quarterly* 5 (January 1933): 131-37; 6 (April, July, October 1933 and January 1934): 25-32, 33-41, 74-95; 7 (April 1934): 24-32. Reprinted in *The Johnnie Heritage*. Winfield, KS: St. John's Alumni Association, 1974.

Describes a college (closed in 1986) unique in the Missouri system, founded as a coeducational liberal arts college by a wealthy businessman, and presented to the church as a gift in 1893.

1507. Stover, Clyde B. and Charles W. Beacham, eds. *The Alumni Record of Gettysburg College, 1832-1932*. Gettysburg, PA: Gettysburg College, 1932.

Contains complete lists and biographical summaries of nearly all alumni and students of the oldest Lutheran college during its first full century. Provides valuable data on the large number of Gettysburg graduates who became founders or faculty members of other Lutheran colleges.

1508. Strietelmeier, John. *Valparaiso's First Century*. Valparaiso, IN: Valparaiso University, 1959.

Presents the early history of the largest Lutheran collegiate institution, from its beginnings as a Methodist school, and its subsequent operation as a proprietary institution. Recounts its purchase in 1925 by a private association of Lutherans and its operation as an independent university, but with close relations to the Missouri Synod.

1509. Studtmann, Henry T. *Concordia of Texas from the Beginning*. Edited by Ray F. Martens. Austin, TX: Concordia College, 1977.

Tells the story of Concordia College in Austin, Texas. Contains additional accounts of early Missouri Synod efforts to establish a school in New Orleans.

1510.   Sutter, Frederic. *Wagner College - Fifty Years on Staten Island.*
New York: Wagner College, 1968.

Contains personal recollections of the pastor who provided
leadership in planting the college on Staten Island after its removal
from Rochester, New York.

1511.   Swain, James E. *A History of Muhlenberg College, 1848-1967.*
New York: Appleton-Century-Crofts, 1967.

Describes a Lutheran college in Allentown, Pennsylvania,
established to promote the ethnic German tradition and provide
classical preparation for pastors, later developing into an institution
emphasizing strong programs in liberal arts and pre-professional
science.

1512.   Veler, Herbert William. "A Life of Ezra Keller, D.D." S.T.M.
thesis. Chicago Lutheran Theological Seminary, 1951. Also in
archives of Wittenberg University, Springfield, Ohio.

Contains extensive excerpts from diaries and articles written
by the founder of Wittenberg University,. setting forth his
educational views and illustrating the influence of the New England
college model. Includes an appendix with reprints of an especially
valuable series of articles by Keller, which appeared in the *Lutheran
Observer* in 1845.

1513.   Walle, Oscar T. *Lest We Forget: A History of Concordia Senior
College, 1955-1977.* Springfield, IL: Privately published, 1978.

Describes the short-lived experiment of the Missouri Synod,
channeling pre-theological graduates of its junior colleges through
two final years in a senior college in Fort Wayne, Indiana,
preparatory to entrance into theological study.

1514.   West, Thomas W. *Marion College, 1873-1967.* Strasburg, VA:
Shenandoah Publishing House, 1970.

Contains the history of the last surviving Lutheran college
for women, to its closing in 1967. Includes appendix containing
college charter and document of dissolution, faculty and alumnae
lists, and enrollment data.

1515.   Wiederaenders, A. G. *Coming of Age: A History of Texas
Lutheran College.* San Antonio, TX: Paul Anderson Co., 1978.

Describes the formation of Texas Lutheran College from the
gradual merging of Lutheran institutions of German, Swedish, and
Norwegian ethnic roots.

Part II: General Literature

1516.   Ahlstrom, Sydney E. "What's Lutheran About Higher Education?
         A Critique." In Lutheran Educational Conference of North
         America, *Papers and Proceedings, 1974*, pp. 8-16.

         Discerns three major post-Reformation currents in the
         tradition of Lutheran higher education: scholastic, pietistic, and
         critical. Asserts that all have persisted through the centuries, with
         the critical tradition having been dominant in the German and
         Scandinavian universities of the 19th century, and having
         contributed the ideals of academic freedom and free investigation.
         Argues that these are aspects of the Lutheran tradition which have
         enriched higher education and scholarly pursuits in both Europe
         and America.

1517.   Baepler, Richard, et al., eds.   *The Quest for a Viable Saga.*
         Valparaiso, IN: Association of Lutheran College Faculties, 1977.

         Contains a collection of essays by faculty members of
         Lutheran colleges, assessing the character of the church-related
         college in an age of pluralism. Examines the "story" or "saga" of
         such colleges and concludes that their future vitality lies in their
         ability to keep their story alive and credible. Contains appendix
         with a useful summary of Lutheran efforts from 1948-77 to
         formulate a philosophy of Lutheran higher education.

1518.   Bergmann, Leola Nelson.   *Music Master of the Middle West.*
         Minneapolis, MN: University of Minnesota Press, 1944.

         Describes the establishment of the choral tradition of the St.
         Olaf Choir by its founder and conductor, F. Melius Christiansen.

1519.   Blegen, Theodore C.   *Norwegian Migration to America: The
         American Transition.*   Northfield, MN: Norwegian-American
         Historical Association, 1940.

         Recounts the social and cultural transition of Norwegian
         immigrants from the Old World to the New. Includes a chapter on
         higher education (pp. 517-42) that reflects the great importance
         placed upon this aspect of their life. Describes the founding of
         academies, colleges, and seminaries by Norwegian Lutheran pastors
         and lay leaders in the Upper Midwest.

1520.   Carlson, Edgar M.   *Church-Sponsored Higher Education and the
         Lutheran Church in America.*   New York: Lutheran Church in
         America, 1967.

         Presents a profile of the college system of the Lutheran
         Church in America in the late 1960s. Contains a valuable chapter
         on the Lutheran rationale for church involvement in higher
         education.

1521.   Carlson, Edgar M. *Public Policy and Church-Related Higher Education.* Minneapolis & New York: The Lutheran Church in America and The American Lutheran Church, 1972.

Contains official statement by two major Lutheran church bodies affirming their support of public assistance to church-related colleges.

1522.   Carlson, Edgar M. *The Future of Church-Related Higher Education.* Minneapolis, MN: Augsburg Publishing House, 1977.

Assesses the role of the church-related college in American higher education. Sees church-related institutions facing a troubled future, but extremely pertinent in the present state of America's social and cultural health. Emphasizes the need for American education to recover a concern for values and for moral and spiritual growth and commitment. Contains a concluding chapter offering an especially suggestive "design for integrity."

1523.   Coates, Thomas. "Making of a Minister." S.T.D. dissertation. Chicago Lutheran Theological Seminary, 1950.

Describes the process of ministerial education in the Missouri Synod, including the preparatory, or college programs. Notes curricular and administrative developments, including the adoption of the junior college structure. Somewhat critical of internal resistance to change.

1524.   Dickinson, Richard C. *Roses and Thorns: The Centennial Edition of Black Lutheran Mission and Ministry in the Lutheran Church-Missouri Synod.* St. Louis, MO: Concordia Publishing House, 1977.

Contains chapter on higher education (pp. 154-71) for Blacks of the churches of the Synodical Conference, but especially of the Missouri Synod. Furnishes overview of the history and offers an insider's perspective on some of the problems.

1525.   Ditmanson, Harold, et al., eds. *Christian Faith and the Liberal Arts.* Minneapolis, MN: Augsburg Publishing House, 1960.

Contains essays prepared by faculty members of midwestern Lutheran colleges, dealing with the relation of the liberal arts to the Christian faith. Explores the theological basis of Christian higher education and the relation of individual academic disciplines to the Christian faith.

1526.   Eisenberg, William E. *The Lutheran Church in Virginia, 1717-1962.* Roanoke, VA: Virginia Synod, L.C.A., 1967.

Provides a comprehensive history of Lutheran work in Virginia from 1717 to 1962. Contains a substantial chapter (pp.

331-85) on Lutheran educational institutions, including theological seminaries, colleges, women's seminaries, and a variety of other schools.

1527.   Fintel, Norman. "The Attitudes of Lutherans Toward Church Colleges." Ph.D. dissertation. University of Minnesota, 1972.

Provides a sampling and analysis of clergy and laity of The American Lutheran Church. Finds a strong sense of loyalty to the colleges of the church and a perception that these institutions are affirming Christian values.

1528.   Gamelin, Francis C. *Church-Related Identity of Lutheran Colleges.* Washington, DC: Lutheran Educational Conference of North America, 1975.

Examines the church-relatedness of 47 Lutheran colleges on the basis of their self-understanding as reflected in catalog statements and studies of church and constituency expectations. Finds variations on a scale ranging from the fully church-owned colleges of the Missouri Synod to the several independent, but voluntarily church-related colleges of the Lutheran Church in America.

1529.   Gamelin, Francis C. "Toward a Master Plan." In *Resources for the Future: Papers and Proceedings of the National Lutheran Educational Conference, 1971.*

Bases a series of proposals on extensive data assembled and analyzed in the crisis year 1970. Urges consideration of a master plan for a consortium of all Lutheran colleges. Includes valuable statistical data on enrollments, curricula, educational policies, facilities, and finances.

1530.   Haussmann, Carl Frederick. *Kunze's Seminarium.* Philadelphia: Americana Germanica Press, 1917.

Furnishes an account of the earliest Lutheran institutional venture in higher education, opened in 1773 by John Christopher Kunze, son-in-law of Henry Melchior Muhlenberg, to provide classical instruction for young men, and forced to close when the British army occupied Philadelphia in 1779.

1531.   Hong, Howard, ed. *Integration in the Christian Liberal Arts College.* Northfield, MN: St. Olaf College Press, 1956.

A well-edited summary of a faculty self-study of St. Olaf College. Deplores the tendency to fragmentation in modern college curricula, even in liberal arts colleges. Describes efforts at integration of learning and experiences, from ancient to modern times, with special emphasis on the Christian principle of the inter-relatedness of all life. Cites the potentialities for integration in the standard areas of the liberal arts curriculum. Outlines a capstone course for senior students.

1532.   Jarchow, Merrill E. *Private Liberal Arts Colleges in Minnesota.* St. Paul: Minnesota Historical Society, 1973.

Presents a series of historical, interpretive profiles of ten church-related liberal arts colleges in Minnesota, of which four are Lutheran: Augsburg, Concordia in Moorhead, Gustavus Adolphus, and St. Olaf. Deals separately with periods, 1850-1900, 1900-1940, 1940-1970.

1533.   Just, Donald. "The Purposes and Performances of the Lutheran Church-Missouri Synod Colleges." Ph.D. dissertation. School of Theology at Claremont, 1981.

1534.   Knudsen, Johannes. *The Formation of the Lutheran Church in America.* Philadelphia: Fortress Press, 1978.

Describes the formation of the Lutheran Church in America in 1962 through the merger of four Lutheran bodies. Includes a chapter on "Seminaries and Colleges" summarizing the effects of the merger on 13 seminaries and 22 colleges and describing the patterns of institutional support and governance in the new church.

1535.   Koehler, John Philipp. *History of the Wisconsin Synod,* Second Edition. Edited by Leigh Jordahl. Sauk Rapids, MN: The Protestant Conference, 1981.

Contains a comprehensive review of the Wisconsin Synod from its organization from 1850 to 1930. Includes several extensive segments dealing with Northwestern College in Watertown, Wisconsin.

1536.   Leonard, R. J., E. S. Evenden, and F. B. O'Rear. *Survey of Higher Education for the United Lutheran Church in America,* 3 vols. New York: Teachers College, Columbia University, 1929.

Summarizes the findings of a comprehensive survey by Columbia University of all collegiate institutions and campus ministries brought together under the Board of Education of the newly-formed United Lutheran Church in 1918. Contains extensive statistical data on all institutions and individual recommendations concerning improvements in faculty, facilities, services, and policies.

1537.   Lindell, Edward. "Implementation of Christian Goals in Selected Lutheran Colleges." Ph.D. dissertation. University of Denver, 1961.

1538.   Lutheran Church in America. "The Basis for Partnership Between Church and College." New York: Lutheran Church in America, 1976.

Affirms the commitment of the Lutheran Church in America to the nurture and support of church-related colleges. Makes a theological and functional distinction between the church and its related colleges. Argues that both perform services pleasing to God, but that the church has the special function of proclaiming God's Word and administering the Sacraments, while the college is primarily an educational community.

1539.   Lutheran Church in America. "The Mission of LCA Colleges and Universities." New York, NY: Lutheran Church in America, 1970.

Presents an official statement of the church concerning its mission in higher education, its standards for recognition of colleges, and the relationship of colleges to the constituent synods of the Lutheran Church in America.

1540.   Lutheran Educational Conference of North America. *Papers and Proceedings, 1968-1987*. In Archives of Cooperative Lutheranism, 360 Park Avenue South, New York, NY 10010.

Comprises one of the most valuable repositories of papers and addresses dealing with contemporary concerns of Lutheran higher education. Contains papers and commentaries at annual meetings, dealing with subjects such as public policy, student life, curriculum, church-related identity, history, educational philosophy, etc. See also National Lutheran Educational Conference, *Papers and Proceedings*, 1919-1940 and 1960-1967.

1541.   Masters, D. C. *Protestant Church Colleges in Canada*. Toronto: University of Toronto Press, 1966.

Describes the special character of church colleges within the Canadian system of higher education. Contains specific segments on Lutheran institutions, such as Waterloo Lutheran University, and Luther College in Regina.

1542.   McCullough, Paul, et al., eds. *A History of the Lutheran Church in South Carolina*. Columbia, SC: R. L. Bryan Co., 1971.

Provides a general history of the South Carolina Synod. Contains accounts (pp. 328-44, 410-17, 511-13) of the founding of Newberry College in 1858, its destruction in the Civil War, and its subsequent restoration and growth.

1543.   Meyer, Carl S. *Moving Frontiers*. St. Louis, MO: Concordia Publishing House, 1964.

Contains a series of excerpted readings and documents relating to the history of the Missouri Synod. Includes several significant segments dealing with the development of the synod's system of higher education.

1544.   Meyer, Carl S. "Secondary and Higher Education in the Lutheran

Church-Missouri Synod, 1839-1874." Ph.D. dissertation. University of Chicago, 1954.

1545.   Mortensen, Enok. *Schools for Life: The Grundtvigian Folk Schools in America.* Junction City, OR: Danish-American Heritage Society, 1977.

Contains a description of the Danish folk school, established in Denmark by Bishop N. F. S. Grundtvig in the mid-19th century, and constituting the distinctive educational contribution of Danish Lutheran immigrants to America. Emphasizes that these schools appealed especially to young adults and sought "to make every Dane an enlightened and useful citizen." Argues that in America the folk schools were pioneers in the field of adult education, using mainly lectures and discussion in history, literature, and public affairs, emphasizing open enrollments, and offering no degrees or diplomas.

1546.   National Lutheran Educational Conference.

Contains records and publications of this oldest inter-Lutheran educational association, dating from 1910, located in the Archives of Cooperative Lutheranism, 360 Park Avenue South, New York, New York 10010. Included are the published *Papers and Proceedings*, 1919-1940 and 1960-1967, and the continued series of the Lutheran Educational Conference of North America, 1967- . See also Item 1540.

1547.   Olsen, Arthur L., ed. *Cooperation for the Future.* Washington, DC: Lutheran Educational Conference of North America, 1976.

Contains the final report of a four-year study by the Committee of the Future, conducted by the Lutheran Educational Conference of North America. Provides summaries of committee studies, including position statements and recommendations on master planning, public policy, and liberal learning. Includes an institutional data study of Lutheran institutions from 1971 to 1975.

1548.   Pannkoke, Otto H. *A Great Church Finds Itself.* Quitman, GA: Privately published, 1966.

Contains descriptive material relating to the numerous financial campaigns conducted by Lutheran colleges during the 1920's in order to establish endowments meeting standards established by regional accrediting agencies.

1549.   Parsonage, Robert Rue, ed. *Church-Related Higher Education.* Valley Forge, PA: Judson Press, 1978.

Contains a chapter (pp. 206-22) on current denominational policies in higher education, including a succinct summary of the policies of major Lutheran church bodies.

1550.	Schmidt, Stephen A. *Powerless Pedagogues.* River Forest, IL: Lutheran Education Association, 1972.

Interprets the history of the Lutheran parochial school teacher in the Missouri Synod, but also provides insights into the programs of the Concordias at River Forest, Illinois, and Seward, Nebraska, colleges specifically designed for teacher training. Shows how the self-image of teachers and the colleges from which they graduated was weakened by the priority given to education of Missouri's clergy.

1551.	Schwiebert, Ernest G. *Luther and His Times.* St. Louis, MO: Concordia Publishing House, 1950.

Contains a description of the German university life and structure experienced by Martin Luther. Provides insight into the historical roots and impulses which were later translated into the higher education institutions of Lutherans in America.

1552.	Sernett, Milton C. "Afro-Americans and Lutheran Higher Education." Resource paper prepared for the History Project of the Lutheran Educational Conference of North America, 1984. 89 pages, including extensive bibliography. In Archives of Cooperative Lutheranism, New York City.

Asserts that with only a few exceptions Lutheran colleges did not become seriously involved in the education of black students until the late 1960s.

1553.	Solberg, Richard W. *Lutheran Higher Education in North America.* Minneapolis, MN: Augsburg Publishing House, 1985.

Provides a comprehensive interpretative survey of Lutheran ventures in higher education in North America from colonial times to the present. Finds the basic Lutheran commitment to an educated clergy rooted in Luther's theology transferred to America through German and Scandinavian immigration. Describes the founding of colleges to meet local needs and traces their development into a system of 50 institutions adapted to the American educational scene, while maintaining a strong loyalty to the church and a firm commitment to liberal arts education.

1554.	Solberg, Richard W. and Merton Strommen. *How Church-Related are Church-Related Colleges?.* Philadelphia: Board of Publications, Lutheran Church in America, 1980.

Presents an interpretive summary of an extensive survey of the images and expectations of 18 LCA-related colleges, held by their supporting constituencies: students, faculty, trustees, parents, clergy, alumni, church leaders, and church members. Finds that 6,728 participants showed notable differences in the expectations of constituent groups, but an overall positive affirmation of the value of the church-related college. The research report itself is available in the Archives of Cooperative Lutheranism, 360 Park Avenue South, New York, New York 10010.

1555.   Wickey, Gould. *Lutheran Cooperation Through Lutheran Higher Education.* Washington, DC: Lutheran Educational Conference of North America, 1967.

Provides a documentary history of the National Lutheran Educational Conference, 1910-1967. Includes lists of officers and leaders, special resolutions of annual meetings, descriptions of services provided by the Conference to colleges and seminaries, and a catalog of papers and addresses organized according to subject categories that furnishes a record of a half-century of major concerns of Lutheran educators.

1556.   Wickey, Gould. *The Lutheran Venture in Higher Education.* Philadelphia: Board of Publications, United Lutheran Church in America, 1962.

Contains an essay on the theology of Lutheran education, followed by brief surveys of Lutheran "ventures" into theological and college education and campus ministry. Lists Lutheran colleges and seminaries existing in 1962.

CHAPTER 20
MENNONITE COLLEGES
Albert N. Keim

1557.   *A Study of Mennonite Higher Education.* Harrisonburg, VA: Study
Commission on Mennonite Higher Education, 1957.

Surveys the status of Mennonite College resources,
curriculum, and faculty. Assesses the long-term needs for
Mennonite higher education. Projects program responses to those
needs.

1558.   Bauman, Harold Ernest. *The Believer's Church and the Church
College.* Ed.D. dissertation. Teachers College, Columbia
University, 1972.

Describes the shape and form of a church college based on
a believer's church theology and tradition. Argues that a believer's
church college will be preoccupied with the campus as an open
Christian community, preparing students for reconciliation
ministries, teaching students how to integrate their faith and
practice in Biblically appropriate ways. The foil is the conventional
"puritan college."

1559.   Deckert, Marion. "What is Liberal Arts Education?" *Mennonite
Life* 34 (March 1979): 4-7.

"How shall I as a Christian live?" asks the author. The
liberal arts hold the promise, not of an answer, but the prospect of
a free search from which may come an answer.

1560.   Epp, Frank H. *Education With a Plus: The Story of Rosthern
Junior College.* Waterloo, Ontario: Conrad Press, 1975.

State-of-the-art history by a master historian. Relates the
seventy year history of a college struggling to navigate the
treacherous shoals of massive cultural change experienced by
Canadian Mennonites.

1561.   *Faculty Dialogue* 6. North Newton, KS: Bethel College, 1986.

A collection of nine essays delivered at a Conference on
Faith and Learning. The focus is on how to create community on
Christian college campuses.

1562.   Friesen, Duane K. *"Peace Studies: Mennonite Colleges in the North American Context." Mennonite Life* 35 (March 1980): 4-7.

Mennonite Colleges are unique in their official commitment to pacifism. Surveys how the Mennonite Colleges incorporate peace studies in their curricula. Peace studies tend to be clustered in the theological and social science departments, with not much attention to the newer quantitative peace research methodologies.

1563.   Hertzler, Daniel. *Mennonite Education: Why and How?* Scottdale, PA: Herald Press, 1971.

This volume comes as close to an official statement of educational purpose and philosophy as the Mennonite Church has developed. The goal of education must be Christian maturity defined as faith in Christ in the context of commitment to Christian community.

1564.   Jansen, Waldemar. *A Basic Educational Philosophy.* Winnipeg, Manitoba: Canadian Mennonite Bible College, 1966.

Addresses the nature of academic freedom, the role of the liberal arts in theological education, and the key goals of religious education at the college level.

1565.   Kauffman, J. Howard, and Leland Harder. *Anabaptists Four Centuries Later.* Scottdale, PA: Herald Press, 1975.

Sociological survey of Mennonite opinions and attitudes including higher education issues.

1566.   Kauffman, Norman Lee. *The Impact of Study Abroad On Personality Change.* Ed.D. dissertation. Indiana University, 1983.

Attempts to measure and report on the effect of the Goshen College Study Service Trimester abroad program. Found that SST students demonstrated significant increases in self-esteem, independence, interest in reflective thought, and concern for the welfare of others as compared to comparison groups at other Mennonite colleges.

1567.   Lederach, Paul M. *Mennonite Youth.* Scottdale, PA: Herald Press, 1971.

Summarizes research findings on Mennonite youth regarding a wide range of values. Provides a basis for Christian nurture and educational strategy for the Mennonite church.

1568.   Lehman, Ruth K. *"The One Thing Lacking ...: The Status of Women At Eastern Mennonite College, 1917-1980."* Honors Thesis. Harrisonburg, VA: James Madison University, 1981.

Thorough and critical historical study of the evolution and

change in the role of women at a small Mennonite college. A story of pathos and sacrificial service. A portrayal of the power of gender discrimination in a religiously conservative academic institution.

1569.   Meyer, Albert J. *Study of Academic Sub-Communities of other Church-Related Academic Resources on University Campuses.* Elkhart, IN: Mennonite Board of Education, 1969.

Purpose of the study is to explore and develop a model, based on Anabaptist-Mennonite theological premises and Mennonite student needs, of a college adjacent to a large public university. The key idea is to take advantage of the vast resources of the university while preserving the communal values held in such high esteem by the Mennonite church. Two models which have emerged since the study are Conrad Grebel College, established as a satellite college on the campus of the University of Waterloo, Ont., and the Messiah College-Temple University Center in Philadelphia.

1570.   Miller, Ira E. *The Development and the Present Status of Mennonite Secondary and Higher Education in the United States and Canada.* Ed.D. dissertation. Temple University, 1963.

An effort to identify the historical and philosophical roots of Mennonite higher education and determine how and whether that history and philosophy is being applied in the contemporary Mennonite college programs.

1571.   Miller, Mary. *A Pillar of Cloud: The Story of Hesston College, 1909-1959.* North Newton, KS: Mennonite Press, 1959.

The Mennonite Church had three junior colleges (one closed recently). This is the story of the largest of the two. Like so many small religious colleges of this era, Hesston College was the work of a few creative and dedicated souls who gave their lives for great ideals, and against all odds, succeeded.

1572.   Pellman, Hubert R. *Eastern Mennonite College, 1917-1967: A History.* Harrisonburg, VA, 1968.

Careful recreation of the often painful transitions of a small sectarian institution struggling through the maze of 20th century change.

1573.   Prieb, Wesley J., and Donald Ratzlaff. *To A Higher Plane of Vision.* Hillsboro, KS: Tabor College, 1983.

History of Tabor College. Data at the end of the volume offer enticing glimpses into the nature of midwestern Mennonite higher education.

1574.   Rediger, Wesley Arnold. *The Achievement of Functional Aims At Eastern Mennonite College as Perceived by Selected Institutional*

Reference Groups. Ed.D. dissertation. Ball State University, 1985.

Focus of the study is on how selected alumni and students of the college perceive the aims of the college to be accomplished.

1575.   Sider, E. Morris. *Messiah College: A History.* Nappanee, IN: Evangel Press, 1984.

Story of a Christian college with a tiny constituency (Brethren in Christ) which reached out beyond that constituency to embrace a wide spectrum of conservative evangelical Christianity, a feat both positive and negative, according to the author.

1576.   Toews, Paul. "Fundamentalist Conflict in Mennonite Colleges: A Response to Cultural Transitions." *Mennonite Quarterly Review* 57 (July 1983): 241-56.

Between 1915 and 1950 Mennonite Colleges were often lightning rods in the struggle between Mennonite progressives and conservatives. The contest was not only a theological controversy, but a complex interplay of personalities, burgeoning denominational organizations and cultural and ethnic changes. As Mennonites moved from agrarian sectarianism to middle-class Protestantism the stresses of change were especially resonant in the colleges.

1577.   Umble, John S. *Goshen College, 1894-1954: A Venture in Higher Education.* Goshen, IN: Goshen College, 1955.

History of the largest of the Mennonite liberal arts colleges, critical, and well written. A college with a strong tradition of scholarship in church history and theology, serving a sectarian church whose commitment to liberal arts has been marginal. The story is thus more dramatic than one finds in many college histories.

1578.   Weaver, Henry. "Its Time For A New Look At Our Mennonite Colleges." *Gospel Herald*, 79, October 21, 1986, pp. 718-19.

Emphasizes the importance of research in church colleges. Argues that the cost of education should be increasingly borne by the congregations who send the students to church colleges. Believes some new innovative organizational arrangements should be developed to enhance the academic and financial viability of Mennonite Colleges.

1579.   Wedel, Peter J. *The Story of Bethel College.* North Newton, KS: Bethel College, 1954.

Bethel College carries the legacy of the Russian Mennonites who came to the United States in the 1870s and 1880s. The College, a conduit for Americanization, has also helped preserve the rich heritage of these Mennonites, whose Dutch, Prussian, and Russian pilgrimage lasted nearly three centuries.

1580. Wiens, Delbert. *From the Village to the City: A Grammar For the Languages We Are.* Winnipeg, Manitoba, 1974.

Acculturation of Mennonite ethnic life in the American setting is powerfully affected by educational enterprises. Using the city as metaphor for the world, the author provocatively suggests how the content of Christian faith and ethnic identity might be transmuted into new forms and new understandings.

1581. Yoder, Lee M. *The Development of Functional Aims of Eastern Mennonite College and a Study of Their Relationship to the Organization of the Curriculum.* Ed.D. dissertation. Temple University, 1979.

Functional aims are the consensus values expressed by the College in its philosophy statement. The purpose is to tease out the essential values in functional terms in order to assess whether the curriculum exhibits the aims in its organization.

1582.   Blair, Marian. "Contemporary Evidence -- Salem Boarding School, 1834-1844." *North Carolina Historical Review* 54 (July 1977): 142-61.

Blair uses the letters received by the 1834 academy principal to picture the life within the school and to provide insights on the conditions within the South which tended to affect the growth of the institution from a secondary school to a college.

1583.   Comenius Medallion Presentation. *Mortimer Adler Convocation.* Bethlehem, PA: Moravian College, 28 February 1984.

Each year Moravian College recognizes a renowned educator who in some way exemplifies the educational leadership of Comenius. Mortimer Adler and Elie Weisel have been recent recipients. Tape recordings of the presentations are available in the college library.

1584.   Fries, Adelaide. *Historical Sketch of Salem Female Academy.* Salem, NC: Crist and Kehln, 1902.

Earliest publication from local historian on beginnings of the academy which eventually became Salem College.

1585.   Gramley, Dale H. *Remembrances of Salem's 13th President.* Salem, NC: Salem Academy and College, 1985.

The President's personal remembrances of life at Salem College during his work there from 1949-1971.

1586.   Griffin, Francis. *Less Time for Meddling: A History of Salem Academy and College, 1772-1866.* Winston-Salem, NC: John Blair, 1979.

Shows how the Moravian girls' school founded on Comenian educational philosophy eventually became a boarding school for girls from prominent southern families.

1587.   Haller, Mabel. "Early Moravian Education in Pennsylvania." *Transactions of the Moravian Historical Society* 15 (1953): 1-409.

Contains exhaustive bibliography of primary sources found within the Moravian Archives. The history covers the development of Bethlehem, Nazareth, Lititz and other extinct Moravian academies. Also covers the Indian missions and the Moravian educational philosophy. Provides insights into the beginnings of Moravian College.

1588. Hamilton, Kenneth, ed. *Records of the Moravians in North Carolina*. Raleigh, NC: 1966.

Contains volumes of historical information on many facets of Moravian life. Volumes 10 and 11 include information on education and Salem College in particular.

1589. Hixon, Ivy. "Academic Requirements of Salem College, 1854-1909." *North Carolina Historical Review* 54 (July 1977): 419-29.

Uses formal college catalogues and issues of *The Academy* as well as Moravian histories to show how the academy evolved into an institution of higher learning.

1590. Kurdybacha, Luktasz. "Comenius Documents in Poland." *School and Society* 98 (November 1970): 446.

Discusses some of the 695 documents in state archives in Poznan. Documents include Comenian letters and documents from the Leszno high school.

1591. Monroe, Will. *Comenius and the Beginnings of Educational Reform*. New York: Charles Scribner's Sons, 1912.

Explains the impact Comenius had on European educational reformers like Francke, Rousseau, Pestalozzi, Froebel and Herbart.

1592. Pope, James D. "Comenius Speaks to Modern Man." *School and Society* 98 (November 1970): 440-45.

Argues that Comenius could help educators reconsider issues such as the proper relationship between school and society, the need for an international language, the role of education in preventing war.

1593. Rights, Douglas L. "Salem in the War Between the States." *North Carolina Historical Review* 27 (July 1950): 277-88.

Shows how and in what manner the Salem girls' school was able to remain open during the war.

1594. Roberts, Paul C. "Comenian Philosophy and Moravian Education from 1850 to the Present Day." Ph.D. dissertation. Rutgers University, 1979.

Concludes that Comenian philosophy may still be present in the elementary schools but is less pervasive in the Moravian College.

1595.   Wenhold, Lucy. "The Salem Boarding School Between 1802 and 1822." *North Carolina Historical Review* 52 (July 1977): 32-46.

Reconstructs the intimate life of the school's first two decades of existence before it evolved into a college.

CHAPTER 22
PENTECOSTAL COLLEGES
Edith L. Blumhofer

A. Assemblies of God

1596.   *Assemblies of God Educator*

Reports trends, enrollments, faculty accomplishments and various statistics pertaining to Assemblies of God colleges; published quarterly by the demomination's Department of Education.

1597.   Collins, Millard E. "Establishing and Financing of Higher Educational Institutions in the Church Body of the Assemblies of God in the U.S.A." Ed.D dissertation. University of Texas, 1959.

Examines the founding of the major Assemblies of God colleges, analyzes the debate over appropriate education and discusses how problems of finance and competition for limited resources were resolved.

1598.   Gray, Donald Paul. "A Critical Analysis of the Academic Evolutionary Development Within the Assemblies of God Higher Education Movement, 1914-1975." Ed.D. dissertation. Southwestern Baptist Theological Seminary, 1976.

Describes the changing attitudes toward denominationally sponsored higher education within the Assemblies of God, examining especially factors pertaining to organization, personnel, and curriculum development.

1599.   Guynes, Eleanor R. "Development of the Educational Program of the Assemblies of God from the School Year 1948-1949 up to the Present." M. A. thesis. Southern Methodist University, 1966.

Reviews the history of Assemblies of God Bible college education in the post-World War II era with an emphasis on educational theory.

1600.   Nelson, Larry. "The Demise of O'Reilly Hospital and the Beginning of Evangel College, 1946-1955." *Missouri Historical Review* 81 (July 1987): 417-46.

Reviews the history of Evangel College, the only Assemblies

of God liberal arts institution, by setting the college's founding in a broader context and dealing with the tensions within a denomination traditionally committed only to Bible college training about endorsing a liberal arts institution.

1601.   Strahan, Richard Dobbs. "A Study to Introduce Curriculum Approaches and Student Personnel Services for Evangel College." Ed.D. dissertation. University of Houston, 1955.

Focuses on early denominational decisions about the direction for liberal arts education in the Assemblies of God and analyzes the school's initial curricular approach.

1602.   Strahan, Richard Dobbs. "The Development of Education in the Assemblies of God." M. Ed. thesis. Southern Methodist University, 1949.

Describes early Assemblies of God attitudes toward education and the founding of institutions that became Bible colleges. Written before the schools fully evolved into colleges and before the denomination's debate over sponsoring liberal arts education was resolved. The thesis represents an early stage in scholarly efforts to assess Assemblies of God education.

B. Church of God (Cleveland, TN)

1603.   Butler, Stanley. "Developing a Manual of Operation for Lee College." Ed.S. thesis. George Peabody School of Education, 1959.

Describes the policy on which Lee College operated to 1959. The author discusses both the written and unwritten policies on which the institution operates.

1604.   Christenbury, Eugene Carl. "Study of Teacher Education in Sixteen Pentecostal Colleges in the U.S." Ed.D. dissertation. University of Tennessee, 1972.

Analyzes 16 Pentecostal colleges representing various Pentecostal denominations to determine the effectiveness of their teacher education programs. He discusses the objectives and organization of the programs; faculty selection and preparation; faculty teaching loads; curriculum development; professional laboratory experiences; student personnel services; library facilities and enrollment trends.

1605.   Conn, Charles Paul. *The Music Makers.* Cleveland, TN: Pathway Press, 1971.

Presents the music program at Lee College. The book profiles the Lee College Singers and the college choir.

1606.   Duncan, Paul E. *On Campus.* Cleveland, TN: Pathway Press, 1977.

Offers guidelines for selecting a college; tips on knowing which Christian college would best suit one's preferences; and guidelines for assuring success in one's college experience.

1607.   Estrada Adorno, Wilfredo. "Reconciliation of Charismatic Pastors and Bible College Professors in the Service of Training for Future Ministry in the Pentecostal Bible College of the Church of God." D. Min. dissertation. Emory University, Candler School of Theology, 1982.

Applies especially to the Church of God's Bible college in Puerto Rico. It analyzes a rift within Church of God ranks that affected both the theology and the "style" of instructors at the school. The thesis discusses the prospects of reconciling old-line pastors of a group known as the Mission Board of Church of God in Puerto Rico with the faculty of the Church of God's Pentecostal Bible College in Puerto Rico.

1608.   Fisher, Robert E. "Follow-Up Study of the Graduates of West Coast Bible College, 1952-1966." M.A. thesis. Fresno State College, 1967.

Analyzes the characteristics of the graduates; discussions of the opinions selected graduates expressed about their educational training; graduates' evaluations of administration, instructional methods, school priorities and the overall school program.

1609.   Gilbert, Earl J. "Some Personality Correlates of Certain Religious Beliefs, Attitudes, Practices and Experiences in Students Attending a Fundamentalist Church College." Ed.D. thesis. University of Tennessee, Knoxville, 1972.

Focuses on students at Lee College in Cleveland, TN; attempts to discover relationships between religious beliefs and attitudes and experiences students encounter in the Pentecostal setting of Lee College.

1610.   Griffith, Wanda. "Study of Students Placed on Academic Probation, 1978-1983." M.S. thesis. University of Tennessee, Knoxville, 1983.

Presents a five-year-long study of students who were placed on academic probation at Lee College during the fall, 1978 semester.

1611.   Horton, E. Gene. *History of Lee Junior College.* N.p., 1953.

Discusses in a general, popular style, the origins of Lee College.

1612.   Hughes, Ray H. "The Transition of Church-related Junior Colleges to Senior Colleges, with Implications for Lee College." Ed.D. thesis.

University of Tennessee, 1981.

Examines the trends within Pentecostal education that led first from short-term Bible institutes to permanent Bible schools, then to junior colleges, and later to four-year colleges.

1613.   Johnson, Robert G. "Establishment and Development of Lee College, 1918-1954." M.A. thesis. Memphis State, 1955.

Describes the general development of Lee College.

1614.   *Look at Lee College.* Cleveland, TN: Pathway Press, 1968.

Provides information about the curriculum and facilities of Lee College, the Church of God, Cleveland's liberal arts college.

1615.   McBrayer, R. Terrell. *Lee College: Pioneer in Pentecostal Education.* Cleveland, TN: Pathway Press, 1968.

Introduces Lee College. The author, a Church of God adherent, presents highlights in the college's history. His purpose in so doing is to analyze the past for direction for the future and to introduce to lay people, using a popular style, what he considers the church's "rich" educational heritage. This book, which was a tribute to the school for its 50th anniversary, was also written to solicit support for the school's continued development. It is directed both to alumni and to prospective students.

1616.   Smith, Henry J. "Development of the Educational System of the Church of God as it Relates to Ministerial Preparation, 1918-1978." D. Min. dissertation. California Graduate School of Theology, 1979.

Examines the development of Church of God training institutions from their inception to 1918 as Bible training institutes to their present role as accredited institutions. Smith emphasizes the role the Bible study plays in Church of God institutions and discusses how this relates to an understanding of the appropriate preparation for Church of God ministries.

1617.   Smith, Henry J. "History of West Coast Bible College." M.A. thesis. Fresno State College, 1970.

Studies the origins, history and development of West Coast Bible College, a Church of God (Cleveland) college in Fresno, California. (The name of the school has since been changed to West Coast Christian College.)

1618.   Spence, G. H. *History of Northwest Bible College.* N.p., 1974.

Sketches the history of Northwest Bible College, a Church of God (Cleveland) school in Minot, North Dakota; directed to the general reader.

1619.   "Teaching From a Christian Perspective." Papers presented at a
        Lee College faculty seminar, 1979.

        Explores the way Christian faith influences classroom
        teaching. These papers, by members of the Lee College faculty,
        offer advice about teaching the Bible, language arts and teacher
        education courses from a Christian perspective in a Christian
        college.

1620.   Underwood, James L. "Historical Development of Lee Junior
        College." M.S. thesis. University of Tennessee, 1954.

        Studies the programs offered through Lee Junior College. Its
        emphasis is on the junior college phase of Lee's development.

CHAPTER 23
PRESBYTERIAN (USA) COLLEGES AND UNIVERSITIES
A. Myrvin De Lapp

Part I. Institutional Histories

1621.   Agnes Scott College (1889)

1622.   McNair, Walter Edward. *Lest We Forget.* Decatur, GA: Agnes
         Scott College, 1983.

1623.   Alma College (1886)

1624.   Stuftin, Joe, Coordinator History Project. *Within Our Bounds. A
         Centennial History of Alma College.* Alma, MI: 1986.

1625.   Arkansas College (1872)

1626.   "Arkansas College 1872-1972." *The Independence County
         Chronicle.* 14 (October 1972): 5-54.

1627.   Austin College (1849)

1628.   Landolt, George L. *Search for the Summit, Austin College Through
         XII Decades, 1849-1970.* Austin, TX: Von-Boechman-Jones Co.,
         1970.

1629.   Barber-Scotia College (1876)

1630.   Cozart, Leland Stanford. *A Venture of Faith.* Charlotte, NC:
         Heritage Printers, Inc., 1976.

1631.   Beaver College (1853)

1632.   Higgins, Ruth L. and Mary S. Sturgeon. *Beaver College: The First
         Hundred Years.* Jenkintown, PA: Alumnae Association, 1954.

1633.   Belhaven College (1883)

1634.   Gordon, James F., Jr. *A History of Belhaven College.* Jackson,
         MS: Belhaven College, 1983.

1635.   Blackburn College (1837)

1636.   McConagha, Glen L. *Blackburn College 1837-1987: An Anecdotal
         and Analytical History.* Carlinville, IL: Blackburn College, 1987.

1637.   Bloomfield College (1868)

1638. Allshouse, Merle F. "Bloomfield College." *Institutional Renewal: Case Histories.* Edited by Douglas Steeples, San Francisco: Jossey-Bass, 1986.

1639. Taylor, Harry T. *Bloomfield College. The First Century. 1868-1968.* Bloomfield, NJ: Bloomfield College, 1968.

1640. Buena Vista College (1891)

1641. Cumberland, William H. *The History of Buena Vista College.* Ames, IA: The Iowa State University Press, 1966.

1642. Carroll College (1846)

1643. Langill, Ellen. *Carroll College, The First Century 1846-1946.* Waukesha, WI: The Carroll Press, 1980.

1644. Centre College (1819)

1645. Craig, Hardin. *Centre College of Kentucky: A Tradition and an Opportunity.* Louisville, KY: Gateway Press, 1967.

1646. Strode, William. *Centre College.* Louisville, KY: Harmony House, 1985.

1647. Groves, Walter A. "Centre College, the Second Phase, 1830-1957." (Reprinted from *The Filson Club History Quarterly.* October 1950, pp. 311-34.)

1648. Hewlett, James H. "Centre College of Kentucky, 1819-1830." (Reprinted from *The Filson Club History Quarterly.* July 1944, pp. 173-91.)

1649. Coe College (1851)

No published history, Cedar Rapids, IA.

1650. Davidson College (1837)

1651. Beaty, Mary. *A History of Davidson College.* Davidson, NC: Briarpatch Press, 1987.

1652. Davis and Elkins College (1904)

1653. Ross, Thomas Richard. *The Diamond Jubilee History* (Davis and Elkins College). Parsons, WV: McClain Printing Co., 1980.

1654. Dubuque, The University of (1852)

No published history, Dubuque, IA.

1655. Eckerd College (1960)

No published history. Unpublished speech by President Peter H. Armacost to Newcomen Society, 1987 for short history,

St. Petersburg, FL.

1656.   Ganado, College of (1901)

       No published history, Ganado, AR.

1657.   Grove City College (1876)

1658.   Dayton, David M. *'Mid the Pines.* Westerville, OH: West-Camp Press, 1973.

1659.   Hampden-Sydney College (1776)

1660.   Bradshaw, Herbert C. *History of Hampden-Sydney College.* Vol. I --to 1856, published privately. Vol. II-- in progress, Professor John Brinkley, Hampden-Sydney, VA.

1661.   Hanover College (1827)

1662.   Baker, Frank S. *Glimpses of Hanover's Past.* Seymour: IN: Graessle-Mercer Co., 1978.

1663.   Millis, William A. *History of Hanover College.* Greenfield, IN: Mitchell Printing Co., 1927.

1664.   Hastings College (1882)

1665.   Weyer, Frank E. *Hastings College Seventy-Five Years in Retrospect 1882-1957.* Hastings, NE: Hastings College, 1957.

1666.   Hawaii Loa College (1963)

       No published history.

1667.   Idaho, College of (1891)

       No published history *per se.* Basic information in the biography of Dr. William Judson Boone. *That Man Boone: Frontiersman of Idaho.* H. H. Hayman. Caldwell, ID: The College of Idaho, 1948.

1668.   Illinois College (1829)

1669.   Frank, Charles E. *Pioneer's Progress, Illinois College, 1829, 1979.* Jacksonville, IL: Southern Illinois University Press, 1979.

1670.   Jamestown College (1883)

1671.   Kroeze, Barend H. *A Prairie Saga.* St. Paul, MN: North Central Publishing Co., 1952.

1672.   Johnson C. Smith University (1967)

1673.   Parker, Inex Moore. *The Biddle-Johnson C. Smith University.* Charlotte, NC: Observer Craftsman Co., 1975.

1674.   King College (1867)

        No published history. Brief brochure only, Bristol, TN.

1675.   Knoxville, College of (1875)

        No published history. Knoxville, TN.

1676.   Lafayette College (1826)

1677.   Gendebien, Albert W. *The Biography of a College.* Easton, PA: Lafayette College, 1986.

1678.   Skillman, David Bishop. *The Biography of a College.* 2 vols. Easton, PA: Lafayette College, 1932.

1679.   Lake Forest College (1857)

        No published history. See Arpee, Edward. *The History of Lake Forest Academy.* Chicago, IL: Alderbrink Press, 1944.

1680.   Lees College (1853)

1681.   Begley, Nancy Stamper. "Had It Not Been for Lees." Special edition of *Recollections.* A Journal of the Appalachian Oral History Project at Lees Junior College, Jackson, KY, 1983, pp. 1-46.

1682.   Lees-McRae College (1900)

1683.   Neal, Margaret Tufts. *And Set Aglow a Sacred Flame.* Banner Elk, NC: Pudding Stone Press, 1942.

1684.   Lewis and Clark College (1866)

        No published history reported. Portland, OR.

1685.   Lindenwood College (1827)

1686.   Templin, Lucinda de Leftwich, compiler. *Reminiscences of Lindenwood College.* St. Charles, MO: 1920. *The Newer Lindenwood in Commemoration of the Dedication of Roemer Hall.* St. Charles, MO: 1921.

1687.   Macalester College (1885)

1688.   Hakala Associates, Inc. *Macalester College, A Century and Beyond.* St. Paul, MN: Macalester College, 1985.

1689.   Mary Baldwin College (1842)

1690.   Waddell, Joseph A., Compiler. *History of Mary Baldwin Seminary.* Staunton, VA: Augusta Printing Corp., 1908.

1691.   Watters, Mary. *The History of Mary Baldwin College, 1842-1942.* Staunton, VA: Mary Baldwin College, 1943.

1692.   Mary Holmes College (1892)

1693.   Pfeifer, Helen F. *Something of a Faith: A Brief History of Mary Holmes College.* West Point, MS: 1967.

1694.   Maryville College (1819)

1695.   Lloyd, Ralph W. *Maryville College: A History of 150 Years. 1819-1969.* Marville, TN: Maryville College Press and Kingsport Press, 1969.

1696.   Millikin College (1901)

          No published history. W. D. Lewis, "Millikin University." Chapter 56 in the *History of Macon County.* Decatur, IL: 1976.

1697.   Missouri Valley College (1889)

          No published history.

1698.   Monmouth College (1853)

1699.   Davenport, F. Garvin. *Monmouth College -- The First Hundred Years 1853-1953.* Cedar Rapids, IA: Torch Press, 1953.

1700.   Crow, Mary with William Urban, Charles Speel, Samuel Thompson. *A History of Monmouth College-Through Its Fifth Quarter Century.* Monmouth, IL: Monmouth Press, 1979.

1701.   Montreat-Anderson College (1916)

1702.   Anderson, Robert Campbell. *The Story of Montreat from Its Beginning 1897-1947.* Kingsport, TN: Kingsport Press, 1949.

1703.   Davis, Calvin Grier. *Montreat-A Retreat for Renewal, 1947-1972.* Kingsport, TN: Arcata Graphics, 1986.

1704.   Muskingum College (1837)

1705.   Fisk, William L. *A History of Muskingum College.* New Concord, OH: The College, 1978.

1706.   Occidental College (1887)

1707.   Rolle, Andrew. *Occidental College: A Centennial History, 1887-1987.* Los Angeles, CA: Castle Press, 1986.

1708.   University of the Ozarks (1834)

1709.   Commemorative publication, Clarksville, AR: University of the Ozarks, Steve G. Edmisten *et al.*, 1984.

1710.   School of the Ozarks (1906)

1711.   Godsey, Townsend and Helen Godsey. *Flight of the Phoenix.* Point Lookout, MO: S of O Press, 1984.

1712. Peace College (1857)

1713. Centennial celebration publication. *Personae: The History of Peace College.* Raleigh, NC: Peace College, 1972.

1714. Pikesville College (1889)

No published history. Pikesville, KY.

1715. Presbyterian College (1880)

1716. Hammet, Ben Hay. *The Spirit of PC: A Centennial History of Presbyterian College.* Clinton, SC: Presbyterian College, 1980.

1717. Queens College (1857)

1718. McEwen, Mildred Morse. *Queens College: Yesterday and Today.* Charlotte, NC: Heritage Printers, Inc., 1980.

1719. Rhodes College (1937)

1720. Roper, James. *Southwestern at Memphis 1948-1975. The College.* (written before name change). Memphis, TN: Southwestern Presbyterian University, 1975.

1721. Rocky Mountain College (1883)

1722. Buhl, Marjorie Carter. *Open Doors.* 75th Anniversary Publications, Billings, MT: The College, 1958.

1723. St. Andrews (1896)

Melton, George E. *St. Andrews: A Brief History.* Twentieth Anniversary publication, Laurinburg, NC: 1981.

1724. Schreiner College (1923)

No published history.

1725. Sheldon Jackson College (1878)

1726. Yaw, W. Leslie. *Sixty Years in Sitka with Sheldon Jackson School.* Sitka, AK: Sheldon Jackson Press and Caxton Press, Ltd., 1985.

1727. Armstrong, Neal A. "Sheldon Jackson Scenes: A Documentary History of Sheldon Jackson Junior College, Sitka, Alaska, 1878-1967." Ed.D. dissertation. George Peabody College for Teachers. Nashville, TN: George Peabody College for Teachers, 1968.

1728. Hinckley, Theodore C. "Sheldon Jackson Junior College: Sitka Alaska's Historic Nucleus of the Presbyterian Enterprise in the Great Land." *Alaska Review.* Alaska Methodist University, 1968.

1729.   Sterling College (1887)

1730.   Buchanan, Christine and Tom Buchanan. *Sterling College: Co-Worker with God.* Sterling, KS: Sterling College, 1987.

1731.   Stillman College (1876)

         No published history reported. Tuscaloosa, AL.

1732.   Tarkio College (1883)

1733.   Ostertag, John, compiler. *Tracing your Roots in the Missouri River Valley.* St. Joseph, MO: AN Foods, 1987.

1734.   Laur, George. "Mule Barn Repertoire." *Rural Missouri.* Jefferson City: Association of Missouri Electric Cooperative, May 1980.

1735.   Trinity University (1869)

1736.   Everett, Donald. *Trinity University. A Record of One Hundred Years.* San Antonio, TX: Trinity University Press, 1969.

1737.   The University of Tulsa (1869)

1738.   Logsdon, Guy William. *The University of Tulsa.* Norman, OK: University of Oklahoma Press, 1976.

1739.   Tusculum College (1794)

1740.   Furhmann, Joseph. *Life and Times of Tusculum College.* Kingsport, TN: Arcata Graphics, 1987.

1741.   Warren Wilson College (1894)

1742.   Jensen, Henry W. and Elizabeth G. Martin. *A History of Warren Wilson College.* Swannanoa, NC: Warren Wilson College Press, 1974.

1743.   Banker, Mark T. *Toward Frontiers Yet Unknown.* Swannanoa, NC: Warren Wilson College Press, 1984.

1744.   Waynesburg College (1849)

1745.   Dusenberry, William Howard. *The Waynesburg College Story.* Waynesburg, PA: The Kent State University Press, 1975.

1746.   Westminster College (1851)

1747.   Parrish, William E. *Westminster College: An Informal History, 1851-1969.* Fulton, MO: Westminster College, 1971.

1748.   Westminster College (1852)

1749.   Gamble, Paul. *History of Westminster College, 1852-1977.* New Willmington, PA: The College, 1977.

1750.   Westminster College (1875)

1751. Nyman, Emil. *A Short History of Westminster College, Salt Lake City: The First Century, 1875-1975.* Salt Lake City, UT: The College, 1976.

1752. Whitworth College (1890)

1753. Gray, Alfred O. *Not By Might: The Story of Whitworth College, 1890/1965.* Spokane, WA: C.W. Hill Printing Co., 1965.

1754. Wilson College (1869)

Books in progress. "History of an Idea." Wilson College Bulletin, Volume XXXII, No. 5, 1869. "Wilson College -- 1870-1910 -- Forty Years of Wilson as told by Her Presidents, Faculty and Students." Compiled by Nettie Hesson Lloyd, Class of 1897, Associate Alumnae, 1910, Repository Press, Chambersburg, PA.

1755. The College of Wooster (1866)

1756. Notestein, Luck Lilian. *Wooster of the Middle West.* 2 vols. Wooster, OH: The Kent State University Press, 1971.

Part II: General Works

1757. Astin, Alexander W. and Calvin B. T. Lee. *The Invisible College: A Profile of Small, Private Colleges with Limited Resources.* Eighth of a Series of Profiles Sponsored by The Carnegie Commission on Higher Education. New York: McGraw-Hill, 1972.

The authors examine both the contributions and the problems facing certain small liberal arts colleges. Religious roots of some colleges have helped their "staying power" but the future looks doubtful.

1757. *(a)* Ben-David, Joseph. *American Higher Education: Directions Old and New.* Second of a Series of Essays sponsored by the Carnegie Commission on Higher Education. New York: McGraw-Hill, 1972.

Is an exceptionally clear discussion of the moral and political implications of liberal education.

1758. Bergethon, K. Ronald. "Background Remarks for General Session of the Presbyterian College Union with the National Task Force on the United Presbyterian Church and Higher Education." Washington, DC: February 4, 1979.

An experienced college administrator and ecclesiastical statesperson points to the need for a new statement by the churches and the colleges indicating where they can move together effectively in the future.

1759.   Berry, Thomas. "The American College in the Ecological Age." *Teachers College Record* 83 (Fall 1981): 89-104.

Utilizing the theoretical base of Teilhard de Chardin, Berry applies it to the American College. He suggests a core curriculum with special attention to a course "on the origin and identification of value."

1760.   Cousins, Norman. "Think of a Man." *Teachers College Record* 85 (Fall 1983): 1-8.

A prominent thinker calls for the academic world to be actors of "informed dedication." He expects higher education to teach people to think and then to act. It is not enough "to wear the garment of religious identification; (one) must accept its ethical and moral obligations and glory."

1761.   Cuninggim, Merrimon. "The Protestant Stake in Higher Education." Council of Protestant Colleges and Universities, 1961.

Study of the place and role of church colleges and universities is grounded in "the educational implications of the major themes of the Reformation." Finding an adequate philosophy of education is an on-going task to which church and colleges are called to participate.

1762.   Cuninggim, Merrimon. "Your Contribution to American Higher Education." An address to the Inaugural Meeting of the Association of Presbyterian Colleges and Universities, Memphis, TN, November 7, 1983.

Reminding church persons about the contribution their colleges and universities have made in practicing candor, demonstrating the importance of leadership and having a knowledge of appropriate priorities serves as a solid ground for moving into the future as a merged church.

1763.   Curtis, Mark H. "Frontiers in Space, Time, Society and Education." Sesquicentennial Papers, edited by Iver F. Yeager. Carbondale, IL: S. Illinois University Press, 1982.

Warning that the dangers to be faced in challenges to the best of the liberal arts are those that are coming from within, the author cites the "sad state of liberal education" and suggests that it will take careful attention by educators in rethinking the ends to be served and how the "pursuit of truth" shall be managed.

1764.   Fisher, Ben C. *An Orientation Manual for Trustees of Church Related Colleges.* 4th edition. Nashville, TN: Education Commission, Southern Baptist Convention, 1980.

Relating effectively to the domination and the academic

community are crucial for responsible trusteeship and academic freedom. Both must be dealt with up-front for the sake of the church and the college.

1765. Fisher, Ben C., ed. *New Pathways: A Dialogue in Christian Higher Education.* Macon, GA: Mercer University Press, 1980.

Voicing diverse concerns, such as Christian unity and diversity to the role of the Church-related college in recovering national purpose, denominational leaders contribute to the dialogue the author desires.

1766. Jonsen, Richard W. *Small Liberal Arts Colleges: Diversity at the Crossroads.* AAHE-ERIC/Higher Education Research Report, Number 4, 1978, American Association for Higher Education, Washington, DC.

A limited but useful exploration of the contribution of small colleges made in the face of drastic changes in the way society perceives their worth.

1767. Moseley, John D. and Glenn R. Bucher. "Church-Related Colleges in a Changing Contest." *Educational Record* 63 (Winter 1982): 46-51.

"Faced with the changes that will come in the 1980's, colleges and universities with religious ties must rethink both their identity and what constitutes the proper college-church relationship."

1768. Murphy, John F. "What About the Next Decades in Church-Related Higher Education?" Address to Presbyterian College Presidents, Washington, DC, February 6, 1981.

Church-related colleges and universities will be required in the next decades to identify and explicate their roles in meeting government, social and ecclesiastical issues.

1769. National Congress on Church-Related Colleges and Universities. 4 vols. Sherman, TX: The Center for Program and Institutional Renewal at Austin College, 1980.

Vol. I: "Affirmation: A Shared Commitment for Creative Renewal."

Basic contentions about the value and contribution of the church-related college, plans for renewal, and a brief description of the activities and processes of the National Congress.

Vol. II: "Mission: A Shared Vision of Educational Purpose."

Conduct of an accepted mission will undergo great changes. The challenge confronting academic institutions and churches is to try to envision what the future may look like. The interrelationships of the factors must be recognized.

Vol. III: "Accountability: Keeping Faith With One Another."

A companion volume to the previous volume. Special attention is given to the increasing litigation matters.

Vol. IV: "Exchange: Sharing Resources for Renewal."

Contains an extensive listing of recent books and articles about church-related higher education and materials available for denominations and colleges.

1770.   New Conversations, published by the United Church Board for Homeland Ministries, 132 West 31st Street, New York, NY, editor Theodore H. Erickson, Vol. 6, No. 1, Spring 1981, "Church-Related Higher Education."

Church and college leaders express their concerns on the nature of church and college relationships and the implications for broader concerns of society.

1771.   New Conversations, published by the United Church Board for Homeland Ministries, 132 West 31st Street, New York, NY, editor Nanette M. Roberts, Vol. 9, No. 2, Fall 1986, "Heritage and Horizon: Higher Education and the Church."

Historical review provides a solid basis for moving into a significant future.

1772.   Parsonage, Robert Rue, ed. *Church Related Higher Education.* Valley Forge, PA: Judson Press, 1978.

Extensive and current exploration of issues and opportunities confronting church-related higher education. Study papers by Smylie, Marty and Cuninggim are unparalleled.

1773.   Presbyterian Panel, Research Division of the Support Agency, United Presbyterian Church, U.S.A., 475 Riverside Drive, Room 1740, New York, NY, 1980, Part II, pp. 11-20.

Questionnaire on attitudes of the Church members toward colleges related to the church and their concepts of desirable characteristics.

1774.   Presbyterian Church Studies. "Faith, Knowledge and the Future. Presbyterian Mission in the 1980's." A Study Paper adopted by the 122nd General Assembly, Presbyterian Church in the United States, Atlanta, GA, 1982.

Goals and recommendations intended for the study of members and institutions related to the Church.

1775. Presbyterian Church Studies. "The Church's Mission in Higher Education." A Report and Recommendations commended for Study in the United Presbyterian Church, USA, February, 1980, Education in Leadership Development, Program Agency, Room 1244J, 475 Riverside Drive, New York, NY.

Theological undergirding revived, historical roots reviewed, and projects for the future laid out.

1776. Sandin, Robert T. *The Search for Excellence.* Macon, GA: Mercer University Press, 1982.

Relating faith and learning effectively continue to be an important task of the "Christian" college. The role of the Christian scholar and the kind of freedom the academy can foster are essential.

1777. Smylie, James H. "Protestant Experiences in America." *Religion, Society and Education, an Ecumenical Symposium at Loyola College.* Edited by Thomas O'Brian Hanley. Baltimore, MD: Loyola College, 1978.

Many changes in church-related education have been part of American history. While Protestant efforts seem more and more marginal, in the business of education in America it is clear that committed clergy and laity have been a constant.

1778. Yeager, Iver F. *Church and College on the Illinois Frontier, 1829-1867.* Prepared in connection with the Sesquicentennial Observance of the Founding of Illinois College. Jacksonville, IL: Illinois College, 1980.

The struggle of the Churches to establish themselves and their colleges took place in less than an inviting atmosphere. Problems and issues faced during the period were not those of Illinois College alone.

CHAPTER 24
REFORMED COLLEGES AND UNIVERSITIES
Peter P. DeBoer

1779.   Armstrong, Robert E. "A Prediction Model of Geneva College, 1956-1976." Ph.D. dissertation. Michigan State University, 1969.

Reviews the kinds of students attending Geneva College and develops a predicting mechanism for determining student enrollment for a regional evangelical college.

1780.   Bos, Gerda. *Trinity Christian College 1959-1984: 25 Years of Service.* Palos Heights, IL: Trinity Christian College, 1984.

Commemorates, in words and pictures, the two planning phases of the college's history, from 1953-56, and 1956-59, followed by a chronicle of significant dates in the quarter century that follows.

1781.   Calvin College Curriculum Study Committee. *Christian Liberal Arts Education.* Grand Rapids, MI: Calvin College and Eerdmans, 1970.

Lays out the curricular reforms and their rationales subsequently adopted by Calvin College. In a day when many colleges were abandoning required cores in general education in favor of electives and "relevance," Calvin reaffirmed its commitment to liberal education through what it termed a "disciplinary view" of "disinterested learning" as a "faith-task" of the Christian community.

1782.   Churovia, Robert M. "An Intercollegiate Athletic History: The Geneva Story." Ph.D. dissertation. University of Pittsburgh, 1978.

Describes sports at Geneva College and the college's input into national intercollegiate sports.

1783.   Covenant College. *Institutional Self-Study Report.* Lookout Mountain, TN: Covenant College, 1986.

Includes a brief history of the college, a statement of purpose that emphasizes the consequences of the doctrines of creation, the fall, and redemption upon mankind's task in this world, and other chapters on faculty, educational programs and the like.

1784.   DeJong, Gerald F. *From Strength to Strength: A History of Northwestern, 1881-1982.* The Historical Series of the Reformed Church in America, No. 9. Grand Rapids, MI: Eerdmans, 1982.

Details the three distinct periods that mark the history of Northwestern: the Academy (1882-1928), the Academy and Junior College (1928-61), and the Four-Year College (1961-1982), with successive attention to setting, physical plant and finances, the faculty and curriculum, and student life and activities.

1785.   DeKlerk, Peter, ed. *A Bibliography of the Writings of the Professors of Calvin Theological Seminary.* Grand Rapids, MI: Calvin Theological Seminary, 1980.

More limited than Lambers' work (see below) because it includes only the writings of professors at the theological seminary, this bibliography is richer because it lists all published works, not just books, monographs and dissertations.

1786.   DeKoster, Lester. "The Liberal Arts in Christian Context." *Reformed Journal,* September 1962, pp. 11-14; February 1963, pp. 17-19; March 1963, pp. 9-11.

Argues that a tension exists among the terms "Christian Liberal Arts," that the "Liberal arts have more often put the Christian tradition to their service, instead of the other way around," and that this endangers the role the Christian college ought to play in American life. DeKoster insists that the future of Christian higher education lies in the Liberal Arts being made the "servile domestics of the Christian mind. . . ."

1787.   DeVries, George Jr., and Earl Wm. Kennedy. "The Reformed Church in America and Higher Education." *Reformed Review* 23 (Spring 1970) 1: 184-95.

Records efforts by the Dutch Reformed to establish schools, from New Amsterdam to Rutgers College (1766) and New Brunswick Theological Seminary (1784) in New Jersey, to Union College (1795) in New York, Hope College (1866) in Michigan, Central (1858) in Pella, Iowa, and Northwestern (1882) in Orange City, Iowa; and critically analyzes the difficulties involved in developing a genuine program of Christian higher education, with special reference to Northwestern Academy and College.

1788.   Donia, Robert J. and John M. Mulder, eds. *Into All the World: Hope College and International Affairs.* Holland, MI: Hope College, 1985.

Traces the influence of Hope College on international affairs, through its graduates. Many of the graduates cited in the study are Reformed Church in America missionaries.

1789.   Dordt College Faculty Committee. *Educational Task of Dordt College.* Sioux Center, IA: Dordt College, n.d.

Constitutes a "statement of purpose" that sets forth the reasons for the establishment of Dordt College in the area of the Reformed Community in which it is located. It outlines the biblically based principles which form the educational philosophy of the college.

1790.   Dykstra, D. Ivan. *Who Am I? and Other Sermons from Dimnent Memorial Chapel.* Holland, MI: Hope College, 1983.

Presents sermons and addresses by a long-time professor of philosophy who served at Hope College from 1947-1980.

1791.   "Educational Credo." *Orientation: International Circular of the Potchefstroom University for Christian Higher Education* 37 (June 1985): 1-3.

Highlights via a preamble, statements of purpose, basis, and educational creed the beliefs of the Institute for Christian Studies in regard to life, scripture, Christ, reality, knowledge, scholarship, and academic freedom.

1792.   "Educational Philosophy." *Orientation: International Circular of the Potchefstroom University for Christian Higher Education* 37 (June 1985): 3-5.

Contains the educational credo of King's College including a statement of principles (in regard to creation; sin; redemption; human life; teaching and learning; and teachers and students), some educational objectives, and educational policies.

1793.   England, Theora Cooper. "An Investigation of the Educational Theatre Programs in the Liberal Arts Colleges Sponsored by the Reformed Church in America." Ph.D. dissertation. University of Minnesota, 1964.

Analyzes, against the background of Calvinism in general and the Reformed Church in America specifically, the history of educational theatre at Hope, Central, and Northwestern colleges, including the growth of the separate departments of speech, drama, or communication; the titles of dramatic productions; and the problems and possibilities encountered.

1794.   Galbreath, C. Ronald. "A Christian College in Contemporary America: Geneva College, 1956-1976." Ph.D. dissertation. University of Pittsburgh, 1981.

Reviews 20 years of recent collegiate history, especially the new evangelical thrust of the Trustees and Administration since 1967.

1795.   Glasgow, William M. *The Geneva Book, Comprising a History of Geneva College: A Bibliographical Catalog of the Alumni and Many Students.* Philadelphia, PA: Westbrook, 1908.

Is considered the authoritative 19th-century history of the college.

1796.   Goehring, Charles Henry. "A Study of the Objectives of Geneva College." Ph.D. dissertation. University of Pittsburgh, 1973.

Examines extensively the foundational concepts of Christian higher education at Geneva College.

1797.   Hubers, Dale. "A History of the Northwestern Classical Academy, Orange City, Iowa, 1882-1957." M.A. thesis. University of South Dakota, 1957.

Describes the history of the academy, until 1961 an integral part of Northwestern College, as the institution approached its seventy-fifth anniversary. The chapter on curriculum development, analyzing the actual curricular changes and the sources of pressure for change coming from outside as well as from within, is especially noteworthy.

1798.   Jellema, William Harry. "Calvinism and Higher Education." In *God-Centered Living: Calvinism in Action,* a symposium by the Calvinistic Action Committee. Grand Rapids, MI: Baker, 1951.

Argues that commitment to Christianity entails responsibility for Christian action in higher education. More specifically, a Christian college like Calvin College is necessary because the *civitas dei* needs a college "in the warfare with the kingdoms of the world; needs a college in order to articulate meaningfully the true answer to the question who God is."

1799.   Jellema, William Harry. "Why We Have No University." *Reformed Journal,* September 1955, pp. 10-11.

Recognizing that the need for a university had been felt for over 50 years, Jellema notes that early on the Christian Reformed constituency had vague ideas about a university while lately its ideas are clear but false. He reviews an old dilemma: that a university must be free (of the church) to be a university, yet if free of the church unlikely to succeed for lack of financial support. Jellema argues that there are more important considerations, especially about priorities, if a university is to be established. It must first aim at scholarly interpretation, "wetenschap," or science. We have a duty "to keep Calvinistic scholarship continuously relevant." Only secondarily ought the university aim at teaching, or educating others, or serving as the top rung of the Christian school educational ladder.

1800.   Jellema, William Harry. "Need For A University: What Is It We Need?" *Reformed Journal,* November 1955, pp. 13-15.

Proposes a university in the form of a Calvinistic Institute for Advanced Studies, out of which a teaching university would eventually grow. Jellema urges that it legally and actually be distinct from Calvin College and Seminary, and also free from the Church.

1801.   Kuiper, Barney. *The Proposed Calvinistic College at Grand Rapids.* Grand Rapids, MI: Sevensma, 1903.

To help fellow Calvinists realize the position they ought to occupy in America, Kuiper briefly recalls their immigrant history from out of the early to middle 19th century, and declares the Calvinist is now called to full participation in American life. To avert the dangers inherent in such involvement (materialism, evolutionism, modernism, secularism) Kuiper argues that the Reformed Calvinist needs more than grammar schools and academies; he needs a college for higher education. Nor will any college do, not even a denominational college: it must be one in which the Bible is recognized as the Word of God and therefore as the highest authority in all the sciences. It must be a Calvinistic College.

1802.   Lambers, Stephen L., compiler. *A Centenary Bibliography: of Books, Monographs, and Doctoral Dissertations Written by Calvin College and Seminary Alumni and Faculty from 1876 to 1976.* Grand Rapids, MI: Calvin College and Seminary, 1976.

Organized by (1) books and monographs, (2) doctoral dissertations, (3) names and locations of graduate schools cited in the doctoral dissertation listing, and (4) listing of authors of doctoral dissertations by subject.

1803.   McIntire, Carl T. "Herman Dooyeweerd in North America." In *Reformed Theology in America,* pp. 172-85. Edited by David F. Wells. Grand Rapids, MI: Eerdmans, 1985.

Contains a concise, non-technical summary of the thought of Dutch philosopher Herman Dooyeweerd, with emphasis on how his thinking was embodied as the core educational philosophy of the Institute for Christian Studies.

1804.   Miller, John. "Pursuing a Global Perspective." *The Church Herald,* September 7, 1984, p. 16.

Affirms that the purposes of academic experiences in foreign countries go well beyond supplementing major fields of study and experiencing something of the world. Miller, from the International Studies Office at Central College, insists that beyond these lies a global perspective, a "view that we are all creatures of God in our diversity, a family of nations and culture very different from one another, and all the more fascinating for our differences."

1805.   Moran, Gerald D. "Normative Library Standards for Evangelical Christian Colleges." Ph.D. dissertation. University of Pittsburgh, 1985.

Presents a history of the Christian College Coalition, with its 63 member libraries, including Calvin, Geneva, Grove City, Whitworth, and Trinity Christian and proposes national norms for evangelical Christian college libraries.

1806.   *Perspective* 15 (September-October 1981): 1-32.

Describes in this, a special 25th anniversary issue of the newsletter of the Institute for Christian Studies, its history, rationale, and programs.

1807.   Plantinga, Theodore. *Rationale for a Christian College.* St. Catherines, Ont.: Paideia Press, 1980.

Explains the distinctiveness of the Christian college in general by focusing on the idea of curriculum, emphasizing selection as the key to Christian uniqueness. The book also devotes some attention to the notion of a scholarly community and deals briefly with Canadian needs and emphases in Christian higher education.

1808.   Report of Special Committee on Reformed Church in American Philosophy on Higher Education. "The Church and its Colleges." In *The Acts and Proceedings of the 163rd Regular Session of the Annual Synod of the Reformed Church in America,* pp. 65-70. New York: The Reformed Church in America, 1969.

Describes the central mission of the colleges in association with the RCA as providing "an excellent education in a Christian context within a revolutionary world." A preamble to a "Covenant of Mutual Responsibilities" defines what that mission means for curriculum, faculty, the teaching of religion, and the like. The "Covenant" within the larger report delineates, in a series of objectives, what the church expects of the colleges, and what the colleges can expect from the church.

1809.   Rooks, Albert J. "Calvin College, Grand Rapids, 1894-1927." *Michigan History Magazine* 11 (October 1927): 532-53.

Divides the history of Calvin College in a fairly unorthodox manner. Most histories begin with 1876, the start of the Theological School. Rooks begins his divisions with 1894 when the trustees decided that students, other than those looking toward becoming pastors, could be admitted to the school. His second division is 1908 when a few students first graduated from the two-year junior college course. His third is 1912 when three students first finished the three-year program. And 1920, when the college began a fourth year of undergraduate studies for the first time, and ushered in the era of the complete college.

1810.   Runner, H. Evan. *The Relation of the Bible to Learning.* Fifth revised ed. Jordan Station, ON: Paideia Press, 1982.

Lays out, by a founder of the Institute for Christian Studies and disciple of the Dutch philosopher Herman Dooyeweerd, the philosophical-theological ideas which underlie the distinctive program of the Institute.

1811.   Seerveld, Calvin. "A Reformed Christian College." Palos Heights, IL: Trinity Christian College, 1960.

Delivered on the occasion of the college's second annual convocation, this address elaborates on these ideas: that Trinity is to be a college, a Christian college, and a Reformed Christian college.

1812.   Semi-Centennial Committee. *Theological School and Calvin College, 1876-1926.* Grand Rapids, MI: Theological School and Calvin College, 1926.

Describes, in a series of articles by 13 different authors, the principles that led to the establishing of Calvin, portrays something of its life and influence, and indicates the ideals which were intended to determine its future development. Especially useful are a version of Rooks' article that has somewhat more detail than the one cited above, and an essay by Professor Louis Berkhof on "Our School's Reason for Existence and the Preservation Thereof."

1813.   Spykman, Gordan J. "Christian Higher Education in Global Perspective: A Call to On-going Reformation." *Pro-Rege* 11 (June 1983): 13-25.

Challenges supporters of Christian higher education to think about Christian scholarship in global dimensions and, while doing so, to capitalize on the riches of the Reformed tradition. Spykman offers four reasons for thinking about Christian scholarship globally: the wide horizons of the creation order; the Biblical idea of universal office; our shrinking world situation; and the cosmic dimensions of the coming Kingdom. To capitalize on the riches of the Reformed tradition requires holistic thinking, honoring classic Christian distinctions like the Creator-creature distinction; the revelation-response distinction; and the structure-direction distinction. Only holistic thinking can help us overcome the dualism-seeking-synthesis patterns embedded in the scholastic traditions of Western Christianity. Finally, Spykman describes the place and task of the Christian academy in light of the complementary principle of sphere-sovereignty and sphere-universality.

1814. Stegenga, Preston J. *Anchor of Hope: the History of an American Denominational Institution, Hope College.* Grand Rapids, MI: Eerdmans, 1954.

Drawn from the dissertation listed below, this volume includes some historical data not found in the dissertation, though it includes no notes and little of the bibliography.

1815. Stegenga, Preston J. "Hope College in Dutch-American Life, 1851-1951." Ph.D. dissertation. University of Michigan, 1952.

Treats Hope College as an exception to the drift of American denominational colleges away from their parent bodies. This is the first of several studies of Hope College.

1816. Stob, George. "The Christian Reformed Church and Her Schools." Th.D. dissertation. Princeton Theological Seminary, 1955.

Traces (in Chapter X, "Education - Not For Ministers Only,") the evolution of Calvin as a college from a mere year added to the high school or academy (in 1900) to a two-year junior college (1906) to a three-year college (1910) to that of a full four-year institution (1921).

Analyzes (in Chapter XIII, "The World, The Flesh, The Devil, and Calvin College,") the suspicions that the young college came under: from outside the church, mistrust regarding the alleged pro-German sympathies of professors; from inside the church, attacks on the school for being too worldly.

1817. Timmerman, John J. *Promises to Keep: A Centennial History of Calvin College.* Grand Rapids, MI: Calvin College and Seminary with Eerdmans, 1976.

Celebrates the events, issues, and most of all the people who have shaped the history of Calvin College from its beginnings as Theological School to its maturity as a Christian liberal arts college, owned and operated by the Christian Reformed Church in North America.

1818. "Trinity Christian College." *Orientation: International Circular of the Potchefstroom University for Christian Higher Education* 37 (June 1985): 8-25.

Details the college's academic credo, including its confessional integrity, integration of faith and learning, Christian social concern in a metropolitan (Chicago) setting, academic excellence, curricular balance, student development and supporting constituency.

1819. VanderZee, Andrew. *Guide to the Archives of Hope College, Holland, Michigan.* Second Edition. Holland, MI: Hope College,

1983.

Serves as a guide to Hope's historical collections which include personal papers of administrators and professors, minutes of college committees, college records, and all college publications.

1820.   Van Dyk, John. "Calvinistic Philosophy and the Relation Between Liberal Education and Vocational Training." *Pro Rege* XV (December 1986): 9-17.

Analyzes the "problem of liberal education" for Reformed Christian colleges by lifting up (1) the distorted sense of office and calling created by the assumption that a hierarchy of professions exists such that those demanding extensive liberal arts education are more highly regarded than others, and (2) the warped understanding of the place of work that results when academic liberal education is separated from vocational training. Van Dyk is confident that "reformational philosophy," by attending to the nature of educational institutions, curricular theory, and instructional theory, can lead the way to new insights and to obedient Christian living.

1821.   Van Halsema, Dick L. "Reformed Bible College, the First Forty Years." *Banner,* March 7, 1980, pp. 6-9.

Identifies the basis for the founding of the college as the Reformed Bible Institute; the relationship of the school to the Christian Reformed Church; and the first members of the board, administrative staff, and faculty. Progresses through a decade by decade description of the evolution of the college from the institute, with an emphasis in 1980 on evangelism, missions, and church education.

1822.   Van Wylen, Gordon J. "What Do We Owe Our Institutional Heirs?" Holland, MI: Hope College Board of Trustees, 1985.

Sets forth, two years prior to his retirement in 1987, the vision of Hope's president (since 1972) for the future of the college. The document was also designed to aid the presidential search committee in their efforts to find a successor to President Van Wylen.

1823.   Weller, Kenneth. "Working Together." *The Church Herald,* September 7, 1984, pp. 12-13.

After describing the relationship between college and church as that of a maturing child and parent, "a relationship which moves from discipline and control to trust and freedom," President Weller, of Central College, outlines what the church can contribute to its colleges, and what the colleges can contribute to the church's identity.

1824. White, John Hugh. "The Integration of Faith and Learning at Geneva College." D.M. thesis. Pittsburgh Theological Seminary, 1977.

Describes efforts to reform Christian higher education at Geneva College.

1825. Wichers, Wynand. *A Century of Hope, 1866-1966.* Grand Rapids, MI: Eerdmans, 1968.

Surveys the college's history in commemoration of the college's centennial celebration in 1966. The author was president of Hope College from 1931-1945.

1826. Wolterstorff, Nicholas P. "The Idea of A Christian College." *Reformed Journal,* September 1962, pp. 15-20.

Argues that Christian higher education, especially college-level education, when conformed to the Christian perspective, is one which -- through teaching, leadership, and scholarship -- must assist in the building of a Christian culture.

1827. Wolterstorff, Nicholas P. "The Mission of the Christian College at the End of the 20th Century." *Reformed Journal,* June 1983, pp. 14-18.

Argues that Christian evangelical and confessional colleges focused, in a Stage I that lasted until after the second World War, on piety and evangelism; argues that in the present Stage II, without losing their concern for piety and evangelism, they have been busy introducing their students to the full breadth of "high" culture through works of natural science, philosophy, art, music, poetry, painting, and the like; and urges Christian colleges to enter Stage III where, without sacrificing past aims, they -- as arms of the body of Christ -- seek to equip their students to live as Christians in society, as instruments of God's justice, for the sake of a suffering humanity.

1828. Zylstra, Henry. "The Junior College Problem." *Reformed Journal,* May 1951, pp. 8-10.

Builds a case against the potential rise of junior colleges within the Christian Reformed constituency by rejecting the notion that what is needed is normal (teacher) training, vocational training, or even terminal liberal education. Zylstra argues that basic liberal education might be acceptable, though he wonders whether the quality of a junior college education, geographically separated from a senior college, would still be "mainly liberal" and "substantially Christian."

1829. Zylstra, Henry. "Are Junior Colleges The Solution?" *Reformed Journal,* November 1952, pp. 5-7.

Argues that the widespread interest in junior college education in the Christian Reformed church is misplaced. Zylstra insists that a junior college, by its very nature, cannot be a good college. The solution is not junior colleges but excellent grammar schools, high schools, and an excellent college.

ACKNOWLEDGMENTS

I want to acknowledge gratefully the assistance of the following persons: Nicholas P. Barker, Vice President for Academic Affairs, Covenant College; Burt P. Braunius, Vice President for Academic Administration, Reformed Bible College; Elton J. Bruins, Dean for the Arts and Humanities, Hope College; Conrad Bult, Assistant Library Director, Calvin College; Justin Cooper, Vice President (Academic), Redeemer College; Douglas M. Eckardt, Department of Theology, Trinity Christian College; Art Hielkema, Director of Ramaker Library, Northwestern College; John B. Hulst, President, Dordt College; Gerald D. Moran, McCartney Library, Geneva College; David Timmer, Department of Philosophy and Religion, Central College; and S. Keith Ward, Academic Dean, The King's College.

CHAPTER 25
SEVENTH-DAY ADVENTIST COLLEGES AND UNIVERSITIES
George R. Knight

Part I: Historical

1830. Ashworth, Warren S. "Edward Alexander Sutherland and Seventh-day Adventist Educational Reform: The Denominational Years, 1890-1904." Ph.D. dissertation. Andrews University, 1986.

   Analyzes the life and work of Adventism's most controversial educational reformer. Also provides insight into Sutherland's contribution to the denomination's philosophy of higher education.

1831. Bower, Donald George. "Fifty Years of Student Employment at Loma Linda University, La Sierra Campus." Ed.D. dissertation. University of California at Los Angeles, 1974.

   A major aspect of Adventist educational philosophy is the combination of useful labor with academic studies. This is one of the few historical studies that examines this philosophy in action over a significant period of time. Not only discusses the factual aspects of the program, but also treats the philosophy of the work-study idea.

1832. Brown, Walter J., comp. *Chronology of Seventh-day Adventist Education.* 2nd ed. Washington, DC: General Conference of Seventh-day Adventists, Department of Education, 1979.

   Outlines, in the order of their development, lists of Adventist schools, administrators, gatherings of note, and educational publications.

1833. Cadwallader, E. M. *A History of Seventh-day Adventist Education.* 4th ed. Payson, AZ: Leaves-of-Autumn Books, 1975.

   Despite its title, this is not a history of Adventist education. It is more of a series of papers on Adventist secondary and collegiate institutions. The volume still has value for understanding Adventist education, even though later works have more fully explored many of the topics treated and in some cases invalidated its conclusions.

1834. Cadwallader, E. M. *Principles of Education in the Writings of Ellen G. White.* Payson, AZ: Leaves-of-Autumn Books, n.d.

Presents an extensive collection of categorized quotations from Ellen White's writings on a wide variety of educational issues. Not interpretive. Based on the author's doctoral dissertation, completed at the University of Nebraska in 1949.

1835.   Cady, Marion E. *The Education That Educates.* New York: Fleming H. Revell, 1937.

Develops a Seventh-day Adventist philosophy of education based on the Bible and the writings of Ellen White.

1836.   Dick, Everett. *Union College of the Golden Cords.* Lincoln, NE: Union College Press, 1967.

Presents the history of one of the denomination's earliest schools. Sheds light on the development of Adventist education in general, and also provides understanding of specific issues such as the church's struggle with accreditation in the 1920s and 1930s.

1837.   *From Vision to Reality: 1905-1980.* Loma Linda, CA: Loma Linda University, 1980.

A pictorial history of the College of Medical Evangelists at Loma Linda, California, and La Sierra College, at Riverside, California, that united in 1961 to form Loma Linda University.

1838.   Gardner, Eva B. Revised by J. Mabel Wood. *Southern Missionary College: A School of His Planning.* 2nd ed. Collegedale, TN: Board of Trustees, [1975].

Presents the history of a school that was both secondary and collegiate for much of its history. Sheds light on conditions in Adventist education at the turn of the century.

1839.   Hodgen, Maurice, ed. *School Bells and Gospel Trumpets: A Documentary History of Seventh-day Adventist Education in North America.* Loma Linda, CA: Adventist Heritage Publications, 1978.

Presents the most complete published collection of documents related to Adventist education. Introductory commentaries provide contextual understanding.

1840.   Hook, Milton R. "The Avondale School and Adventist Educational Goals, 1894-1900." Ed.D. dissertation. Andrews University, 1978.

Provides the history of the first six years of the school that Adventists look to as the "ideal model" of their brand of reform education. Hook's analysis separates the universal principles undergirding the Avondale School from the particulars of time and place that provided the school's immediate context.

1841.   Knight, George R. "Battle Creek College: Academic Development and Curriculum Struggles." Unpublished manuscript, Andrews University, Adventist Heritage Center, 1979.

Presents the catastrophic difference between the philosophy and the curriculum of Adventism's first academic institution in its historical context. The results of the issues faced at Battle Creek continue to influence Adventist education at all levels.

1842. Knight, George R., ed. *Early Adventist Educators.* Berrien Springs, MI: Andrews University Press, 1983.

Presents the contributions of eleven of the most important educators to the denomination's educational system during its formative period (1867-1900). In lieu of a formal history, this volume is the most comprehensive treatment of nineteenth-century Adventist education available.

1843. Knight, George R. "Oberlin College and Adventist Educational Reforms." *Adventist Heritage* 8 (Spring 1983): 3-9.

Demonstrates that the "unique" aspects of Adventist educational reform in the period from 1870-1900 had been tried and had been given up at Oberlin in the 1830s and 1840s. Further argues that Adventist education must not lose touch with its impulse to reform.

1844. Knight, George R. "Seventh-day Adventist Education: A Historical Sketch and Profile." In *Religious Schooling in America*, pp. 85-109. Edited by James C. Carper and Thomas C. Hunt. Birmingham, AL: Religious Education Press, 1984.

Summarizes the most salient features of the history of Adventist education from the 1840s through the early 1980s. Provides a profile of contemporary Adventist education.

1845. Lindsay, Allan G. "Goodloe Harper Bell: Pioneer Seventh-day Adventist Christian Educator." Ed.D. dissertation. Andrews University, 1982.

A well-documented account of the first "successful" Adventist teacher. Highlights not only Bell's contribution to the theory and practice of Adventist schooling, but also his contribution to the development of the Adventist Sabbath school and textbooks for English classes.

1846. Neff, Merlin L. *For God and C. M. E.: A Biography of Percy Tilson Magan Upon the Historical Background of the Educational and Medical Work of Seventh-day Adventists.* Mountain View, CA: Pacific Press Pub. Assn., 1964.

Provides a biography of one of Adventism's most illustrious educational reformers. Presents the early Magan as a radical reformer of the Sutherland school and the later Magan as the denomination's foremost educator of medical personnel.

1847. Neufeld, Don F., ed. *Seventh-day Adventist Encyclopedia.* Rev. ed. Washington, DC: Review and Herald Pub. Assn., 1976.

Presents a large number of articles on Adventist educators and educational institutions. Many of the other articles provide contextual understanding of the development of Adventist education.

1848. Otto, Leroy. "An Historical Analysis of the Origin and Development of the College of Medical Evangelists." Ed.D. dissertation. University of Southern California, 1962.

A history of the medical and nursing programs at what is now Loma Linda University from their inception early in the century up through the early 1950s. Also contains a chapter dealing with the development of the schools of dietetics, medical technology, x-ray technology, and physical therapy. Not covered is the development of the school of dentistry, which was not begun until the early 1950s. Deals somewhat with the philosophy of Adventist medical education.

1849. Reye, Arnold Colin. "Frederick Griggs: Seventh-day Adventist Educator and Administrator." Ph.D. dissertation. Andrews University, 1984.

Analyzes the contribution of the Adventist administrator who had the most impact on the formation of the denomination's administrative and curricular development as its scattered institutions were developed into a system in the first decade of the twentieth century.

1850. Reynolds, Keld J. "The First Twenty Years: An Historical Sketch of La Sierra College." 1944. Mimeographed.

Presents a history of La Sierra College in southern California from 1922 to 1942. Seeks to capture something of the spirit and experience of the founders. A large amount of the material is based on oral history provided by the founders.

1851. Robinson, Dores Eugene. *The Story of Our Health Message: The Origin, Character, and Development of Health Education in the Seventh-day Adventist Church.* 3rd ed. Nashville, TN: Southern Pub. Assn., 1965.

Provides a history of the development of health-related topics in Adventism and the development of health education in the denomination.

1852. Sandborn, William Cruzan. "The History of Madison College." Ed.D. dissertation. George Peabody College of Teachers, 1953.

Discusses the development of the school that became the mother of a large number of self-supporting Adventist educational and medical institutions throughout the world, but particularly in the southeastern United States.

1853.   Schwarz, Richard W. *John Harvey Kellogg, M. D.* Nashville, TN: Southern Pub. Assn., 1970.

Treats the life, work, and thought of Adventism's foremost health educator. Kellogg influenced Adventist education at every level. An adaptation of Schwarz's doctoral dissertation, completed at the University of Michigan, 1964.

1854.   Simmons, Marion Seitz. "A History of the Home Study Institute (Seventh-day Adventist Church)." M.A. thesis. University of Maryland, 1953.

The only history of the development of Adventist theory and institutions related to correspondence study at the elementary, secondary, and collegiate levels.

1855.   [Spalding, Arthur Whitefield]. "Lights and Shades in the Black Belt." [1913.] Unpublished manuscript, Andrews University, Adventist Heritage Center.

A contemporary study of the development of black Adventist education in the South between 1890 and 1913.

1856.   Spalding, Arthur Whitefield. *Origin and History of Seventh-day Adventists.* 4 vols. Washington, DC: Review and Herald Pub. Assn., 1961-1962.

Offers an interpretation of the historical development of Adventist education within the context of general denominational history. Devotes several chapters to the growth of Adventist educational thought and institutions.

1857.   Sutherland, E. A. *Living Fountains or Broken Cisterns: An Educational Problem for Protestants.* Battle Creek, MI: Review and Herald Pub. Assn., 1900.

Argues that the hope of Protestantism and republicanism lies in the proper education of the youth, and that this education is to be found in the principles delivered to the Jews, demonstrated by Christ, and revived by the Reformation.

1858.   Sutherland, E. A. *Studies in Christian Education.* Nashville, TN: Nashville Agriculture and Normal Institute, 1915.

Argues that Adventist education must not make the educational mistakes of other Protestants, such as Oberlin College which backslid from its program of the 1830s and 1840s. Contends that manual labor, self-supporting missionary work, the Bible, and simplicity in such areas as diet should be at the heart of Christian education.

1859.   Syme, Eric. *A History of SDA Church-State Relations in the United States.* Mountain View, CA: Pacific Press Pub. Assn., 1973.

Chapter nine presents an overview of the Adventist position on church-state relationships that affect education. Included are such issues as prayer in public schools and state aid to church-related schools. The book is a revision of Syme's doctoral dissertation, completed at American University, 1969.

1860.   Thurston, Claude, et al. *60 Years of Progress: The Anniversary History of Walla Walla College.* College Place, WA: The College Press, [1952].

Presents the history of an institution that was as much a secondary school as a college for much of its early period. Provides a great deal of human interest material regarding faculty, students, and life in general at a late nineteenth and early twentieth century Adventist school.

1861.   Utt, Walter C. *A Mountain, a Pickax, a College: A History of Pacific Union College.* Angwin, CA: Alumni Association of Pacific Union College, 1968.

Argues in the early chapters that Healdsburg Academy--which later became Healdsburg College and Pacific Union College--began with a reformed educational program that was not evident in the denomination's first educational institution--Battle Creek College.

1862.   Valentine, Gilbert Murray. "William Warren Prescott: Seventh-day Adventist Educator." 2 vols. Ph.D. dissertation. Andrews University, 1982.

Discusses the role of Adventism's leading educator of the 1880s and 1890s. Analyzes Prescott's significant contributions to Adventist education during its formative period.

1863.   Vande Vere, Emmett K. *The Wisdom Seekers.* Nashville, TN: Southern Publishing Association, 1972.

Discusses the history of Adventism's first educational institution from its inception as a private non-denominational Adventist school in the late 1860s, through its development as Battle Creek College (1874-1901), Emmanuel Missionary College (1901-1959), and Andrews University (from 1960). Provides a great deal of necessary background for understanding Adventist education.

1864.   Walter, Edwin Carlan. "A History of Seventh-day Adventist

Higher Education in the United States." Ed.D. dissertation. University of California, 1966.

Surveys the development of each Adventist institution of higher education in the United States. The histories of the various institutions, unfortunately, are not integrated into a unified whole, but are a series of related histories.

1865.   Wehtje, Myron F. *And There Was Light: A History of South Lancaster Academy, Lancaster Junior College, and Atlantic Union College.* South Lancaster, MA: The Atlantic Press, 1982.

Develops the history of an important early Adventist educational institution. The first few chapters shed light on the implementation of Adventist educational philosophy.

1866.   White, Arthur L. *Ellen G. White.* 6 vols. Washington, DC: Review and Herald Pub. Assn., 1981-1986.

Presents the biography of the most influential person in the development of Adventist educational theory and practice. Several chapters discuss education as their primary goal, while other chapters treat it incidentally.

1867.   White, Ellen G. *Counsels on Education: As Presented in the Nine Volumes of Testimonies for the Church.* Mountain View, CA: Pacific Press Pub. Assn., 1968.

Presents in one volume the educational writings of Ellen White that were published in *Testimonies for the Church* to guide Adventism's developing educational system between 1872 and 1909. Ellen White, it should be noted, was the most influential person in the development of the denomination's educational thought and practice. She continues to hold that position through her writings.

1868.   White, Ellen G. *Counsels to Parents, Teachers, and Students Regarding Christian Education.* Mountain View, CA: Pacific Press Pub. Assn., 1913.

Sets forth the general principles of Christian education. Focuses on the application of principles.

1869.   White, Ellen G. *Education.* Mountain View, CA: Pacific Press Pub. Assn., 1903.

Expounds upon a biblical philosophy of education. The most important book in the formation of Adventist educational ideals. Holds that the purpose of Christian education is the restoration of God's image in fallen humanity.

1870.   White, Ellen G. *Fundamentals of Christian Education: Instruction for the Home, the School, and the Church.* Nashville, TN: Southern Pub. Assn., 1923.

Sets forth the general principles of Christian education. Focuses on the application of principles.

Part II: Contemporary

1871.   Dudley, Roger L. *Why Teenagers Reject Religion and What To Do About It.* Washington, DC: Review and Herald Pub. Assn., 1978.

Presents the basic causes of youth alienation from Christian values. Forcefully demonstrates, from an Adventist philosophic perspective, the role of the home and school in fostering a healthy attitude toward religion.

1872.   General Conference Department of Education. "Handbook for Seventh-day Adventist Higher Education," 1974. Mimeographed.

A general working policy for Adventist higher education. Very long and comprehensive. Provides administrators with official denominational policies along with position papers on selected topics.

1873.   [Harder, F. E. J.] *A Statement Respecting Seventh-day Adventist Philosophy of Higher Education.* Washington, DC: General Conference of Seventh-Day Adventists, 1973.

Provides an official statement of Adventist philosophy of higher education that articulates and accentuates the uniqueness of Seventh-day Adventist colleges and universities.

1874.   Hilde, Reuben. *Showdown: Can SDA Education Pass the Test?* Washington, DC: Review and Herald Pub. Assn., 1980.

An evaluation of contemporary Adventist education by an official of the General Conference Department of Education. Basically defensive in regard to "the system." Argues against those who, like Raymond Moore, demand more radical approaches to educational reform.

1875.   Knight, George R. *Myths in Adventism: An Interpretive Study of Ellen White, Education, and Related Issues.* Washington, DC: Review and Herald Pub. Assn., 1985.

Argues that if Adventism is to be faithful to its educational goals, it must separate the unchangeable principles enunciated at its founding from the particulars of time and place that formed its original context. These principles must then be applied with understanding to a late twentieth century context. Analyzes several misconceptions in Adventist education that are based on false assumptions, and illustrates the hermeneutical method it proposes in such areas as recreation and literary study.

1876.   Knight, George R. *Philosophy and Education: An Introduction in*

Christian Perspective. Berrien Springs, MI: Andrews University Press, 1980.

Surveys traditional and modern philosophers of education and evaluates them from a biblical perspective. Part III presents the biblical grounding for the Christian approach to education that forms the foundation of Adventist educational thought.

1877.   Moore, Raymond S. *Adventist Education at the Crossroads.* Mountain View, CA: Pacific Press Pub. Assn., 1976.

Argues that Adventist education should be more faithful to its philosophy as expounded by Ellen White--especially in such areas as work-study programs. This book is built upon a skewed and inaccurate view of Adventist educational philosophy, but it is important because it represents the views of a sizable portion of "fundamentalist" Adventists in the tradition of E. A. Sutherland.

1878.   *Official Report: North American Division Quadrennial Council for Higher Education.* Washington, DC: General Conference Department of Education, 1968.

Presents minutes, addresses, and papers read at a meeting held for teachers working in North American Adventist colleges and universities. Many of the papers deal with critical issues in Adventist higher education and in the various subject matter fields.

CHAPTER 26
UNITED CHURCH OF CHRIST COLLEGES AND UNIVERSITIES
Verlyn L. Barker, Joseph T. McMillan, Jr., and James A. Smith, Jr.

The United Church of Christ was formed in 1957 with the union of the Congregational Christian Churches and the Evangelical and Reformed Church. Each of these was the result of an earlier union of two denominations: The General Council of the Congregational and Christian Churches was formed in 1931 by the union of the National Council of the Congregational Churches and the General Convention of the Christian Church; the Evangelical and Reformed Church was formed in 1934 with the merger of the Reformed Church in the United States and the Evangelical Synod of North America.

The most appropriate general term to describe the relationship of the colleges to the United Church of Christ would be "associated with, at time of founding." The nature of the relationship includes the Congregational tradition with strong conviction that colleges should *not* be under the control of an ecclesiastical body but under the control and supervision of a Board of Trustees independent of state and church. At the other end of the spectrum was the tradition of the Reformed Church in the United States which established its colleges by vote of its national judicatory to which the colleges were accountable and which elected the governing boards of the colleges.

The American Missionary Association was formed in 1846 by Christian persons committed to the freedom and education of all persons, initially those freed from slavery. Since the founders and supporters were mostly of the Congregational churches, the organization associated with the Congregational mission agency in 1865 and carried a major role in providing primary, secondary and higher education for Blacks in the South.

Because Presbyterians and Congregationalists cooperated during the westward development of the nation in the early 19th century, some of the colleges in this chapter also have Presbyterian roots. Several of the colleges, because of mergers, are now related to other denominations as well as to the United Church of Christ. In 1987, 30 of the colleges and universities included in this entry continue a relationship with the United Church of Christ through its Council for Higher Education, as do the Divinity Schools of Harvard, Yale and Howard Universities.

Part I: Institutional Histories

A. Congregational Churches

1879.   Amherst College (1821)

1880. Fuess, Claude Moore. *Amherst, The Story of a New England College.* Boston: Little, Brown, 1935.

1881. LeDuc, Thomas. *Piety and Intellect at Amherst, 1865-1912.* New York: Columbia University Press, 1946.

1882. Tyler, W. S. *History of Amherst College During its First Half Century.* Springfield, MA: Clark W. Bryan and Company, 1873.

1883. Beloit College (1846)

1884. Ballard, Lloyd. *Beloit College, 1917-1923: The Brannon Years.* Beloit, WI: Beloit College, 1971.

1885. Eaton, Edward D. *Historical Sketches of Beloit College.* New York: A. S. Barnes & Co., 1928.

1886. Bowdoin College (1794)

1887. Hatch, Louis Clinton. *The History of Bowdoin.* Portland, ME: Loriag, Short & Harmon, 1927.

1888. Helmreich, Ernst Christian. *Religion at Bowdoin College: A History.* Brunswick, ME: Bowdoin College, 1982.

1889. Carleton College (1866)

1890. Headley, Leal A., and Merrill E. Jarchow. *Carleton: The First Century.* Northfield, MN: Carleton College, 1966.

1891. Leonard, Delavan L. *The History of Carleton College: Its Origin and Growth Environment and Builders.* Chicago: Revell, 1904.

1892. Case Western Reserve University (1826)

1893. Cramer, Clarence H. *Case Western Reserve University: A History, 1826-1976.* Boston: Little, Brown, 1976.

1894. Thwing, Charles F. *Notes on the History of the College of Women of Western Reserve University for Its First Twenty-Five Yeras, 1888-1913.* Cleveland, OH: Western Reserve University Press, 1913.

1895. College of California (1868) - Became University of California, Berkeley

1896. Ferrier, William W. *Origin and Development of the University of California.* Berkeley: The Sathergate Bookshop, 1930.

1897. Stadtman, Verne A. *The University of California 1868-1968.* New York: McGraw-Hill, 1970.

1898. Willey, Samuel H. *A History of the College of California.* San Francisco: Samuel Carson and Co., 1887.

1899. Colorado College (1874)

1900.   Hershey, Charlie Brown. *Colorado College, 1784-1949*. Colorado Springs: Colorado College, 1952.

1901.   Norlin, George. *A Voice from Colorado's Past for the Present: Selected Writings of George Norlin*. Boulder: Colorado Associated University Press, 1985.

1902.   Reid, J. Juan. *Colorado College: The First Century, 1847-1947*. Colorado Springs, CO: Colorado College, 1979.

1903.   Riley, Graham. *The Colorado College: An Informal History*. New York: Newcomen Society in North America, 1982.

1904.   Dartmouth College (1769)

1905.   Chase, Frederick. *A History of Dartmouth College and the Town of Hanover, New Hampshire*. Cambridge: Wilson and Son, 1891-1913.

1906.   Daniell, Jere R. *Eleazor Wheelock and the Dartmouth College Charter*. Hanover, NH: Dartmouth College, 1969.

1907.   *History of Dartmouth College*. 2 vols. Hanover, NH: Dartmouth College, 1932.

1908.   Lord, John K. *History of Dartmouth College, 1769-1909*. 2 vols. Concord, NH: n.p., 1913.

1909.   McCallum, James D. *Eleazor Wheelock, Founder of Dartmouth College*. Hanover, NH: Dartmouth College Publications, 1939.

1910.   Richardson, Leon Burr. *An Indian Preacher in England*. Hanover, NH: Dartmouth College Publications, 1933.

1911.   Smith, Baxter Perry. *The History of Dartmouth College*. Boston: Houghton, Osgood and Co., 1878.

1912.   Doane College (1872)

1913.   *The History of Doane College, 1872-1912*. Crete, NB: Doane College, 1957.

          In memory of David Brainard Perry, first President; Arthur Babbet Fairchild and John Sewell Brown, Professors.

1914.   Drury College (1873)

1915.   Clippinger, Frank W. *The Drury Story*. Springfield, MO: Drury College, 1982.

1916.   Pope, Richard M. "Drury College: An Interpretation." Ph.D. dissertation. University of Chicago, 1955.

1917.   Roulet, Paul. *History of Drury College at Springfield, Greene County, Missouri; with a Sketch of the Early Educational Efforts by the Settlers of South West Missouri, Before the War.* Springfield, MO: 1899. Unpublished.

1918. Grinnell College (1846)

1919. Adams, Ephraim. *The Iowa Band.* Boston: n.p., 1868.

1920. Grinnell, Josiah Bushnell. *Men and Events of Forty Years.* Boston: n.p., 1891.

1921. Magown, George F. *Asa Turner, A Home Missionary Patriarch and His Times.* Boston: n.p., 1889.

1922. Magown, George F. President, 1865-1884. *The Past of Our College.* Grinnell, IA: Grinnell College, 1895.

1923. Nollen, John Scholte. *Grinnell College.* Iowa City: State Historical Society of Iowa, 1953.

1924. Payne, Charles E. *Josiah Bushnell Grinnell.* Iowa City: n.p., 1938.

1925. Harvard University (1636)

1926. Bentinck-Smith, William, ed. *The Harvard Book: Selection from Three Centuries.* Revised edition. Cambridge: Harvard University Press, 1982.

1927. Morison, Samuel Eliot. *Harvard in the Seventeenth Century.* 2 vols. Cambridge: Harvard University Press, 1936.

1928. Morison, Samuel Eliot. *The Founding of Harvard College.* Cambridge: Harvard University Press, 1935.

1929. Morison, Samuel Eliot. *Three Centuries of Harvard 1636-1936.* Cambridge: Harvard University Press, 1936.

1930. Quincy, Josiah. *The History of Harvard University.* 2 vols. Cambridge: John Owen, 1840.

1931. Howard University (1867)

1932. Dyson, Walter. *Howard University, The Capstone of Negro Education, A History: 1867-1940.* Washington, DC: The Graduate School, Howard University, 1941.

1933. Holmes, Dwight O. W. "Fifty Years of Howard University, Part I." *Journal of Negro History* 3 (1918).

1934. Howard, Oliver Otis. *Autobiography of Oliver Otis Howard.* Vol. II. Freeport, NY: Book for Libraries Press, 1971. Founder of the University.

1935. Logan, Rayford W. *Howard University - The First One Hundred Years, 1867-1967.* New York: New York University Press, 1969.

1936. Illinois College (1829)

1937.   Frank, Charles E. *Pioneer's Progress: Illinois College, 1829-1979.* Carbondale: Southern Illinois University Press, 1979.

1938.   Johnson, Daniel Thomas. "Puritan Power in Illinois Higher Education Prior to 1870." Ph.D. dissertation. University of Wisconsin, 1974.

1939.   Rammelkamp, Charles Henry. *Illinois College: A Centennial History, 1829-1929.* New Haven: Yale University Press, 1928.

1940.   Willis, John R. *God's Frontiersmen: The Yale Band in Illinois.* Lanham, MD: University Press of America, 1979.

1941.   Yeager, Iver F. *Church and College on the Illinois Frontiers: 1829-1867.* Jacksonville, IL: Illinois College, 1980.

1942.   Knox College (1837)

1943.   Calkins, Ernest E. *They Broke the Prairie: Being Some Account of the Settlement of the Upper Mississippi Valley by Religious and Educational Pioneers, Told in Terms of One City, Galesburg, and One College, Knox.* New York: n.p., 1937.

1944.   Muelder, Hermann R. *Missionaries and Muckrakers: The First Hundred Years of Knox College.* Urbana: University of Illinois Press, 1984.

1945.   Webster, Martha F. *Seventy-five Significant Years: The Story of Knox College, 1837-1912.* Galesburg, IL: Knox College, 1913.

1946.   Marietta College (1834)

1947.   Andrews, Israel Ward. "A Discourse on the History of Marietta College." Delivered on the celebration of the fiftieth anniversary, 1885. Marietta, OH: Marietta College, 1885.

1948.   Beach, Arthur C. *A Pioneer College: The Story of Marietta.* Chicago: John F. Cuneo Co., 1935.

1949.   Middlebury College (1800)

1950.   Lee, W. Storrs. *Father Went to College: The Story of Middlebury College.* New York: Wilson-Erickson, 1936.

1951.   Stameshkin, David M. *The Town's College.* Middlebury, VT: Middlebury College Press, 1985.

1952.   Milwaukee-Downer (1851). Now part of Lawrence University.

1953.   *Annals of Milwaukee College, 1848-1891.* Prepared by William W. Wight. Milwaukee, WI, 1891.

1954.   Kieckhefer, Grace Norton. *Milwaukee-Downer College, 1851-1951.* Milwaukee, WI: The College, 1951.

1955.   Mount Holyoke College (1837)

1956.   Cole, Arthur C. *A Hundred Years of Mount Holyoke College: The Evolution of an Educational Ideal.* New Haven: Yale University Press, 1940.

1957.   Green, Elizabeth A. *Mary Lyon and Mount Holyoke: Opening the Gates.* Hanover, NH: University Press of New England, 1979.

1958.   Mount Holyoke College. *The Centenary of Mount Holyoke College.* South Hadley, MA: The College, 1937.

1959.   Stow, Sarah D. *History of Mount Holyoke Seminary During Its First Half Century, 1837-1887.* Springfield, MA: Springfield Printing Co., 1887.

1960.   Northland College (1892)

1961.   Dexter, Nathaniel B. *Northland College: A History.* Ashland, WI: Northland College, 1968.

1962.   Oberlin College (1833)

1963.   Ballantine, William G. *Oberlin College, Oberlin Jubilee, 1833-1883.* Oberlin, OH: E. J. Goodrich, 1883.

1964.   Barnard, John. *From Evangelism to Progressivism at Oberlin College, 1866-1917.* Columbus: Ohio State University Press, 1969.

1965.   Burroughs, Wilbur. "Oberlin's Part in the Slavery Conflict." *Ohio History* 20 (1911): 269-334.

1966.   Carlson, Ellsworth C. *Oberlin in Asia: The First Hundred Years, 1882-1982.* Oberlin, OH: Oberlin Shansi Memorial Association, 1982.

1967.   Fairchild, J. H. *Oberlin: The Colony and the College 1833-1883.* Oberlin, OH: 1883.

1968.   Fletcher, Juniata D. *Against the Consensus: Oberlin College and the Education of American Negroes, 1835-1865.* Washington, DC: n.p., 1974.

1969.   Phillips, Wilbur H. *Oberlin Colony: The Story of a Century.* Oberlin, OH: Oberlin Printing Co., 1933.

1970.   Warford, Malcolm L. "Piety, Politics and Pedagogy: An Evangelical Protestant Tradition in Higher Education at Lane, Oberlin, and Bere, 1834-1904." Ed.D. dissertation. Teachers College, Columbia University, 1973.

1971.   Olivet College (1844)

1972.   Riethmiller, M. Gorton. *Upon This Hill: My Affair with Olivet.* Detroit: Harlo, 1982.

1973.   Williams, Wolcott B. *A History of Olivet College.* Olivet, MI: n.p.,

          1901.

1974.   Pacific University (1849)

1975.   Eells, Myron, ed. *A History of Tualatin Academy and Pacific University, Forest Grove, Oregon, 1848-1902*. Forest Grove, OR: Pacific University, 1904.

1976.   Hitchman, James H. *Liberal Arts in Oregon and Washington, 1862-1980*. Bellingham, WA: Center for Pacific Northwest Studies, Western Washington University, 1981.

1977.   Johnson, Paul. *A Brief History of Pacific University*. Forest Grove, OR: Pacific University, 1931.

1978.   Long, Walt A. "A History of Pacific University." Ph.D. dissertation. University of Oregon, 1932.

1979.   Piedmont College (1897)

1980.   Jenkins, Frank E. *Anglo-Saxon Congregationalism in the South*. Atlanta: The Franklin-Turner Company, 1908. Chapter on "Piedmont College," 185-?.

1981.   Raintree, George W. "Piedmont College: Its History, Resources and Programs." Ph.D. dissertation. University of Georgia, 1965.

1982.   Pomona College (1887)

1983.   Brackett, Frank P. *Granite and Sagebrush: Reminiscences of the First Fifty Years of Pomona College*. Los Angeles: Ward Ritchie Press, 1944.

1984.   Lyon, Elijah Wilson. *The History of Pomona College, 1887-1969*. Claremont, CA: The College, 1977.

1985.   Sumner, Charles Burt. *The Story of Pomona College*. Boston: Pilgrim Press, 1914.

1986.   Ripon College (1851)

1987.   Dexter, Frank N., ed. *A Hundred Years of Congregational History in Wisconsin*. Fond du Lac, WI: n.p., 1933.

1988.   Merrell, Edward H. *Ripon College: An Historical Sketch*. Ripon, WI: Ripon Free Press, 1893.

1989.   Pedrick, Samuel M. "Early History of Ripon College." *Wisconsin Magazine of History* 8 (September 1924): 22-37.

1990.   Rockford College (1847)

1991.   Cederborg, Hazel Paris. "The Early History of Rockford College." Master's thesis. Wellesley College, 1926.

1992.   *Profiles of the Principles of Rockford Seminary and President of*

Rockford College. Rockford College, 1947.

1993. Rocky Mountain College (1878)

1994. Buhl, Marjorie Carter. *Open Doors, 1958.* Unpublished history of higher education in Montana, 1883-1958. Written on occasion of 75th Anniversary of Rocky Mountain College.

1995. Rollins College (1885)

1996. Hanna, Alfred Jackson. *The Founding of Rollins College.* Winter Park, FL: Rollins College, 1935.

1997. Jenkins, Frank E. *Anglo-Saxon Congregationalism in the South.* Atlanta: The Franklin-Turner Company, 1908. Chapter on Rollins College, 163-84.

1998. Schauffler College (1886) - Now part of The Defiance College

1999. Reynolds, Ward M., compiler. "A History of The Defiance College." Unpublished history of The Defiance College, March 14, 1958. Schauffler College merged with The Defiance College.

2000. Scripps College (1926)

2001. *Ellen Browning Scripps Papers.* Scripps College Archives.

2002. Smith College (1871)

2003. Hanscom, Elizabeth Deering and Helen French Green. *Sophia Smith and the Beginnings of Smith College.* Northampton, MA: Smith College, 1925.

2004. Mendenhall, Thomas C. *Chance and Change in Smith College's First Century.* Northampton, MA: The College, 1976.

2005. Seelye, Laurenus C. *The Early History of Smith College, 1871-1910.* Boston: Houghton Mifflin, 1923.

2006. Washburn University (1865)

2007. Hickman, Russell K. "Lincoln College - Forerunner of Washburn Municipal University." *Kansas Historical Quarterly* 18 (1950). Pt. I: "Founding of a Pioneer Congregational College," 20-54. Pt. II: "Later History and Change of Name," 164-204.

2008. MacVicar, Peter. *An Historical Sketch of Washburn College.* Unpublished pamphlet by President of Washburn University at dedication of Boswell Library Building and Holbrook Hall, October 23, 1886.

2009. Zimmerman, James Frederic. *The Washburn Story.* Unpublished manuscript in Washburn University archives. Details history to 1966.

2010. Wellesley College (1875)

2011.   Converse, Florence. *Wellesley College: A Chronicle of the Years, 1875-1938.* Wellesley, MA: Hathaway House Book-Shop, 1939.

2012.   Glascock, Jean, ed. *Wellesley College, 1875-1975: A Century of Women.* Wellesley, MA: Wellesley College, 1975.

2013.   Hackett, Alice Payne. *Wellesley, Part of the American Story.* New York: E. P. Dutton, 1949.

2014.   Westminster College of Salt Lake City (1875)

2015.   Nyman, Emil. *A Short History of Westminister College, Salt Lake City: The First Century, 1875-1975.* Salt Lake City. UT: Westminister College, 1976.

2016.   Webster, Lewis G. *A History of Westminister College of Salt Lake City, Utah, 1875-1969.* Logan: Utah State University, 1970.

2017.   Wheaton College, Illinois (1860)

2018.   Askew, Thomas A. *The Liberal Arts College Encounters Intellectual Change.* (A Comparative Study of Education at Knox and Wheaton Colleges, 1837-1925.) Evanston, IL: n.p., 1969.

2019.   Bechtel, Paul M. *Wheaton College: A Heritage Remembered, 1868-1984.* Wheaton, IL: Shaw Publishers, 1984.

2020.   Whitman College (1859)

2021.   Anderson, Florence Bennett. *Leaven for the Frontier: The True Story of a Pioneer Educator.* Boston: The Christopher Publishing House, 1953.

2022.   Penrose, Stephen B. L. *Whitman: An Unfinished Story.* Walla Walla, WA: Whitman Publishing Co., 1935.

2023.   Williams College (1793)

2024.   Botsford, E. Hubert. *Fifty Years at Williams.* 5 vols. Pittsfield, MA: McClellan Press, 1928-1940.

2025.   Rudolph, Frederick. *Mark Hopkins and the Log: Williams College 1836-1872.* New Haven: Yale University Press, 1956.

2026.   Spring, Leverett Wilson. *A History of Williams College.* Boston: Houghton, Mifflin Co., 1917.

2027.   Yale University (1701)

2028.   Kelly, Brooks M. *Yale: A History.* New Haven: Yale University Press, 1974.

2029.   Pierson, George Wilson. *Yale College, an Educational History, 1871-1921.* New Haven: Yale University Press, 1952.

2030.   *Yale: A Short History.* New Haven: Office of the Secretary, Yale

University, 1976.

2031.   Yankton College (1881)

2032.   McMurtry, William J. *Yankton College: An Historical Sketch.* Yankton, SD: n.p., 1907.

2033.   Stewart, Edgar I. *Yankton College: The Second Twenty-five Years.* Yankton, SD: n.p., 1932.

B. The Christian Church (not to be confused with The Christian Church, Disciples of Christ)

2034.   Antioch College (1852)

2035.   Antioch College. *Dedication of Antioch College and Inaugural Address of its President, Hon. Horace Mann.* Yellow Springs, OH: A.S. Dean, 1854.

2036.   Straker, Robert Lincoln. *Brief Sketch of Antioch College (1853-1921).* Yellow Springs, OH: Antioch College, 1954.

2037.   Straker, Robert Lincoln. *The Unseen Harvest: Horace Mann and Antioch College.* Yellow Springs, OH: Antioch College, 1955.

2038.   Vallance, Harvard F. "A History of Antioch College." Ph.D. dissertation. Ohio State University, 1936.

2039.   The Defiance College (1850)

2040.   Reynolds, Ward M., compiler. "A History of The Defiance College." Unpublished history of The Defiance College, March 14, 1958.

2041.   Elon College (1889)

2042.   Stokes, Durward T. *Elon College: Its History and Traditions.* Elon College, NC: Elon College Alumni Association, 1982.

Southern Union College (1922) - Now Southern Union State Junior College

2043.   Phi Theta Kappa. *Tap Roots: A Historical Account of Southern Union State Junior College and Areas in Randolph County.* Roanoke, AL: The Roanoke Leader, 1976.

C. The Reformed Church in the United States (German Reformed Church)

2044.   Catawba College (1851)

2045.   Keppel, Alvin Robert. *A College of Our Own: A Brief History of Catawba College, 1851-1951.* Salisbury, NC: Catawba College,

1951.

2046.   Leonard, Jacob Calvin. *History of Catawba College.* Salisbury, NC: The Trustees, 1927.

2047.   Cedar Crest College (1867)

2048.   Klein, Harry M. *Cedar Crest College, 1867-1947.* Allentown, PA: Trustees of Cedar Crest College, 1948.

2049.   Franklin and Marshall College (1787)

2050.   Dubbs, Joseph Henry. *History of Franklin and Marshall College.* Lancaster, PA: Franklin and Marshall College Alumni Association, 1903.

2051.   Klein, Frederick S. *Since 1787: The Franklin and Marshall Story.* Lancaster, PA: Franklin and Marshall College, 1968.

2052.   Heidelberg College (1850)

2053.   Williams, E. I. F. *Heidelberg: Democratic Christian College, 1850-1950.* Menasha, OH: Benta, 1952.

2054.   Hood College (1893)

2055.   Dutrow, Katharine E. "Hood Through the Years, 1893-1968." Unpublished manuscript, 1968.

2056.   Lakeland College (1862)

2057.   Jaberg, Eugene C. and Roland G. Kley, eds. *A History of Mission House - Lakeland.* Philadelphia: The Christian Education Press, 1962.

2058.   Ursinus College (1869)

2059.   Yost, Calvin Daniel. *Ursinus College: A History of Its First Hundred Years.* Collegeville, PA: Ursinus College, 1985.

D. Evangelical Synod of North America

2060.   Elmhurst College (1871)

2061.   Baltzer, Frederick. *Alma Mater: A Story of College Life Written in Commemoration of the Fiftieth Anniversary of Elmhurst College at Elmhurst, Illinois.* St. Louis: Eden Publishing House, 1921.

2062.   Banzhaf, Richard Franklin. "The Eight Colleges of the Evangelical and Reformed Church: A Study in Changing Religious Character." 2 vols. Ed.D. dissertation. Teachers College, Columbia University.

2063.   Stanger, Robert. "The First Hundred Years, (1871-1971). *Elmhurst College Magazine* 4 (1971).

2064.   Deaconess College of Nursing (1889)

2065.   Rasche, Ruth W. "The Deaconess Sisters: Pioneer Professional Women." In *Hidden Histories of the United Church of Christ*. Barbara Brown Zikmund, ed. New York: United Church Press, 1984.

E. American Missionary Association

2066.   Atlanta University (1865)

2067.   Adams, Myron W. *A History of Atlanta University*. Atlanta: Atlanta University Press, 1930.

2068.   Bacote, Clarence A. *The Story of Atlanta University: A Century of Service, 1865-1965*. Atlanta: Atlanta University Press, 1969.

2069.   Berea College (1855)

2070.   Brown, Dale W. *Berea College: Spiritual and Intellectual Roots*. Berea, KY: Berea College Press, 1982.

2071.   Fairchild, E. H. *Berea College, Kentucky: An Interesting History*. 1875.

2072.   Hutchins, Francis S. *Berea College*. New York: Newcomen Society in North America, 1963.

2073.   Nelson, Paul David. "Experiment in Interracial Education at Berea College, 1858-1908. *Journal of Negro History* 59 (January 1974): 13-27.

        Reports on the experience of Berea in interracial education long before the nation struggled with universal integrated education as national policy.

2074.   Peck, Elizabeth S. *Berea's First Century*. Lexington: University of Kentucky Press, 1955.

2075.   Peck, Elizabeth S. *Berea's First 125 Years, 1855-1980* (with final chapter by Emily Ann Smith). Lexington: University Press of Kentucky, 1982.

2076.   Rogers, John A. R. *The Birth of Berea College*. Philadelphia: H.T. Coates & Co., 1903.

2077.   Warford, Malcolm L. "Piety, Politics and Pedagogy: An Evangelical Protestant Tradition in Higher Education at Lane, Oberlin, and Berea, 1834-1904." Ed.D. dissertation. Teachers College, Columbia University, 1973.

2078.   Dillard University (1869)

2079.   New Orleans University. *Seventy Years of Service, New Orleans*

University. New Orleans: Faculty of New Orleans University, 1937.

2080. Fisk University (1866)

2081. Eaton, James Nathaniel. *The Life of Erastus Milo Cravath. A Guiding Light in an Era of Darkness.* Nashville, TN: Fisk University, 1959.

Cravath was first president of Fisk, 1875-1900.

2082. Hopkins, Alphonso A. *A Life of Clinton B. Fisk.* New York: Funk and Wagnalls, 1890.

Biography of founder for whom Fisk was named.

2083. Merrill, James G. *Fisk University.* Nashville, TN: n.p., c1899.

2084. Richardson, Joe Martin. *A History of Fisk University, 1865-1946.* University, AL: University of Alabama Press, 1980.

2085. Hampton University (1868)

2086. Jackson, L. P. "The Origin of Hampton Institute." *Journal of Negro History* 10 (1925): 131-49.

2087. Peabody, Frances Greenwood. *Education for Life: A Story of Hampton Institute.* Garden City, NY: Doubleday, Page, and Co., 1919.

2088. Robinson, William Hannibal. "The History of Hampton Institute, 1869-1949." Ph.D. dissertation. New York University, 1955.

2089. Huston-Tillotson College (1876)

2090. Jones, William H. *Tillotson College from 1930 to 1940, A Decade of Prayers.* Austin, TX: n.p., 1940.

2091. Shackles, Chrystine I. *Reminiscences: The Story of Tillotson College and Samuel Huston College, 1928-1968.* Austin, TX: Best Publishing Co., 1973.

2092. LeMoyne-Owen College (1862)

No institutional histories.

2093. Talladega College (1867)

2094. Butler, Addie Louise Joyner. *The Distinctive Black College: Talladega, Tuskegee, and Morehouse.* Metuchen, NJ: Scarecrow Press, 1977.

2095. Kimball, Solon T. *The Talladega Story: A Study in Community Process.* University, AL: University of Alabama Press, 1954.

2096.   Miller, Joseph Herman. *Talladega College: Retrospect and Prospect.* Talladega, AL: Talladega Alumni, 1950.

2097.   Tougaloo College (1869)

2098.   Campbell, Clarice T. *History of Tougaloo College.*   Ph.D. dissertation. University of Mississippi, 1970.

F. United Church of Christ

2099.   Hawaii Loa College (1963)

No institutional histories.

2100.   New College (1961) - Now part of the University of South Florida

2101.   Arthus, Furman C. *The Merger Years of New College, 1973-75.* Sarasota, FL: 1978.

2102.   Elmendorf, John. *Transmitting Information about Experiments in Higher Education: New College as a Case Study.* New York: Academy for Educational Development, 1975.

2103.   Glasser, Kay E. *The New College Story.* Sarasota, FL: 1977.

2104.   Prescott College (1960)

2105.   Parker, Charles Franklin, ed. *Emergence of a Concept, a Dynamic New Educational Program for the Southwest.*   Prescott, AZ: Prescott College Press, 1965.

2106.   Trombley, William. "The Prescott Experiment."   *World Book Encyclopedia Yearbook, 1973.* 180-88.

Part II: General Literature

A. Denominational Histories

2107.   Douglass, H. Paul. *Christian Reconstruction in the South.* Boston: The Pilgrim Press, 1909.

Develops the role of the Congregationalists in their "mission" outreach into the South, following the Civil War, including a good analysis of the initiatives in the education of the freed slave.

2108.   Dunn, David, ed. *A History of the Evangelical and Reformed Church.* Philadelphia: Christian Education Press, 1961.

Brings together the histories of the Reformed Church in the United States and the Evangelical Synod of North America in their union to form the Evangelical and Reformed Church.   The definitive history of the Evangelical and Reformed Church.

2109.   Fagley, Frederick L. *The Congregational Churches.* Boston: The

Pilgrim Press, 1925. Pp. 132-33.

Outlines the intent of the Christian Churches in education, including a listing of institutions founded as early as 1811, as well as the Congregationalists' commitments to education.

2110.   Good, James I. *History of the Reformed Church in the United States in the Nineteenth Century.* New York: Board of Publication of the Reformed Church in America, 1911.

2111.   Good, James I. *History of the Reformed Church in the United States, 1725-1792.* Reading, PA: n.p., 1899.

Gives, in these two books, detailed information about the formation and development of The Reformed Church, including helpful comments on concerns about ethnic identity and about the perennial issue of authority in churches in a voluntary society. The authoritative historical accounts of The Reformed Church in the United States.

2112.   Gunnemann, Louis M. *The Shaping of The United Church of Christ.* New York: United Church Press, 1977.

Suggests that the formative ecclesiastical principles, which were at work in the two uniting churches which formed the United Church of Christ, were derived from a common Reformed tradition, rooted in Continental European and English reformation movements; provides a narrative account of the church-union process itself.

2113.   Gunnemann, Louis M. *United and Uniting: The Meaning of An Ecclesiastical Journey.* New York: Pilgrim Press, 1987.

Brings his earlier denominational history up to date, concentrating on the United Church of Christ, 1957-1987.

2114.   Schneider, Carl E. *The German Church on the American Frontier.* St. Louis: Eden Publishing House, 1939.

Writes the definitive history of the (German) Evangelical Church in the settlement of the midwest, to the time of its union with the German Reformed Church in the United States in 1934.

2115.   Scott, William T. *A Brief History of the Christian Church.* Elon, NC: Elon College, 1956.

Argues that the groups that formed The Christian Church, while with different beginnings, had a common passion for Christian union and carried within them the distinctive marks of the awakening in the frontier settlement.

2116.   Stanley, J. Taylor. *A History of Black Congregational Christian Churches of the South.* Ltd. ed. New York: United Church Press,

1978.

Brings together into one cohesive and comprehensive account the history of the Black congregations from the Congregational Christian traditions that became a part of the United Church of Christ.

2117.   Stokes, D. T. and William T. Scott. *A History of the Christian Church in the South.* Elon, NC: Elon College, 1975.

Compiles former historical accounts of The Christian Church and focuses on the 20th-century development of the denomination, to the time of the union with the Congregational Churches in 1931. The most complete history of The Christian Church.

2118.   Walker, Williston. *The Creeds and Platforms of Congregationalism.* New York: Charles Scribner's Sons, 1893.

Collects and discusses the statements of belief and major organizational statements of agreement which emerged within the settlement and development of Congregationalism in the New World.

B. Higher Education - General

2119.   Bullock, Henry Allen. *A History of Negro Education in the South: From 1619 to the Present.* Cambridge: Harvard University Press, 1967.

Offers a dependable and comprehensive overview of the commitments, purposes and forms for the education of the Negro in the South, from the early 17th century into the middle of the 20th century.

2120.   Cremin, Lawrence A. *American Education: The Colonial Experience, 1607-1783.* New York: Harper & Row Publishers, 1970.

Traces the origins of American education to the European Renaissance, depicting the transplantation of educational institutions to the New World as part of the colonizing efforts of the seventeenth and eighteenth centuries.

2121.   Franklin, John Hope. *From Slavery to Freedom.* New York: Alfred A. Knopf, 1947.

Traces the education of Negroes in colleges before the Civil War, e.g., at Bowdoin, Oberlin, Franklin, Rutland.

2122.   Hofstadter, Richard and Wilson Smith. *American Higher Education,* 2 vols. Chicago: The University of Chicago Press, 1961.

Includes a discussion of the role of Congregational ministers in the founding of the public university. ("Henry P. Tappan on University Education," 488-511. Tappan was President of the University of Michigan.)

2123.   Holbrook, Stewart. *Yankee Exodus*. New York: The Macmillan Co., 1950.

Emphasizes the influence of Yale, Dartmouth, Amherst and Williams (New England denominationally founded colleges) on the colleges of the west, e.g., Western Reserve, Oberlin, Illinois, Grinnell, Beloit, Carleton.

2124.   Horowitz, Helen Lefkowitz. *Alma Mater: Design and Experience in the Women's Colleges from the Nineteenth-Century Beginnings to the 1930's*. New York: Alfred A. Knopf, 1984.

Presents extensive research and analysis of the role of women's colleges in the development of higher education in America.

2125.   Perry, Charles M. *Henry Philip Tappan*. Ann Arbor: University of Michigan Press, 1933.

Sets forth the ideas and commitments of the Congregational minister, Henry Tappan, who became President of the University of Michigan.

2126.   Sack, Saul. *History of Higher Education in Pennsylvania*. Harrisburg: Pennsylvania Historical & Museum Commission, 1963.

Traces, in Chapter 5, the role of the clergy of the established churches in the formation of the University of Pennsylvania, 106-39.

2127.   Shipton, Clifford K. "The Puritan Influence on Education." *Pennsylvania History* 3 (July 1958): 223-33.

Seeks to balance the excesses of New England enthusiasts' interpretation of New England's influence on higher education and the excesses of the "secular" historian (e.g., J. T. Adams, Beard, Parrington, Jernigan, and Wertenbacher) who discuss the influence as a failure; also discusses the difference in the concept of "veritas" as the search for truth, not the "revealed truth" of Christianity.

2128.   Sloan, Douglas, ed. *The Great Awakening and American Education: A Documentary History*. New York: Teachers College Press, 1973.

Includes a discussion of the pervasive impact of the Great Awakening on American institutions; important for understanding the founding of the colleges which came out of the Great Awakening, e.g., Dartmouth.

2129.   Smith, Timothy L. "Protestant Schooling and American Nationality, 1800-1850." *Journal of American History* 53 (1966-67): 679-795.

Seeks to correct the tendency of historians to read twentieth century distinctions between the public and private back into the nineteenth century, in discussing the relationship between the denominations and the colleges associated with them.

2130.   Solomon, Barbara Miller. *In the Company of Educated Women: A History of Women and Higher Education in America.* New Haven: Yale University Press, 1985.

Offers a comprehensive historical account of the untold story of the role of women in the development of higher education in America, including the place of the colleges for women.

2131.   Stevenson, Louise L. *Scholarly Means to Evangelical Ends: The New Haven Scholars and the Transformation of Higher Learning in America, 1830-1890.* Baltimore: Johns Hopkins University Press, 1986.

Assesses the impact of Yale on the expansion of American higher education, including the "Yale Band."

2132.   Tewksbury, Donald G. *Founding of Colleges and Universities Before the Civil War.* New York: Teachers College Press, 1932.

Assumes a close relationship between the denomination and the colleges, which developed in the first two centuries of America, a relationship challenged by later historians of education; the classic treatise on the numerical expansion of colleges in the nineteenth century.

2133.   Williams, George H. *Wilderness and Paradise in Christian Thought.* New York: Harper & Brothers, 1962.

Traces, in Part II, the evolution of the idea of the university as a paradise of learning, with focus on Harvard College whose founders preserved the medieval conception of the *translation studies* and were conscious of the assignment laid upon them in transferring to the New World the disciplines of learning, in a tradition that stretched, by way of Old Cambridge, Paris, and Athens to Jerusalem; from the schools of the Israelite prophets to the wilderness of America.

2134.   Williams, George H. *The Theological Idea of The University.* New York: Commission on Higher Education, National Council of Churches of Christ, 1954.

Builds what is perhaps the enduring foundation for understanding the common and distinctive functions and responsibilities of the church, the commonwealth and the college in establishing and developing higher education in America; presented in imagery of the City of Jerusalem (sustained by the love and tutelage of redemptive faith), the City of Athens (sustained by a commitment to pursue truth to the very brink of human perception), and the City of the Civic Person (sustained by its grounding in law which safeguards constitutionally the rights of diverse voluntarist associations gathered within the City, including the rights and privileges of the two historic communities of scholarship and faith).

2135. Williams, George H., ed. *The Harvard Divinity School.* Cambridge: Harvard University Press, 1954.

Concentrates on the tradition of one institution in order to clarify its experience and to identify certain theological or quasi-theological motifs that already belong to or may be appropriated by other academic institutions in America where the problem of religion and higher education is under discussion.

C. United Church of Christ Related Colleges

2136. The Armstrong League of Hampton Workers, eds. *Memoirs of Old Hampton.* Hampton, VA: The Institute Press, 1909.

Describes the circumstances which led to the founding of Hampton Institute, the philosophy of Samuel Chapman Armstrong (the founder and first principal), and the early experience and reflections of Armstrong and several early teachers.

2137. Armstrong, Samuel Chapman. *A Paper Read at the Anniversary Meeting of the American Missionary Association, Held in Syracuse, NY, October 24, 1877.* Hampton, VA: Normal School Press, 1877.

Tells the story of the founding of Hampton Normal and Agricultural Institute of 1868 as the first school planted by the North for the education of the children of slavery. Author was founder.

2138. Baltzer, Adolf C. S. *Recollections of a Missouri-Bred Preacher.* Rio de Janeiro, Brazil: Artes Graficas, 1939.

Reflects autobiographically about his college (Elmhurst), Eden Seminary and pastorate in the Evangelical Synod. Author is son of Synod president-general, Adolf Baltzer, and brother of late Synod head, John Baltzer.

2139. Banzhaf, Richard Franklin. "The Eight Colleges of the Evangelical and Reformed Church: A Study in Changing Religious Character." Ed.D. dissertation. Teachers College, Columbia University, 1973.

Describes the diversity of the ecclesiastical traditions which formed the Evangelical and Reformed Church, in terms of its related colleges and their historical roots and involvement.

2140. Beard, Augustus Field. *Crusade of Brotherhood, A History of the American Missionary Association.* Boston: Pilgrim Press, 1909.

Discusses the conditions out of which the American Missionary Association was created; traces the history of the American Missionary Association, including commentary on the persons responsible for it and on the principles of the Association which guided its work in education and evangelization. An early authoritative history of the Association. Recounts the American Missionary Association involvement in the founding of Fisk.

2141. Berens, Helmut Alan. *Elmhurst: Prairie to Tree Town.* Elmhurst, IL: Elmhurst Historical Commission, 1968. Pp. 77-79, 112-26.

Gives an account of the Elmhurst Community's early days, including the story of Thomas Barbour Bryan whose gift of property to the Evangelical Synod made Elmhurst College possible.

2142. Brawley, James P. *Two Centuries of Methodist Concern: Bondage, Freedom, and Education of Black People.* New York: Vantage Press, 1974.

Includes in Part IV, "Historical Accounts of Individual Institutions," narrative histories of Dillard University and the forerunner institutions of New Orleans University and Straight University, which merged in 1930; also, Huston-Tillotson College and the forerunner institutions of Samuel Huston College and Tillotson College, which merged in 1952.

2143. Brownlee, Fred L. *Heritage of Freedom: A Centenary Story of Ten Schools Offering Education in Freedom.* Philadelphia: United Church Press, 1963.

Reflects on the race relations commitment of the American Missionary Association and its decision to charter primary and secondary schools, during the mid-nineteenth century, as "colleges and universities"; provides historical vignettes on ten of the AMA's institutions which celebrated their centenaries between the late 1950's and the early 1970's; and ends with "ten specific things that can be done to counteract the evil influences of racial prejudice and to bring about improved race relations in America."

2144. Brownlee, Fred L. *New Day Ascending.* Boston: Pilgrim Press, 1946.

Sounds a clarion call to advance the new day ascending toward the abolition of segregation and unjust discrimination; tells the story of the American Missionary Association as a prophetic movement which spearheaded freedom and justice for minority groups - Negroes, Southern Highlanders, Jamaicans, Hawaiians, Orientals, Indians, Eskimos, and Puerto Ricans.

2145.   Campbell, Clarice T. and Oscar Allan Rogers, Jr. *Mississippi: The View from Tougaloo.* Jackson: University Press of Mississippi, 1979.

Places the extended role of Tougaloo in the context of its cultural milieu, thus reinforcing its role in educating the community and relating its own tradition and commitments to societal change.

2146.   Carpenter, John A. *Sword and Olive Branch.* Pittsburgh, PA: University of Pittsburgh Press, 1944.

Presents a good biographical study of the life of General Oliver Otis Howard, founder of Howard University.

2147.   Chrystal, William G. "Possessing Your Inheritance: Elmhurst College, The Evangelical Synod and the Niebuhrs." *In Thy Light* (1986). Elmhurst College Monograph.

Connects the history of Elmhurst College not only with its ecclesiastical heritage but also with the theological tradition of Richard and Reinhold Neibuhr, two of its distinguished graduates who became germinal theological thinkers and writers in the mid-20th century.

2148.   DeBoer, Clara Merritt. "The Role of Afro-Americans in the Origin and Work of the American Missionary Association, 1839-1877." 2 vols. Ph.D. dissertation. Rutgers University, 1973.

Documents the leadership of Black Americans in the missionary organizations which united to form the American Missionary Association and the subsequent involvement of more than 500 black men and women in the Executive Committee of the AMA and as early teachers and missionaries in the South.

2149.   Drake, Richard Bryant. "The American Missionary Association and the Southern Negro, 1861-1888." Ph.D. dissertation. Emory University, 1957.

Provides a fascinating account of the philosophy and involvement of the American Missionary Association in the education of Southern Blacks, during the Civil War and Reconstruction period, with an emphasis on documentation of the receipts and expenditures of the AMA, the Freedman's Bureau, and other Freedmen's Aid Societies.

2150.   Engs, Robert Francis. *Freedom's First Generation: Black Hampton, Virginia, 1861-1890.* Philadelphia: University of Pennsylvania Press, 1976.

Presents a study of Black post-bellum Hampton during the period of the Civil War and the decades after slavery to the 1890s and argues that the relationship between northern Whites and former slaves resulted in economic and political advancement that were not equaled anywhere in the South.

2151. Fisher, Isaac. *The Unique Educational Philosophy of Samuel Chapman Armstrong, Founder of Hampton Institute.* Unpublished manuscript, 1924. P. 246.

Exhibits the profound commitments of Hampton's founder to education as central to the future welfare of the children of slavery.

2152. Frissell, Hollis Burke. *Hampton Institute From Servitude to Service: Being the Old South Lecturers on the History and Work of Southern Institutions for the Education of the Negro.* Boston: American Unitarian Association, 1905. Pp. 115-52.

Recalls for the liberal Northern benefactors, the phenomenal impact of their commitment and financing to the lives of southern Blacks as the result of their educational opportunities.

2153. Gilpin, Patrick J. "Charles S. Johnson: An Intellectual Biography." Ph.D. dissertation. Vanderbilt University, 1973.

Focuses on the work of the first black president of Fisk University and his work in the field of race relations, national and international affairs, and higher education.

2154. Hinkle, Gerald Hahn. *The Theology of the Ursinus Movement: Its Origins and Influence in the German Reformed Church.* Ann Arbor, MI: University Microfilms, 1964. (Ph.D. dissertation. Yale University.)

Divides into four sections: the Palantinate heritage, Bomberger's career and College, Bomberger's "Old Reformed" dogmatics, and the broadening of the Ursinus tradition; includes bibliographic essay and extensive bibliography.

2155. Hosford, Herbert Chamberlain. *This Good Life: A Biography of Henry Hallock Hosford.* Erie, PA: Herbert C. Hosford, 1966.

Follows the life of a professor of science at Doane College.

2156. Hotchkiss, Wesley A. "The College-Church-State-Triangle." Unpublished manuscript of the General Secretary of the Division of Higher Education and the American Missionary Association, United Church Board for Homeland Ministries, March, 1980.

Develops the thesis that the distinctive mark of the Congregationalists in America was their clear definition of the discrete functions of the school, the state, the church.

2157.   Hotchkiss, Wesley A. "Congregationalists and Negro Education."
         In *The Journal of Negro Education* 29 (Summer 1960): 289-98.

         Outlines the foundations of the American Missionary
         Association's commitment to "equal brotherhood in the family of
         Christ" and its implications for education.

2158.   Hotchkiss, Wesley A. "The Prophetic Academy: An Historical
         Perspective on UCC Related Colleges." In *A Unique Role in A
         Unique Time*. New York: Council for Higher Education, 1977.

         Discusses the diverse traditions in higher education of the
         four denominational lineages that constituted the United Church
         of Christ.

2159.   Hotchkiss, Wesley A. "To Grow and Take Wings." In *Council for
         Higher Education Journal* (December 1963). A publication of the
         United Church Board for Homeland Ministries.

         Sets forth the United Church of Christ's advocacy for
         education that insists on freedom of inquiry and probing the moral
         questions of the meaning of knowledge.

2160.   Hughes, Jerome W. *Six Berea College Presidents: Tradition and
         Progress*.

         Illumines the history of Berea through the work of six of its
         presidents.

2161.   Johnson, Clifton H. "The American Missionary Association,
         1846-1861: A Study in Christian Abolitionism." Ph.D. dissertation.
         University of North Carolina, 1958.

         Analyzes the commitment of the American Missionary
         Association to address "the Negro problem" in the U.S. by
         establishing schools and colleges in the South during the Civil War
         and Reconstruction period and offers the first attempt to give a
         detailed account of the organization's ante-bellum history based on
         extensive use of manuscript materials.

2162.   Jones, Howard. *Mutiny on the Amistad*. New York: Oxford
         University Press, 1987.

         Shows how the abolitionist's argument put the "law of
         nature" on trial in the U.S., as such leaders as Tappan refused to
         accept a legal system claiming to dispense justice while permitting
         artificial distinctions based on race or color; the story of the
         Amistad Mutiny in 1839, the event which gave rise to the formation
         of the American Missionary Association in 1846.

2163.   Lundy, Harold W. "A Study of the Transition from White to Black
         Presidents of Three Selected Schools Founded by the American
         Missionary Association." Ph.D. dissertation. University of

Wisconsin, 1978.

Treats the issue of transition in leadership in three American Missionary Association Colleges - Fisk, Dillard and LeMoyne-Owen - that had followed the traditional pattern of white administrators in black colleges, and the outcomes of this black leadership in the development of the respective colleges.

2164.   Marsh, J. B. T. *The Story of the Jubilee Singers; With Their Songs.* Boston: Houghton, Mifflin and Co., 1876.

Recalls the story of the formation, in 1871, of the Jubilee Singers of Fisk University who, knowing the experience of bondage, took the name from the Old Testament's Year of Jubilee and sang of their deliverance, world-wide; a continuing group into the present day.

2165.   McCulloch, Margaret C. *Fearless Advocate of the Right: The Life of Francis Julius LeMoyne, M.D., 1798-1879.* Boston: The Christopher Publishers House, 1941.

Traces the early history of LeMoyne Institute, from 1860's to early 1900's and examines the educational and religious philosophy of Dr. LeMoyne. LeMoyne gave funds for rebuilding the school in 1866, following it being burned in one of the riots which followed the Civil War.

2166.   McFeely, William S. *Yankee Stepfather: General O. O. Howard and the Freedmen.* New Haven: Yale University Press, 1968.

Tells the story of General Howard, Chief Commissioner of the Freedmen's Bureau, who founded Howard University.

2167.   McKinney, Richard I. *Religion in Higher Education Among Negroes.* New Haven: Yale University Press, 1945; reprint ed. New York: Arno Press and the New York Times, 1972.

Analyzes the religious interests and forces that have been the primary determining factors in the rise and perpetuation of higher education institutions for Black Americans; concludes that men and women representing various religious organizations sought to lay the foundation for the education of the Negro which embody definite religious principles.

2168.   McMillan, Joseph T., Jr. "The Development of Higher Education for Blacks During the Late Nineteenth Century: A Study of the African Methodist Episcopal Church; Wilberforce University; the American Missionary Association; Hampton Institute; and Fisk University." Ed.D. dissertation. Teachers College, Columbia University, 1986.

Utilizes the research technique of narrative history to

describe and analyze the contributions of the African Methodist Episcopal (AME) Church and the American Missionary Association of the Congregational churches to the higher education of blacks; discusses the philosophies of liberal and industrial education of these sponsoring bodies; and notes the financial resources made available for the higher education of blacks.

2169.   McPherson, James. "White Liberals and Black Power in Negro Education, 1865-1915." *The American Historical Review* 35 (June 1970): 1337-1386.

Discusses the efforts of blacks to gain greater control of the freedmen's schools and colleges founded by Northern abolitionists, missionaries, and other "white liberals" interested in advancing the status of blacks and improving race relations through education.

2170.   Morris, Robert C. *Reading, 'Riting, and Reconstruction: The Education of Freedman in the South, 1861-1870.* Chicago: The University of Chicago Press, 1981.

Presents a comprehensive survey of educational activities of the Freedmen's educators from the early years of the Civil War through 1870 in seventeen states and the District of Columbia.

2171.   Nelson, Paul David. "Experiment in Interracial Education at Berea College, 1858-1908." *Journal of Negro History* 59 (January 1974): 13-27.

Reports on the experience of Berea in interracial education for over a century.

2172.   Oedel, Howard T., ed. *Daniel Hand of Madison, Connecticut, 1801-1891.* Madison, CT: The Madison Historical Society, Inc., 1973.

Tells the life story of Daniel Hand, a native of Madison and long time resident of Augusta, Georgia, where he had gone as a young man in the employment of his uncle and eventually become self-employed in such a successful venture that he was able to contribute one million dollars for the education of deserving blacks in the South.

2173.   Patterson, Joseph Norenzo. "A Study of the History of the Contribution of the American Missionary Association to the Higher Education of the Negro - With Special Reference to Five Selected Colleges Founded by the Association, 1865-1900." Ph.D. dissertation. Cornell University, 1956.

Discusses the higher education of blacks as exemplified in the five American Missionary Association colleges founded during Reconstruction - Atlanta University, Fisk University, Hampton, Straight, and Talladega.

2174.   Qualls, J. Winfield. "The Beginnings and Early History of the LeMoyne School at Memphis, 1871-1874." M.A. thesis. Memphis State University, 1952.

Covers the founding of LeMoyne Normal and Commercial School in 1871, including its difficulties during the Yellow Fever epidemics; follows the various changes of leadership of the early teachers sent by the American Missionary Association.

2175.   Richardson, Joe Martin. *Christian Reconstruction: The American Missionary Association and Southern Blacks, 1861-1890.* Athens, GA: University of Georgia Press, 1986.

Studies the efforts of the American Missionary Association to bring blacks into the mainstream of American life by providing the opportunity for them to acquire an education.

2176.   Sturtevant, Julian M., ed. *Julian M. Sturtevant: An Autobiography.* New York: n.p., 1896.

Expresses the commitments of the "Yale Band" whose members were pledged to devote themselves to religion and education in the West; written by president of Illinois College who fought to keep the college free from sectarian control though church related.

2177.   Sylvester, Ben F. and Ruth M. Sylvester. *A Man and His College: The Butler-Doane Story.* Crete, NB: Doane College Press, 1954.

Tells the story of U.S. Senator Hugh Butler and his role in the development of Doane College.

2178.   Talbot, Edith Armstrong. *Samuel Chapman Armstrong: A Biographical Study.* New York: Doubleday, Page and Co., 1904.

Studies and discusses the life of the founder of Hampton Institute.

2179.   Tingey, Joseph Willard. "Indians and Blacks Together: An Experiment in Biracial Education at Hampton Institute (1878-1923)." Ed.D. dissertation. Teachers College, Columbia University, 1978.

Discusses one of the earliest endeavors for biracial higher education in America.

2180.   *Twenty-Two Years of the Hampton Normal and Agricultural Institute at Hampton, Virginia.* Unpublished manuscript, 1893.

Reviews the records of Negro and Indian graduates of Hampton Institute, with personal sketches and testimony on important race questions.

2181.   Ursinus College. *The Reverend John H. A. Bomberger, Doctor of Divinity, Doctor of Laws, 1871-1890.* Philadelphia: Publication and Sunday School Board of the Reformed Church in The United States, 1917.

Provides the biography of Bomberger, including early life, student days, pastorates and church activities, founding and presidency of Ursinus College.

2182.   Welch, Eloise Turner. "The Background and Development of the American Missionary Association's Decision to Educate Freedmen in the South, with Subsequent Repercussions." Ph.D. dissertation. Bryn Mawr College, 1976.

Demonstrates the effect of the American Missionary Association's philosophy of providing education for freed blacks, following the Civil War, instead of supporting repatriation plans and efforts; cites examples of the educational philosophy and standards at its schools during the late nineteenth century; and suggests the relevance of various aspects of the AMA's educational model for contemporary American education.

CHAPTER 27
UNITED METHODIST COLLEGES AND UNIVERSITIES
Charles S. McCoy

Part I: Institutional Histories

2183. Akers, Samuel Luttrell. *The First Hundred Years of Wesleyan Colleges, 1836-1936.* Macon, GA: Wesleyan College, 1976.

2184. Allen, Paul F. *A History of Martin College.* Pulaski, TN: Martin Methodist College, 1970.

2185. Allison, Vista Royse. *Methodist History of Adair County, Kentucky 1782-1969.* Tompkinsville, KY: Monroe County Press, 1972.

   This book contains a section giving the history of Lindsey Wilson College, Columbia, Kentucky. See pp. 209-320.

2186. Arail, James M. *Columbia College 1912-1968.* Columbia, SC: Columbia College, 1969.

2187. Ault, Warren O. *Boston University. The College of Liberal Arts, 1873-1973.* Boston, MA: Boston University, 1973.

2188. Bartlett, Willard W. *Education for Humanity: The Story of Otterbein College.* Westerville, OH: Otterbein College, 1934.

2189. Berendzen, Richard. *Is My Armour Straight? A Year in the Life of a University President.* Bethesda, MD: Adler & Adler, 1986.

   The President of American University gives a sometimes wry account of the trials, tribulations, temptations, and potentialities of a university president on the battlefiled of contemporary higher education.

2190. Blaha, Nan. *History of Hamline University, 1880-1912.* Special Honors thesis. St. Paul, MN: Hamline University, 1933.

2191. Brandstadter, Dianna Puthoff. "Developing the Coordinate College for Women at Duke University: The Career of Alice Mary Baldwin, 1924-1947." Ph.D. dissertation. Duke University, 1977.

2192. Brawley, James P. "A Brief Historical Account of the Founding and Development of Bennett College." In *Two Centuries of Methodist Concern: Bondage, Freedom, and Education of Black People*, pp. 153-72. New York: Vantage Press, 1974.

2193.   Brawley, James P. *The Clark College Legacy*. Atlanta, GA: Clark College, n.d.

2194.   Breukelman, Fred Nieveen. *The College That Refused to Die*. Dover, DE: Wesley College, n.d.

2195.   Brill, H. E. *Story of Oklahoma University*. Oklahoma City, OK: Oklahoma City University Press, 1938.

2196.   Brown, Irving Frederic. *Indiana Asbury University: DePauw University, A History*. Cincinnati, OH: Monfort, 1914.

2197.   Buhl, Marjorie Carter. *The History of Higher Education in Montana, 1883-1958*. Billings, MT: Rocky Mountain College, 1958.

         Provides helpful material on Rocky Mountain College and its predecessor institutions.

2198.   Bullock, Henry M. *A History of Emory University*. Nashville, TN: Parthenon Press, 1936.

2199.   Chaffin, Nora Campbell. *Trinity College, 1839-1892: The Beginnings of Duke University*. Durham, NC: Duke University Press, 1950.

2200.   Clary, George E., Jr. *Paine College, August, Georgia: An Account of Its Beginnings (1882-1903)*. Brunswick, GA: Lemmond Letter Shop, 1975.

2201.   Cobb, Alice. *"Yes, Lord, I'll Do It": Scarritt's Century of Service*. Nashville, TN: Scarritt College, 1987.

2202.   Corley, Robert G., and Samuel N. Stayer. *View from the Hilltop: The First 125 Years of Birmingham-Southern College*. Birmingham, AL: Birmingham-Southern College, 1981.

2203.   Cornelius, Roberta D. *"Randolph-Macon Woman's College, Its Origins and Development."* *The Iron Worker* 16.1 (Winter, 1951-2): 1-13.

2204.   Cornett, John S. *Fifty Years of Kansas Wesleyan University: 1886-1936*. Salina, KS: Padgett's Printing House, 1936.

2205.   Coursey, Oscar William. *A History of Dakota Wesleyan University for Fifty Years, 1885-1935*. Mitchell, SD: Dakota Wesleyan University, n.d.

2206.   Craig, Marjorie. *This History of Brevard College; and Its Forerunners*. Brevard, NC: unpublished manuscript, 1955.

2207.   Crowell, John Franklin. *Personal Recollections of Trinity College North Carolina 1887-1894*. Durham, NC: Duke University Press, 1939.

2208.   Cunningham, John Thomas. *University in the Forest: The Story of*

Drew University. Florham Park, NJ: Afton Publishing Co., 1972.

2209.   Custard, Leila Roberta. *Through Golden Years, 1867-1943: A History of Centenary College Published for the Seventy-Fifth Anniversary.* New York: Lewis Historical Publishing Company, 1947.

2210.   Dees, Jesse W. *The College Built on Prayer: Mary McLeod Bethune.* Daytona Beach, FL: Behtune-Cookman College, 1963.

2211.   Dickie, Samuel. "A History," *Old Albion 1861-1909.* Edited by LeRoy E. Kimball. Albion, MI: Albion College, 1909.

2212.   Early, James. *On the Frontier of Leadership: The Centennial Story of the University of Puget Sound.* Tacoma, WA: University of Puget Sound, 1987.

2213.   Ellison, Rhoda Coleman. *History of Huntingdon College 1854-1954.* Tuscaloosa, AL: University of Alabama Press, 1954.

2214.   Ellison, Rhoda Coleman. "Huntingdon College 1860-1865." *Alabama Review* 8 (January 1954): 3-21.

2215.   *Emory Magazine.* A Sesquicentennial Issue 1836-1986. March 1987.

This edition of the magazine published by Emory University contains an interesting collection of articles that trace the history of the university from its founding as Emory College, provides an attractively illustrated time-line setting forth the main events for Emory's past, gives a vivid account of the impact of the "Death of God" controversy that rocked the school in the 1960's, and includes the sesquicentennial address of President James T. Laney.

2216.   English, Thomas H. *Emory University 1915-1965: A Semicentennial History.* Atlanta, GA: Emory University, 1965.

2217.   Fall, Delos. "History of Albion College." *History of Calhoun County.* Edited by Washington-Gardner. Vol. 1. Chicago: Lewis Publishing Company, 1913.

2218.   Fennimore, Keith J. *The Albion College Sesquicentennial History: 1835-1985.* Albion, MI: Albion College, 1985.

2219.   Feutcher, Clyde. *A History of Baldwin University and German-Wallace College.* Enlarged and revised by Herbert L. Heller. Berea, OH: Baldwin-Wallace College, 1973.

2220.   Galpin, W. Freeman. *Syracuse University, Volume I -- The Pioneer Days.* Syracuse, NY: Syracuse University Press, 1952.

2221.   Galpin, W. Freeman. *Syracuse University, Volume II -- The Growing Years.* Syracuse, NY: Syracuse University Press, 1960.

2222.   Galpin, W. Freeman, and Oscar T. Barck, Jr. *Syracuse University,*

Volume III -- The Critical Years. Revised and edited by Richard Wilson. Syracuse, NY: Syracuse University Press, 1984.

2223.   Garber, Paul Neff. *John Carlise Kilgo: President of Trinity College, 1894-1910.* Durham, NC: Duke University Press, 1937.

2224.   Garst, Henry. *The History of Otterbein University.* Dayton, OH: Brethern Publishing Company, 1907.

2225.   Giddens, Paul. *Recollections of A. G. Bush and His Associations with Hamline University.* St. Paul, MN: Hamline University, 1975.

2226.   Gifford, James F. *The Evolution of a Medical Center: A History of Medicine at Duke University to 1941.* Durham, NC: Duke University Press, 1972.

2227.   Gildart, Robert. *Albion College, 1835-1960, A History.* Chicago: Donnelley Lakeside Press, 1961.

2228.   Gingrich, F. W., and E. H. Barth. *A History of Albright College: 1856-1956.* Reading, PA: Albright College, 1956.

2229.   Gobbel, Luther L. *Greensboro College 1935-1952.* Greensboro, NC: Greensboro College Alumni Association, 1977.

2230.   Goerig, Violet Miller. *Dakota Weslyan University, 1885-1960.* Vermillion, SD: University of South Dakota Press, 1970.

2231.   Gregg, Robert D. *Chronicles of Willamette.* Volume II. Portland, OR: Durham & Downey, Inc., 1970.

2232.   Haggard, Theodore M. *Florida Southern College: The First 100 Years.* Lakeland, FL: Florida Southern College Press, 1985.

2233.   Hall, John Gladden. *Henderson State College: The Methodist Years, 1890-1929.* Arkadelphia, AR: Henderson State College Alumni Association, 1974.

2234.   Hancock, Harold. *The History of Otterbein College.* Kansas City, MO: Yearbook Publishing Co., 1971.

2235.   Harrison, Daniel W. "Madison College, 1851-1858: a Methodist Protestant School." *Methodist History* 17 (January 1979): 90-105.

Describes an unsuccessful attempt of the Methodist Protestant Church to operate a college that had previously been Presbyterian, including the circumstances surrounding and possible reasons for its failure.

2236.   Haught, Thomas W. *West Virginia Wesleyan College, First Fifty Years, 1890-1940.* Buckhannon, WV: West Virginia Wesleyan, 1940.

2237.   Hay, Fanny A., Ruth E. Cargo, and Harlan L. Freeman. *The Story of a Noble Devotion.* Adrian, MI: Adrian College, 1944.

2238. Hendricks, Marvin L. *From Parochialism to Community: A Socio-Historical Interpretation of Indiana Central University 1902-1975.* Indianapolis, IN: Indianapolis, 1977.

2239. Hicks, John. "My Six Years at Hamline." *Minnesota History* 39 (November 1965): 678-90.

2240. Holter, Don W. *Flames on the Plains.* Nashville, TN: Parthenon Press, 1983.

 This book emerges from the Methodist experience in Nebraska and includes material on Nebraska Wesleyan University.

2241. Hubbart, Henry Clyde. *Ohio Wesleyan's First Hundred Years.* Delaware, OH: Ohio Wesleyan University, 1943.

2242. Irby, R. *History of Randolph-Macon College.* Richmond, VA: Whitter and Shepperson, 1898.

2243. Jeffrey, H. N., editor. *Historical Sketch and Alumni Record of Iowa Wesleyan College.* Mt. Pleasant, IA: Iowa Wesleyan College, 1917.

2244. Johnson, David. *Hamline University, A History.* St. Paul, MN: North Central Publishing Co., 1980.

2245. Jones, Glendell A., Jr. *Mid the Pine Hills of East Texas: The Methodist Centennial History of Lon Morris College.* Jacksonville, TX: Progress Publishing Co., 1973.

2246. Joy, James Richard, editor. *The Teachers of Drew, 1867-1942.* Madison, NJ: Drew University, 1942.

 This book is a commemorative volume issued on the occasion of the 75th anniversary of the founding of Drew Theological Seminary and provides interesting historical material on Drew University.

2247. Key, David M. "Historical Sketch of Milsaps College." *The Southern Association Quarterly* 10 (November 1946): 560-76.

2248. Lance, T. J. *History of Young L. G. Harris College.* Atlanta: Brown Publishing Co., 1936.

2249. Lefall, Delores C., and Janet L. Sims. "Mary McLeod Buthune -- The Educator; also Including a Selected Annotated Bibliography." *The Journal of Negro Education* 45 (Summer 1976): 342-59.

 The article not only provides a short account of the life and work of Mary McLeod Bethune, the founder of Bethune-Cookman College, but also an excellent bibliography on Mrs. Bethune that includes some good sources on the college.

2250. Lester, James E., Jr. *Hendrix College: A Centennial History.* Conway, AR: Hendrix Centennial Committee, 1984.

2251.   Lever, Oscar W. "Kentucky Wesleyan College, Owensboro, Kentucky, 100th Anniversary, 1858-1958." Pamphlet. Owensboro, KY: 1958.

2252.   Lowrey, Walter. *Centenary College of Louisiana Sesquicentennial 1825-1975.* Shreveport, LA: The Centenary College Alumni Association, 1975.

2253.   Manhart, George Born. *DePauw Through the Years.* Greencastle, IN: DePauw University, 1962.

2254.   Mansfield, Stephen. "Virginia Wesleyan College." In *Higher Education in the Southeastern Jurisdiction of the United Methodist Church,* pp. 109-11. Edited by DAn F. Brewster and G. Ross Freeman. Atlanta, GA: Parthenon Press, 1984.

2255.   Marigold, W. G., ed. *Union College 1879-1979.* Barbourville, KY: Union College, 1979.

2256.   Marsh, Daniel L. "The Founders of Boston University." *Bostonia* 5 (March 1932): 224-38.

2257.   Martin, LeRoy Albert. *A History of TWC, 1857-1957.* Athens, TN: Tennessee Wesleyan College, 1957.

2258.   Medary, Marjorie. "The History of Cornell College." *The Palimpsest* 34 (April 1953): 145-208.

2259.   Meriwether, Robert W. "Galloway College: The Early Years, 1889-1907." *Arkansas Historical Quarterly* 40 (Winter 1981): 291-337.

2260.   Milhouse, Paul W. *Oklahoma City University: A Miracle at 23rd and Blackwelder.* Oklahoma City, OK: Oklahoma Heritage Association, 1984.

2261.   Mills, Frances F. *Early History of Baldwin-Wallace.* Microfilm edition. Berea, OH: Berea Enterprise, 1937.

2262.   Mims, Edwin. *History of Vanderbilt University.* Nashville, TN: Vanderbilt University Press, 1946.

2263.   Mitchell, Bernita Breon. *Prologue to the Future: Kansas Wesleyan 1962-1986.* Salina, KS: Arrow Printing, 1986.

2264.   Morgan, James Henry. *Dickinson College: The History of One Hundred and Fifty Years, 1783-1933.* Carlisle, PA: Dickinson College, 1933.

2265.   Nelson, Edward T., ed. *Fifty Years of History of the Ohio Wesleyan University, Delaware, Ohio, 1844-1894.* Cleveland, OH: The Cleveland Printing and Publishing Co., 1895.

2266.   Nelson, William Hamilton. *A Burning Bush and a Flaming Fire: The Story of Centenary College of Louisiana.* Nashville, TN:

Methodist Publishing House, 1931.

2267.   Nute, Grace Lee. *In Hamline Halls, 1854-1954*. St. Paul, MN: Hamline University, 1954.

2268.   Olmsted, Ralph. *From Institute to University*. Evansville, IN: University of Evansville, 1973.

2269.   Osbourne, Yost. *A Select School, The History of Mount Union College and an Account of a Unique Educational Experiment, Scio College*. Alliance, OH: Mount Union College, 1953.

2270.   Parks, Joseph H., and Oliver C. Weaver. *Birmingham-Southern College, 1856-1956*. Birmingham, AL: Birmingham-Southern College, 1956.

2271.   Perkins, Nell. *Dry Ridge: Some of Its History, Some of Its People*. Weaverville, NC: Miller Printing Co., 1962.

    This book provides good information about Weaver College, a Methodist school in western North Carolina that is a predecessor institution of Brevard College.

2272.   Perry, Wilbur Dow. *A History of Birmingham-Southern College, 1856-1931*. Birmingham, AL: Birmingham-Southern College, 1931.

2273.   Phelps, Jon. *"I have selected Duke University...." A Short History*. Second edition. Durham, NC: Duke University, 1977.

2274.   Porter, Earl W. *Trinity and Duke 1892-1924*. Durham, NC: Duke University Press, 1964.

2275.   Pouncey, Temple. *Mustang Mania: Southern Methodist University*. Huntsville, AL: Strode Publishers, 1981.

2276.   Price, Carl F. *Wesleyan's First Century*. Middletown, CT: Wesleyan University Press, 1932.

2277.   Reynolds, John R., and Joanne E. King. *Highlights in the History of The American University*. Washington, D.C.: The American University, 1976.

2278.   Savory, Jerold J. *Columbia College: The Ariail Era*. Columbia, SC: Columbia College and R. L. Bryan Company, 1979.

2279.   Scanlon, James Edward. *Randolph-Macon College: a Southern History, 1825-1967*. Charlottesville, VA: University of Virginia Press, 1983.

2280.   Sellers, Charles Coleman. *Dickinson College: A History*. Middletown, CT: Wesleyan University Press, 1973.

2281.   Shields, M. Carrington. *"Historical Sketch of Randolph-Macon Woman's College." The Southern Association Quarterly* 3 (November 1939): 590-99.

2282.   Smith, C. Q. *Building for Tomorrow: The Story of Oklahoma City University.* Nashville, TN: Parthenon Press, 1961.

2283.   Smith, Ernest Ashton. *Alleghany -- A Century of Education, 1815-1915.* Meadville, PA: The Alleghany College History Company, 1916.

2284.   Smith, Matthew D. *Ventures in Christian Education under Five Flags.* Mitchell, SD: Dakota Wesleyan University, 1973.

2285.   Snyder, Henry Nelson. *An Educational Odyssey: Adventures of a President of a Small Denominational College.* New York and Nashville: Abingdon-Cokesbury Press, 1947.

         A prominent southern educator and president of Wofford College from 1902 to 1942 writes this lively autobiography that includes not only an account of his life illustrated with charming stories but excellent insights into the processes of higher education as well.

2286.   Stevenson, George J. *Increase in Excellence: A History of Emory & Henry College 1836-1963.* New York: Appleton-Century-Crofts, 1963.

2287.   Sutherland, Gretchen R. *On the Education of Women at Cornell College, 1853-1953.* Mount Vernon, IA: Cornell College, 1982.

2288.   Swain, Christie. "History of Simpson College." *Zenith* (1935): 82-105.

2289.   Sweet, William Warren. *Indiana Asbury-DePauw University, 1837-1937: A Hundred Years of Higher Education in the Middle West.* New York: Abingdon, 1937.

2290.   Thomas, Mary Martha Hosford. *Southern Methodist University: Founding and Early Years.* Dallas, TX: SMU Press, 1974.

2291.   Tippens, Jerry. *Voice of the Tiger: A History of the Dakota Wesleyan University Forensics Department.* Mitchell, SD: Dakota Wesleyan University, 1952.

         In the case of many schools, there are not only histories of the institution as a whole but also accounts written of particular divisions.   Here is an example of a department rather than a professional school.

2292.   Tolley, William Pearson, editor. *Drew University, 1867-1925.* Madison, NJ: The Seminary, 1926.

2293.   *Trustee Handbook: Alaska Pacific University.* Anchorage, AK: Alaska Pacific University, 1987.

2294.   Turrentine, Samuel B. *A Romance of Education.* Greensboro, NC: Piedmont Press, 1964.

2295. VanDerhoof, Jack Warner. *The Time Now Past: 1886-1961.*
       Salina, KS: Arrow Printing, 1962.

2296. Wallace, David Duncan. *History of Wofford College, 1854-1949.*
       Nashville; TN: Vanderbilt University Press, 1951.

2297. Wallace, Paul A. W. *Lebanon Valley College: A Centennial
       History.* Annville, PA: Lebanon Valley College, 1966.

2298. Walton, W. C. *Centennial History of McKendree College,
       1828-1928.* Lebanon, IL: McKendree College, 1928.

2299. Ward, E. F. *Story of Northwestern University.* New York:
       Appleton-Century, 1924.

2300. Winship, F. Loren. "Early History of Nebraska Wesleyan
       University." Unpublished Master's thesis. Lincoln, NE: University
       of Nebraska, 1930.

Part II: General Literature

2301. *A College-Related Church: United Methodist Perspectives.*
       Nashville, TN: National Commission on United Methodist Higher
       Education, 1976.

2302. Addo, Linda, and James D. McCallum. *To Be Faithful to Our
       Heritage: A History of Black United Methodism in North Carolina.*
       Winston-Salem, NC: Harris Publishing Company, 1980.

2303. Blackburn, William. *The Architecture of Duke University.*
       Durham, NC: Duke University Press, 1936.

2304. Boaz, Hiram Abiff. *Eighty-four Golden Years: an Autobiography
       of Bishop Hiram Abiff Boaz.* Nashville, TN: Parthenon Press, 1951.

2305. Brawley, James P. *Two Centuries of Methodist Concern: Bondage,
       Freedom, and Education of Black People.* New York: Vantage
       Press, 1974.

       This study of Black higher education contains sketches
       relating to the history of development of many Methodist and
       United Methodist institutions.

2306. Brewster, Dan F., and G. Ross Freeman, editors. *Higher Education
       in the Southeastern Jurisdiction of the United Methodist Church
       1787-1984.* Atlanta, GA: Southeastern Jurisdictional Conference
       Council on Ministries, 1984.

2307. Brubacher, John S., and Willis Rudy. *Higher Education in
       Transition: A History of American Colleges and Universities,
       1636-1968.* New York: Harper & Row, 1968.

2308. Butts, R. Freeman, and Lawrence A. Cremin. *History of Education
       in American Culture.* New York: Henry Holt & Co., 1953.

2309.   *Chapel-Duke University.* Photography by Richard Cheek; text by William H. Willimon; introduction by Reynolds Price. Durham, NC: Duke University Stores, 1986.

2310.   Cummings, A. W. *The Early Schools of Methodism.* New York: Phillips and Hunt, 1886.

2311.   Day, Heather F. *Protestant Theological Education in America: A Bibliography.* Metuchen, NJ: Scarecrow Press, 1985.

Because theological education and theological dimensions have been important for United Methodist colleges and universities, this bibliography is a crucial supplement to those interested in the areas of Methodist higher education.

2312.   Drury, Clifford M. "Church-Sponsored Schools in Early California." *Pacific Historian* 20 (Summer 1976): 158-66.

2313.   Duvall, Sylvanus M. *The Methodist Episcopal Church and Education up to 1869.* Contributions to Education No. 284. New York: Teachers College, Columbia University, 1928.

2314.   Godbold, Albea. *The Church College of the Old South.* Durham, NC: Duke University Press, 1944.

2315.   Gross, John O. *Methodist Beginnings in Higher Education.* Nashville, TN: Division of Educational Institutions, Board of Education, The Methodist Church, 1959.

2316.   Hofstadter, Richard, and Wilson Smith, eds. *American Higher Education: A Documentary History.* Chicago: University of Chicago Press, 1961.

2317.   Hohner, Robert A. "Southern Education in Transition: William Waugh Smith, the Carnegie Foundation, and the Methodist Church." *History of Education Quarterly* 27 (Summer 1987): 181-203.

2318.   Knight, Edgar W., editor. *A Documentary History of Education in the South Before 1860: Volume IV, Private and Denominational Efforts.* Chapel Hill, NC: University of North Carolina Press, 1953.

2319.   Limbert, Paul M. *Denominational Policies in the Support and Supervision of Higher Education.* New York: Teachers College Press, 1929.

2320.   McCoy, Charles S. *The Responsible Campus: Toward a New Identity for the Church-Related College.* Nashville, TN: Division of Higher Education, Board of Education, The United Methodist Church, 1972.

2321.   McCoy, Charles S. "The Churches and Higher Education." In *Foundations for Christian Education in an Era of Change*, pp. 259-70. Edited by Marvin J. Taylor. Nashville, TN: Abingdon,

1976.

2322. McCoy, Charles S. and Neely D. McCarter. *The Gospel on Campus: Rediscovering Evangelism in the Academic Community.* Atlanta, GA: John Know Press, 1959.

2323. Naylor, Natalie A. "The Ante-Bellum College Movement: A Re-Appraisal of Tweksbury's Founding of American Colleges and Universities." *History of Education Quarterly* 13 (Fall 1973): 261-74.

This article offers a helpful perspective on colleges and universities founded prior to the Civil War and provides a possible corrective to the account of Donald G. Twekbury that has been virtually canonized by many.

2324. Pace, C. Robert. *Education and Evangelism: A Profile of Protestant Colleges.* New York: McGraw-Hill Book Company, 1972.

Though a part of a distinguished series of studies of higher education supported by the Carnegie Corporation, this contribution is disappointing because of the narrow, inadequate theological perspective of church-related colleges that informs the author's research and reporting.

2325. Parsonage, Robert Rue, editor. *Church Related Higher Education: Perceptions and Perspectives.* Valley Forge, PA: Judson Press, 1978.

2326. Pattillo, Manning M. and Donald M. Mackenzie. *800 Colleges Face the Future.* St. Louis, MO: Danforth Foundation, 1965.

2327. Patillo, Manning M. and Donald M. Mackenzie. *Church-Sponsored Higher Education in the United States.* Washington, D.C.: American Council on Education, 1966.

2328. Rankin, Robert, editor, with Myron B. Bloy, Jr., David A. Hubbard, Parker J. Palmer. *The Recovery of Spirit in Higher Education: Christian and Jewish Ministries in Campus Life.* New York: The Seabury Press, 1980.

Drawing on the traditions and perspectives of the major religious traditions in the United States, the participants in this project of the Danforth Foundation make a significant contribution to colleges and universities of all denominations by focusing on: the discovery and nurture of the life of the spirit on campus; the close relation of contemplation and action; and what religious ministry means today in higher education.

2329. Ringenberg, William C. *The Christian College: A History of Protestant Higher Education in America.* Grand Rapids, MI: Eerdmans Publishing Company, 1984.

2330.   Schmidt, George P. *The Liberal Arts College: A Chapter in American Cultural History.* New Brunswick, NJ: Rutgers University Press, 1957.

2331.   Snavely, Guy E. *The Church and the Four-Year College: An Appraisal of Their Religion.* New York: Harper & Row, 1955.

2332.   Tewksbury, Donald G. *The Founding of American Colleges and Universities Before the Civil War.* New York: Teachers College Press, 1932; reprinted, New York: Archon Books, 1965.

2333.   Thomas, James S. "Methodism's Splendid Mission: The Black Colleges." *Methodist History* 22 (April 1984): 139-57.

         An excellent, brief account of the Black colleges of the United Methodist Church. Started as missionary enterprises and integrated on the trustee and faculty level from the beginning, have produced a significant number of leaders in the church and in society despite generally precarious financing.

2334.   *To Give the Key of Knowledge: United Methodists and Education 1784-1976.* Nashville: National Commission of United Methodist Higher Education, 1976.

2335.   *Toward 2000: Perspectives on the Environment for United Methodist and Independent Higher Education.* Nashville: National Commission on United Methodist Higher Education, 1976.

2336.   Underwood, Kenneth. *The Church, The University, and Social Policy: The Danforth Study of Campus Ministry.* Two volumes. Middletown, CT: Wesleyan University Press, 1969.

2337.   Wicke, Myron F. *The Church-Related College.* Washington, DC: Center for Applied Research in Education, 1964.

         Written by a former college dean and long-time Methodist executive in higher education, this book contains an analysis informed by experience and seasoning. Wicke writes: "The insistent question is whether or not the church-related colleges has in fact a unique and essential role to play in American higher education" (p. 2).

CHAPTER 28
WESLEYAN COLLEGES
John C. Holmes

The Wesleyan Methodist Church and the Pilgrim Holiness Church merged in 1968 to form the Wesleyan Church.

2338.   Allen, Richard Doyle. "An Investigation of the Religious Climate at the Four Liberal Arts Colleges Related to the Wesleyan Church." Ph.D. dissertation. Michigan State University, 1984.

Surveys 640 students and 100 faculty members with modified Gough's "Survey of College Environments." Finds a significant difference between resident and non-residential students at Bartlesville Wesleyan with no significant difference at Houghton (NY), Marion (IN), and Central Wesleyan (SC). Discovers significant difference between freshmen persisters and leavers. Claims religiousity was found to be "appropriate to and comparable with" the Wesleyan Church. Recommends that the colleges emphasize their religious commitment in all promotional efforts.

2339.   Boyce, Harold Walter. "Relationship Between College Majors and Eventual Employment of Marion College Alumni." Ed.D. dissertation. Indiana University, 1974.

Reviews the graduates of Marion College from 1950 to 1969. Eighty percent were in the fields of their majors with Elementary Education more likely at 88% than Social Science with 60%. Those who majored in Theology were morely to still be in their major than those who majored in Religion. Marion alumni who were later graduates (of the 1960's) are more likely to be in employment related to their degree than those from prior years. Alumni who made career decisions before college are more likely to be in related work.

2340.   Taylor, Charles Winthrop. "History of the (Higher) Educational Movement of the Wesleyan Methodist Church of America." Ph.D. dissertation. Indiana University, 1959.

Details the development and operation of Wesleyan Methodist Church (now part of the Wesleyan Church) colleges since 1843. Includes founding of church; educational views of founding leaders; why colleges failed; or transferred sponsorship--Adrian (MI) College and Wheaton (IL) College. Concludes that the colleges need professional educators, rather than ministers, for presidents.

2341.   Thomas, Clifford William. "A Descriptive Study of Ministerial Education in the Wesleyan College." Ph.D. dissertation. Michigan State University, 1968.

Examines (1) curricula of existing programs; (2) the nature of professional training among ministers; and (3) expectations held by Wesleyan ministers, administrators and educators. Finds inadequate financial support, deficiency of adequately trained faculty and diversity of levels of expectation. Points out that seventy percent of the ministers were not satisfied with the level of their training and that there was only a limited interest in developing a Wesleyan seminary.

2342.   Thomas, Paul Westphal and Paul William Thomas. *The Days of Our Pilgrimage.* Marion, IN: The Wesley Press, 1976.

Provides early pictures and descriptions of God's Bible School of Cincinnati and other early colleges of the Pilgrim Holiness Church in Greensboro, NC; Owosso, MI; Beulah Park near Allentown, PA; Carlinville, IN; Pilgrim Bible College in Pasadena, CA; and Colorado Springs, CO. Examines the forming of Central Pilgrim College in Bartlesville, OK from a merger of Colorado Springs Bible College and Western Pilgrim College in El Monte, CA in 1958. The Pilgrim Holiness Church existed from 1897 to 1968 and is now part of the Wesleyan Church.

CONTRIBUTORS

Contributors are listed in order of their appearance in the book.

THOMAS C. HUNT received the Ph.D. from the University of Wisconsin. He is Professor of Foundations of Education at Virginia Tech. His major interest is history of American education with an emphasis on religion and schooling. He is the co-editor of *Religion and Morality in American Schooling* (1981), and co-edited, with James C. Carper, *Religious Schooling in America* (1984), and (with Carper and Charles S. Kniker) *Religious Schools in America* (1986). His articles have appeared in *Educational Forum, The Journal of Church and State, Momentum, The Catholic Historical Review, Paedogogica Historica, Journal of Presbyterian History, Religious Education, Methodist History, National Association of Episcopal Schools Journal,* and *High School Journal.* He received the Thayer S. Warshaw award in 1986 for his essay on "Religion and Public Schooling: A Tale of Tempest."

JAMES C. CARPER earned the Ph.D. from Kansas State University. He is on leave from Mississippi State University while serving as Director of the Education and Society Division in the Office of Research of the U.S. Department of Education. His articles have appeared in *Kansas Historical Quarterly, Mid-America, Education Forum, Journal of Church and State, Review Journal of Philosophy and Social Science,* and *Journal of Thought.* He recently co-edited (with Thomas C. Hunt) *Religious Schooling in America* and (with Hunt and Charles R. Kniker) *Religious Schools in America: A Selective Bibliography.* His scholarly interests include the history of American education and religious schools, particularly Christian day schools.

JENNINGS L. WAGONER, JR. is Professor of History of Education and Policy Studies in the Curry School of Education at the University of Virginia. He received the B.A. from Wake Forest, M.A.T. from Duke, and Ph.D. from Ohio State University. He is author of *Thomas Jefferson and the Education of a New Nation* (1976), co-editor of *The Changing Politics of Education* (1978) and has published extensively in scholarly journals. Professor Wagoner is a past president of Division F of the American Educational Research Association.

TIMOTHY W. KENNEY received his B.A. and M.A. degrees in history from James Madison University. He is currently a doctoral student in higher education at the University of Virginia. Mr. Kenney served in the U.S. Marine Corps and has worked as an archivist at the George C. Marshall Research Foundation.

JAMES F. HERNDON is Professor of Political Science at Virginia Polytechnic Institute and State University. He received his Ph.D. from the University of Michigan. His research and publications concern church-state issues, mathematical applications in political science, legislative behavior, and interest groups.

RALPH D. MAWDSLEY, Administrative Counsel at Liberty University, is a graduate of the University of Illinois College of Law. In addition, Dr. Mawdsley holds a Ph.D. in Educational Administration from the University of Minnesota where he holds Adjunct Professor status and teaches a course, Tort Liability for Vocational Educators. He has written extensively in legal periodicals and is a frequent conference speaker on educational law topics. Dr. Mawdsley is on the Board of Directors for the National Organization on Legal Problems of Education (NOLPE) and the Society of Educators and Scholars, and is a member of the Editorial Advisory Committee of West's Education Law Reporter. His book *Legal Problems of Religious and Private Schools* has been used as a textbook in graduate school law courses and his monograph, *Legal Aspects of Plagiarism*, has become a model for designing university policies on plagiarism.

JERRY M. SELF is Assistant Director of the Education Commission of the Southern Baptist Convention, Nashville, TN.

HAROLD D. GERMER is Director of the Collegiate Education Services located in Valley Forge, PA. He is the Staff Person in the Division of Christian Higher Education, Educational Ministries, American Baptist Churches, USA.

VIRGINIA LIESON BRERETON teaches history at the Winsor School in Boston. Her doctoral dissertation deals with the history of the Bible schools between 1880 and 1940, and she has published a number of essays on this subject and on religious training schools. She is currently at work on a book manuscript on American women's conversion narratives between 1800 and the present.

MARY A. GRANT is Director of the Health Education Resource Center, College of Pharmacy and Allied Health Professions, St. John's University, New York. She has earned a Master's degree in Library Science and a Ph.D. degree in Educational Administration and Supervision from St. John's. In her professional career Ms. Grant has been a classroom teacher and a director of secondary library media centers in the New York and Philadelphia areas. She has served as a library consultant on the diocesan level and presently is library consultant for Winston Prep School in New York City. Her professional activities include serving as Vice-President and President of the national Catholic Library Association from 1983 to 1987. As immediate past president of the Association, she continues to serve on its Executive Board.

D. DUANE CUMMINS is an author, educator and churchman. He was written thirteen books and numerous articles, and served as Darbeth-Whitten Professor of American History at Oklahoma City University. Since 1978 he has been president of the Division of Higher Education of the Christian

Church (Disciples of Christ). He received his Ph.D. from the University of Oklahoma. For his publication scholarship, he has been recognized in Who's Who in America, Contemporary Authors and the Directory of American Scholars.

ROBERT E. HOOPER is Chairman of the Department of History and Political Science at David Lipscomb College, Nashville, Tennessee.

ROBERT J. MATTHEWS received his Ph.D. from Brigham Young University. In the past he has been Professor of Ancient Scripture and Dean of Religious Education at BYU. He is now Director of the Religious Studies Center at the same University. He is ecclesiastical leader in The Church of Jesus Christ of Latter-day Saints and a lecturer and frequent contributor of doctrinal and historical treatises in LDS Church publications.

MURRAY L. WAGNER is Professor of Historical Studies, Bethany Theological Seminary, Oak Brook, Illinois, and Adjunct Professor of Religion, Elmhurst College, Elmhurst, Illinois. He studied at the Free University, Berlin; Comenius Theological Faculty, Prague; and received the Th.D. at the Chicago Theological Seminary.

HAROLD E. RASER is Associate Professor of the History of Christianity at Nazarene Theological Seminary, Kansas City, Missouri. He is an ordained minister in the Church of the Nazarene and is a member of the American Academy of Religion, the American Society of Church History, and the Wesleyan Theological Society. He is the author of *Phoebe Palmer, Her Life and Thought* (1987) as well as articles and reviews appearing in several church publications and scholarly journals.

ARTHUR BEN CHITTY received a B.A. from the University of the South and M.A. from Tulane University. Historiographer of the University of the South since 1954, he became president of the Association of Episcopal Colleges in 1965, served 11 years, and is now President Emeritus. He founded the National Episcopal Historians Association in 1961. He has written or edited five books of Sewanee history and edited its alumni publication and the Association of Episcopal Colleges newsletter. He serves on the boards of *Anglican and Episcopal History*, the *Anglican Digest*, and the *St. Luke's Journal of Theology*, and has contributed numerous articles on Episcopal Church colleges to journals. He has been a trustee of four Episcopal colleges and holds honorary degrees from two of them.

ELIZABETH NICKINSON CHITTY received the B.A. and M.A. from Florida State University. She has been associated with the University of the South for most of the years between 1946 and the present, including associate editorship of the *Sewanee News* 1946-1962 and managing editorship of the *Sewanee Review*. She became Associate Historiographer in 1980, following 10 years as director of financial aid and career services. She has been co-editor of four volumes of Sewanee historical material.

CLARK WHITING DIMOND III has graduate degrees in English, religion and education. He has held appointments in the parish ministry and on the

English faculty at Virginia Tech.

JOHN C. HOLMES earned the standard ministerial diploma at Mt. Vernon
Bible College (OH), an A.B. at Spring Arbor College (MI), M.A. in Ed. at the
University of Akron (OH), and an Ed.D. at Pepperdine University at Los
Angeles. He has served as a pastor, college instructor and Christian schools
superintendent. Currently Dr. Holmes and his family live in Westminster,
Maryland where he pastors a Foursquare Gospel Church. He also serves as
Assistant for Government Information, Office of the Executive Director,
Association of Christian Schools International. Dr. Holmes' doctoral
research, completed in 1983, was entitled: "A Comparison Among Black,
Hispanic and White Parental Expectations of the Evangelical Christian
School."

CLAYTON L. FARRADAY is a retired teacher of biology and assistant
Headmaster at Friends' Central School in Philadelphia, PA. He is Chairman
of the Executive Committee of the Friends Council on Education, past
President of the Pennsylvania Association of Private Academic Schools
(PAPAS) and a member of Board of Directors of the Council for American
Private Education (CAPE). He is also Instructor in biology, Delaware
County Community College, Media, PA.

GEORGE C. PAPADEMETRIOU received his Ph.D. from Temple
University. He is Associate Professor and Director of the Library at Hellenic
College/Holy Cross Greek Orthodox School of Theology. Since 1960 he has
served the Greek Orthodox Archdiocese as a priest. He is the author of
Introduction to St. Gregory Palamas and has also written numerous articles
for scholarly journals.

WILLIAM C. RINGENBERG is Chairman, Department of History and
Director of the Honors Program at Taylor University, Upland, Indiana,
where he as been a member of the faculty since 1968. He is the author of
Taylor University: The First 125 Years (1973) and *The Christian College: A
History of Protestant Higher Education in America* (1984) both published by
Eerdmans Press of Grand Rapids, Michigan. He presently serves as vice
president and president-elect of the Conference on Faith and History.

HAROLD S. WECHSLER is a communications specialist for the National
Education Association. The author of *The Qualified Student: A History of
Selective College Admission in America*, and the coauthor, with Paul
Ritterband, of a forthcoming book on the history of Jewish learning in
American universities, he has taught at the University of Chicago, Teachers
College, Columbia University, and the State University of New York at
Buffalo. He is the Editor of the *History of Higher Education Annual.*

RICHARD W. SOLBERG is a retired Lutheran pastor and educator living
in Thousand Oaks, California, where he serves as Adjunct Professor of
History at California Lutheran University. He is a graduate of St. Olaf
College and Luther Northwestern Theological Seminary, and holds a Ph.D.
in American history from the University of Chicago. He taught at St. Olaf
College, Augustana College (South Dakota), served as Vice President for

Academic Affairs at Thiel College in Pennsylvania, and until his retirement, was Director for Higher Education for the Lutheran Church in America. He is the author of *Lutheran Higher Education in North America* (1985), *How Church-Related are Church-Related Colleges?* (1980), *God and Caesar in East Germany* (1961), an account of church-state relations in East Germany, 1945-59, and *As Between Brothers* (1957), a history of world Lutheran relief efforts after World Wars I and II.

JON DIEFENTHALER received his Ph.D. under Sidney Mead in American Religious History in 1976 at the University of Iowa. Prior to this, he graduated from Concordia Seminary, St. Louis, and was awarded his M.A. by Washington University. In 1981-1982, he worked with Timothy L. Smith as a postdoctoral fellow in the department of History at the Johns Hopkins University. Over the course of his career, Diefenthaler has served as both a seminary professor and parish pastor. For three years he was a member of the Department of Historical Theology at Concordia Theological Seminary, Springfield, Illinois. More recently, he has been a visiting professor at Lutheran Theological Seminary in Gettysburg, teaching courses in American Lutheranism. He is currently pastor of Bethany Lutheran Church located in the Shenandoah Valley at Waynesboro, Virginia. Published in 1986 by Mercer University Press is his book, *H. Richard Niebuhr: A Lifetime of Reflections on the Church and the World*. Work on Niebuhr still in progress involves an anthology that collects essays and articles from his early years. Diefenthaler's research in the area of American Lutheranism has focused on education, and his essay on "Lutheran Schools in America" was published in 1984 as a chapter in *Religious Schooling in America* edited by James C. Carper and Thomas C. Hunt.

ALBERT N. KEIM is Professor of History at Eastern Mennonite College, Harrisonburg, Virginia. He received the Ph.D. from Ohio State University in recent American history. He is the author of *Compulsory Education and the Amish: The Right Not to Be Modern* (Beacon Press, 1975), and numerous articles on church-state issues.

BEATRICE E. NAFF received her doctoral degree from Virginia Tech. She also holds a Masters in Theology from Bethany Theological Seminary. She has taught for four years in the Virginia public schools and two years in the Chicago Network of Alternative Schools. She is now Assistant Professor at Mercer University in Georgia.

EDITH L. BLUMHOFER received the B.A. and M.A. degrees from Hunter College of the City University of New York. Her Ph.D. degree is from Harvard University (American religious history). She is project director for the Institute for the Study of American Evangelicals and assistant professor of history at Wheaton College. Her publications focus on the emergence and development of American Pentecostalism.

A. MYRVIN DE LAPP retired after twenty-five years service with the Division of Higher Education of the Board of Christian Education of the United Presbyterian Church, U.S.A. and its successor, the Program Agency of the United Presbyterian Church, U.S.A. He has also been a Visiting

Lecturer at Princeton Seminary since 1963. He served as Chaplain and Dean of Men, Lake Forest College, Lake Forest, Illinois; Presbyterian University Pastor at Kansas State University, Manhattan, Kansas and pastor of Second Presbyterian Church, Lincoln, Nebraska. After graduating from Macalester College he received a degree from McCormick Theological Seminary. His Doctor of Divinity degree was also from Macalester College. Dr. De Lapp served in the United States Army Medical Corps for four and a half years (1941-45). His discharge rank was Captain.

PETER P. DEBOER has a Ph.D. from University of Chicago. He is Professor of Education and Director of Adult and Continuing Education at Calvin College. His areas of special interest include Protestant schools in North America, and Christian philosophy of education, especially an understanding of curriculum and pedagogy. He is author of *Shifts in Curricular Theory for Christian Education* (1983); he has contributed articles to the *History of Education Quarterly, American Journal of Education*, the *Christian Scholar's Review*, and the *Reformed Journal*, among others.

GEORGE R. KNIGHT has been Professor of Church History at Andrews University since 1985. Previously he was Professor of Educational Foundations at the same institution from 1976-1985. His major publications include: *Philosophy and Education: An Introduction in Christian Perspectives* (1980); *Issues and Alternatives in Educational Philosophy* (1982); *Early Adventist Educators* (editor, 1983); *Myths in Adventism* (1985); and *From 1888 to Apostasy: The Case of A. T. Jones* (1987).

VERLYN L. BARKER holds the Ph.D. degree in American Studies from Saint Louis University and theological degrees from Yale University. He is Secretary for Higher Education Programs and Resources, Division of Education and Publication, United Church Board for Homeland Ministries. Mr. Barker coordinated the research for the United Church of Christ chapter.

JOSEPH T. McMILLAN, JR. holds the Ed.D. degree in Higher Education Administration from Teachers College, Columbia University, as well as a master's degree from Howard University. He is Secretary for Higher Education Relationships, Division of Higher Education and Publication, United Church Board for Homeland Ministries.

JAMES A. SMITH, JR. holds the Ph.D. degree in the Sociology of Religion from Boston University and theological degrees from Yale University. He is Coordinator of Church-College Relations, United Church Board for Homeland Ministries.

CHARLES S. McCOY received his B.A. degree from the University of North Carolina, Chapel Hill, his B.D. from Duke Divinity School, and his Ph.D. from Yale University. At present, Dr. McCoy is Robert Gordon Sproul Professor of Theological Ethics and Higher Education at Pacific School of Religion and the Graduate Theological Union, Berkeley. His publications include *The Responsible Campus, When Gods Change*, and *Management and Values*. He was a member of the Supervisory Commission of the Danforth Study of Campus Ministries and has taught at the University of Munster,

Germany, as Fulbright Senior Lecturer.

AUTHOR INDEX

SUBJECT INDEX

Abilene Christian College 1012, 1025, 1036
Abilene Christian College Lectureship 1009
Academic Computing and the Information Society 492, 662
Academic Freedom 272, 810, 812, 813, 825, 840, 854, 868, 891, 1398, History of 12
Accountability 110, 1769
Accreditation and Licensing Requirements 127, 348, 362, 377, 388
Adler, Cyrus 1434, 1446
Adler, Mortimer 1583
Administrators, Clergy as 554
Admissions Standards, (SATs) 131
Adrian College 2237, 2340
Adult Higher Education 874, 909, 941
Adventist Sabbath School 1845
African Methodist Episcopal Church 2168
Agnes Scott College 1621, 1622
Alaska Pacific University 2293
Albertus Magnus College 926
Albion College 2211, 2217, 2218, 2227
Albright College 2228
Alderson-Broaddus College 430
All Saints' College 1106, 1107
Alleghany College 2283
Alma College 1623, 1624
American Association of Bible Colleges 689
American Baptist Association 491
American Baptist Convention and Higher Education 573
American Catholic Colleges and Universities (ACCU) 916,
917
American Church Institute for Negroes 1141, 1198, 1307, 1312, 1314, 1326
American Civil Liberties Union 77, 294
American Education Society (AES) 18
American Indian Education 2179, 2180
American Jewish Historical Society 1449
American Lutheran Church, The 1527
American Missionary Association 2140, 2143, 2144, 2148, 2149, 2157, 2161, 2162, 2168, 2173, 2175, 2182
American Philosophical Association 942
American University, The 2277
Amherst College 15, 1879-1882, 2123
Amistad Mutiny, The 2162
Anderson College 456
Andrews University 1863
Antioch College 2034-2038
Aquinas College 922
Arkansas Christian College 1013
Arkansas College 1625, 1626
Armstrong, John Nelson 1033
Armstrong, Samuel Chapman 2136, 2151, 2178
Asbury College 1418
Ascending Liability 328, 341
Ashland College 1076
Assemblies of God Higher Education 1596-1602; History of 1597-1599, 1602; Reports on 1596
Association of Episcopal Colleges 1308, 1324, 1334